DEVELOPMENT OF INTERACTIVE ABILITIES IN CHILDREN

DEVELOPMENT OF INTERACTIVE ABILITIES IN CHILDREN

V.K. NANDA

ANMOL PUBLICATIONS PVT. LTD.

NEW DELHI - 110 002 (INDIA)

ANMOL PUBLICATIONS PVT. LTD.
4374/4B, Ansari Road, Daryaganj
New Delhi - 110 002
Ph.: 23261597, 23278000
Visit us at: www.anmolpublications.com

Development of Interactive Abilities in Children

ISBN 81-7488-834-9

PRINTED IN INDIA

Published by J.L. Kumar for Anmol Publications Pvt. Ltd., New Delhi - 110 002 and Printed at Mehra Offset Press, Delhi.

Contents

Preface

"Child is the father of man," thus future of a nation depends on the development of children. 'Child development' in its diverse aspects is elaborately discussed in the present encyclopaedia.

Organised in five volumes, the first volume of the encyclopaedia contains information on 'Principles of Child Development.' 'Child Development Counselling' is the theme on which learned articles are compiled and collated in the volume second. Volume three consists of useful and authoritative material on Nutrition and Health for Child Development. Teaching Methodology and Child Development is the major theme of volume four. Volume five of the encyclopaedia is devoted to Development of Interactive Abilities in Children.

All the articles are judiciously selected from authoritative sources. We are grateful to all the learned authors and academicians whose writings are cited or substantially made use of in these volumes. Students, teachers, researchers, administrators, policy planners and professionals from different streams of disciplines will find this encyclopaedia informative and useful.

V. K. Nanda

1
Communication and Child Development

Because the process of verbal communication relies on signals that can be heard or seen, something physical must happen when a message is to be transmitted. This requires mechanical performances. A mental element shines through, but physical skills become indispensable. These skills are performed at varying degrees of efficiency but, like all skills, can be improved.

Speaking, handwriting, punctuating, and spelling differ in the extent to which they are mechanical as well as in the proportion of physical and mental ingredients involved, but all can be improved through practice.

SPEECH

Normally the processes of thinking and speaking coordinate so smoothly and swiftly that nobody reflects on the complexity of the situation. Neurons and muscles function harmoniously. But when some phase of the process operates at low efficiency or draws unfavourable attention to itself people become aware of the mechanics involved. The difficulties range from being wholly physical and easily corrected to being psychophysical and having pathological overtones.

Motivations for improving speech are strong because children want to be understood and listened to. In the upper grades a pupil begins to realise the great truth that his speech ranks along with his appearance in a person's impression of him and that among his friends his speech may be the most important factor in establishing their opinion of his personality.

Physical Skills of Speech

In every grade a teacher pays attention to enunciation, pronounciation, loudness, posture, and related physical aspects of speech. She hopes to improve them through classroom guidance, although children impeded by handicaps like cleft palate, stuttering, aphasia, cerebral palsy, and deafness usually require help from surgeons and psychiatrists.

Estimates vary of the number of children needing some kind of aid in the physical aspects of speech. Variables exist in the ages of pupils and the situations in which problems occur. Also people disagree on what constitutes a speech defect, although most would admit that a deficiency exists when speech attracts unpleasant attention. There is general agreement that about 8 or 10 per cent of the children in an average class need some kind of help. Of course, half may be expected to have serious defects. Articulation difficulties, particularly stuttering, usually predominate. It is important for a teacher to identify cases requiring special help. Also a teacher should recognise difficulties that children normally outgrow in a few years.

Emphasis on improving a particular skill varies with the grade and the immediate situation. In pitch and voice quality, for example, only limited development can be expected in certain grades, and improper articulation of some phonemes need cause little concern while pupils' front teeth are missing. Childhood's troubles with sounds represented by *l*, *r* and *s* will be outgrown. Posture, breathing, and loudness deserve attention in every grade, although recommendations regarding them differ according to whether the pupil is conversing informally or is preparing an announcement at the school assembly.

Varying amounts of emphasis on the speech difficulty should relate to the temperament and sensitivity of the child. With some the best results come from suggestions given privately and rather casually. Tape recordings, used tactfully, give pupils authentic impressions of their speech (without gesture and posture) and stimulate interest in self-improvement. Samplings of good speech can be heard repeatedly from records and tapes.

Classroom attention should concentrate on developing the aspects of speech which pupils need most urgently. The ratio between the time expended and the probable benefits is a consideration. Time would be more or less wasted in trying to wean children from dialectal features that prevail in a region, conspicuous though those features may be to a teacher from another area. The teacher may as well accept the dialect if it is spoken by the cultured people of the community. The teacher should, of course, work toward replacing any substandard patterns of articulation, pronunciation, and gesture.

Normally a teacher feels justified in working with any of the key aspects of speech discussed below. Improvement in these is certain to compensate for the time expended. The aspects are interrelated and improvement in one favours development in others.

Control of Lips and Tongue. The lips and tongue, aided by the teeth, palate, and jaw, control articulation of the approximately nine vowels, three semivowels, and twenty-one consonants basic in English speech. If lips are "lazy" or unduly thick, if the tongue lacks nimbleness, or if the jaw is less relaxed and responsive than it should be, speech sounds are formed inadequately. Lisps (misarticulation of one or more sibilant consonants, affecting *s* and *z* most frequently), obscured consonants, and "thick" speech result. Words then become difficult to understand because their consonant sounds, usually more important than vowel sounds in identifying words, are muffled.

"Tongue-twisters", yawning routines for relaxing the jaws, and tongue and lip drills are standard types of remedial exercises. For purposes of drill the tongue can be moved rapidly in and out of the mouth, it can be folded to form a groove longitudinally along its middle, or its tip can be curled back of the upper teeth. Lip movement may be exaggerated by protrusion or puckering. Pupils can say various phonetic combinations and take care to distinguish between combinations resembling each other.

Children born into a non-English language need retraining if their language differs from English in its manner of using the lips, tongue, teeth, jaw, and palate.

Breathing. Breath control affects speech rhythms, resonance, and the degree of body or "thinness" of the voice. Speech books suggest exercises for developing good breathing and for diaphragm support of speech. A typical exercise asks the pupil to inhale generously and then exhale in a series of controlled puffs, as if he were blowing out a candle in five or six puffs. After some experience he should increase the number of puffs to ten or more. Sometimes he can speak a syllable with each puff. In another exercise, a pupil breathes deeply, then, holding a feather or piece of thin paper in front of his mouth, exhales slowly, saying a sibilant like *s* or *z* and trying to keep the feather or paper quivering as long as he can sound the sibilant.

By means of tape recordings the class can hear the effects of breathing on speech and notice how truly the voice rides upon the breath.

Posture. Naturalness in posture is desired. If the pupil stands free of the desk, a major temptation to slouch or "drape" is thereby removed. Related problems—notably for boys—are what to do with the hands and how to keep the hands away from the mouth.

A video tape provides the best study of posture. Lacking such tape, a pupil can observe his posture in a large mirror.

When reading aloud a pupil usually holds his book or paper so low that he directs his voice toward the floor. His communication improves greatly if he holds his script high enough so that he can project his voice toward his listeners, yet not so high as to eclipse his face.

Posture and breathing are interrelated. Classroom guidance which improves either of them is likely to improve the other.

Pronunciation of Interior and Final Syllables. There is a widespread and natural tendency to slur unaccented final syllables of words and to omit unstressed interior parts of long words. *Walking* becomes *walkin, government* becomes *goverment, miniature* becomes *minature.* In moderation this tendency is normal as part of the shortcuts and fluidity of informal speech, but there is a point beyond which it sounds slovenly. Carelessness, "lazy" lips, and undue rapidity of speech are among the causes of such slovenliness. Inaccurate listening and defective hearing may be causes too, by giving the child incorrect impressions of how words are supposed to sound.

Suggested remedies (provided hearing is normal) include choral speaking, dramatics, and listening to standard speech on recordings. It is helpful also to practice clear pronunciation of a specific sound or syllable as it occurs at differing positions in different words—at the beginning of one word, in the middle of another word, and at the end of another (*ruin, February, grew*).

Improvement in the full pronunciation of words tends to reduce the speech of children who talk too rapidly. It also removes a major cause of poor spelling.

Resonance. Nasalisation and denasalisation result from improper opening and closing of nasal passages. What is somewhat misleadingly called "nasality" occurs when there is incomplete closure of the velopharyngeal area. The imperfect closing is due to either lack of sufficient structure or inability to make the structure operate properly. Consequently a person sounds as if he were "talking through his nose".

Denasality usually is caused organically by an obstruction of the back part of the nasal passage or nasopharnyx. The obstruction may result from enlargements of some portion or from growths or allergies. This abnormality affects nasal phonemes most, but makes all speech sound as if the speaker had a head cold.

The true nasal phonemes, represented by the letters *m* and *n*, are continuant sounds and should have resonance in the nose. When they are uttered correctly the cartilage of the nose vibrates sufficiently for the speaker to feel the vibration if he places his fingers on the cartilage.

Speech textbooks offer varied drills for increasing the resonance of *m* and *n* and for reducing nasality in other phonemes. Vowel nasality can be reduced if the pupil alternately sounds *ab* and *ng*, being careful that he utters *ab* without use of nasal passages and *ng* with abundant resonance in the nose. Vowels require no nasal resonance, and if properly uttered their sound is affected very little when the speaker closes his nostrils with the thumb and forefinger. This fact provides an easy way for pupils to check whether their vowels are free from nasality. Children can sound the vowels first with their nostrils free, then with the nostrils held closed. Ideally the vowels should sound about the same in both circumstances.

Variations in Pitch and Volume. Droning monotony is much more common in oral reading and in reciting from memory than in spontaneous speech. It also is more frequent in classrooms than on playgrounds.

If in spontaneous speech a pupil's "speech profile" is unduly flat, he should be encouraged to make his voice go up and down and become louder and softer in natural response to feelings and situations. The likelihood is that on the playground his modulation is good. Children naturally have somewhat limited ranges of pitch and volume, but they can avoid monotony.

Puppetry based on stories having lively dialogue and contrasting characters induces children to modulate the voice. Other forms of dramatics and choral speaking also serve well. Tape recordings reproduce pitch and volume faithfully enough to be very revealing to a speaker.

Rate of Speech. Some speech is too rapid and some (often the too-rapid type) lacks the pauses needed for a change of pace. If a pupil's nervousness and tension are causes, the teacher may be able to relax the situation. Tape recordings help pupils analyse problems related to pauses and rate. They also reveal that an increase in the volume of sound and the pounding of a desk are not the only ways to emphasise a word or idea. Changes in the rate of speech and the use of pauses are two other ways, and good ways, too. Choral speaking, dramatics, and puppetry encourage children to vary the tempo and employ pauses effectively.

Rapid speech may be acceptable if it is uncluttered and spoken with a rhythm that fits the intonation patterns of the English language. There is a natural interplay between rate of speech and the extent to which words are slurred, compressed, or spoken fully.

Gesture and Facil Expression. In spontaneous speech, children use abundant facial expressions and bodily gestures; they speak with their total selves. But when reading orally and when speaking from memory they usually lapse into inexpressiveness; they do not put in the kinesic elements used in spontaneous speech. Even in spontaneous conversation a few pupils remain inexpressive.

The loss is great when readers or speakers merely utter words. In speech so much is said through vocal qualifiers, gestures, posture, and related types of signals that some estimates credit to words themselves only about 30 per cent of the total communication.

Miming, dramatic play, and speaking lines and operating strings for lively marionette characters are among the best developers of expressive faces and bodies. Video tape, where available, lets the pupil see himself in action.

At the other extreme, gestures and facial expressions which are excessive or are distracting for some other reason also interfere with communication. They can be reduced rather easily through watchfulness, provided they do not reflect nervousness or traumatic disturbances.

The Manner of Speaking. The quality that may be called the "manner" of speech includes a number of elements. Linguistics recognises a great many of them. People notice tones of kindness (or of unkindness); overtones of impatience, boredom, and fatigue; and the timbre of whining. There are courteous (and discourteous) ways of asking "what?" saying "no", and calling "mother" or "dad". Certain mental and emotional ingredients help establish the manner, but physical factors like pitch, volume, accent, and rhythm operate too, imposing special meanings on the basic phonology and grammar. Details of their nature and influences can be found in discussions of paralanguage and paralinguistics.

Here again a tape recorder is revealing. Attention to this aspect of speech is important because the characteristics grouped under "manner of speaking" will be exceedingly influential in the pupil's social and business contacts throughout his life.

Serious Speech Disorders

Speech abnormalities related to stuttering, muscular disturbance, aphasia, cleft palate and other malformations of the mouth, tongue, teeth, or larynx require help from either a speech clinician or a surgeon or both. Most such difficulties are physiological, but stuttering cases are likely to have important psychological elements. The informed teacher identifies the several types of serious speech disorders for what they are and knows which cases need professional assistance in addition to the help she can give.

Books on speech therapy identify the types of difficulty. Articles on kinesics—now a lively aspect of studies in communication—tell what kinds of bodily responses are symptomatic of certain mental and emotional disturbances.

The teacher has much to do even after referring a case to someone else. Here is the problem of helping the child feel at ease, yet face his handicap realistically. On the problem of selecting out-of-school clinicians and therapists, teachers and parents can obtain guidance from the American Speech and Hearing Association, 1001 Connecticut Avenue, N.W., Washington 6, D.C.

Stuttering is the most frequent type of serious speech disorder, being present in about one pupil out of every hundred. It is progressive, usually starting in the preschool period and becoming worse during grade-school and high-school years. It also demands the most careful cooperation between the teacher and therapist. Its origins are complex, often bordering on the traumatic; the processes of its cure may be equally complex.

The stutterer should be encouraged to participate in normal speech responses: roll call, answering questions, and reporting. Sometimes he can be given the option of speaking, raising his hand, or writing in response to roll call or questions, but only if such option is given to his classmates also. Frank, calm discussions of the situation should bring the problem out into the open and lead to a casual attitude of the stutterer toward his disability. There even may be a request from the therapist that the pupil purposely be allowed to stutter so as to change his emotional and muscular behaviour slowly rather than abruptly. Such a request is likely to surprise teachers who think that the change should be made quickly. A tape recorder may help, as some stutterers speak smoothly on tape, especially if they can be entirely alone when recording.

In connection with stuttering there has been much speculation on whether a forced change in a child's handedness is likely to bring on the speech impediment. Present opinion holds that changing handedness, of itself, does not cause stuttering but that circumstances attending the change—especially the unreasonableness of a dictatorial parent who forces the change—might lead to tension and hesitancy.

Cleft palates or lips, malformed tonsils, enlarged adenoids, chronic natal ailments, and thickened vocal bands generally respond to surgery. Speech difficulties arising from them rather than from psychological causes usually clear up quickly after an operation. Malocclusions resulting from abnormal tooth arrangement can be improved by dentistry; those caused by a protruding or receding jaw may respond to orthodontic treatment and special articulation exercises.

A cleft palate makes all phonemes sound nasal because they pass directly to the nose. It also prevents a speaker from forming the plosives *(p, b, t, d, k)* because he cannot build up pressure in his mouth. The lack of control of air in the mouth causes trouble also with sounds represented by *f, s, v, w, sh, zh* and the voiced and unvoiced *th*.

Speech organs that had been malformed need special training after correction, and, in some cases, during the process of correction. Muscles may require limbering, retraining, or coordinating. For such training purposes many speech games and exercises have been devised and made available in books on speech correction.

WRITTEN PUNCTUATION

Kindergarten children punctuate abundantly when they speak. They do it with intonations, faces, hands—in fact, with their whole bodies. They understand very well the punctuation signals in the speech of other people. In infancy they began learning oral punctuation—watching it, listening to it, practicing it. But of written punctuation they know little or nothing.

In order to write, pupils must learn a second set of punctuation signals—a system of marks and spacings used to represent, in so far as possible, the signals of the voice and body. Learning this second system poses one of the major problems connected with the enterprise of writing.

Pupils' early school experiences with written punctuation occur in connection with chalkboards or experience charts. Casually, yet systematically, teachers comment as they write: "Now we are asking a question, so I'll put this mark here to show that I wrote a question", or "Here I'm putting a dot to show that an ordinary sentence ends". She may draw analogies from traffic signals, speaking of "stoppers", "starters", "interrupters", or "direction signs".

When pupils begin writing from dictation, teachers continue their observations on punctuation and pupils record the appropriate marks. Gradually pupils learn the importance of written signals just as, in very early childhood, they discovered the importance of pauses, the rise and fall of the voice, and accents in speech.

Limitations of Written Punctuation

Pupils soon realise that the six or seven written signs are quite inadequate for representing the rich punctuation occurring in speech. Much that is expressed through gesture, facial expression, intonation, and tempo of speech cannot be shown. That is a major reason why writing is often a weak approximation of what happens in language. These shortcomings must seem the more frustrating to a child because they prevent him from representing adequately those very aspects of language which were most communicative for him in early years.

If writers could use the full notation system devised for linguistics and kinesics, they could record intended communications more faithfully. With such a system, as employed in *The First Five Minutes*, writers can represent "the pronunciation of successive words, the intonation, the location and duration of pauses, hems and haws, sighs, gasps, coughs and throat-clearings, and such variables as rate of speech, register, volume, and tone-quality". Bodily movements, too, can be indicated. But since no such system is in general use, the pupil, like writers in general, must try to do as well as he can with periods, commas, question marks, exclamation points, quotation marks, and other standard signals.

Word Position as an Aid. Under guidance the young writer may discover that he can compensate partly for shortcomings of written punctuation by being more careful of the position of words, phrases, and clauses when he writes than he is in ordinary speech. In conversation and oral discussion the speaker is right at hand to explain ambiguities, clarify what is obscure, correct misstatements, repeat items, indicate shades of meaning or feeling with shades of the voice, and—again with play of the voice—establish pronoun references and the proper connections of certain clauses which, in writing, might seem misplaced or dangling. The writer has none of those opportunities. Once he has recorded his statement, his script must stand as it is and communicate what it can. Therefore, position is extraordinarily important.

Difficulties with Complex Sentences

In upper grades, the pupil adds colons, semicolons, dashes, parentheses, and underlining to his instruments. His greatest trouble comes in grades 4, 5, and 6 when he attempts to write sentences that contain subordinate clauses. He has spoken complex sentences lucidly for some years and has heard them ever since infancy, but when he starts writing them he meets the problem of deciding whether to put in a comma or not, and whether to use a comma or a period. Adverbial clauses trouble him especially. In addition he is likely to be unsure about what constitutes a sentence, particularly a written sentence. Uncertain where one sentence ends and another begins, he puts commas where periods belong and vice versa. The results are fragmentary sentences, run-on sentences, and distorted phrasings so characteristic of grades 4 to 6.

Capitals

As for learning the use of capitals, that is far simpler than learning the subtleties of commas and periods. By the end of the second grade most children employ capitals when writing the names of people, days of the week, months of the year, names of cities and streets, and when starting a sentence. In the later grades they begin using capitals in titles of books and stories, at the beginning of a line of poetry, in the names of holidays, and in proper adjectives. They may be surprised to see how widely people vary in their use of capitals and that there is a tendency to put in too many capitals rather too few.

Self-Correction

For checking on the correctness of written punctuation, the oral test is best. The pupil should read his sentences aloud, saying them as he would if he were talking spontaneously. Spontaneity is important because a monotonous, deadpan reading would reveal nothing about punctuation. In this way he can check whether the important auditory signals of the voice are matched by some kinds of visual signals on the page. For example, his voice will tell him whether he should write his statement as, "The boy said the man is here" or "The boy said, 'The man is here'," and whether he wants to say, "The girls who were here yesterday have gone" or "The girls, who were here yesterday, have gone." To help him the teacher should be acquainted with junctures and superfixes as described by linguistics.

The accuracy of self-correction is greater if a few hours or even a few days elapse between the writing and the correcting. Class discussion and correction of recurring errors is profitable. So, too, is the experience of proofreading for a school newspaper.

How a young learner can make punctuation a dynamic instrument in constructing ideas with language?

HANDWRITING

Clear handwriting is a courtesy to readers and a measure of enlightened self-interest for the writer. It is a courtesy because it helps readers pick up the communication rapidly and easily; it is advantageous for the writer because it predisposes readers in his favour. Both of these benefits are appreciated by children, and therefore can become incentives for pupils to improve their penmanship.

Handwriting is a skill requiring both muscular readiness and practice. It therefore demands time for developing muscular coordination in the arm, wrist, and hand, and for the practice required to establish the quick neuromuscular responses needed for rapid writing.

Before entering the first grade all children scrawl words, alphabetic letters, and numbers, and a good many learn to write or letter their names. Also they see samples of writing and many printed words on television, in advertisements, on toys, and on food packages. In school they see their teacher write words and hear her comment on the lettering, neat arrangement, and spacing. Consequently most children have good background for their first systematic efforts in handwriting.

Manuscript Writing

In about 90 per cent of the schools, instruction in handwriting begins with manuscript form. This form is easy for children because it is based on circles, straight lines, and combinations of circles and straight lines. Each stroke used in making a letter can be drawn separately, and the child need not link one letter with another. It is generally considered easier than cursive for children to learn. Furthermore, manuscript writing resembles the printing children see in books. It may contribute to good spelling and reading, but the evidence remains inconclusive. Opinion is divided on whether it reduces the speed of writing. Its major disadvantage is the necessity of switching to the cursive form.

Usually in their first handwriting lesson children watch the teacher letter a name or names on the blackboard. The next day they watch again, and perhaps help the teacher draw the lines. Soon a child does the writing on the blackboard, with the teacher as director, and then each child tries it, with less and less guidance from the teacher. Writing on paper begins as soon as feasible.

During the time of venturing into handwriting, and even prior to it, children profit by having blackboard space on which they feel free to write when they like. A number of classrooms provide "scribble board" for children to use.

The Shift to Cursive Writing

The shift from manuscript writing to cursive is generally favoured in grade 3, as by that time most children have sufficient hand and wrist development to shape letters and maintain a flow of movement from letter to letter. A few third-grade children, though, do not yet have enough coordination to make the change.

Teachers who wish to defer the shift are confronted with the public's disinclination to consider manuscript writing real writing. "When is he going to learn to write?" parents ask when their child is still using manuscript form. That they should ask this question is somewhat inconsistent with adult experiences, inasmuch as most grown-ups are directed to use manuscript writing (by a request which says "please print") when filling application forms for car and driver's licenses, mail orders, and tax returns. The poor quality of the lettering and spacing produced on such forms suggests that attention to manuscript writing might be desirable throughout school years and into adulthood.

When wishing to have the class make the transition, the teacher starts using the cursive form herself for writing on the chalkboard. Then she directs children to slant their manuscript letters somewhat. Next she shows how certain cursive letters differ from manuscript letters, with special attention to the ones that differ most: *b, e, f, h, r,* and *s*. Finally, she teaches the pupils to unite the letters. The transition is easier if children start with words made up of letters having practically the same shapes in both manuscript and cursive forms.

Troublesome Letters

In cursive writing a few letters and letter combinations cause trouble. Concentrated attention on the troublesome ones is strategic, yielding maximum benefits for the time and energy expended.

Much is gained from practice on *a, b, e, h, i, r, t,* and *cl.* Some teachers would add *o, n,* and *s.* Letters *a, e, r,* and *t* are especially troublesome. Slote picked out a list of "scarlet letters", analysed the causes of trouble, and showed how the writing of those letters could be improved. Her list and recommendations are printed here from her book, *Improve Your Handwriting.*

Most children can improve their handwriting conspicuously by following a few simple, specific rules:

Keep the loop well open in letters that are supposed to have loops: *b, e, f, g, h, k, l, q, y, z.*

Avoid making a loop in letters that are supposed to have strokes: *d, i, p, t.*

Extend the curve of *d* until it meets the vertical stroke. This will distinguish it clearly from *cl.*

Cross every *t* on the *t;* dot every *i* over the *i.*

Round the tops of *m* and *n* so that these letters will be distinct from *i, u,* or *w.*

Flatten the top of *r* to distinguish the letter from *s* or an undotted *i.*

Close the curve of *a* so that *a* will not resemble *u.*

Capitals, Spacing, and Slant

Capital letters, spacing, and slant are key items too. Capitals should be definitely larger than lowercase letters. This is especially necessary for letters that, in cursive writing, can have identical shapes in capital and lowercase forms: *A, C, G, M, N, O, S, U, V, W, Y, Z.*

Spacing is important between lines and between words. Between lines the space should be large enough so that the lower halves of letters like *g, j, f,* and *q* do not become enmeshed with the upper halves of letters like *b, f, h,* and *l* in the line below.

Spaces between words ought to be well defined. There should be no break between any two letters of one word because such breaks confuse a reader by making him think that he is looking at two words instead of one.

The slant of letters should be reasonably uniform; a mixed slant is confusing. For speed in writing, a moderate forward slant is best for the right-handed writer; a moderate backward slant, for the left-hander. Excessive slant reduces legibility.

Alignment is important also, but it causes little trouble when pupils use ruled paper and try to make all letters rest on the line.

Numerals

Numerals require special care in writing. Unlike a letter in a recognisable word, a number cannot be deciphered from context. As Slote says:

> Unlike letters, numbers cannot acquire legibility in context. For instance, you may write a perfectly miserable *p*, but when it shows up in something like "appearance", there isn't much question that it is a *p*.
>
> Not so with numbers. Write a thousand numerals correctly and slip up on one; the rest won't throw any light on that number.
>
> Each number must be legible by itself.
>
> In short, if you write every number with a vivid picture of what can go wrong if it isn't understood, you're pretty certain to lick the numbers problem.

The numerals 0, 2, and 5 require most attention.

Left-handed Writers

Because from 5 to 10 per cent of her pupils are likely to be either left-handed or ambidextrous, every teacher needs a workable policy regarding the sinistral child. Theories differ regarding the causes of left-handedness, the dangers of urging a child to shift to right-handedness, and the possible effects of such shift on speech and reading, but experience and research suggest that a pupil should be allowed to write with the hand that is dominant when he comes to school. A left-handed child needs help in finding satisfactory body and paper positions for writing and in using equipment designed for the right-handed majority.

For a left-handed person a backhand slant is natural, and should be allowed. Some teachers provide a chart of the alphabet written in backhand to prevent a sinistral pupil from attempting the forward slant. To avoid a hooked position of the hand and its attendant smudging of the lines, the pupil should reverse the slant of the paper.

Drills and Scales

Although children write best when they have a practical reason for doing so, drills have a place in handwriting instruction. A definite period for handwriting seems to be desirable throughout the grades. But drills should be directed toward specific motor skills or particular aspects of letter formation. They are most successful when associated with a project in which pupils want to write well, and when the teacher's advice is specific. Traditional "writing exercises" usually deteriorate into purposeless copying and produce little improvement.

Given a self-help chart, pupils can diagnose and remedy some of their own handwriting difficulties. Tidyman and Butterfield offer a very workable chart, classifying faults and remedies under seven heads: "line colour", "size", "slant", "letter spacing", "beginning and ending strokes", "word spacing", and "alignment". For each identified fault there is a specific remedy.

The Zaner-Bloser chart on *Handwriting Faults and How to Correct Them* provides ways of testing for legibility, slant, spacing, alignment, size of letters, and quality of line, and enables a pupil to check himself on these qualities. The chart is a development from the *Freeman Chart for Diagnosing Faults in Handwriting*.

Commercial handwriting scales offer a standard for judging the quality of penmanship. Sampling one of them, gives an impression of their usefulness.

Format

The margins, indentations, title, placement of items on the page, size and shape of the paper, and general makeup are, like handwriting, matters of courtesy to the reader and self-interest to the writer. Noting a pleasant format, the reader feels good about approaching the material on the page and is predisposed in favour of the writer.

By the time they learn to write, children have already had several years of experience with format. They have seen margins, spacing, alignment, and other layout elements in newspapers, books, magazines, and posters. They noted the appearance of letters and observed frames and mattings around pictures. Perhaps they gave little conscious thought to those elements, but they surely felt that certain effects were "nice", "pretty", or "not pretty". Inevitably upon reaching second grade they have some appreciation of the appearance of a written or printed page.

Early school impressions of format come from experience charts. The teacher strengthens those impressions if she says something about why she puts the words and sentences where she does and explains that she spaces them to make the sheet attractive.

A teacher can insist on neatness and still escape the very real danger of having pupils criticise her for being "fussy" or "cranky". This she can do by getting children to notice how the format of a paper affects their classmates, sets the tone of a reader's reception of the paper, and gives an impression of the writer's work habits. If the paper is untidy, its bad effects may be likened to those of a person coming to a party sloppily dressed. In these reasons the writer sees that he should be careful for his own sake, not because the teacher insists.

This viewpoint is doubly influential; it provides strong motivation for the pupils, and it protects a teacher's relationship with the children by reducing the likelihood that she will be considered overfastidious for insisting on neatness.

Preplanning and the Angle of Viewing

Two additional viewpoints can be established in the class. One is the idea that planning the format saves time and reduces the need for recopying. It pays to think beforehand about the size and shape of the paper in relation to what is written and the purpose of the writing.

The second idea is the awareness that a writer sees his paper from one angle only while the reader sees it from another. The writer, while writing, has a slanting view of the paper; the reader has a perpendicular one. Moreover, the writer has seen his papers from his writing angle so often and so long that he tends to accept the appearance as all right, regardless of how untidy it might be. It looks normal to him.

Four things can help him view his paper as others see it. He can sit in good posture when writing, thus giving himself an adequate view of his paper. He can lift up the paper, look at it from the perpendicular, and thereby try to judge it as a reader sees it. He can hold the paper upside down and view its general layout. And he can hold the paper in reverse toward a light, looking at it from the back. These means of checking, and especially the third and fourth, give him fresh views of his manuscript and tell him much about the appearance of his paper. Irregular margins or crude arrangements or spacing then show up as the blemishes they are. Elementary school pupils and college students alike are surprised by what they discover about their manuscripts through unaccustomed views of the pages.

SPELLING

Teachers have strained their ingenuity to aid boys and girls in the perennial skirmishes with spelling in English. They have tried all sorts of strategy, with varying results. Research has experimented and probed. Yet spelling continues to be a formidable redoubt for writers to conquer. Ingenuity and research have smoothed the approaches to the stronghold and reduced somewhat the noxious effects of its presence; they have not conquered the citadel itself—the phonetic inconsistencies of English spelling.

Linguistic scientists are the most recent assailants. Theirs is a frontal assault. They reject the "global recognition" and "see-and-say" approaches to spelling. Outfitted with a rigorous mastery of phonetics they attack the central wall. They see—as others saw—that there are many regularities in English spelling. But, more than others, they see some order among the disorders of spelling, some regularity in the irregularity. Thus they try to reduce the enemy by analysing and partially neutralising his forces.

Spelling attracts research and experiments. Its persistence as an unconquered area invites exploration. Also, even more than the area of reading, it offers tangibles to work with. Words are distinct units, readily seen, heard, and counted. Control groups and experimental groups can be established easily. Results are measurable. Experiments therefore have been numerous, and present-day teaching of spelling is the more efficient because of them. But it is not yet easy.

In Chaucer's day a teacher of spelling would have had a relatively light task because pronunciation and spelling were more nearly in agreement than now; a word was spelled pretty much as it sounded. Furthermore the public had not yet put a high premium on "correct" spelling; it accepted variant spellings of words. Since 1400, English pronunciation and spelling have changed considerably, with pronunciation changing more rapidly than spelling, thereby setting up most of the phonetic inconsistencies which trouble spellers today. Retarding factors in the evolution of spelling were the rise of printing and the development of dictionaries. Society—perhaps with a touch of snobbishness—increased the pressure on writers by sharpening its demands for "correct" spelling and taking a person's spelling (particularly his "incorrect" spelling) as an index of his education and culture, even of his intelligence.

When to Introduce Spelling

This is one of the less complicated questions associated with spelling, although there is no clear-cut answer in terms of pupil age or grade. Spelling is needed as soon as a pupil begins to write. Normally some attention is directed to spelling in the latter part of the first-grade year, but the start there is gradual and almost casual, perhaps in connection with experience charts, invitations, or personal notes. In the second grade, spelling instruction is more systematic and direct but based on pupils' needs in writing rather than on a spelling textbook.

All pupils are not equally prepared for spelling instruction in the second grade. Some remember how to spell a number of the words introduced in the first grade; others are not ready for good achievement even at the end of the third year. Children should have a start in reading before attempting much work in spelling. It is desirable also that they be able to enunciate words clearly, write alphabetic letters correctly, and understand the meanings of words they attempt to spell.

Hildreth is one of many believing that systematic work in spelling should not begun until the pupil has attained a mental age of 7½ years or more, developed a speaking vocabulary of some 5,000 words, and can recognise and pronounce 300 to 400 of the commonest words met in reading. Further, she believes that the pupil ought to have had an introduction to the phonics of the commonest words and should be able to copy simple words correctly and write a few easy words from memory.

Betts, specifying "minimum conditions" for spelling, says that a word must be in the pupil's reading vocabulary before it is to be studied for spelling and that the child must know the names of the letters he is using and must have eye-hand coordination.

Which Words to Study

The words taught in the spelling classes of the country come primarily from two sources: textbooks based on lists of words that appear most frequently in children's and adults' writing, and the teacher's and pupils' homemade lists of words needed for writing in the room or grade. A majority of teachers rely almost entirely on textbooks; others, using no textbook, build up their lists from local needs.

In 1915 Leonard Ayres pioneered in word-count research by publishing a list of 1,000 words occurring most frequently in adult correspondence and literary selections. E. L. Thorndike and Ernest Horn extended such research to cover additional types of adult writing. Horn's study, published in 1926, showed about thirty-six thousand different words found in a total of 5 million running words that had been tabulated.

Corresponding studies of words used by children or by children and adults were made by Henry H. Rinsland, B. R. Buckingham, and James A. Fitzgerald. Rinsland's study had an enormous scope, embracing more than 100,000 specimens of writing of all types from grades 1 to 8 in 416 localities all over the United States, and containing more than 6 million running words. Its final list gives the 14,671 words which occurred at least three times at some grade level.

Analyses of those lists and of words in spelling books show conspicuous disagreement among the lists but also a core of agreement. The core of agreement among the lists consists of words that everybody uses very frequently. Most of these words are very short.

Folger, analysing the Rinsland list, concluded that 10 words from the list accounted for 25 per cent of all words which children use; 25 words, for more than 36 per cent; 50 words, for over 40 per cent; 100 words, for more than 60 per cent; 2,000 words, over 95 per cent. Rinsland's most frequent are: *a, and, I, in, it, of, the, to, you, we.*

From data it is clear that no textbook lists will meet all the needs of a particular classroom. Teachers and pupils must build up supplementary lists according to needs of the class and individuals. The need of supplementary lists increases with the influx of new words into children's vocabularies through television, rocketry, space exploration, and other factors which popularise words that either had low frequency or did not exist when the major lists were compiled.

Swenson and Caldwell, counting misspelled words in children's letters, found that 28 per cent of all word errors were concentrated in a mere 4 per cent of all words misspelled. These 4 per cent totalled fewer than 50 words. Fitzgerald identified 222 spelling "demons" by checking through 700,000 running words, and observed that those trouble-some words caused 65 per cent of spelling errors in grades 2 to 6.

Teachers soon discover that they cannot teach all the words their pupils need. After the first 1,000 to 1,500 words on frequency lists, there is much divergence in needs, just as there is divergence among the lists. A total of about 2,500 words is a good objective for the end of the sixth grade, provided the words are chosen with attention to their usefulness. That is a fair start toward the 10,000 which, it has been estimated, constitute the lifetime spelling needs of the average person.

The first words attempted in the early grades should be phonetically regular, having as far as possible a one-to-one relationship between the sounds (phonemes) and written symbols (alphabet letters or graphemes). Words having irregularities between the sound and written symbol should come later. Some fairly difficult words must be learned early though, because children use them often. *Dear, mother, father, received,* and *Halloween* are examples.

Each child must practice self-help, assuming some responsibility for learning the spelling of the less frequent words that he wishes to write. In school his best sources of such help are the classroom word box and the dictionary.

Major Causes of Trouble in Spelling

Certain causes of poor spelling seem to be mentioned very frequently. They are:

1. Irregularities in the way the English orthography represents English sounds.
2. Homonyms (or homophones).
3. Differences between the names of alphabetic letters and the word sounds or phonemes which they represent.
4. Contractions and other abbreviations.
5. Possessives.
6. Incorrect hearing of words.
7. Mispronunciation.
8. Poor handwriting.

9. Ignorance of the meaning of a word.
10. Mental limitations.

Of these, the first three inhere in the phonetic structure of the English language; the fourth and fifth arise from special forms of certain words; the last five result from pupils' personal shortcomings.

Irregularities. The irregularity of English spelling is the greatest single cause of trouble. About 15 or 20 per cent of all words are irregular, about 80 or 85 per cent regular. But the irregulars include many words that pupils use most frequently—up to 85 per cent of the time, according to some high estimates. Young spellers do not go very far before meeting bafflers like: *take, break; head, bed; break, head; walked, caught; cough, off; gate, wait; label, table; receive, believe; bean, green; play, weigh; go, gem, jelly; few, you, view; -able, -ible.*

Also there is the problem of so-called "silent" letters—the *b* in *debt* and the *p* in *pneumonia,* for instance, and the final *e* in the second of each of the pairs: *hat, hate; fat, fate; not, note; bit, bite.* (Commonly referred to as "mute *e*", this *e* is not actually "silent" in the sense of having no function or effect. It is faintly discernible in the spoken word and in a written word it signals a specific value of the preceding vowel. Children can recognise its function and see that this *e* is not actually an irregularity.) Inconsistencies like *first, physics* and *sick, psychology* confront writers in upper grades.

The main reason for these irregularities is numerical. English speech uses approximately thirty-six basic sounds (phonemes) and the English alphabet offers only twenty-six symbols (plus a few diagraphs) for representing those sounds. There are not enough symbols to meet the need. Even if the symbols were used at highest efficiency, the same symbol would have to be employed (in different syllables) to represent more than one sound. No one-to-one relationship is possible between each symbol and some one (and only one) corresponding sound.

In addition the available symbols are not used efficiently. Consequently English spelling is even more inconsistent than it needs to be. As a result the following conditions prevail: *A given sound in English speech is likely to be shown in writing by any one of several letters or combinations of letters.* And conversely, *a certain letter or combination of letters appearing in the spellings of different words is likely to represent, all told, more than one sound because in the spelling of one word it stands for one sound; in the spelling of another word, for another sound.* Those are basic conditions. Every pupil who thinks his way through the phonetic situation until he understands those conditions will at least be aware of the problem he faces.

Regional dialects can cause special complications, particularly when a teacher speaks a dialect conspicuously different from that of her pupils. Trouble occurs in vowels more frequently than in consonants because vowels are more affected by dialectal variations.

Differences between the Name of a Letter and the Sound the Letter Represents. If children are confused by differences between names of alphabetic letters and the speech sounds which these letters represent in writing, the previous classroom instruction in phonics was inadequate. The relationship between spoken sounds and the names of the alphabet should be analysed. Alphabetic marks used in writing have names (which the child utters when saying "the a, b, c's"), but each mark stands for some spoken sound which usually differs from the sound of the mark's name. That spoken sound is part of the phonetic continuum or flow constituting a word. In the continuum it blends with other sounds as *t* in *at, bit, cat, water*.

Homonyms. Homonyms (or homophones) are a form of alphabetic inconsistency employed to show differences in meaning (morphemic differences). A few homonyms are used early in a pupil's writing and ought to be studied as soon as needed. *Their, there; here, hear; to, too, two;* and *write, right* have their places in the second and third grades.

Homonyms usually are studied in pairs or triads, and always in sentences which reveal their usages. But Schonell, a British writer on spelling, does not favour teaching all the homonyms together. Instead he would put each homonym with some other word that sounds and looks like it, or that looks like it but sounds slightly different, or that resembles it in having the same silent letter in common.

Contractions, Possessives, and Abbreviations. The placement of the apostrophe is usually the difficulty in writing contractions and possessives. Contractions that give trouble should be analysed so that pupils see what parts of the full word or set of words were omitted to form the contraction. Spellers are well on the way toward mastering a contraction when they understand the reason for the apostrophe and why the mark belongs where it is. By analysis they can reduce, also, the widespread confusion between the contraction *it's* and the possessive *its*.

As for general abbreviations, a few are necessary in early grades. *St., Ave., Mr.,* and *Mrs.* are typical. Explanations of their origin and reviews of their use should clear up difficulties.

Possessives can be analysed too with profit. Seen in historical evolution, they are a variety of contraction. Earlier English (Chaucerian, for example, and even more recent writing) shows that there had been an *-es* case ending to signal the possessive *(milleres,* not *miller's).* The pronunciation of the word at that time gave full value to the *-es* ending. Gradually the sound represented by the *e* in the ending was dropped from speech and also from spelling. No apostrophe was used. But later, grammarians and spellers decided that the omitted, unpronounced *e* ought to be represented by an apostrophe. That decision prevails today.

The possessive apostrophe is omitted very often nowadays in advertisements, posters, signs, and letterheads: *means clothing, ladies shoes, teachers college.* The trend, apparently growing, is a leading cause of confusion for young spellers. Children see examples of it almost every day in school as well as elsewhere.

Is the use of the apostrophe of possession on its way out? Is it actually unnecessary as a signal in written English? Those are questions which teachers cannot escape if they think of the long evolution of English pronunciation and spelling.

Pupil's Shortcomings. Troubles in spelling may develop from personal causes. Most of them are related to deafness, careless listening, slovenly pronunciation, poor penmanship, ignorance of word meanings, or mental limitations.

Incorrect hearing of words and incorrect pronunciation are related. Both cause incorrect spelling. The incorrect hearing may be due to a pupil's careless listening, defective hearing, or exposure to someone else who mispronounces the word. Incorrect spellings follow: *prehaps* for *perhaps, except* for *accept, chimley* for *chimney, atheletic* for *athletic, pencnil* for *pencil, use to* for *used to, suppose to* for *supposed to, fastinate* for *fascinate, another words* for *in other words, a rear egg* for *a raw egg*. The teacher must first identify the cause. Correction then is usually easy, unless mispronunciations of particular words have been firmly established through years of practice.

Careless penmanship makes spelling appear worse than it is. Some ambiguous letter shaping is not due to carelessness, however. Occasionally a writer, unsure of a spelling, deliberately makes the doubted letters obscure, hoping that readers will interpret them according to correct spelling, and therefore in his favour.

When children do not know the meaning of a word which they are learning to spell they are working in a partial vacuum. The handicap of this somewhat unrealistic situation is avoidable because meanings always can be obtained and learned. However, some advocates of the phonetic method of teaching are far less disturbed by this circumstance than are devotees of the "global recognition" or "see and say" approach. They hold that pupils who know English phonetics and orthography are able, without any ill effects, to spell words whose meanings they do not know. Such ability to project from known spellings to the spellings of unknown words is, they believe, one of the practical benefits from phonetic study.

Mental limitations are a permanent handicap in spelling, as in other aspects of language arts. There is no positive coordination between intelligence and accurate spelling—for many poor spellers are people of high intelligence—but low intelligence can be an insurmountable hindrance in learning to spell.

Procedures in Teaching Spelling

Methods of teaching take into account the difficulties which exist in English spelling. Common sense suggests that a child be encouraged to know the meanings of words he is expected to spell. It suggests further that a pupil ought to hear the word correctly and pronounce it accurately, and that the first words which he attempts to spell should be both short and phonetically regular. To learn a word, particularly a word having phonetic irregularities, he should hear the word pronounced, say it, look at it, visualise it with his eyes closed, spell it aloud, study it to analyse its spelling, and notice whether it shows any resemblances or contrasts with words that he can spell, and whether the spelling fits any rule that he knows. Then he will be prepared to write the word and check and recheck his accuracy until he has learned the word.

The procedure mentioned above is widely followed. It represents a practical strategy. Details in working it out vary with pupils' ages and abilities. The test-study-test sequence is used in many classrooms, especially in grade 4 and beyond, because it saves time that otherwise would be spent on words which pupils already know. The contrasting sequence—teach-study-test—seems preferable in the second and third grades and with slow-learning pupils in all grades. It is practical also whenever a teacher knows that most of the words to be taught are new to the class.

Progress is best when lessons concentrate on words which children need at the time, and when the day's programme is so arranged that words recently studied are used in some natural, practical way. Special drills speed up the mastery of difficult words and of such troublesome parts of words as *-al, -le; -ie-, -ei-; -ence, -ance; -ent, -ant; -able, -ible.*

There is a question whether special attention should be directed to difficult parts of words by the use of coloured chalk, underlining, or syllabication. Some kind of warning or analysis may be helpful. The dangers are obvious if a teacher-overstresses the difficulty or speaks a syllable so unnaturally that the pronunciation of the word is absurdly distorted.

Phonetic Irregularities. When pupils begin to spell words that are phonetically irregular (*cough, puff*) a frank discussion of the situation reduces the confusion. Any child has a great advantage when he is aware that a speech sound (which he hears or utters in a word) is likely to be shown in writing by any one of several letters or combinations of letters, and that, conversely, a given letter or combination of letters which he sees in a word (on the page or chalkboard) is likely to represent any one of a number of sounds. This awareness alerts the pupil to the difficulties in spelling. The situation should not be stressed to the extent of confusing pupils needlessly, but any speller may as well face the truth. In doing so he escapes blind fumbling. Knowing what conditions exist, he can do something constructive to meet them in both spelling and reading.

Typing and Proofing. The use of a typewriter seems to improve spelling among children of seven years or more. The experience of proofreading is definitely helpful. Materials to proof can be obtained from various sources, in school and out.

Grouping. Great consideration, especially in upper elementary grades, is given to the grouping of children. As a time-saver, each group should consist of children who are about the same in spelling needs and achievement. There should be flexibility to readjustment as the pupils' problems or achievements necessitate.

Pupil Interest. The spelling programme of a class takes a strong step forward when pupils join the teacher in planning their goals, discussing the reasons why correct spelling is important, and noting the penalties for poor spelling in daily life. There is a gain, too, when each pupil knows his personal record in spelling and wants to improve it. Lists spelled by pupils should be corrected as soon as possible—often by the pupils—because early returns on test performance are more stimulating to the class than delayed reports.

Individual Lists. Pupils should learn how to help themselves in finding the spellings of words because no word list, published or homemade, can anticipate all their needs. To this end they ought to build up personal word lists and habitually use dictionaries and the word boxes maintained for the entire class or for group. A child whose first language was not English needs to make a special list after he has had linguistic help in pronunciation and word analysis.

Phonetics and Linguistics in Teaching Spelling

The potential of phonetics as an aid in teaching spelling are being developed. Recent studies are more positive than earlier ones in suggesting that phonetics can be helpful.

Linguists urge a vigorous phonetic approach to spelling, as they do to reading. They would have instruction begin with consonant phonemes, which have a high degree of regularity in spelling. They would teach the vowel symbols of short words that are free of irregularities. Irregular words would be approached through ones that the pupils use most frequently. In the irregularities of spelling they look for patterns or "sets". Thereby they group the deviates according to types of deviation, reducing the confusion. Some deviates fit into no set, and must be analysed and learned individually.

Familiar Sounds and Words. An additional suggestion on method comes from linguistics. No time need be spent teaching speech *sounds* to pupils since normal children of school age know the sounds already. Time devoted to such instruction is wasted. What children must learn is the set of written symbols (alphabetic letters) used to represent those sounds. The same is true of words that pupils know. It is a misuse of time to "teach" words like *rain, sun, walk,* or *dog*. The energy should go toward recognising the written symbols for the sounds which constitute those words.

Applied Phonetics. Equipped with accurate phonetic knowledge, a child can pronounce and spell words which are new to him, linguists say. He understands that spelling has an alphabetic basis and that there are correlations between sounds and letters. Without such knowledge the child finds that every new word is one more isolate to be learned almost as if it were a Chinese character.

Robert Hall sees nothing wrong with what is called "word-calling" (pronouncing words whose meanings are unknown) if pupils do it by applying phonetic principles. In *Sound and*

Spelling in English he states his belief that pupils able to pronounce new words through phonetic analysis are excellently equipped for reading and spelling.

Likewise, Hall believes that a pupil should be commended, not criticised, for applying analogical reasoning to spell a word according to the pattern of another word similar in sound. A child writing *munny* for *money* by analogy with *funny* or *rane* for *rain* by analogy with *sane* and *Jane* "is not being stupid; on the contrary he is using his intelligence to extend the patterns of spelling that he has already learned." He must be guided into learning correct spellings, but in such manner that he will continue to think intelligently and analogically, and not resort to blind memorisation.

Patterns within Irregularities. Hall develops the search for regularity within irregularities of spelling. Asserting (as do practically all linguists) that phonics systems in conventional spelling and reading series are based on incomplete and unscientific analyses of English sounds, he presents the phonemic classification which is established by rigorous procedures of linguistics. His table shows thirty-six single phonemes and eleven combination phonemes (such as /*ay*/,/*oi*/, and /*yuw*/) having special spellings or graphemic representations in English. Along with each phoneme he gives the variant spellings found for it in English words—a total of 176 variants for the thirty-six single phonemes and forty-two variants for the eleven combination phonemes.

Having charted all the phoneme-grapheme relationships found in English, Hall lists the ones that are regular and points out certain patterns of "regular irregularities" among some of the irregular ones. He believes that editors of reading and spelling series too often overemphasise the irregularities of English spelling, overemphasising them either out of limited knowledge of the phonemic facts or as an excuse to promote the "see-and-say" or "global recognition" method of teaching.

Syllabication. Provided the syllables are observed as part of the whole word, syllabication is generally approved in the linguistics approach. There is strong opposition to over-emphasising a syllable so much that pronunciation is distorted.

In some words the division between syllables is hard to establish. Hall explains that often when a word has a single consonant phoneme between two vowels a person cannot say whether the consonant goes with the preceding vowel or the following one. In his examples, *demon* and *water,* the divisions could be *de-mon* or *dem-on* and *wa-ter* or *wat-er*. Such uncertainty exists whenever the "lowest point of sonority" between two syllables falls right in the middle of a single consonant between vowels. (The "lowest point of sonority" is the signal which marks divisions between English syllables.) Dictionaries offer syllabic divisions, but many of the choices are arbitrary.

Requests for Pronunciations

Linguistics urges teachers to use phrasings like "What word do these letters stand for?" or "What sound is this the sign of?" instead of the conventional "How do you pronounce this?" "How are these letters pronounced?" or "How do you pronounce *-ing?*" The two ways of phrasing have very different implications. The former implies the actual facts: spoken language is the starting point in all spelling, and written spelling is a method of using graphemes to represent the spoken word. The latter phrasing suggests, falsely, that written words have, within themselves, a pronunciation, and that perhaps they have priority. For a pupil who is trying to learn pronunciation and spelling, the former is the more illuminating; it keeps the record straight on relationships between speech and writing.

Rules for Spelling

The irregularities of English spelling limit the number of workable rules. A rule requires a generalisation, and, in the face of irregularities, generalisation either reaches an end or the rules become so heavily qualified by exceptions that they are impractical. Nobody could formulate a rule that would differentiate between *grammar* and *hammer* or between *label* and *table*.

To be worth emphasising, a rule should apply to a good number of words, be subject to few exceptions, and be understandable to children of the grade in which it is being considered. For a rule to be timely, the class ought to know a number of words to which it applies. In some instances children can generalise on their own, thereby arriving at a rule. Having learned a rule, they must alert themselves to exceptions, in order to avoid errors.

Teachers familiar with linguistics and pupils acquainted with accurate phonetic analysis can generalise more extensively than those not thus informed.

Five or six is about the total number of rules that most teachers find worth the time and effort of teaching. Those rules relate to plural endings *(cat, cats; wish, wishes)*, the final *e* that is dropped when an ending which begins with a vowel is added *(state, stating)*, the *u* which regularly follows a *q* in English words *(quick)*, what happens in pluralising a word that ends in a consonant or *y (fly, flies)*, the doubling of the last consonant if it is preceded by a vowel and is to be followed by an ending that begins with a vowel *(jet, jetted)*, and the *e* and *i* combinations *(receive, believe)*.

The rule covering words like *control, controlled* and *worship, worshiped* (based on whether the word accent is on the last syllable or the first) should be introduced when needed.

For capitals, which are related to both spelling and writing, there are rules, but they are not practiced uniformly.

Measuring Achievement in Spelling

The spelling which a pupil gives to a word is open for everybody to see or hear. Being observable, the performance is measurable, and the testing which is done tells something about a pupil's achievement, although the reasons why a child has difficulty with spelling may remain undisclosed.

Spelling tests take several forms, notably teacher-made (informal or formal), standardised, and the informal measurements of the performance of a pupil when he is spelling words in his normal writing. The last is the ultimate and best demonstration. A teacher's homemade test has the advantage of being tailored to the local situation. Standardised tests, such as the Morrison-McCall Spelling Scale and the Metropolitan

Achievement Test, tell a teacher where her class stands in relation to other pupils in the local school system and the nation. Each of those standard tests presents the words in context rather than as isolates.

The purposes of testing vary, too: pretesting, to reveal which words are known and which require study; diagnostic testing, to identify which pupils are weak in spelling and which kinds of spelling errors are most frequent in the group; and achievement testing, to determine progress in spelling. In addition, teachers use check-up tests in the test-study-test and study-test sequences to measure progress in the immediate spelling lesson.

Tests yield best instructional benefit when pupils correct the tests themselves, particularly if the correcting occurs soon after the test is finished.

Relation between Spelling and Writing

A pupil in a third grade is writing about the class visit to an apple orchard. In his second sentence he wants to use a word that he cannot spell. What will he do? Break away from writing and look up the word in the room's word box or dictionary? Obtain help from the teacher? Spell the word as well as he can? Leave a blank space to be filled in later? Use another—perhaps less suitable—word, but one that he can spell?

Each of these recourses is used, with varying effects. Interruption of his writing to look up the word may break the flow of thought, especially if he is writing something creative. Use of another word, primarily because he can spell it, may weaken his statement by depriving it of the word that would have been "just right".

To meet this problem of spelling in the midst of writing, teachers may encourage pupils to leave a blank space temporarily, so that the rush of ideas will not be interrupted. Or they may try to anticipate difficulties by making a chalkboard list of hard words that the class is likely to need for the immediate project. Teachers might walk among the writers, giving help when asked, responding in a whisper or writing the requested word on a slip of paper.

Positive correlation exists between spelling ability and writing ability, and one of the rewards of good achievement in spelling is a growing confidence in writing.

PUPIL ACTIVITIES

1. In a piece of paper or cardboard cut a small slot that will show only one or two letters of a word when you lay the piece over a word. Then lay the paper over a sample of your handwriting. Can your friends recognise the alphabetic letter or letters they see through the opening without seeing the whole word? Try it on someone else's writing. Why should each letter of a word be written so clearly that a reader can recognise it without needing the rest of the word to help him know or guess what it is?

2. When a speaker does not say his words completely we have trouble understanding him. We say that he slurs his words. When he writes and does not make the letters clear or complete we have trouble reading what he wrote. Do you think that we could say that careless handwriting is like slurring in speech? Ask seven or eight friends for their opinions on this.

3. Here are some of the punctuation marks that we use when we write:

? “ ”

,

. :

Each of them is a signal telling something to people who read what we write.

Imagine that each of them is talking to readers. It says what it is doing. The (?) might say, “I am asking a question”. The (“ ”) might say, “Somebody said this”. Decide what the other marks say.

Perhaps you know a few punctuation marks not shown here. If you do, think what they tell a reader.

4. Invent a new mark that you could use in place of a comma in a sentence. Also invent a new mark to put where we use a period; a question mark; an exclamation point.

Would the marks you invented be as handy for writers to put down as the ones we now use?

5. "Punctuation is part of good manners in writing". This is what someone said. Could you give a three- or four-minute talk on that remark? What illustrations would you use?

6. Sally had just come in. She said, ". . ."

Sally had just come in. She said that she. . . .

If you finish the first sentence you will be giving Sally's exact words. If you finish the second sentence you will be telling in your own words what Sally said.

It is very handy for us to have these two ways of writing what somebody says. Do you see how punctuation helps us in this?

7. Get one of your friends to make a short tape recording in which the voice shows the pauses, ends of sentences, and questions very clearly. Then copy his words as you listen to the tape, and try to put in written punctuation marks that will show how he said his words and sentences. Next have him look at your copy. Does he agree with your punctuation?

If he originally had written out what he was going to record, you could compare your copy with his.

8. Have someone make a tape recording in which he speaks very monotonously, showing no pauses, ends of sentences, or signs of a question or exclamation. As you listen to the tape, notice how much trouble you have in catching the meaning. How could a page of writing that is very poorly punctuated be likened to this troublesome recording?

9. From a story pick out a passage of seven or eight lines containing conversation. Copy those lines but omit all commas and quotation marks.

Then ask someone to read those lines aloud to you. Does that person have trouble deciding how to read the passage? Why?

10. Give yourself the experience of doing some proofreading. That will be easy if your school has a newspaper.

Or the editor of your town newspaper might give you a few columns for proofing.

After you have done some proofreading, do you find that you are more careful about punctuation and spelling than you had been before?

11. Make a dictionary of your own by cutting some sheets of paper to the size you like and stapling them at the edge. In your dictionary put words that you want to learn to spell. Perhaps you will find some such words in advertisements or in magazine and newspaper articles.

12. For one month keep a list of words that you misspell. How many words are on the list by the end of the month? How many of those words did you misspell because you had mispronounced them?

13. Listen to a phonograph or tape recording or a broadcasting by somebody who speaks very distinctly. Would you find it easier to spell words correctly when hearing him pronounce them than if they were spoken by someone who speaks less clearly? Do you pronounce words clearly enough to help your classmates when they want to spell words that you have spoken?

14. Sometimes a reader thinks that we have misspelled a word when we really haven't. The trouble was in our handwriting because a letter did not look like the one we had meant it to be. Look at the words marked wrong in your writing. Do you find any that you had spelled correctly but that looked as if they were misspelled? Ask your friends about their experiences with handwriting in relation to spelling.

15. Pronounce the words *cow* and *bough.* When we say those words, the last parts of the two words sound alike. But we spell those last parts differently. In one we show the sound with the letters *ow;* in the other we use *ough.*

There are other sounds that are spelled in more than one way in different words. Can you think of four or five such sounds?

16. Look at the words *bough* and *cough*. Each word has in it the combination of letters *ough*. But in the spelling of one word *ough* stands for one sound and in the spelling of the other word it stands for a different sound.

In the spellings of many other words we find that a certain letter or combination of letters stands for different sounds in different words. Watch for examples of such spellings. Can you find ten?

17. Talk with people who receive many letters. Those people might be in the school office or in business offices elsewhere. Ask them what they think of the writer when they see words misspelled in letters. What happens if they see misspellings in letters of applications for work?

How do the office people avoid having misspelled words in letters that they mail?

18. Many people say that they can see a misspelling in a word more quickly and more surely when they type than when they write by hand. Perhaps you can experiment to see whether that is true of you.

19. People who proofread for newspapers say that they learn to be good spellers and to see misspellings very quickly. Why might that be true? Try it out for yourself if you can do some proofreading of somebody's letters or for the school paper. Your local newspaper office might be willing to give you some galleys or pages for you to proof.

STUDY ACTIVITIES FOR TEACHERS

1. How often do you find that statements which are clear when heard from speech become ambiguous when written word-for-word as spoken? Does the ambiguity exist because the writing does not show pitch, accent, oral junctures, or other speech signals?

What, for instance, is the meaning of *fast* in "I wonder how fast workers can do this"? Or of *thinking* in "What thinking moviegoers do about this film I cannot say"? Or of *hanging* in "There I saw the hanging tree"?

In speech various intonations of the voice would convey the intended meaning. Is there any way of avoiding ambiguity when writing those sentences?

2. Thirty years ago a teacher of writing said to his class: "Written punctuation is very inadequate for representing the subtle signals of spoken language. In order to record the richness of speech we need additional marks. The resulting notation would be the equivalent of a musical score."

Today the markings used in linguistics and kinesics provide a much fuller notation system. Do you see in them an equivalent to a musical score or to choregraphy?

3. Some people say that handwriting has deteriorated during the last forty years. Others insist that it has not, believing that the *average* person today writes better than the *average* person did early in the century. What evidence is available on this in old school files, courthouse records, and family letters?

4. What are some words that rather recently became popular with elementary school children and that children want to use often inwriting? How many of them are on the Rinsland list?

5. A classroom word count could be made from all papers written by a class during a week or more. What is the likelihood that it would show an influx of some words not widely known in the grades fifteen years ago? Of some words not in existence when professional word counts were made?

6. British and Canadian spellings and those in the United States differ quite consistently in words like *labour, labor; centre, center; mould, mold; glamour, glamor; learnt, learned.* Do pupils become confused by the differences now that international television programme and news photographs show the variant spellings?

7. "How do you pronounce this?" "How is this pronounced?" and "What does this word say?" are habitual remarks. To be correct linguistically a person should say: "What word does this stand for?" or "What sounds does this represent?"

How persistent is the habit of the older phrasing when you try to adopt the newer?

Might children's spelling improve if all teachers used only the newer phrasing?

8. "Silent" letters and "mute *e*" are spoken of often in discussions of spelling and pronunciation. According to estimates, at least forty thousand words in an unabridged dictionary contain at least one so-called "silent" letter as in *fight, would, knight, double, half, mute,* and *tale.* How many "silent" letters in common words really represent no sound? How many signal the nature of the sound represented by some other letter in the written word?

9. What words do first-grade children know how to spell because of their experiences with television commercials? What words not on any frequency list, and probably more difficult than any words on such a list, can fifth graders spell for the same reason?

10. Check the spelling (including the presence or absence of the possessive apostrophe) in commercial letterheads, signs in stores and public buildings, and posters. What spelling rules that you teach seem to be ignored most frequently?

11. What would be suitable titles for four or five spelling boxes that you and your faculty colleagues might set up for yourselves? The boxes would contain cards listing words whose spellings sometimes give you trouble. Pupils do well by using titles like "Home Words", "Animal Words", "Language Words", "Art and Music Words", "History Words", "Arithmetic Words", and "Science Words". How might the faculty titles differ from those?

VIEWPOINTS TO EMPHASISE THROUGH TEACHING AIDS

1. *We punctuate when we write because we punctuate when we speak.*

   (a) Tape recordings of conversations and oral reports. Listening to them several times, pupils notice how people punctuate when speaking.

(b) Three cardboard or paper disks, one on top of the other, are fastened at the center on the same pin or paper fastener. The bottom disk is the largest—10 inches in diameter, for example. The middle one is slightly smaller, perhaps 9 inches in diameter. The top one is about 1½ inches in diameter.

On the bottom disk are a number of sentences written from the outer edge toward the center, and separated a little from each other. The second disk has in it a slot long enough and wide enough to reveal the longest sentence on the bottom disk. On the small top disk are the sentence-end punctuation marks (. ! ?) in a circle around the centre.

By turning one of the larger disks a pupil brings different sentences into the slot opening, and by rotating the small disk he places different punctuation marks after the open sentence. He thus notices how written punctuation can represent different ways of saying certain groups of words.

(c) A poster showing the standard punctuation marks:

. : — —

, ? ( )

! ; " "

Captions: These help you talk on paper *or* It makes a big difference which of these we use.

2. *Readers want to know where quotations and information come from.*

(a) On a poster or chalkboard is a quotation given without naming the source. Its nature makes the pupils wonder where it comes from. Caption: What did the writer forget? *or* We wish the writer had given the source.

(b) Projector, television, or poster demonstrations of how sources should be shown.

3. *Handwriting will improve if we watch six or eight strategic points of penmanship.*

(a) A motion picture film showing posture, placement of

paper, nature of strokes, characteristics of individual alphabetic letters, and other elements of handwriting.

(b) A large picture of a pupil writing in proper lighting and posture and with the paper at a satisfactory slant.

(c) Charts showing manuscript and cursive forms of all alphabetic letters.

(d) On a poster is the statement: Do these and watch your handwriting improve. Beneath are two vertical columns of letters, one column containing letters that require a loop *(b, e, f, g, h, j, k, l, q, y, z)*; the other, the letters with strokes *(d, i, p, t)*. To the right of the first column is a statement like, "Keep your loops in these", and opposite the second column, "No loops in these". A variant caption: Loops and strokes for better handwriting.

(e) Over a handwritten word is a card that has a narrow slot through which only one or two of the word's letters are visible. The arrangement is shown on an opaque projector. Can pupils identify the letters without the help of seeing more of the word? If not, what is wrong? And how could those letters be written so as to be recognisable through the slot?

The card can be placed over various words.

(f) A test like *e*, above, for numerals.

4. *Spacing and neatness help both the writer and the reader.*

(a) Two contrasting letters or class papers mounted on a poster. One is attractively laid out; the other is untidy. Beneath them is the question: Which one of the writers would you rather meet?

(b) Two contrasting copies as in *a*, above. Caption: It pays to recopy, *or* Your papers never stop telling about you.

(c) A poster showing that there are Party Manners, Table Manners, and Writing Manners.

(d) Displayed on a shelf: a small school trophy on a

pedestal, a picture in a frame, and a class paper and a letter having good margins and spacings. The question on an accompanying card:

A pedestal
A frame
A margin } Why each of these?

(e) Pictures and statues in the room or halls and pages of newspapers, magazines and books are used to demonstrate that frames, mats, and pedestals do for pictures and statues what margins do for printed and written papers.

5. *Spelling is handy as a way of putting a word in writing.*

   Several objects either on display or pictured on a poster. Statement beneath objects or pictures: Spelling helps us put the names of these on paper.

6. *A speech sound, when shown in writing, is likely to be represented by any one of several different alphabetic letters or combinations of letters.*

   Appropriate examples on posters or the chalkboard: *deer, dear,* for instance, or *fluff* and *-ough.*

7. *A letter of the alphabet, or a combination of letters, is likely to represent any one of several speech sounds in the spellings of different words.*

   Appropriate examples on posters or the chalkboard: *mi-* as in *misery* and *might,* for example, or *-ough* as in *cough, borough,* and *bough.*

   Tape recordings and television materials can be coordinated with poster and chalkboard examples.

8. *Letters of the alphabet have names, but often the sounds represented by those letters are different from the names.*

   Chalkboard and poster illustrations showing this difference—the name of the letter *b,* for example, together with a few words using the sound represented by that letter, as in *able, job, below;* or *h* and the words *have, hit,* and *behave.*

9. *Careful pronunciation and careful listening help a person in spelling.*

Tape recordings of people speaking clearly and of others speaking indistinctly and mispronouncing words. Which type of speaking would lead to the better spelling?

10. *Incorrect spelling is a blemish on a page.*

(a) Letters and classroom papers shown through opaque projectors or on posters. Some are free of spelling errors; others contain misspellings.

(b) Two letters of application are mounted on a poster. They are much alike, but one contains two misspelled words. Caption: Which letter wins the job?

11. *A person can learn to pick out quickly the words that are incorrectly spelled.*

Repeated experiences of proofreading pieces of prose, printed, types, or handwritten. The class, as a group, can proofread the same piece if the manuscript is shown through an opaque projector.

12. *Some words change their last letter when spelled in the plural.*

A series of drawings, making an animated cartoon, showing what happens, under certain conditions, to the final *-e* in spelling when an *-ing* comes along, as in *skate, skating*. The strip can be pulled through a box movie or opaque projector.

INQUIRIES AND PROBLEMS FOR STUDENTS

1. Demonstrate to yourself that a transition from manuscript writing to the cursive form is rather easy.

2. How often, during a year, do you and your parents have occasion to letter ("print") a name and address? How well is the lettering done as regards consistency of letters and spacing?

3. Collect a dozen handwriting specimens that are hard to read. What specific features make the reading difficult? How much would the legibility have been increased if the writers had kept all loop letters open and all stroke letters closed, and had distinguished clearly between *d* and *cl*?

4. "My handwriting deteriorated in college". So say many college students. What are your observations on college handwriting? What factors might cause deterioration? How can they be countered?

5. Society is exacting in its demands for accurate spelling. Is it overexacting? Is there an element of snobbery in the attitude? To what extent might the emphasis be strong because spelling is a skill that is readily observable and easy to check on?

6. Do errors of punctuation and spelling show up for you more readily on a typed paper than on a handwritten one? What do your classmates say about this? Would you favour having grade children use typewriters in school?

7. It is said that single-consonant phonemes are most nearly regular of all phonemes in spelling. Do you find this to be true in your experiences with spelling? How can the phonemes represented by *k, j, f,* and *s* be troublesome at the beginnings of words?

8. Demonstrate differences between the names of letters of the alphabet and the sounds that those letters represent in the flow of speech. Do you see a corresponding situation in numerals: the pronunciation of the numbers 3 and 4 alone, for example, and then in the number 34?

9. List the ten words that you think occur most frequently in English. Select them on the bases of your speaking and writing, of what you hear and read, and, if you have time, of a word count of several thousand running words in general prose. Compare your findings with the ten nominated as most frequent by Godfrey Dewey, Leonard Ayres, Ernest Horne, and Henry Rinsland.

10. List ten or twelve words that you tend to misspell. Can you identify some reasons why those words give you trouble? Are there evidences of mispronunciation or mishearing?

Make a similar analysis of fifteen words frequently misspelled by grade school children. Of ten words misspelled by your classmates.

11. How many of the following terms can you explain and illustrate? *Diphthong, digraph, homonym, homophone, phoneme, morpheme, grapheme, homograph.*

12. After reading Robert Hall's *Sound and Spelling in English,* examine the phonics sections of several spelling-book and reading-book series widely used in schools. Do those sections contain the flaws that Hall found in some series?

Also see whether you can identify some "sets" or patterns in the irregularities of irregular spellings.

13. Design a series of frames for programmed instruction in spelling. Think of your material as being intended for a homemade type of teaching machine.

14. During the next month try to observe five or six cases of speech abnormality. Of those, which do you think could be cared for by a classroom teacher? Which need a speech pathologist?

2

Development of Structure

With grammar transformed and resurgent in high schools after a generation of neglect, with foreign languages flourishing in all grades, and with the science of linguistics burgeoning, the elementary programme in language arts is in a new era. Courses of study are being redesigned and teachers have occasion to employ a wide knowledge of English and other languages. Instruction in usage and structure continues, but in a larger framework than previously.

Emergent Policies

The spacious dimensions of this new framework spring from policies now emergent. A number of the policies may seem revolutionary, but all prove to be sensible and natural in the analytical intellectual climate of today. Six of them are mentioned below. Their total effect is a considerable accumulation of linguistic knowledge during elementary years. They are not "formal" grammar extended into the grades, but observations about what language is made up of and how it works. Their presence contrasts with the older situation in which elementary schools deliberately avoided not only formal grammar but also almost any discussion of language as language.

Pre-school Knowledge of Language. Children entering kindergarten and first grade are now credited with considerable knowledge of their native tongue. It is recognised that they have mastered the basic sounds and structure. Language arts instruction can use that background is a springboard for extension and refinement of that knowledge.

This viewpoint, promoted by studies in psychology and linguistics, is a notable change from an earlier attitude which considered the child ignorant of grammar, largely, perhaps, because he could not state the rules and had not mastered the irregularities of the language.

Language as a Code. In the new pedagogy, a language is discussed as a code or system made up of units arranged in accepted sequences and embodying numerous signals that mean something to people acquainted with the language. So well defined is each system that a child who once knows its basic structure can understand a sentence that he never heard or saw before and can also compose a new sentence himself.

As a corollary to this viewpoint is the evident fact that anyone using the code must use it acceptably well if he wants people to understand him. A language has within itself an authority which must be respected. This is a most persuasive argument supporting good usage.

Conventional grammar said little about these fruitful thoughts on language.

Discussion of Language. It is now recognised that the English language, in itself, offers a body of material to observe and talk about. Direct and frank discussions can relate to how the language code is constructed, how it works, how listeners and readers know what it says, the various degrees of correctness which one hears and sees in language usage, how the statement of an idea can be changed or modified, and how one can construct ideas or compose in language.

Such discussions contrast with the negative viewpoint which held that nothing which might be considered technical about language should be introduced in elementary grades. It contrasts with textbooks, too, which declared, apparently with pride, that their pages included nothing technical.

That retreat from language may have been a natural reaction from the aridity of unrealistic textbook material, workbooks, and rote instruction by teachers who knew the rules of grammar but had a limited knowledge of language.

Whatever the reasons, it was a kind of self-negation practiced in no other branch of the curriculum.

The newer practice is natural in the light of linguistics. And in being willing to speak forthrightly about her medium, the teacher of language arts is merely doing what her colleagues in the musical and visual arts have been doing all along to the benefit rather than to the detriment of their arts.

Language as Used. Anyone who looks upon language as an instrument for practical communication will shift emphasis from textbook English to the speech and writing of daily life. This leads to a testing of rules by the realities of actual usage. Valid rules survive this test, but that is not the fortune of those which never had a foundation in language history or which, though out of date, had been perpetuated from one textbook to another.

This kind of perspective on language leads to discussion of usage levels, standard and substandard. It also arouses the conversations who oppose innovation in language.

Knowledge of Other Languages: Teachers of English now have several windfalls because of current linguistic developments. Thousands of elementary school children are learning French, German, Russian, or some other non-English language. Many hear a foreign language spoken at home. Thousands also hear foreign languages on television or radio and see signs and banners written in various languages. Children exchange letters with pen pals abroad. In addition, exotic personal names and place names from foreign lands appear in the daily news. On all these linguistic experiences of her pupils a teacher can capitalise.

Contact with an unfamiliar language encourages pupils to view languages—including English—as codes that must be used correctly. It also heightens an alertness to the function of inflections, the influence of word order, and the importance of correct conjunctions and prepositions. Modern linguistics shows how knowledge of one language can be used to strengthen the understanding of another. Thus situations that had generally been considered liabilities now can be converted into assets.

Resources of the Language. Collectively the preceding policies open an inventory of English resources. This gives a dimension of depth. Any language offers a large variety of elements and features for speakers, listeners, writers, and readers to use. Children entering school know some of them but have yet to become acquainted with many, especially in writing and reading.

The inventory viewpoint, though inspiring and valuable throughout life, was rarely suggested by the older grammar.

OBJECTIVES IN TEACHING STRUCTURE AND USAGE

The practices and policies mentioned above indicate the main objectives in teaching structure and usage. The pupil should extend his knowledge of language, discover and use advantageously the resources of English, perceive language as a systematic code, and understand why he will benefit from speaking and writing the code acceptably. Standards hoped for will vary from grade to grade and from pupil to pupil.

Two especially rewarding objectives are an understanding of the way the position of a word or phrase influences the meaning of an English sentence and an awareness of the flexibility which English allows in the placement of phrases and words. They can be developed in connection with the nature and resources of language. Through a knowledge of them the pupil can avoid ambiguous statements, adjust a sentence until it says what he wants it to say, and get a start in the direction of a pleasing style.

Several happy features distinguish the objectives established by the newer outlooks on language. All the objectives have long-range values. Attained, they continue paying dividends throughout school and college years and into adulthood. They are reasonably damageproof, should the pupil meet unenlightened teaching of grammar in junior or senior high school. Most rewarding of all can be the discovery that language itself, viewed in the newer perspective, is exciting to work with. Children may find it as exciting as clay, building blocks, or colours. Though less tangible than those media, insofar as it cannot be touched and can be seen in a superficial way only, language is recognisable as an instrument having many possibilities. The discovery may come as a by-product of other objectives. Most surely of all it comes through contact with teachers who, themselves, find language exciting.

A teacher's objectives are influenced by the extent of her knowledge of language and the framework of the local curriculum. Her knowledge is more influential than the curriculum because if she is well informed on the nature of language and the interplay between language and people she can transcend limitations of the local course of study.

PUPIL BACKGROUND FOR STUDYING STRUCTURE AND USAGE

Children come to school with considerable language background, whether entering sixth grade or kindergarten. Already they are well along with one of life's major enterprises—learning the language. Pedagogically the situation is favoured by the pupils' needs and interests to which teachers can relate instruction.

Most of what children bring constitutes an asset, a capital of built-in motivations, interests, and experiences that can be used and extended. A few items are liabilities to be cleared up, and a good many children learn substandard usages from home and neighbourhood environments. Generally the linguistic backgrounds and needs of pupils can be matched by offerings of a language arts programme. The successful teacher manages to do the matching.

Basic Structure of English

By the time they enter kindergarten, children are quite experienced in combining words into statements. In infancy, before starting to put words together, they listened to other people's sentences. Also they babbled a wide variety of sounds, emitting them in an appreciable range of intonations. Gradually they sorted out such sounds and intonations as they heard used in speech and began using words and sequences of words meaningfully. They developed a fair mastery of the English structure pattern. In the earliest grades pupils know the sound system of the language, the subject-verb object sequence of statement sentences, the inverted sequence and sustained intonation of questions, the patterns of command and exclamation, the placement of the adjective before the noun, the forms signaling tense, singular and plural number, possession, and such vocal signals as pitch, stress, volume, pauses, and tempo. So well developed is this knowledge that a child in the earliest grades generates sentences to meet all his needs. He has yet to master the more complicated patterns of sentences.

The implications of word position are known, too. Statements like "The dog bit the raccoon" and "The raccoon bit the dog" stand in contrasted meanings for any pupil.

There is also a feel for the several classes of words or parts of speech. Before the age of five, and in some cases a year or two earlier, children sense the "nounness" of nouns and the "verbness" of verbs in sentences. A basis exists likewise for an understanding of adjectives, adverbs, conjunctions, and prepositions.

Regularisation

The first five or six years of life provide time to learn the dominant patterns of English but not all the irregular ones. Consequently children regularise irregular forms of nouns, verbs, and pronouns. They apply the structure patterns they know to forms that happen to be exceptions. By leveling off declensions and conjugations in the direction of forms used most frequently they say *sheeps* for *sheep, swimmed* for *swam.*

Children are not unique, however, in this behaviour. Adults, even well-educated adults, show the same tendency. Between children and adults the differences in tendency to level off irregularities in language are in degree rather than in kind.

Linguistic Play

Children have fun with language. They doodle with sounds, repeat syllables, and distort words. Hearing a word that appeals to them they are likely to repeat it often, perhaps with variations in phoneme and stress. Young people like to see what can be done with any linguistic resource which they know, just as they want to see what they can do with a stick or a pile of blocks.

Experiments with pig Latin and other "secret" languages flourish perennially among groups of children. Related to those experiences are impressions of signal systems in scouting, the military services, diplomacy, and aviation.

All such experiences prepare a background for discussions of the English language as a code. They open the way to experimenting with a flexible medium which permits varied combinations and yields a spectrum of effects.

Interest in Communication

Throughout their pre-school years children have strong motives for using language reasonably well. They want to understand others and to be understood. Their social survival depends upon this. Such motivations continue in school, giving a teacher a most advantageous leverage for encouraging good usage.

PUPILS' DAILY EXPERIENCES WITH STRUCTURE AND USAGE

Of all aspects of language arts, the linguistic one pervades most fully the entire day. Continually, in some form, language is an instrument of academic and social survival in school and out. In school it has no limitation of period or subject. A teacher is disposed to be even more gratified when pupils use English effectively in a science or health class than when they do equally well in the language arts period. Conversely it is the heartbreak of an English teacher to see a deterioration as soon as the language period is over.

Outside of the classroom the experiences with language continue to dominate the day. They abound in corridors, on playgrounds, and at home. Their linguistic quality varies, but tends to be somewhat below that of the classroom. On playgrounds, in numerous communities and homes, and in bilingual homes it usually is substandard.

The language which a child sees in public print is spotty too. Along with well-phrased, accurately punctuated statements, he meets crude, ambiguous ones. In the practice of using an apostrophe to signal the possessive case he finds great confusion, notably in the *it's—its* contrast and the misuse of the apostrophe in noun plurals having strong z sounds.

Language flourishes throughout fifteen or sixteen hours of each pupil's day. The five or six hours in the controlled conditions of school must be weighted quite heavily to counter the ten or more wakeful hours spent elsewhere, not to mention Saturdays, Sundays, and vacations.

DIFFICULTIES IN TEACHING STRUCTURE AND USAGE

The linguistic environment of children outside of school, unhappy circumstances associated with traditional grammar, a long-term curricular neglect of language instruction, teachers' limited information about language, and the complexities of the English language cause difficulties in the teaching of structure and usage. Linguistic environment is a problem because, as mentioned above, children spend most of their time outside of school, subject to whatever standards happen to exist there. Only in a minority of cases do those standards equal those advocated in the classroom.

Traditional Grammar

For years formal grammar had been deferred to junior high school or early senior high school, but, through feedback influences, the unhappy circumstances in those advanced years reacted unfortunately on elementary grades. With so much of the textbook material and instruction arid and uninformative regarding the essentials of language, all thought of possibly teaching something about language in elementary grades was dropped. The result was a generation without serious efforts to extend children's acquaintance with basic aspects of language.

Even with good teaching, traditional grammar suffers from two elements: the efforts of early grammarians, who knew and admired Latin, to fit English (a Germanic language) into Latin patterns, and the Latin origin of grammatical terms. Both of these elements impede teachers and pupils in every grade. Descriptive linguistics now provides grammars that fit the English language. But terms remain troublesome. Names like *adjective, pronoun, compound, passive,* and *interrogative*—all self-explanatory when pupils knew Latin—now seem foreign and difficult.

Teachers, administrators, pupils, and parents were disappointed with the results of traditional grammar. They saw little correlation between the amount of formal grammar taught and the quality of English usage. Much was said about the "awful grammar" spoken and written and about students not knowing the structure of their native tongue. The latter complaint came especially often from teachers of foreign languages.

Meanwhile grammar gathered around itself some of the least pleasant of all school time memories. "It's a pity", says Kluckhohn, "that so few of us have lived down our childhood struggles with grammar. We have been made to suffer so much from memorising rules by rote and from approaching language in a mechanical, unimaginative way that we tend to think of grammar as the most inhuman of studies."

Curricular Neglect

The feedback from the unfortunate situation in advanced grades discouraged language instruction in elementary years. The curriculum gave slight support, and textbooks did not pick up and carry forward such linguistic mastery as children already possessed. Little was done to prepare pupils for the sudden plunge into grammar in later grades.

This curricular vacuum still impedes the teaching of structure and usage. A regenerated language programme in junior and senior high schools should improve the attitude in earlier years, opening the way for considerable linguistic instruction there. At present there remains a gap to overcome.

Limited Information

To teach English structure and usage well a person needs to know about the nature of language, how the English code is constructed, and how it works. That kind of knowledge was not really provided by the older type of grammar text, and was rarely acquired by the elementary school teacher. Though able to speak and write satisfactorily, the teacher may not have been articulate about the structure and operation of the language. Native speakers are notoriously unable to describe their own language unless acquainted with descriptive linguistics.

Complexities of English

Not to be ignored are the difficulties which the English language imposes through its irregularities in noun, pronoun, and verb forms. This type of instructional difficulty is not unique to English. No natural language had been blue printed or otherwise engineers for regularity in an early planning stage. Troubled by these irregularities children and adults try to regularise the language by leveling off the exceptions to conform with dominant or regular patterns. Consequently a surprisingly large percentage of the energy expended in teaching usage goes toward preventing speakers and writers from following the centuries-old drift toward regularisation. The big task is to bolster the maintenance of irregularities.

SPECIAL PROBLEMS RELATED TO USAGE

Usage is the production line supported by linguistic knowledge. It is a person's grammar in action. It also becomes an exhibit, revealing to school people and the public the effectiveness of language instruction. Because it is on exhibition it is the centre of controversy between purists and those more liberal in language usage. It is a teacher's major concern and a leading cause of despair.

Controversies over Standards

Admitting the existence of several "levels of usage" they feel satisfied if a pupil attains what seems to be a realistic level for the child's ability and linguistic environment. On the opposite side are those who consider almost any change a corruption. Between the two groups vituperative exchanges abound.

Siding with neither extreme but tending toward the liberal side are the students of linguistics. Noting that several levels of usage exist, they quickly point out that certain usages are substandard. Further, they show that a speaker or writer defeats himself if he distorts the language code so badly that listeners or readers become displeased or confused. When language signals are inaccurate the message is blurred. But linguists say that on matters of pronunciation, syntax, choices of inflectional forms, and vocabulary a person feels more comfortable and responds better when hearing or reading usages which he knows and likes than when encountering others. For this reason they recommend such usages as will win the most favourable and cooperative response from people whose response is desired. They add that everybody, including purists and teachers of grammar, employs several levels of usage, the level differing with the place, type of listeners or readers, and other circumstances associated with the occasion when speaking or writing occurs. However, on an item like "them apples" they would say that the school should teach a child to say "those apples" even if his family and friends say "them apples".

Personal Factors

For children reared and living amid substandard English the mastering of standard forms is equivalent to learning a new dialect. Almost, it is like learning a new language. For bilingual children it is especially difficult.

Social factors may encourage the use of substandard English. This is well illustrated in a report by Golden, who asked students in grades 11 and 12 why they avoided standard forms. The three reasons given most frequently were, "They'd think I was putting on air", "They wouldn't understand me", and "They'd think I was better than they." Miscellaneous reasons included "When I talk to my family and friends I talk like them", "Because I have always used it" (substandard form), "My parents would think I was crazy!" and "Just carelessness". These are compelling reasons, and they can prevail among elementary school children as well as in upper grades.

Choice of Items

A number of considerations affect a teacher's choice of an item for remedial attention. Chief among them are a realistic appraisal of controversial arguments on the item, the pupil's home and neighbourhood environments, the vocational prospects of the pupil, the grade in which the item would be taught, whether the questioned usage is part of evolutionary changes which occur in English, and the relative frequency of the usage.

Selection of specific items is important because best results are obtained by concentrating on a few errors instead of attempting to remedy a large number of errors at the same time. For this policy to succeed, the teachers of several grades should coordinate their remedial schedule so that each important usage receives attention sometime and receives it in a suitable grade. Pooley's suggested allocation of items has been widely reprinted and followed, but schools can establish schedules of their own, based on local needs. Allocations must consider both oral and written usages because the items for the two differ.

The relative frequency of errors tends to be consistent. Notable is the confusion of past tense and past participle of common irregular verbs like *be, run, write, see, come, drink, break, begin, lie, do, go, sit, sing, ring,* and *take*. Also high on the frequency list are subject-verb agreement and case forms of pronouns. Below them come a scattering of miscellaneous errors.

Attainable standards vary with local linguistic environments of the pupils, but by the middle grades children should be reasonably correct in their use of *see, take, do, go, come,* and *know,* verbs ranking next to *be* in frequency of usage. This achievement should include the use of the correct past-tense form after pronoun subjects *(I saw, he did that)* and the use of the past participle forms after the auxiliaries *have* and *has*.

Middle graders can also attain accuracy in subject-verb agreement, in forming complete sentences, and in saying "Sam went" rather than "Sam, he went". Likewise they should outgrow "himself" and "youse".

Reasons for Substandard Usage

Usage problems can be handled most wisely through a knowledge of why the substandard form came into being and how it fits into the evolutionary trend observable from King Alfred's time down through the Chaucerian and Shakespearean periods to the present. Regarding each item the following questions can be asked: Is it part of the long-range tendency to level off irregularities? (*He don't for he doesn't,* for example.) Is it an old usage which is no longer considered desirable? *(He hasn't got nothing.)* Or is it a genuine error in the use of the English code—a misuse that will confuse the listener or reader? (A misplaced phrase or pronoun, causing ambiguity; or disagreement in number between subject and verb.)

The controversial "it's me", for example, can be discussed more satisfactorily if the teacher knows the following five reasons for the popular adoption of the "incorrect" expression:

1. Most English sentences have a noun or pronoun in the objective case following the verb. They conform to the subject-verb-object pattern. This pattern is so strongly stamped on people's speech habits that the objective case form *(me)* is chosen, even after the intransitive verb *is* or *was.*

2. Many people are acquainted with the French expresion *C'est moi.*

3. "It's me" or "It is me" is easier for the vocal organs to form and utter than "It's I" or "It is I".

4. "It's me" is formed farther front in the mouth than is the other expression. Its adoption accords with a long-range English tendency to front (i.e., to sound farther front in the mouth) certain sounds, notable vowels.

5. Americans are influenced by the very wide usage of "It's me" in British speech.

Likewise a teacher finds that there are linguistic reasons for the increasing use of *who* in place of *whom.* And by a little careful listening she will see that usages can be started by the general human tendency to shorten long words and mishear and mispronounce unfamiliar words or phrases.

To obtain information on language evolution and reasons for innovations in usage one must turn to histories of language and especially to modern linguistics. Conventional grammars give little help, restricting themselves to rules and prohibitions. Once informed on an item, a teacher need not sanction its usage, but she is prepared to develop an intelligent pedagogy in relation to it.

Prediction of Trends. Seeing the evolution of English in perspective, a teacher can estimate which of the usages not now sanctioned have good chances of being considered standard in the next fifteen or twenty years. She notes that certain usages are coming in, others fading out. She distinguishes between what is basically corrupt English find what is formal linguistic change. Thus she is not inclined to misdirect her energies or to battle a usage that is almost certain to be fully accepted by the time her pupils reach maturity. She is not likely to set on the wrong horse.

Procedures in Teaching

The *how* as well as the *what* of teaching usage is a school-wide enterprise. A programme has a strong likelihood of succeeding when the whole faculty follows a concerted plan.

As increasing number of teachers avoid the prescriptive grammarian's blunt "That's wrong", "That's awful English", or "You must say it this way. . . ." They prefer to help children discover that there are several ways of saying certain things and that many people like to hear or read them stated in one way rather than another. To this end these teachers encourage children to observe usages in the neighbourhood and discuss their findings. If both "he don't" and "he doesn't" happen to be reported, the teacher is careful to explain that both forms are widely used but that "he doesn't" is the standard form and that educated people prefer to hear it rather than the other.

This policy is considerate of human values. Under it, no child need feel that his father, mother, and friends are linguistic outcasts. By thus reducing the conflict between in-school and outside-of-school usages, a frank approach is more likely than a dogmatic one to achieve its objective.

Advocates of this procedure consider themselves realistic. It is futile, they believe, to aim for high-level usages among children who hear substandard English approximately 83 per cent of each week when they are outside of school. Also, if the gap between actual usage and what is taught is too arbitrary, pupils conclude that something is wrong in the classroom.

Drill. Classroom drill on correct forms is necessary. Incidental corrections of substandard usages do not suffice. But drills easily deteriorate into busywork and mechanical repetition. Mere filling in blanks and worksheets does little to develop good usage. Drill periods accomplish most when short and frequent. They succeed best when supported by pupils' observations on how people use varying kinds of language according to circumstances, and by classroom discussions of why the variations occur.

Oral drill ranks high as a means of improving usages in verb forms, subject-verb agreement, redundancy, sentence sense, and other items which function in speech as well as in writing. Tape and disk recordings help pupils develop a feeling for usages that "sound right". Once a preferred usage sounds natural to a child, that usage has a good chance of being employed.

Tape recorders offer several advantages. Pupils can record a correct usage a number of times, then listen to it repeatedly. They also can have the experience of judging correctness if they listen to a tape containing a variety of usages, some correct, some incorrect.

Instruction in usage succeeds best when it is individual and personal. Any grouping of pupils should be according to similarities in need.

Correct Use of a Code. A strong approach to improving usage can be made through discussions of English as a code. Thinking of their language as a coded system pupils realise that they must use it correctly if the message is to be understood. Again their experiences with secret languages and semaphores link the subject with their lives. Pupils see that correct usage of a code is important to everybody. If a sentence is wrong grammatically it is wrong because its construction confuses the hearer or reader, not just because a "book says so". Any child who realises this fact has reached a commendable stage of linguistic maturity. Also he finds it a most convincing argument for improvement of his usage.

In any classroom the teacher finds many occasions to point up the values of using the code correctly. There are sentences and longer statements which tell their messages especially well, and deserve special attention because of that. In contrast there are sentences which cannot be understood readily. They need restating (or recording). And there are occasions when the whole class is especially anxious to have their announcement, invitation, or news item understood correctly by people attending school assembly, listening to the public address system, or reading the school newspaper. Then, if ever, the attainment of correct usage becomes a total class enterprise.

LINGUISTICS AS AN AID IN TEACHING STRUCTURE AND USAGE

The science of linguistics is an altogether natural development of the twentieth century. It meets the current interest in finding out how things work and what they are made of. In contemporary spirit it analyses the phenomenon called language. Its procedures and findings, far from being mysterious or remote, are realistically sensible.

Linguistics identifies the basic components of a language and describes the patterns by which those components operate to convey information. It therefore is interested in phonemes, morphemes, classes of words (or parts of speech), arrangements of words in sentences, the development of various sentence patterns, and the signals which indicate meaning. It shows that language has many signals: vocal signals such as pitch, stress, loudness, duration, and breaks between words or part of words; visible signals in the forms of facial expressions and bodily gestures; grammatical signals like tense, number, case; and syntactic signals through word arrangement and position. There are punctuaton signals used in writing only, but these are relatively few—too few to signal the richness of meanings expressed in spoken language.

To linguists, a language is fundamentally a continuum of sound, encoded according to a system that a society understands. Speech is considered the primary form; writing, a secondary or derived one.

Linguistics tries to explain how sentences can be generated and made to grow (or transformed) in various directions through the addition of qualifying phrases and clauses. It also attempts to bridge the gap between structure and meaning. To do this it prefers to start from structure and proceed to meaning rather than use the route of traditional grammar from meaning to structure. In justification it says that, up to a point, the structure determines meaning more than meaning determine structure, even if, beyond a certain point, a recognition of the meaning becomes important.

Thus linguistics prepares a blueprint showing what the language is made up of, how it conveys meaning, and what resources it offers to people who use it. Its approach is descriptive, illuminating important aspects that conventional grammar leaves unexplored. It represents a shift from classification of language items to description of how the items combine in use. It rounds out the picture of language. Eventually it arrives at grammatical rules, but inductively and by offering a broad view in addition. Perhaps one can say that conventional grammar and linguistics view language from opposite ends of a telescope.

Background for Teachers

For teachers of language arts, linguistics provides two kinds of help: informational background and a viewpoint which enrich the approach to all aspects of language, from kindergarten through high school and college; and certain linguistic facts which can be taught in appropriate grades. The former contribution is exceedingly important for teachers in elementary schools, where pupils form persistent attitudes toward the study of language.

In any grade, throughout the school system, a teacher can present English from either of two perspectives: a rather narrow one, established by the prescribed rules of a book, or a broad one, in which the teacher sees and helps pupils see English as an example of the great human phenomenon of language, with patterns of arrangement, signals (spoken and written), a large inventory of resources, and standards of usage, all employed as a mean of communication. Linguistics furnishes this latter perspective by giving information that traditional grammar leaves either obscure or unexplored.

The older, prescriptive system of grammar gives security to people who either want something very definite to prescribe or are not confident in their own knowledge of the nature and behaviour of language. Linguistics appeals to those who welcome a modern, bold assault on problems of teaching and learning language.

Contributions to Instruction

The kinds of things that linguistics explores are practical and easy to talk about in the grades. Also, the how-language-is-made and how-language-works activities appeal to children.

The inductive approach helps, too. "It offers a method of inquiry that is *in itself* satisfying and liberating to the student", declares Postman. This method, he continues, "sensitises" people to the structure of language, but in the method of traditional grammar a pupil who is given the definition of a noun, for instance, "is neither encouraged nor equipped to reflect on its truth or falsity".

The extensive helpfulness of linguistics in teaching usage was evident in the preceding section of this chapter and need not be restated here. But linguistics contributes to instruction in other aspects of language.

Attitude toward Language. The findings of linguistics encourage people to see language as a live, dynamic system made up of structures and signals and vital in people's lives. Pupils and teachers can observe English objectively, thus opening the way for linguistic fun and linguistic truth. The situation contrasts with that in a traditional grammar class which treats language so impersonally that everything seems remote and dissociated from daily life.

Communication systems and codes éxcite children' interest. The popularity of "secret" languages demonstrates that. Some of this excitement can be transferred to the English language. Children note the code nature of English in both speech and writing. Conspicuous are the *s* sounds to show plural in nouns and singular in verbs. Also easy to notice are such signals of the voice as pauses, accents, rise and fall, and loudness and softness. Pupils see some signals on experience charts of the first grade. Later they can have fun with the code by covering a part of a sentence with a card and then, after reading the first part of that sentence, trying to guess what signals are in the portion that is covered. Points out some of the signals used in English.

For a number of reasons the linguistic approach is a promising one for getting pupils excitedly involved in language. It interweaves the structure of language with the pattern of life.

Resources of English. People are not accustomed to think of language as something that offers resources, but the viewpoint is fruitful. Having attained it, a pupil sees all the elements of language in a new light. Before him are many items for him to use. The simple fact that they exist is an inducement for him to see what he can do with them. "Other people use them, so why shouldn't I?" he concludes.

The descriptive approach to language is best for attaining this viewpoint because it carefully identifies the components of language. Linguistics also encourages pupils to listen, watch, and read in order to note what other people accomplish with language. Tape recordings and efforts to use new resources in writing make the discoveries personal with each child. Pupils tend to respond because they have a native eagerness to try anything new and to see what they can do with it.

Upon entering school, children already have command of numerous language resources, particularly of those related to speaking and listening. But they can find many more in oral English and in connection with writing and reading. Discovery of previously unused language resources and of how people use them can be an accomplishment that will pay dividends throughout a lifetime.

Discovering unused resources is, in a sense, equivalent to improvement in usage. For all poor usage is not related to grammar and syntax; some of it results from personal poverty in language patterns. There are people who speak and write in correct syntax but with limited effectiveness because they do not know what can be done with language. They do not know the resources. The result is either ambiguity or monotony, or both. The remedy is greater acquaintance with what language offers.

Punctuation. Both oral and written punctuation receive great attention in linguistics because all punctuating is a form of signalling. By identifying the superfix elements of stress, loudness, and juncture, linguistics explains the basis of most oral punctuation. For written punctuation it urges oral testing to see whether commas and other written signals show the places where sizable junctures and certain intonations occur in speech.

Linguistics also points out and explains the poverty of written punctuation compared with subtleties of speech. For their special needs, linguists devised systems of full notation which record practically all aspects of intonation, gesture, and kinesics, as well as the precise phonemic values of the words. Children cannot be expected to use such notations but they can appreciate the intent and value when they see a specimen.

The Importance of Position. In sentences like "Sally rocked the doll" (contrasted with "The doll rocked Sally") children readily see that the position of a word influences the meaning of a statement. But they meet sentences in which the effects of word or phrase position are more subtle. A pupil might say or write a sentence like "I ate the apple that I bought in the car". Class discussion would be needed to help some children see that "in the car" could refer to either the eating or the buying. Further discussion would test other ways of arranging the sentence and point out the meaning of each arrangement.

Almost any sentence that has dangling words, phrases, or clauses (often yielding absurd meanings) or that is ambiguous for another reason can be improved by changes in the positions of certain parts. Incorrect references by *who, which,* or *that* usually are remedied by placing the pronoun as close as possible to the noun to which reference is intended. The words *only* and *alone* also raise problems of position.

Attention to position is more crucial in writing than in speech. In speech the intonations and pauses usually make the intended meaning clear.

Position invariably receives attention when linguists study any language. In English it has become increasingly important since Anglo-Saxon times in proportion as the language lost case endings in nouns and conjugational endings in verbs. Linguists call modern English a positional language, as contrasted with inflectional languages like ancient Latin and Greek. In highly inflected languages words may stand some distance apart, yet be united by related inflectional endings. When inflectional signals become scarce in a language, position takes over.

Alertness to the importance of position is therefore extremely rewarding for any student of English. Linguistics, through its grammar of word order or position, provides information to help develop that alertness.

Linguistic Flexibility. A tolerance exists even in the somewhat fixed structure of a positional language. Varied phrasings (with corresponding changes in meaning) are linguistically admissible in a majority of statements. Between flexibility and the importance of position there is an interplay which can be likened to a linguistic dance; flexibility makes possible the advantageous placing of words, phrases, and clauses, while the importance of position gives value to flexibility. Linguistics describes the limits within which flexibility is admissible in English structure. Once a pupil resolves to take advantage of the flexibility of the English language he has made a decision which will have long-range influenes on his precision and his style.

Word Classes. Linguists prefer the term *word classes* over the conventional grammar designation, *parts of speech.* Their name, they think, is more descriptively fitting than the other, somewhat enigmatic one.

Pupils, too, seem to think in terms of classes or types of words. Before starting school they become aware of noun types and verb types. Using the linguistic descriptions of word classes, a teacher can refine that awareness, together with the feeling for the other types of words. She may wish to follow linguistics in reclassifying several of the minor types under headings called *connectors, operators, function words,* and *determiners.*

Instruction in word classes develops the "grammar readiness" that junior high school teachers hope for. More significantly it helps children realise what elements make up the language and how those elements operate to convey meaning.

Functional Shift of Words

The *race* is over.

The boys *race* from the barn to the house.

He won the *race.*

This is a *race* horse.

He keeps the *racing* records.

Words can resemble chameleons. Above, the word *race* changes in nature or class when its function shifts. Such functional shifts confuse pupils who are trying to understand word classes.

Linguistics reduces the confusion by describing standard sentence patterns and showing that each place in the sentence is occupied by a certain class of word. Correspondingly any word put into a particular place and having a particular intonation becomes thereby a member of the word class associated with that location and intonation pattern. The shift occurs automatically.

This behaviour of words is interesting to observe. Incidentally it provides a framework for studying and testing the usage of correct case forms of personal pronouns.

Beginnings of Grammar. There is no need, they believe, to wait until the seventh or eighth grade before talking about how the language works. Some generalisations about the use and patterns of English will make sense to younger pupils.

The descriptive approach to language reveals much that is easy to see and explain. For example, there can be discussion on how a person hearing somebody say "Joan bought the books" knows that Joan is the one who bought the books, that she had bought the books already, and that she purchased more than one book. There can be experiments with the meanings of vocal signals—pauses, rise and fall, stress, and tempo—all of which children have heard and used.

From linguistics comes help in teaching what a sentence is, through attention to how the rise and fall of the voice and the breaks (junctures) tell where a sentence ends and whether it is a statement, question, command, or exclamation.

If a teacher has occasion to explain the nature of a noun she can turn to linguistics. There she will find that a word or construction is a noun if it meets the following specifications: (1) it can be pluralised; (2) it can be made to show possession; (3) it can be used with such noun makers as *a, the, his, their;* (4) it can be used in certain places or slots in a sentence; and (5) it receives certain voice intonations when the sentence in which it appears is spoken. All this is far removed from the conventional (and fallible) statement about a noun being "the name of a person, place, or thing", but it is more explanatory and more defensible.

In correspondingly descriptive manner linguistics explains other classes of words.

Carried forward over a number of years through a planned progression from grade to grade, observations on how the English language works lead to considerable knowledge by the end of grade 6. With the new and interesting information available there is no longer any excuse for backing away from grammatical instruction in early grades.

Bilingual Problems. When teaching English structure and usage to a bilingual child a teacher has a great advantage if she knows the structure, sentence patterns, and intonation system of the non-English language. She can get such information from linguistics. Then, if she knows the linguistics of her own language, she realises the language problems which her pupil faces in switching from his language to English. Her advice can be efficient and practical.

Preparation for Other Languages. Such linguistic knowledge is convertible to the study of German, Russian, Japanese, Latin, or other curriculum offering. It is much more convertible than the substance of traditional grammar. Rules and definitions conventionally given for English do not fit other languages, but the linguistic concepts mentioned above prevail among languages everywhere.

Teachers of foreign languages declare that their students could learn the language better if they knew English grammar. Their statement is only partly true. Not English grammar in the traditional sense of the term, but English grammar as set forth in structural and descriptive linguistics is what is needed.

PUPIL ACTIVITIES

1. The message "Raise the flag at once" must be signalled to some people who are on a nearby hill. You are to do the signalling. The people can see you, but they are too far away to hear you. Therefore you must send the message by a code made up of signals that they can see.

What code will you use? One you learned in scout activities? One you make up yourself? Put the message into the code that you decide to use.

2. Make a guess as to how many times you need to use language for some practical purpose during one hour of a day. You can choose an hour at school or an hour at home.

After you have made your guess, try to keep a record for an hour. On a small card you can make a mark for each time you talk or write.

If one of your friends does the same experiment, you can have fun comparing notes.

3. The next two times you go shopping for groceries, try to make a count of how often you must use language during the trip.

4. Watch somebody closely for ten minutes to see how often the person uses language. Count every time he or she talks, writes, or uses sign language. Perhaps you can do this without letting that person know that you are watching.

5. Two people are talking about automobiles, but they do not know English grammar very well. They do not know how to show the difference, by words, between one automobile and more than one automobile. That is, they do not know how to change a word to make it plural. Also they do not know the differences in meaning between the words *and* and *or*.

Make up some of their conversation. Do you discover what troubles they have in saying what they want to say?

6. The *duck* has oil on its feathers.
I counted five *ducks*.
There is oil on a *duck's* feathers.
There is oil on *ducks'* feathers.
There is oil on the feathers *of a duck*.

As you look at the italicised words can you see how our written language shows whether we are talking about one duck or about more than one duck? Can you see, also, what sign or signal the English language uses to show that something belongs to a duck?

You will find a different kind of signal in the sentences below; it shows the time when some things happened. Do you also find one kind of signal that is like one in the sentences above?

One child went skating.
I saw five children skating.
I wanted the child's book.
They opened the children's books.

7. Think of how many ways people say "You'll be sorry". Notice all the different meanings people give to that sentence by making or holding certain words or parts of words longer than other words, and by making the voice go up or down. Try the sentence yourself, on a taperecorder, and then, as you listen to yourself, notice how your voice uses certain signals to show the meaning.

Do you find that people also say the word "yes" in various ways, giving different meanings to it? Do facial expressions and gestures help?

How many of the different meanings of "you'll be sorry" and "yes" can you show by punctuation when you write?

8. People who write telegrams think carefully about the way they state their sentences and also about punctuation. Can you tell a few reasons why they must be careful? Look at some telegrams and write several, to test your reasons.

9. Take sentences containing pronouns such as *that, which, who, she, they,* or *he.* Sentences like "I bought the book which I saw in the window" or "The man brought the dog that he had trained" would be fine. Draw a line from the pronouns to the words that they refer to. In these sentences you would draw lines from *which, that,* and *he* to the proper words. Put an arrow on the line to show the direction of the reference.

10. In museums and libraries you can see some language codes other than English. Perhaps they will be ancient picture writing, Egyptian hieroglyphics, Arabic, German, Japanese, or Russian. You probably cannot read them.

As you look at them, do you think of the fact that any language is a code, and that both the person who writes and the one who reads must know how to use it if the message is to be understood?

11. Have you ever thought of comparing the English language to a construction set—a Tinkertoy set, for example? You can tell what different kinds of pieces are in a construction set and what various things you can make out of the set by putting certain pieces together. Also you know that pieces can be put together in many different ways, to make many different things.

So, too, if you think carefully about our English language, you can tell that there are different kinds of "pieces" or parts in it. You will notice words, sentences, alphabet sounds, and many other parts which you use when you talk or write. How many "pieces" can you find?

Then notice how the different pieces of language, like pieces of a construction set, can be put together in many ways so as to have different meanings and to make various kinds of sentences and paragraphs.

12. While your bicycle is running well you do not think very much about it. You just keep on giving it good care and handling. But when the chain breaks or a tire goes flat, you and your friends give it a lot of attention. You want to repair it.

Have you noticed that the use of language is somewhat like that? As long as you speak or write correctly, nobody says much about it. People enjoy your good language, but they don't give it special attention. But when something goes wrong with your grammar, they notice it and want you to repair it.

Does grammar get more attention when it is incorrect than when it is correct? Do people take good grammar for granted and pay little attention to it?

13. A "never-again" list is a useful thing to have. On that list people put all the kinds of mistakes in grammar and spelling that they find themselves making.

Then once in a while they look through the list and see which mistakes they no longer make and which ones must still be watched. They also check through the list when they are revising papers that they want to hand in or when writing letters for mailing.

What items would be on your never-again list?

One or more of your classmates can plead the case for the expression, and another one or more can argue against it. You can easily arrange for a judge and jury.

STUDY ACTIVITIES FOR TEACHERS

1. A planeload of English-speaking people makes a forced landing in a jungle area of New Guinea. The natives understand no English, and the passengers know nothing about Papuan languages. The friendly natives talk much among themselves and try to communicate with the strangers. By the second day the stranded travellers have observed enough about how the native language works to understand a fair amount of what is said.

What features of the language would the travellers watch for and analyse in order to break the code? What features regarding words? Regarding word order? About the rise, fall, tempo, and stress of the voice?

To what extent would these people be doing what a linguistic scientist does when he analyses and describes a language?

2. Listening to various languages—English, German, French, Spanish, Russian, Italian, Swedish, Danish, Chinese—can you notice that each language has its unique speech melody? If someone turns down the volume of a radio programme until the words cannot quite be understood, can you nevertheless tell, by the speech melody alone, which language is being spoken?

3. After a little practice you can listen to a news broadcast in a special way: concentrate on the spoken sounds, not on the news that is being announced. Then the announcer's statements become an orchestration of sounds only—a flow of phonetics grouped variously, with pauses, risings and fallings of pitch and volume, and modulatins of stress, the whole producing a patterned, understandable code.

The experience helps people understand why some linguists say that spoken language may be considered as "a noise made by the face". The "noise" is, of course, a controlled, patterned one.

4. In *Mirror for Man,* Clyde Kluckhohn observes that language, through its system of signals, says to people who hear or read it: "Notice this", "Always consider this separate from that", "Such and such things belong together".

How strongly aware are you that grammatical forms and other signals of language, in themselves, tell much? As Kluckhohn comments, persons trained from infancy to respond to those signals "take such discrimination for granted as part of the inescapable stuff of life."

5. For what reasons does a page of prose or verse in a language that you cannot translate make you realise that language is a code?

6. The English language uses various ways to show

relationships among ideas or among words representing those ideas in sentences. Can you find ten ways illustrated in one column of a newspaper?

How many additional ways might have been employed if the sentences in that column had been *spoken* with the full dynamics of speech?

7. "This poem stirs the imagination. Do not all good poems stir the imagination's fire?"

How could this idea be stated by means of picture writing only? After having drawn the pictures, speculate on how they might evolve, if they were used by several generations of writers. Might they be streamlined, stylised, and perhaps even reduced to abstract symbols?

8. Can you get through a half hour or more of active life without using an adjective? a noun? a verb? an exclamation?

9. Have someone delete every fifth or sixth word in a selection of normal prose. By reading what remains, can you guess the words that have been deleted? Or, at least, can you determine the class (or kind) of word in each deletion? In how many instances can you determine the class of word from the language structure alone, without much attention, if any, to the thought?

If you can make these guesses fairly accurately, what does that accuracy imply regarding:

(a) The presence of a well-established structural pattern in language?

(b) The existence of predictability or probability in word sequence?

(c) A certain amount of redundancy in the language?

10. People generally say "a raise in wages" or a "wage raise" rather than the traditionally correct "rise in wages" or a "wage rise". Yet they speak of a "price rise" or a "rise in prices".

Is it likely that phonetic influences operate here? Does the *a* sound in *wages* tend to encourage *raise* in place of *rise?* And does the *i* sound in *price* tend to retain the correct form *rise?*

11. Here is an experience that is illuminating to people who expect a living language to change, but disturbing to those who imagine that a language can be frozen at its *status quo.*

The time of King Alfred (tenth century Anglo-Saxon or Old English)

The time of Chaucer (Middle English of 1400)

Shakespearean (1600)

Contemporary

VIEWPOINTS TO EMPHASISE THROUGH TEACHING AIDS

1. *The English language is a code for use in sending and receiving messages.*

(a) Poster showing a semaphore code in use by boy scouts or on a railroad. Shown along with this is a sentence being spoken by someone to a listener.

(b) Cartoon drawings showing an American tossing a sentence, made up of English words, to another American. The second American catches it readily. Also shown is a Frenchman tossing a sentence, made up of French words to a Frenchman. The Frenchman catches the sentence. This can be developed further by indicating that the American probably would have difficulty catching the sentence tossed by the Frenchman and the Frenchman might likewise fumble the English sentence.

2. *The English language, like any code, uses a set of signals or signs according to a definite plan to show the meaning.*

(a) On a poster, opaque projector, or overhead projector present sentences like:

The rabbit's nose *is* pink.

The hunter tri*ed* to keep *his feet* warm.

The words and letters that are italicised here should be shown in red. Caption: The red parts are signals. What does each one show?

(b) On a poster write two or three sentences like those in *(a)*, above. Space them generously. Put small paper flaps over some of the signals. Caption: Guess what the signals are? Why do you need them?

(c) Take advantage of the signal system that is in any artificial or "secret" language which happens to get started among the pupils.

3. *In our everyday use of language we sometimes are senders, sometimes receivers.*

A poster with drawings of transmitter and receiver, as in television or radio. Sketches of persons sending and receiving semaphore signals. By additional sketches or by words, point out the fact that in speaking and writing, too, people are transmitters and receivers.

4. *We must know how to use the words and signals of the English language if we are to send or receive a message correctly.*

(a) A poster showing transmitter and receiver, as in 3, above. But transmitter and receiver are not in tune with each other, or are set for different channels. The message does not get across.

(b) A picture showing a boy scout signalling a message and another scout picking it up. Caption can emphsise that the message gets through when the sender knows how to handle the signals and the receiver knows what the signals mean.

(c) A tape or phonograph recording of a language which the children do not understand. A few seconds of listening to it demonstrate that the message is not understood because the listeners do not know the words and signals of that language.

(d) A few pupils who already know or are learning some non-English language converse briefly in front of the class. They understand each other; members of the class do not understand them.

5. *The English language is important to us many times every day.* On a poster:

	100 times	
	300 times	
	400 times	
You speak, listen, read, or write	600 times	a day?
	1,000 times	
	50 times	

Caption: Which number is nearest to yours?

6. *The way we speak and write our language tells people much about us.*

(a) Tape recordings of the speech and conversations of children and adults not known to the pupils. Pupils listen to the recordings and notice that they form some idea of the speaker from the way he or she uses language.

(b) Radio speech, listened to for the purpose mentioned in *a*, above. Television speech is workable, too, especially if the listener avoids looking at the screen. After having gained an impression, the listener can look at the image and see whether his impression was correct.

(c) The sound of people's speech in an adjoining room or around a corner, listened to for the purpose in *a*, above.

(d) Opaque projector showings of letters and other writings done by people whom the children do not know. What impressions do we form of the writer when we look at the written language?

7. *The subject and the predicate of a sentence must fit together.*

On chalkboard, opaque projector, or poster are sentences like: The beaver swims cautiously. Beavers swim cautiously.

The beavers that built the dam in the creek swim cautiously. Caption: Subject and predicate sometimes are close together, sometimes far apart, but they should always agree.

Arrow lines from *close together* to the two short sentences; and from *far apart* to the long sentence.

8. *A sentence is made according to a plan or structure.*

(a) A poster showing a pile of bricks that had been casually tossed together, and also a brick wall that is nicely built. Shown, too, are some words *(forests, we, our, campfires, careful, being, by save, with)* and the sentenec: We save our forests by being careful with campfires. Caption: They can't just be tossed together.

(b) Sentences pasted on a blueprint. Caption: Sentences, too, have a plan.

(c) On an opaque projector, show a series of sentences in ribbon-sign manner. Sentences are on long strips of paper that are pulled through the projector. The structural plan of the sentences is easy to observe and discuss when the pupils see part after part of the sentence.

(d) On a chalkboard or poster is a sentence. Part of the sentence (subject part or predicate) is underlined. Pointing to this part is an arrow line which starts from the caption: There's a reason why this part of the sentence is here.

9. *Each kind of pronoun has its special way of working.*

(a) An overhead-projector drawing or an animated-cartoon type of sketch is good for demonstrating that (1) *who, that,* and *which* tend to link up with the noun that comes earlier and is nearest in the sentence; and (2) *he, she, it,* and *they* tend to refer to a previously mentioned person, thing, or idea which fits with the particular pronoun and which the phrasing of the sentene or paragraph has made most important.

A pronoun is pictured as a cowboy twirling a lasso. The lasso catches the word that it refers to. Some pronouns lasso the preceding name that is close to it. Others catch a preceding name that stands out as especially important.

(b) A poster or an opaque projector sheet carrying a sentence or paragraph marked with lines that extend out from the pronouns and show the references.

(c) In a paragraph the word (or words) naming the idea, person, or thing that the statement makes seem most important to the reader is written in large letters, so as to be conspicuous. The personal pronoun *(he, she, it,* or *they)* that follows somewhere in the paragraph would link up with that word.

(d) Projected sentences show that sometimes a comma and the number of the noun or verb are signals to help show what a pronoun like *who, which,* or *that* refers to:

There are animals living on the prairie which are called coyotes.

There is an animal living on the prairie, which is called a coyote.

There is an animal living on the prairie which is called a coyote.

Discussion can point out that the *positions* of words in sentences give hearers or readers excellent signals:

On the prairie lives an animal which is called a coyote.

On the prairie lives an animal called a coyote.

10. *The pronoun form which we use when it is alone as the subject of a sentence should stay the same even when something else is added to the subject.*

On a poster or through a projector:

I did the work.
Henry and *I* did the work.

11. *Sentences, clauses, and phrases differ from each other.*

Flannel board, overhead projectors, chalkboard, and opaque projectors can present examples showing differences between a statement that is complete in itself, one that is a clause-type part of something larger, and one that is a phrase-type part of something larger. Captions and discussions clarify the differences.

12. *We have four kinds of reasons for talking or writing something.*

A poster or opaque projector layout showing that we *tell;* we *ask questions;* we are *surprised;* we *ask people to do things.* Under each of the four is an example of its particular kind of statement (declarative, interrogative, exclamatory, imperative). A picture or drawing can be added to each, showing a situation in which that particular kind of statement is naturally used.

13. *Other aspects of language, as stated among audio-visual suggestions in earlier chapters on speech and writing, and in following chapters on words and composing.*

INQUIRIES AND PROBLEMS FOR STUDENTS

1. Do you believe that language is too often studied solely as a medium for communicating? Does that emphasis cause students to neglect thinking of the English language as a dynamic and interesting entity in itself?

Is there an analogy between language and the following statement about a line in art? "A line is too often thought of as something that encloses form or colour. People forget that a line can be a dynamic thing in itself."

2. Are you bilingual in English? Or perhaps even trilingual? Do you have one brand of English for formal situations, another for ordinary conversations, and a third for play or very informal situations? Can you think of additional gradations?

3. Find samples of language usage which are substandard because they result in ambiguous statements. Ones which are incorrect grammatically but not necessarily ambiguous. Ones which are both incorrect and ambiguous.

4. Find examples of substandard usage to illustrate each of the following types: survival of forms which once were acceptable but now no longer are considered standard; usage which is part of a long-range drift or tendency to level off irregularities in case forms (nouns and pronouns) or in conjugation forms of verbs; usage which always has been considered substandard.

5. How often do you find cultivated adults using illiteracies when in a playful mood?

6. "Some purists admit that language will change but don't like the kind of people who change it."

This was said by a student of language. Do you agree?

7. The ratio between the number of times a pupil makes an error and the number of times he has opportunity to make that kind of error has been called the "quotient of error". Try to determine the quotient of some common type of error that you select.

8. Ask ten adults, ten junior high school students, and ten senior high school students about their memories and current impressions of grammar. What do their responses suggest regarding the status of grammar as a school subject?

9. Ask some children, high school students, and adults several questions about the elements that make up English language and how those elements work. For example: How the personal pronouns *they, it, he, she* operate when used in a sentence (i.e., how they select their antecedent). How the relative pronouns *who, that, which* operate. Or why, in our language, there is need of the classes of words we call "nouns" and "verbs".

How much basic knowledge of the native language is reflected in the responses? Do people seem to be surprised, even baffled, by your questions?

10. Think out three reasons why grammar teaching is likely to deteriorate into mechanical routine.

11. But the three words *eat, let's,* and *John* together in two different sequence, and intonation patterns. Noting the differences in meaning among the versions, reflect on the following statement from linguistics: "If you put linguistic elements together in a certain way, they can mean only one thing."

12. What possibilities do you see for the use of teaching machines for instruction in the English language?

3

Development of Word Meaning Discourse Analysis

Introduction

The hope of psycholinguistics is that if the meaning of an utterance can be specified, then it should be possible to tell whether children understand the meaning. But it is very difficult to specify the meaning of an utterance without going beyond units of analysis like sentence or sentence-part (de Beaugrande 1980) to the consideration of context-dependent meanings (Strawson 1950, Searle 1975, Grice 1968). This necessarily involves taking into account not only the speaker's intention in selecting his words, but the range of expressive powers that those words might have for a listener under those particular circumstances (Bennett 1976, 253-64). This means going beyond highly formal dictionary-dominated models to open the lumber-room of pragmatic rules which, like all lumber-rooms, has to be put in order. Recently both psychologists and philosophers have come up with some quite precise formulations. Rules for defining presupposition (e.g. Langendoen 1971, Oh and Dinneen 1979, Gazdar 1979), and Grice's (1975) work on rules for distinguishing between conventional and conversational implicatures, suggest that pragmatics might indeed be orderly if we had a sufficiently detailed and technical analysis.

Psychology is not only concerned with how pragmatic aspects of meaning can be brought into line with other aspects, but also with the question of how communicants can form a mental representation of an extended series of interchanges, a 'shared discourse', as it is often termed. We suggest, in what follows, that discourse analysis too can lead to highly formal models of cognition, to frame-analysis, the structure of scripted knowledge, and the like. We began the work reported here with an apparently clear case of children failing to grasp the meaning of simple utterances. We came to recognise that their unadult responses were quite rational from a discourse point of view.

From Word Meaning to Word Use

The relation between what a word means and the rules for its appropriate use has remained problematic ever since Frege (1892) initiated modern linguistic logic. Clearly there is a device by which one can present the meaning of words without classifying their rules of use: it is called a dictionary. Dictionaries have a long history; formulations of their underlying principles are more recent. Modern linguistics (de Saussure 1966) treats words as having fixed core meanings with restricted rules of variation around the core. One can find the core meaning of a word by constructing a semantic field in which the word is positioned in relation to other words which are agreed to be its relatives. For example, 'up' is *contrary* to 'down', *orthogonal* to 'left', has a *dual existence* as word and particle in 'put up with', and so on. Lyons (1977) presents a beautiful analysis which sustains one's intuition that the meaning of a word is *contrastive* in nature, and he systematises many contrasts. Yet Miller and Miller (1979) showed, *inter alia*, that it cannot be assumed that we know the conditions under which Lyons's contrasts have psychological reality. To take a more general view: when do the relationships which are given in dictionaries register in the mind of someone hearing one or more words which supposedly exemplify the relationships?

For example, it is easy to see that the words 'beer' and 'wine' have something in common; but it is less easy to see when this relationship has psychological reality and when it does not. Jacoby, Craik and Begg (1979, 585) point out that 'the meaning of an event is determined by the set of contrasts *generated during initial processing*' (italics added). Put less formally, the work which a word does in a given context can be defined by the distinctions that it conveys in that context, and to that extent is context-dependent. 'If "beer" is initially encoded as an alcoholic beverage, it may be poorly distinguished from "wine" or "vodka", but if "beer" is encoded as a good third-quencher after baseball, it may be poorly distinguished from orange juice or Cocacola. Consequently it is impossible to specify the distinctiveness of an event without specifying the alternatives in question' (Jacoby *et al.* 1979, 598). Thus, even the contrastive or intensional specification of the meaning of a word cannot be defined independently of the context or occasion of its use: 'the point is that meaning is not a static characteristic of individual words, but is rather a variable set of interpretations depending on the distinctions the word is intended to convey' (Jacoby *et al.* 1979, 597).

It follows, then, that at least part of the proper study of word meaning is the study of interlocutors' ability to agree on (a) the set of applicable distinctions it is reasonable to draw, and (b) the selection rules for discrimination within the set. Coming to such agreement is a social act with conventional rules, and this is what our account is about. The first step is to focus on the phrase 'the distinctions that the word is intended to convey'. Talk of intentionally threatens to lead us into an epistemological minefield, but even the most basic distinction-words like 'same/different' exemplify the case. Here is some recent evidence.

Early research on children's comprehension of 'same' and 'different' (Donaldson and Wales 1970) reported that children failed to distinguish between them, treating them both, apparently, as if they meant 'same'. This was taken to be evidence of incomplete semantic acquisition, and was interpreted within a theory of context-free lexical marking by Clark (1970). However, as Glucksberg, Hay and Danks (1976) showed, the assumption was unwarranted. They adopted the paradigm for use with adults. This time, references to 'same' and 'different' items were made by a stooge ostensibly engaged in the task of repairing a taperecorder. When the stooge held up a screwdriver and asked for a 'different one', adults interpreted this as a request for another screwdriver: a different token of the same type. They therefore responded identically to 'same' and 'different' requests, since there was only one available screwdriver: a perfectly reasonable interpretive strategy in the context. As with Frege's classical analysis of the morning/evening star, two *semantically distinct* referring expressions can be made to have the same *referential function* because their interpretation depends upon conventional rules of use of words in a discourse context.

The experiment serves to bring out a crucial point. To understand the way a speaker intends an utterance to be *used* in context requires agreement over a *frame of reference.* The point is not new: it was made nearly three centuries ago by John Locke (1690). In sections 7-9 of the chapter on Simple Modes, he deals with the field of reference indexed by the term 'same place'. If a company of chessmen remain on the squares of the board where they have been placed, they may be described as being in the same place, even if the board has been carried into another room 'because we compared them only to the parts of the chess board, which keep the same distance one with another'. Locke argues that place-specifications are developed by 'common use', by making 'reference to these adjacent things which are best served to their present purpose, without considering other things which, to another purpose, would better determine the place of the same thing'. In short, 'our idea of place is nothing else but such a relative position', a landmark specification within a frame of reference determined by the speaker's purpose. Nothing in the formal semantics of 'same place' will guarantee an appropriate understanding without a grasp of the speaker's purpose and intended frame of reference. William James (1892) generalised Locke's point: 'Reasoning is always to attain some particular conclusion. . . . conceiving [the datum] rightly means conceiving it by that one particular abstract character which leads to the one sort of conclusion which it is the reasoner's temporary interest to attain.'

The common image of developmental psychologists is precisely one in which they invite children to reason 'to attain some particular conclusion', noting whether or not the appropriate conclusion is in fact attained, thereby inferring something about the child's reasoning capacities. Only recently have psychologists questioned whether or not the child's reasoning processes were governed by the same 'particular abstract character' as that which referentially framed the conclusion from the experimenter's point of view; whether the child's 'temporary interest' really did coincide with the experimenter's. The notion of 'temporary interest' is well expressed by Chafe (1976, 28) when he points out that rules for organising conversation in context depend upon assumptions that speakers make about 'temporary states of the addresse's mind'. Context-specific rules for understanding have been explored in perspective-taking (Hughes 1978, Light 1979), conversation (McGarrigle and Donaldson 1975, Sinha and Walkerdine 1978a, Sinha and Carabine 1980), comprehension of spatial terms (Grieve *et al.* 1977, Walkerdine and Sinha 1978), and class inclusion (McGarrigle *et al.* 1978, Finn 1979). It is however, only fair to note that such rules may not always strongly show up (Freeman, Sinha and Stedmon 1981); and we do not yet have adequate methods for measuring the effects of 'socio-dialogic sense' (Karmiloff-Smith 1979), 'social logic' (Sinha and Walkerdine 1978b) or 'human sense' (Donaldson 1978) upon comprehension of words in context.

The task is formidable. The 'same/different' problem (and the other areas briefly referred to above) shows that nothing in the formal semantics of linguistic descriptions alone will guarantee that interlocutors 'will intepret a word in the same way' without their 'temporary interests' coinciding. Appeals to shared background knowledge, common presuppositions, reciprocal development of purposes seem essential, yet they only loosely embrace the solution to the problem. It is clear that the problem is one of how we are to formulate the use by interlocutors of an extended representation of knowledge. The structure of such knowledge is incredibly difficult to guess at. At the very least, *context-specific frames of reference* must be set up during social negotiation, and must be extended and coherent enough to integrate linguistic and non-linguistic information. They must also be sensitive to conventional rules regulating conversation, and must contain procedures for making some alternatives of interpretation more salient than others, so that the interlocuters can find a ready route for agreement over what to concentrate on.

To develop these last points further, let us return to the beverage example. Suppose someone appears poorly to distinguish beer from a blank sheet of cardboard, would that not strain any account of communicative competence? Not necessarily. Suppose A were to say: "A beer would refresh us now, what a pity there isn't any", and B were to hand A a cardboard sheet with every expression of goodwill. B's response might be intelligble as an act resulting from framing the utterance in terms of its original purpose: acquiring a means of cooling down. In this context, a piece of cardboard used as a fan is an appropriate alternative means to the same end (airstreams have psychological reality as reinforcers for creatures as lowly as rats). The intelligibility of B's response depends upon (a) the assumption that the topic of the utterance is not beer, but means of refreshment (b) the framing of 'beer' within a contrast set constituted not by 'other drinks' but 'other means of refreshment'. So the example of Jacoby *et al.* moves from word meaning to word use, but only works to draw the contrasts they propose if the word use coincides with the word as topic. This is a notion taken from discourse analysis, and that deals not with words but with whole sets of utterances in context. So many analyses of word meaning are built upon completely unrecognised assumptions about regulations governing conversation. It is high time to unpack some.

This chapter, then, is concerned with discourse rules as ways of representing local knowledge. In particular, we shall be concerned with the notion of discourse topic, as a means of access to the appropriate referential framing of context, and consequently to the determination of the implicit contrast set for a referring expression. We shall show that children may appear not to comprehend a word because the adult speaker unwittingly fails to convey the topic of the discourse to the child, and thereby fails to secure agreement over the appropriate frame of reference. First, however, we shall examine further the concept of discourse topic.

From Utterance Meaning to Utterance Use

The Discourse Topic

As the title of this section shows, we are going to parallel the previous section on a higher plane of analysis. dealing with even more unwieldy 'units' such as whole sentences and utterances in context. The area is called 'discourse analysis'. It might as well be called 'homilectics'—the art of holding converse and delivering extended messages. That is what many psycholinguistic experiments on children are really about. But, as Chafe (1976) discussed, how do we decide 'what a sentence is really about'? According to him, the topic of a sentence is just that. There are many devices for assigning, emphasising, shifting and maintaining topic. These range from the canonical topic-as-subject/comment-as-predicate construction, to cleft and pseudo-cleft devices handling phonic reference and foregrounding, relativisation and so on. Amid the proliferation of overlapping concepts and distinctions available in the literature, the concept of topic is the one upon which there has been maximal recognised and unrecognised convergence.

Linguists have held out the promise that the key to identifying the topic of discourse lies in the classification of the linguistic distinctions and devices noted above. We suggest that, while it is necessary to do so, it is not sufficient. Purely linguistic analyses are about as much use in discourse as in word-meaning analyses. Take for example a simple declarative of transparent meaning: 'The cat is climbing into the fridge'. What does it mean? Since the subject is 'cat' and the predicate '. . . . fridge', is the topic the cat and the comment its undesirable location? It could be, but one would like to go beyond linguistics and say that the case would be stronger *if background knowledge were presupposed:* the fridge is on and contains tonight's dinner. The conjunction between linguistic analysis and some formalisation of knowledge structures might hold the key. Let us reveal the true state of affairs: the fridge is indeed open and contains tonight's dinner, but it had been left open over the weekend and the kippers have gone mouldy. The cat is only one more disaster: the overall topic is the state of the fridge. The fact that the cat is climbing in is only a comment upon the parious state of affairs obtaining within a wider frame than the single utterance. The proper study of topicalisation procedures is the relationship between conventional rules of delivering linguistic information, the background knowledge credited to the interlocutors and the presuppositions which are triggered as antecedents of the target utterance. How far can one get by dividing the information in the utterance into what can be taken as already given and what is genuinely new?

Bates (1976) cuts the gordian knot by legislation: the topic/comment distinction maps onto the given/new distinction of Haviland and Clark (1974), not to mention the new/old distinction of Chafe (1976), the figure/ground distinction of MacWhinney (1974) *et tutti quanti.* Miller (1979) also collapses some of these. Hornby (1972) is more circumspect: topic is 'the part of the sentence which constitutes what the speaker is talking about, the rest of the sentence—the comment—providing new information about the topic'. But packing down dichotomies is not the same as integrating them, as we now show by unpacking the relation between devices previously thought of as having a topicalising function and theories of information-processing in sentence-comprehension.

Haviland and Clark (1974) and Clark and Haviland (1977) in formulating the 'given/new contract', analysed the information content of an utterance in terms of the use made by a cooperative speaker of syntactic devices for conveying the difference between (a) knowledge presumed to be known by the listener and (b) knowledge provided by the speaker as presumed to be currently unknown to the listener. Bates (1976) assumes that topicalisation procedures are equivalent to devices for highlighting new information. Clark and Haviland, however, did not suggest that an utterance *in isolation* conveys the sense of given and new information, but rather that the listener is able to gain access to the essential antecedent information by building inferential links from an existing knowledge-base. Hence, given and new information are interpreted within an *extended* representation of knowledge having the status of a presuppositional structure. Clearly then, topic, while being strongly related to given information, is not to be equated with it, nor with the subject slot which may realise both. We make the entirely formal proposal that topic be conceived of as *that particular frame of reference which (a) is accessed by the given information, (b) instantiates a set of presuppositions enabling the listener to integrate the new information with the antecedents of the linguistically-given information.*

This is close to the proposal of Keenan and Schieffelin (1976) that topic be defined as a propositional representation, but diverges on one crucial point. Keenan and Schieffelin locate topic as the (set of) proposition(s) about which the speaker is giving or requesting information. We propose that topic does two jobs: (a) delimits the appropriate presuppositional pool, i.e. those aspects of the context which the given information refers to, in such a way that new information can be added to the pool, and (b) linguistically encodes the given information itself. Formally, the topic frame itself organises the links by making default assignments (inferential bridges) which complete its internal construction.

So topic is a big concept upon which others converge. What saves it from thereby being analytically useless in generating evidence? There are three answers to that. The first will be left to the rest of this chapter on a 'proof of the pudding' basis. The second is that there are a number of powerful formalisms which describe knowledge macro-structures and which can be focused. These include Reiter's (1980) logic for default reasoning to formalisms for how a knowledge-base can be used to pair mental representations with functional processes: the episodes of Schank (1975), the plans and scripts of Schank and Abelson (1977), and the frames of Minsky (1974 and 1975), Kuipers (1975), Goffman (1974) and Winograd (1975). All the above accounts attempt to produce models for the extended representation of knowledge, and hence address a common problem area. Finally, it is in itself advantageous to have a clearing-ground for related phenomena:

1. CONTRASTIVENESS

Chafe (1976) points out that devices of stress and syntax often mark a contrast between what is explicitly stated and what has been left unstated, so that relevant presuppositions can be contrastively defined—hence implicating the set of applicable distinctions as in the beverage example. The device of foregrounding consists in the selection of a *particular* referent from a set of plausible options.

2. EXTENDED DISCOURSE SEQUENCES

If topic is to be treated as the extended representation to which a current input is assimilated, this makes sense of the wide variety of devices above the single-utterance level identified by Keenan and Schieffelin (1976). Devices such as collaborative topic-maintenance in question/answer sequences, topic-incorporation by shifting topic to update a frame of reference under the impact of new information, and the like, need a formalism of background knowledge.

3. REPRESENTING LINGUISTIC AND NON-LINGUISTIC INFORMATION IN A COMMON FORMAT

Minsky (1975) supplies a frame analysis for the organisation of information from disparate input sources. The concept of topic draws attention to the need for a common format for integrating information, and permits the scaling of linguistic and non-linguistic cues in cases where the sense and reference of a linguistic unit may not seem easily relatable one to another (Stedmon and Freeman 1980b).

4. PLAUSIBILITY OF RELATIONS WITHIN A TOPIC FRAME

Canonical relations amongst objects being referred to may bias representation (Freeman 1980), perhaps via the operation of circumscription rules upon the set of predicates used to express the facts (see McCarthy 1980). Again, what is given linguistically may well have a central organising function in leading the listener to access stored knowledge, and may serve as an expectancy cue. But successful communication demands that salience should be assigned to the new information that is to be incorporated. We conclude with a formal definition: topic frame is an organised and structure for representing knowledge from the immediate linguistic and contextual input, such that a presuppositional background can be activated which assigns maximum salience to the new information.

The rest of chapter is devoted to giving concrete examples and new evidence on these rather abstract points.

A case of children's miscomprehension—produced by their word-use or utterance-use problems?

Now we have the necessary tools to analyse an intriguing study. Donaldson and Lloyd (1974) showed 14 4-to-5-year-olds' collections of cars and garages like those in Table 3.3. There was a spare car or an empty garage, and the task was to verify whether 'all the cars are in the garages' or, on other occasions, whether 'all the garages have cars in them'. Five children always assented to both statements with four garages and five cars, thus in effect ignoring the spare car. These and a further one always dissented from both statements given a spare garage. 'Watching children and listening to them, one had the powerful impression that the empty garage was somehow salient for them, and that they intepreted everything in ways affected by this salience' (Donaldson 1978, 67).

So a spare car is not salient enough, and a spare garage is too salient. In itself this cuts out one formal linguistic explanation. Suppose that the children obey a rule that 'a universal affirmative quantifier in the subject slot generalises to the predicate'. So 'all the cars are in the garages' is processed as 'all the cars are in [all] the garages', leading to over-exhaustive search for one-to-one relations between the sets. This would account for the extra-garage salience, but obviously not the lack of extra-car salience. So let us go to the other extreme of explanation. Assume that the only function of the utterance is to trigger background knowledge. Children might think to themselves that a garage's customary job (canonical function) is to contain cars, and all utterances get referred to that single criterion. Therefore, there might be a bias towards expecting words like 'some' or 'most' rather than the 'all' with which they have to deal.

Indeed this point, in more analytic form, will become relevant shortly. For the present, all we need to note is that many studies show how powerfully expectations about object-relations and usage can operate in 'word-comprehension tests' (Baldwin 1975, Grieve *et al.* 1977, Freeman, Sinha and Condliffe 1981, Wilcox and Palermo 1975; see also the chapter by Bridges in theis volume). So will the concept of canonical function give the key to the problem? Are children really construing the situation as one in which the topic is the rules of use of garages, thus falling prey to adventitious cognitive 'human sense'?

A Study of Canonical Relations Between Sets

The obvious step is to make clear that the objects will often *not* be put to customary use, in a systematic replication of the Donaldson-Lloyd study. Thus one can arrange cars on top of garages, make tables have vases under them, etc. Table 3.1 shows the design: for each canonical relationship of *in, on,* or *under,* there is a contrasting non-canonical relationship. This is important in case the garage-salience be specific to containment (*in*-ness) more than canonicality. So we can check the Donaldson-Lloyd study of spatial relations, to see whether it is really a fragment of the study of canonicality, containment or whatever.

The garages, fireplaces, tables and bridges can be thought of as the *fixed objects* (FO) in relation to which the smaller *moveable objects* (MO) can be placed. This distinction has psychological reality: it is more natural to describe a moveable car as being near a fixed garage than the reverse. Fixed objects are landmark reference objects: see Bowerman (in press) and Macrae 1978 for an analysis of semantic, syntactic and pragmatic considerations. At the moment we shall use FO and MO as a notation, and later analyse its role in the evidence.

Table 3.1: Combinations of Objects and Spatial Relations about which the Children were Questioned

Fixed objects	*Moveable objects*	*Implicit spatial contrast*	*Canonical relation*	*Non-canonical relation*
garages	cars	IN/ON	IN	ON
fireplaces	clocks	IN/ON	ON	IN
tables	vases	IN/UNDER	ON	UNDER
bridges	boats	ON/UNDER	UNDER	ON

The procedure was always that four FOs were put on the table, then either three or five MOs were placed at the FOs, leading to one spare +FO or one spare +MO, respectively. On each trial we explained that the rest of the objects were 'not in the game', so that it was only what was on the table that was 'being talked about'. On each trial the child was asked, 'Are all the MOs [at] the FOs?' *or* 'Have all the FOs got MOs [at] them?' Each child had 32 trials, to cover the whole matrix of possibilities, in counterbalanced order.

The results from 32 5-year-olds were particularly clear. The frequency of correct answers was unaffected by canonicality (compare the columns in Table 3.2) or by particular spatial relations (compare each row in Table 3.2). Minute breakdown of the data gave no different pattern. Neither did replication of the study on another 59 children in the two-year age-bands above and below 5 years. So the children's judgment-error has impressive generality over categories which could provide explanations which would compete with the one shortly to be promoted. But this is only a start: now to reconsider the data.

Table 3.2: Classification of the Data in Terms of Canonicality and Spatial Relationship. Maximum Number of Possible Correct Responses Per Cell is 128

Implicit spatial contrast instantiated by array	*Spatial relation instantiated by array items*	*No. of correct responses for canonical instantiations*	*No. of correct responses for non-canonical instantiations*
IN/ON	IN	72	78
	ON	72	69
ON/UNDER	ON	73	71
	UNDER	66	73

One needs data at the individual level: 'the sheer numbers of right answers is much less informative than the pattern of their occurrence' (Donaldson and Lloyd 1974). Add another step (from a study of spatial relations): treat "all the patterns as legitimate variants. . . . it is imposible to score single responses as correct or incorrect' (Tanz 1980). We shall employ two shorthand notations: response-patterns will be referred to as 'strategies', and individual responses will be referred to as 'correct/incorrect' to mean 'like/unlike adult responses', the notation to be unpacked in a study shortly to be discussed. We tabulate the children's patterns of 'yes/no' in terms of the relative salience accorded to the FO or MO sets of referent items. Three easily-identifiable strategies emerged, according to an arbitrary criterion of accounting for 90 per cent of the indivdual's responses. The first strategy is that of providing information about whether all the FOs are paired with MOs, i.e. topicalising FOs. Table 3.3 shows how this and the other strategies were identified. The reverse strategy is that of topicalising MOs. Finally, some answers were about the mismatch between the sets: a joint topicalisation strategy. Always saying 'yes', whatever the question, and 'random' strategies also occurred, as usual.

Table 3.3: Evidence for Identifying Stable Strategies. Key: = Fixed Object (FO); X = Moveable Object (MO); ☒ = MO at FO

Strategy	*Array*	*Code*	*Response to either question*
Topicalising fixed	☒ ☒ ☒ ☒ ×	+ MO	Yes
elements	☒ ☒ ☒ ☐	+ FO	No
Topicalising moveable	☒ ☒ ☒ ☒ ×	+ MO	No
elements	☒ ☒ ☒ ☐	+ FO	Yes
Joint Topicalising both fixed and moveable elements	☒ ☒ ☒ ☒ ☒	+ MO	No
(mismatch strategy)	☒ ☒ ☒ ☐	+ FO	No

The results are shown in Table 3.4 for all 91 subjects studied, from 3-8 years of age. We feel reasonable confident that the characterisation is accurate, from post-test discussions with the individuals. The empty-garage-salience strategy is here labelled 'topicalisation of FOs' and clearly, as in the Donaldson-Lloyd study, is stronger than the MO strategy: 42 children compared with 12. It is the dominant response mode. But topicalising MO *did* occur, and presumably it was their small sample size which prevented Donaldson and Lloyd from noticing it.

It is now clear that the salience of the empty garage does not derive from its spatial role as a cavity-bearer nor from its canonical function. Instead, most children seem to use a general-purpose strategy cutting across a wide variety of object-pairs and spatiofunctional relations. Two questions are now raised. The first is what it is in the situation which leads statistically to a modal bias towards fixed objects. The other is—to hard back to an earlier briefly-made point—whether some of the answers are *really* wrong in adult terms. A useful step would be to find a situation in which adults too used similar strategies. This we now do as the first step in the long process of solving the modal-response puzzle.

Table 3.4: Number of Children Falling into Each Strategy Group, for Our Results and Those of Donaldson and Lloyd (1974)

Strategy	*Rsults of Experiment 1*	*Results of Donaldson and Lloyd's (1974) experiment reanalysed*
Responding yes to all questions	7	2
Topicalising the fixed object	42	5
Topicalising the moveable objects	12	0
Joint topicalising both sets of objects	11	1
Alternative 'random' strategies	19	6
Total	91	14

TOPICALISATION PROCESSES UNDERLYING ADULTS' COMPREHENSION OF QUANTIFIERS

All that needs to be done is to find a situation in which adults find it natural 'erroneously' to reply 'yes' to the question, 'Are all the MOs [at] the FOs?', even given an extra MO; and 'no' when there is an extra FO (cf. Table 3.3). Again Donaldson

(1978, 66) gives a lead: if we say, 'Have you put all the knives and forks on the table?' we are at least as likely to mean 'all the knives and forks that are going to be needed' as 'all the knives and forks that are kept in the drawer': the choice of meaning will depend upon the total context. Responsiveness to a perceived purpose will provide the listener with *appropriate reasons* for an answer which is only wrong according to timeless context-free criteria of the logic of truth-values. These reasons, *grâce à* John Locke, are ingredients of topic-setting processes in the listener's mind.

We drew two naively realistic pictures. In one, four saucepans served as FOs relative to four saucepan-lids plus one lid lying next to the cooker amongst vegetables and a knife. In the other, four saucers served as the FOs, with three of them having a cup on. Twenty non-psychology students were accosted in a public place and spun an almost-true tale. In effect, they were told that the experimenter was designing a language comprehension test for children, but had been surprised at their performance. In view of this, she was seeing whether adults found the situation clear. The two pictures they would be shown came from test batteries concerned with domestic scenarios of mother either cooking or laying the table for tea. They were then shown the pictures and asked: (1) 'Are all the lids on the saucepans?' (2) 'Are all the cups on the saucers?'

The results were clear. Sixteen subjects replied 'yes' to question 1 (*P* .006, Binomial) and 17 replied 'No' to question 2 (*P* .001). Only one subject expressed any feelings of ambiguity but still gave the modal responses. So the results replicate the 'errors' of children. Since adults can reasonably be credited with comprehension of the formal semantics of the questions, it must be concluded that their interpretation of quantified expressions depends upon conventional rules of use which encompass the perceived purposes and intentions of the speaker. This is very like the Glucksberg *et al.* study (1976), outlined in section 2, on the semantics of 'same'.

Adults did not interpret the referring expression 'all the cups' to means 'all the cups visible in the picture', rather to mean 'all the cups which ought to be present'. Similarly, a nonfunctional lid is not assumed to be a member of the referent set encoded in the phrase 'all the lids'. The hypothesis to be evaluated is that children could conceivably understand the formal semantics of, say, 'all the cars' but still have to rely upon conventional rules to decide *which* set of cars the speaker had in mind. But there is a huge gap between the cookery lesson and the 'garage-salience' data. If we are to appeal to conventional rules to bridge it, we have next to describe some of these rules, then to find out whether that leads us to gain an analytic grip on the 'garage-salience problem' so as to predict a new effect. To anticipate, it does.

Conventional Rules for Interpreting Quantified Expressions

When a speaker asks a question about the presence of 'all the Xs', he is implicitly requesting the hearer to carry out an exhaustive search to check that no X is missing. Asking someone such a question is only legitimate 'socio-dialogically' if there is at least a possibility that some X is (or some Xs are) in actuality missing. The conventions underlying asking such a question therefore presuppose not only that the size of the intended referent set is potentially larger than the contemporaneously present set of Xs, but that such knowledge is potentially available to both interlocutors.

If the hearer's task is to check the context for cues which might indicate the absence of one of the items, then there is a conventional discourse bias towards giving a negative reply. *Effectively the situation provides a context for plausible denial (Wason 1965) in view of the speaker's apparent concern that nothing is missing*. Furthermore, if the children thought that the search was instigated for a particular purpose it would hardly be relevant for them to mention any extra referents lying outside the set identified within the discourse context. Hence answering a question about 'all the Xs' is likely to entail ignoring irrelevant Xs and searching for cues which indicate a mising X. Both the empty garage in Donaldson and Lloyd's experiment and the unpaired saucer in the adult experiment could be taken to show that an item of the intended discourse referent set must be missing. Again, when an item referenced by 'all the Xs' is ignored, clearly the quantifier does not operate with the logical scope of embracing a univesal set of Xs: rather, 'all the Xs' is taken to mean 'all the Xs which ought to be present' or 'all the Xs which the speaker intends to be present'. In other words, adult comprehension is guided by the listener's assumptions about the speaker's temporary interests, which may be *inferred by default,* from real-scene knowledge, including knowledge of what have come to be called event-scripts and scenarios. In the child experiments, this leads to the testable alternatives that the children are construing the experimental situation in such a way that either (a) a purpose can be attributed to that particular experiment, as in Locke's argument outlined early on, or (b) it can be taken for granted that *any* speaker would naturally be topicalising the garages. Since the garages are fixed, four in number in a row, this forms the natural set for checking that nothing is missing. This is, at the moment a guess: data come shortly.

Now there is a gap between the adult and the child studies. In the former, real-world knowledge is obviously called up in the subjects' minds, and gives a rational basis for their replies. In the child study, we cannot be sure, yet, whether this holds true. So the next step is to 'naturalise' the artifical child task, taking care to set the topic in such a way that we can be reasonably sure that the children understand that we are attempting to share a common purpose (a temporary interest) with them. In the Donaldson-Lloyd, and our first, experiment, the speaker was attempting to use the rather unconventional rule of employing a quantified expression to refer solely to the immediate visible array. This runs foul of the 'context of plausible denial' effect. In the next study we deliberately provide two differing plausible contexts for conventional rules of 'reasoning to attain a conclusion'.

The Effect of Setting a Topic with Children

There is a useful analysis of establishing a topic set out in the Keenan and Schieffelin (1976) model: in our terminology, the referents which are intended to be talked about should be included in the topic frame triggered by the utterance. It was shown in section 4b that adults' procedure for finding the referents of quantified noun phrases depends on the interlocutors constructing the same background knowledge schemes for intepreting the target utterance. When the context instantiates a highly familiar even or set of activities, utterances may be quite economical: many of the referents involved will already be incorporated into a scripted knowledge-frame (Nelson and Greundel 1979), and so need not even be mentioned. It can safely be assumed that the listener knows the ingredients of a cookery scene. If children, like adults, can interpret quantified expressions as referring to a set of items other than those immediately present, they must somehow have constructed a topic frame which includes either a larger or smaller set of items than those present in the array. As yet we have no real idea of the cues by which children make the fixed objects the salient entry in a topic frame, nor the cues which might lead them to swing over to entering the moveable object into this slot instead. Yet if the rules of interpretation set out in the previous section are anywhere near the mark, it ought to be easy to do so.

Here is a simple experiment which feeds children with a great deal of knowledge and thereby swings the strategy of individuals from topicalising fixed objects to topicalising moveable objects. The arrays were exactly as in the Donaldson-Lloyd study, only using cows and cowsheds. The experimenter, Tony Fehler, told 9 4-year-olds a story focused either upon the naughtiness of cows or upon the propensity of cowsheds to burn down. At crucial moments in the story, acted out with the toys, the child had to verify the quantified expressions. The results, scored for strategy as in section 4a, were unambiguous. When the cows (MOs) were topicalised by the experimenter, 8/9 children topicalised them in an answering strategy. When the cowsheds (FOs) were topicalised by the experimenter, 7/9 children topicalised them in their answers.

So the 'garage-salience effect'—the FO salience effect noted in the big experiment—can be reversed in the same individuals. It should also be recalled that adults too could be led to give entirely reasonable 'wrong' answers. So we have found a rational basis for the Donaldson-Lloyd effect and reversed it under conditions predicted by discourse analysis. But it is not yet a very satisfactory state of affairs. It is one thing to demonstrate theoretically that the problem of quantifiers is not primarily one of word-meaning but conventional discourse rules and topic-setting procedures, and it undeniably helps to get adults to give child-like answers and children to reverse their strategies; but it is another thing to demonstrate that this is what went on in the simple 'garages tasks'. Yet this is now easy to do: let us scrutinise the 'garages study' for potential topic-setting cues, then manipulate them to reverse the children's strategies. This brings the evidence together over quite a wide range.

Numerical Invariance as a Topic-setting Cue for Children

The Donaldson-Lloyd results appeared as an *unadultlike* pattern induced by *fixed objects* acting as *containers* in *canonical* mode. We now know that none of the italicised ingredients is essential, though we do not know the conditions under which any or all may assume importance. The strongest case for the adequacy of a theory would be to find the simplest condition under which none of those variables exerted any effect. It is daunting to try to do so all in one swoop. What seems an easier option is to scrutinise the arrays in terms of these few concepts which have come out as theoretically the most basic ones, and this should lead us to the unique variable underlying the action of those we have investigated. Thence manipulation of the variable should enable us to reverse individual strategies.

At the risk of being repetitious, the argument which follows applies a discourse analysis to the task. This means that it is not regarded as a test of language comprehension but of children's problems with a shared topic. The children's answers to the experimenter's questions indicate that they seem to have identified the garages as that aspect of the array which is topicalised by the experimenter's utterance. Possibly our previous guess that numerical invariance might mark the intended topic set is on the right lines. If the experiment be repeated with an invariant set of four MOs and a variable set of three or five FOs, the children ought to switch to topicalising the MOs.

From the 5-year-olds in the big canonicality study, we selected 23 who had on 90 per cent of their trials topicalised the fixed objects in each array (as set out in Table 3.3). After a fortnight's interval we retested them with the moveable objects now held invariant in number, as shown in Table 3.5, bottom two rows (the top two rows contain the configurations used in the canonicality test, for ease of comparison). In this study, only 24 trials were given, since we held back the cars and garages. After the 24 trials were over, the four garages and three/five cars were reintroduced as a post-test to see whether the children would swing back to fixed-object topicalisation when the invariance cue was returned to the fixed objects.

With the moveable objects invariant, only 5/23 stuck to this fixed-object topicalisation strategy. Five gave 'random' patterns, leaving 13 who now did take account of the moveable objects: 6 switching to topicalising them and 7 adopting a joint-topicalisation (mismatch cue) strategy. It was noteworthy that 11 of these 13 then reverted to fixed-object topicalisation with the post-test of invariant garages. What seems to be happening is that the invariance cue does work, but against the background of some bias towards fixed objects, rather than moveable. Of course this might be due to the selection of previously-biased subjects for the strategy-reversal experiment; or there may be an inherent bias towards topicalising fixed objects. Either account is reasonable in view of the analysis offered here, but needs further testing. We have done experiments in which the child handles either the fixed set or the moveable set, when each set in turn is made invariant, and it is possible to scale a number of cues for topic-setting within this general paradigm. These studies will be written up separately, from the report by Stedmon and Freeman (1980a).

Table 3.5: Comparison of the Arrays from the Canonicality Study and the Invariance-cue Study on 5-year-olds. Key: = Fixed Object (FO); X = Moveable Object (MO); ☒ = MO at FO

Task structure over trials	*Array type*	*Array structure*
Experiment 1 Fixed objects invariant in number for all 32 trials	+ MO + FO	☒ ☒ ☒ ☒ × ☒ ☒ ☒ □
Experiment 2 Moveable objects invariant in number for all 24 trials	+ MO + FO	☒ ☒ ☒ × ☒ ☒ ☒ ☒ □

This is straightforward work. The more challenging task is to alter the referential form of the utterances to provide varying degrees of information about the referents, and to check these forms to see if they operate as linguistic topic-setting cues. Our discourse analysis provides a way of formalising relations amongst different cues. Karmiloff-Smith (1979) has presented an analysis of child language which provides an empirical basis for scaling the identifying strengths of various linguistic forms. Accordingly Stedmon and Freeman (1980b) amalgamated one of Karmiloff-Smith's designs with modifications of the Donaldson-Lloyd design, and showed that scaling linguistic and non-linguistic topic cues against one another led to very orderly data. In the next section we analyse the role of just the non-linguistic cues in order to generalise the account beyond quantifiers.

How the Context Supplies Topic-setting Cues

There are two rather different but related ways in which context and utterance jointly supply information about topic. First, cues from context and utterance may help the listener to identify the intended referent-set to which the speaker is apparently addressing his or her concerns. This can range from a disordered refrigerator to unhoused cars, from a chessboard to an apparently faulty taperecorder. Through this *referential* function of topic-setting, listener and speaker can negotiate a common frame of reference, and a common set of interests with respect to that frame. Second, cues from utterance, external context, and internal frame of reference may help the listener to identify what particular information must be added to their current representation, if they are to give an informative reply. This *informative* function of topic-setting enables the listener to update his or her topic frame to bring it into line with that apparently held by the speaker.

Linguistic devices for signalling both the referential and informative aspects of topic-setting are well documented. Non-linguistic cues have been grossly neglected. A consequence of this neglect is that we are still in the dark as to the relative salience of linguistic as opposed to non-linguistic cues for young children. In the absence of previous comparative data over a wide range, miscomprehension of linguistic form has been attributed to children in cases where a ready alternative explanation consists in positing a rational use of non-linguistic information in a discourse context.

There are now two days in which one can recognise cases of misidentification of the topic—cross-purposes between the interlocutors. It would occur either through inadequate decoding of the adult utterance at a semantic-syntactic level, or through the rational application of alternative discourse conventions by the child. This enables one easily to dig out premises for a purely linguistic account of the Donaldson-Lloyd study. One would have to assume that when the syntax of the utterance is altered from 'all the cars. . . .' to 'all the garages. . . .', the surface change in grammatical subject from the moveable to the fixed objects is enough to mark a change in discourse topic.

However, it is critically important to note that marking implicit topic-changes by linguistic means will ensure a change in the truth value of the response if, and only if, the items referred to in the utterance have been identified by the listener as those which are momentarily present in the physical array. Any psychological bias on the part of the child towards widening or narrowing the identified set (remember the cookery experiment in section 4b, and the 'cowshed' one) will upset the experimenter's calculations.

Let us now compare two analyses of the evidence. The first is in terms of faulty semantic processing. Children fail to decode the syntactic distinction which conventionally assigns the topic to the grammatical subject. They therefore cannot make use of the subject-predicate construction to identify the topic, and search for some non-linguistic, perceptually salient cue to 'make human sense' of the utterance. They do not notice the error of this procedure, and will defend their verdicts because they fail to recognise the syntactic constraints for restricting the scope of the quantifier to those precise items referred to in the noun phrase in which it occurs. This failure is equivalent to failure to comprehend a quantifier.

The second is a discourse analysis which captures the general tenor of Donaldson's more recent work (e.g. Donaldson 1978), that children try to understand what people mean, not only what words mean. This is the 'context of plausible denial' sort of approach. With simple declaratives,the subject-predicate distinction is certainly the canonical device for linguistic encoding of the topic-comment distinction (for the referential use of language). By convention it is also the canonical device for encoding the distinction between given and new information (for the informative use of language). But herein lies the rub. As we noted earlier, when the subject-predicate distinction is used to encode a given/new distinction, nothing entails that this has to map onto an underlying topic/comment distinction. Rather, topic may be *identified by inference* from that part of the utterance which is the syntactic realisation of the given information. So there are two distinctions which the surface form of the utterance, subject-predicate, can encode; and one needs pragmatic rules for relying on one or other distinction as being communicatively more reliable. It may well be the case that adults would often tend to treat subject-predicate as the surface realisation of topic-comment, and there is a set of studies on linguistic intuition in parsing waiting to be done. (The work of Bock (1977) and Hornby (1972) provide a lead here.) But children might regard the informative use of language—the request for information from the controller of the situation—as a more reliable discourse-maintenance function, and thereby apply a pragmatic rule for identifying topic. Their replies provide information about this construed topic, rather than the referential content of the subject noun-phrase in the adult utterance. The adult *thinks* that she is requesting information about cars in the array because she has taken care to start off by saying 'all the cars', but the child *knows* that garages are the topic. *Once garages have been established within the topic slot, the topic frame assigns by default a numerical value to the variable set. This value is precisely the number of items needed to match the topic-set in accordance with the conventional meaning of the word 'all'*. Under such a condition even adults will reliably ignore an extra lid or concentrate upon a spare saucer. To be sure, they understand the restrictive nature of 'all', but they have to look to the array to make up their minds about which set of referent items is intended, and this may be taken to be more or less than those physically present. Whenever a situation gives a listener access to background knowledge, whether in the form of scripts or knowledge frames about themes such as cookery, or in the form of noticing what the speaker has apparently taken care to make perceptually salient, or to keep invariant, in the situation, a frame of reference is set up. Making reference to a set of items within a frame is never enough to establish *joint* reference between two people unless the different conventional rules of discourse coincide.

Whenever children give strange answers in such studies, it is up to the psychologist to *prove* that he or she has really established joint reference with the child in the way that was intended, if faulty semantic/syntactic comprehension is to be invoked as an explanation. It is essential to work towards independent evidence of this, and it is not sufficient to say that children must have miscomprehended the semantics *solely* on the grounds of a context-free truth-value violation somewhere. As Locke showed so long ago, truth-values can be relative things—relative, surely, to the set of distinctions one is trying to get the listener to draw. Collaborative focus on a topic is the children's key to the world of communication. They may not always find the lock for themselves. Only if there is independent evidence that the relevant frame of reference has been set up, and the relevant distinctions have been drawn, and that *still* the answer is wrong, are we on safe ground in producing a purely linguistic analysis. It is an uphill task, and one in which few research lines have managed to achieve enough altitude for a bird's-eye view to be possible.

4
Development of Attitudes Towards Language

From earliest times the principal means of studying how children think has been to ask them questions—there is every reason to believe that its popularity will continue. But what happens when we have the answers? In particular, how do we deal with the two related problems: does the child understand me? and how do I intepret what he says? Specifically, what does it mean to believe the child when he says that we only have snow for children to play in, that clouds more because pedestrians drag them along as they walk, that quantity changes with visual appearance?

The topic of this chapter is the way children acquire the ability to make basic logico-mathematical judgments, how they come to move from giving the wrong answer to giving the right answer. The way I want to approach this topic is by consideration of what we should do with the wrong answers. Some would focus on the child's deficiencies as an information processor (e.g. Klahr and Wallace 1976, Klausmeier 1979). But the approach I will be adopting here begins by asking whether the incorrectness resides in the way the child construes the question and in the principles on which he frames his judgment. Without wishing to become involved at this point in the wrangle about whether one is an epiphenomenon of the other, let me just say that concentrating on this latter, linguistic-interpretive question is at least an sensible as making models of the child's 'information' handling.

Let us consider the possibility that the younger child's judgment is divergent because he does not possess a notion of 'correctness' versus 'incorrectness' that is sufficiently like our own. He may indeed not have fully distinguished language in imaginative play from language in the communications of publicly corrigible fact. Perhaps he is giving something that we would call an opinion when we would like him to make an attempt at 'the answer'. The child, in short, may be regarding verbal propositions in a radically different way to the way we do. It is not that his semantics or syntax is primitive—although they may be—rather it is his attitude to the implicit criteria which sustain the truth of such judgments that is radically divergent. We do not have to look very far for a term to describe this divergence. The philosophical literature contains the term 'propositional attitude', and it is used there in a way that is analogous to how I will be using it here. The term is derived from Brentano's concept of the 'propositional act', our attitude of mind towards propositions such as thinking, fearing, doubting, hoping, expecting *that*. This is sometimes known as the 'dyadic-relation' theory of propositions, because a distinction is made between the act of proposing and the statement itself. J. M. Baldwin (1901) elaborated such a view and Gilbert Ryle (1929) argued that there can be a notion of 'the proposition' which is the neutral invariant against which different 'propositional attitudes' can be taken by different people and by the same person at different times.

Let me provide an illustration of how successful verbal communication depends on the listener and speaker sharing an appropriate propositional attitude *as the term will be intended here.* Two people are discussing a film. A says, 'I enjoyed *The Fiend without a Face*', B says, 'You can't have enjoyed it because it isn't an enjoyable film'. If A does not (implausibly) interpret this answer as mere boorishness and if A is (almost as infuriatingly) of an analytical turn of mind, he may reply in the vein that saying he enjoyed the film is making a statement about his own experience, not essentially about the film; that although some films can be said to be more enjoyable than others nobody can tell him that he did *not* enjoy a film; that when we are considering enjoyment there is always the possibility of being in a minority of one—some kinds of masochist probably are. . . . and so on. That is, B does not know that the appropriate propositional attitude is 'subjective'.

In contrast, what if A says, 'I saw *The Terror of Tiny Town* at the Rialto last Thursday evening' and B says, 'You can't possibly have seen it, it was only shown on Wednesday/it was on at the Plaza/I saw you at the match that evening/it's The *Tenor* of Tiny Town. . . .'? Here the two will be arguing about objective fact. If A says that it does not matter to him whether the film really had been shown and the main thing is that he *thinks* he saw the film and that's where the issue should rest, then it is now he who lacks the appropriate propositional attitude-of-objectivity.

There is a steadily growing body of evidence that young children *do* have propositional attitudes which are divergent from ours. The work of Martin Braine has much the same pioneering status here as in the field of language development. In two ingenious experimental studies (Braine and Shanks 1965a and b) he showed that the natural interpretation which 5- to 7-year-old children give to questions about shape and size is a phenomenalistic one. That is, when asked whether a stick which appears bent by light refraction when placed in water has changed its shape, or whether a cube is larger under a magnifying glass, they will answer affirmatively, despite the fact that most *can* frame a realist interpretation by age 5 given a sufficiently unambiguous context. And of course Bruner (1966) made a similar point about the nonconservation judgment a little later, claiming that the nonconserving child is telling us about 'how things look to him' rather than 'how they are really'.

A related point about interpretations is made by the work of Margaret Donaldson and her associates (see Donaldson 1978). For many years now Donaldson has been insisting that any judgment a young child makes in an experiment is a function of both his construal of what is expected of him by the experimenter and the way that the materials support different construals. Some recent examples of the Donaldson approach developed in interesting directions are to be fund in Sinha and Carabine 1980 and Light *et al.* 1979. The orientation that these workers share is that the child's thought is labile (c.f. Werner 1948) relative to our own: it is coloured by the insertion of a single adjective in the instructions and canalised by the smallest manipulation of experimental materials. It is, in short, determined by what linguists call 'pragmatics'—communicative intent within the practical context. Needless to say, other workers (notably Rose and Blank 1974) have produced comparable data.

My own approach has differed from this only in emphasis. It has been to try to tease out pragmatic-interpretive failure by employing non-Piagetian problems in order to study directly the variable of instruction intepretation (Russell 1975, 1976) and by presenting Piagetian problems nonverbally rather than modifying the instructions or materials (Russell 1979). About conservation at least my conclusions have been that: (a) nonconservers can fail by linguistic misinterpretation *prior to* witnessing any transformations of the materials; (b) nonconservers may use conservation language to describe their own performance, but its use by the experimenter distorts their judgments in the direction of nonconservation; (c) nonverbal competence in conservation can be found as early as 4 to 5 years if an appropriate transfer of learning design is used. (Other nonverbal tests of conservation have found only small effects with children who are in any case practically or actually within the concrete operational age range (e.g. Miller 1979, Weldall and Poborca 1980).)

Why, in particular, does a nonconserver, when asked why he chose the (correct) pair of transformed pencils on a transfer condition, say that he chose the ones that were 'the same size' but then perform like a nonconserver again on the standard (verbal) post-test. In the Russell 1979 experiment, the only essential difference between the two situations was that it was the *experimenter* who used the phrase in one case. My speculation was that the nonconserving child cognises length equality through transformation in a 'subjective' or 'private' manner. He cannot appreciate that when *another* person uses a phrase such as 'the same size' he and that person can hold a common reference not only to the simple perceptual fact of protrusion, but to a length identity which is manifest in the covariance of two dimensions (one pencil protrudes but another trails, therefore length constant). He does not know that length judgments, at least, can refer to this privately-cognised invariance. Public criteria for invariance of physical properties can, he thinks, only be one-dimensional and 'perceptual'.

The picture which begins to emerge before those who are at all sympathetic to this line of thought is that of the young child having a propositional attitude that is phenomentalist/labile/pragmatic/subjective/private/perceptual. (All these words are, of course, more or less unsatisfactory because this is not a state of mind that adults have to refer to—by definition.) On this model the main developmental task is the progressive socialisation of the child's judgments, their tuning in with those of the adult by means of the appropriate public criteria. The attainment of intersubjectivity is the *necessary* (but of course not sufficient) condition for the objectivisation of thinking. As I have indicated elswhere (Russell 1978), although such a conception gained philosophical currency by way of Wittgenstein and the Pragmatists and has recently been elaborated by David Hamlyn (1978), it was J. M. Baldwin (1861-1934) who first spelled out the implications of such an assumption for developmental theory.

But how does all this accord with Piagetian theory? Of course, Piaget is a notoriously protean and eclectic thinker—some might find in Piaget's famous notion of egocentrism a conceptualisation akin to that being sketched here. But, that said, I believe the attempt to explain judgmental deficiencies by divergence of propcsitional attitudes is fundamentally opposed to the Piagetian orientation. This incompatibility comes into sharp relief when we consider the Piagetian account of how *social* processes are supposed to function in the equilibration of mental structures. This is best seen in Piaget's book *The Psychology of Intelligence* (1950). In a fascinating penultimate chapter Piaget compares "intellectual" interaction between individuals to 'a vast game of chess, which is carried on unremittingly and in such a way that each action carried out with respect to a particular item involves a series of equivalent or complementary actions on the part of the opponent; laws of grouping are nothing more or less than the various rules ensuring the reciprocity of the players and the consistency of their play' (165). Piaget is here drawing something far stronger that a mere analogy between preoperational children as individuals and the individual centrations of preoperational children. Just as centrations are equilibrated through reciprocal *inter*-individual cognitive conflict, so judgments are socialised by the equilibration of reciprocal *inter*-individual cognitive conflict. The empirical implications is there to be extracted. social interaction between cognitive *equals* (e.g. fellow preoperational children) can be the *sufficient* social experience for the objectivisation of thought.

The theory is that egocentrism is dissolved through the child's having to cooperate with other children who necessarily adopt different perspectives from his own: the reciprocal coordination of mental perspectives. Piaget had introduced a similar conception much earlier in his work on moral development; in any event it is a notion absolutely at the heart of his theory. According to equilibration theory knowledge is not transmitted to the child, it is constructed by him both individually and in concordance with others (the two processes are indissociable). In principle, therefore, preoperational children do not require *exposure* to the concrete operational judgments to construct them—the equilibration machinery will see to that. My crucial (Gedanken!) experiment here would be to ship a group of healthy preoperational children to a desert island and leave them there for about four or five years; if Piaget is correct they should have constructed a system of concrete operations by then out of the exigencies of social cooperation.

The critical point that I want to make is this: for such a process to function, the preoperational children who find themselves making conflicting judgments must be capable of regarding these judgments *as* conflicting. What if they do not? What if their pragmatic/subjective/etc. propositional attitudes direct that they will be like two film fans who have the *appropriate* propositional attitudes and are reporting to each other whether they enjoyed the film rather than discussing who directed it? To illustrate, within equilibration theory two non-conservers may come to coordinate liquid conservation by the following kind of dialectic. They are sharing out a drink: one child boasts that he has more because the liquid in his (thinner) glass comes higher up; the other child counters with the claim that *he* has more because his drink is wider. Eventually they come to agree that neither of them is correct and fall back on the fact that both drinks came out of (say) full glasses of the same shape: they hit upon the principle of identity via that of the necessary incompatibility of unidimensional judgments. Naturally, this is a gross characterisation of a process which Piaget would regard as having a much finer grain than this. But my point is that, on the non-Piagetian approach being developed here, if such a conversation ever took place it would not be about reality and truth, it would be about something more akin to appearance and opinion. The children would not engage in a dialectic at all: the conversation over their glasses would have more in common (in logicality if not style) with that of two wine tasters considering whether 'tart' or 'piquant' is the appropriate adjective. Two children with such propositional attitudes would never attempt to coordinate their perspectives, any more than adults ever really discuss whether a film is 'enjoyable'—yes or no.

We cannot ship children off to desert islands to test the implications of the equilibration model, but we can test dyads to see whether such conversations and such coordinations do indeed take place. And fortunately we do not have to rely on Piagetian exegesis for the framing of this 'cognitive conflict hypothesis'. Willem Doise (see especially Doise 1978) of Geneva and his associates have been performing experiments since about 1974 as demonstrations of just this thesis. Principally they have been concerned with the facilitatory effect of having two spatially 'egocentric' children cooperating on a model landscape reconstruction task based on Piaget and Inhelder's (1956) tasks. They report (e.g. Doise *et al.*, 1975) that conflicts of centration between children result in performance at a higher cognitive level than either child is capable of when performing solo. Despite this, it was Piaget's formulation which motivated our research project on dyadic interaction, which began in 1978. (In fact it could not have been otherwise, because I did not come across Doise's work until after that phase of the project was complete!)

The aim of the project was to pair children whose performance was preoperational on a specific task in such a way that they would approach the problem from (sometimes literally) different perspectives. We also paired children who succeeded on the pre-test with such children in order to examine the possible transmission of the principle from one child to another. Altogether we tested around 150 dyads in the age range of 4 to 8 years. In those dyads who contributed to the grouped data the children were of the same sex, within 6 months of age and (usually) from the same class at school. All were tested in the department's developmental laboratory, being left alone in a room containing a remote-control video camera which filmed their reflection in an observation mirror. Speech was recorded by a ceiling microphone. Each dyad performed either 5 or 6 tasks together in one half-day session, which gave us around 22 hours of tape by the end. Two check lists were drawn up from pilot tapes which were meant to be applicable to any dyadic performance of a concrete operational task: an 'epistemic' list which scored behaviour in terms of its correctness and logical characteristics, and a 'pragmatic' list which descriptively recorded events in the stream of social behaviour (questions, counters and so on).

Conservation

Figure 4.1 represents the arrangement of two children who have to decide on an answer to the standard length conservation question. The post-transformation display is shown here. If both are nonconservers than a direct perspective mismatch is virtually guaranteed, because child A will judge pencil x to be bigger and child B will judge pencil y to be so. We can then compare this kind of dyad with one which contains a conserver and a nonconserver. Additionally, because the resolution of disputes is to a greater or lesser degree a function of what is loosely known as social dominance as well as of certainty about the answer, all children were given a task which was supposed to indicate something about the relative dominance of the partners. This task employed the 'Etch-a-Sketch' toy which is like a miniature TV screen containing a drawing stylus that can be guided by two dials: one dial moves the line horizontally and the other dial moves it vertically. The partners took a dial each and were instructed to copy a step-like figure. As pilot tapes had shown, in this situation one of the children tends to take charge and instruct his partner to 'turn', 'stop' and so on. Therefore, we employed the (admittedly crude) measure of which child gave the more task-relevant instructions as the index of relative dominance. We also used a story completion task for the same purpose, on the assumption that the suggestion for finishing the story of the more dominant child would tend to be adopted. The procedure in the conservation study was that the experimenter would pose the conservation question after transformation, tell the children that they had to agree on *one* answer, and that they should shout 'ready' when they had finished, and then leave the room.

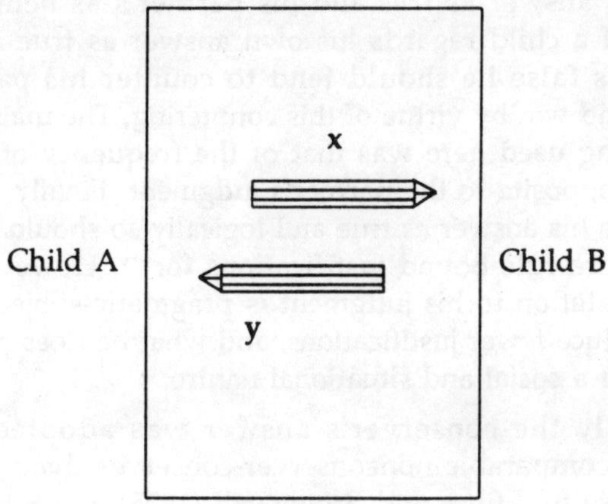

Fig. 4.1. Diagram of the post-transformation display in the conservation study.

Two kinds of question were asked by means of this design: (a) does the pairing of non-conservers result in success by virtue of perspective coordination as compared to nonconserver/conserver dyads? (b) does the dyadic behaviour of nonconservers evince the kind of propositional attitude sketched above? The criteria for (a) were simply the relative amount of post-test improvement in the two groups, on three post-tests over five weeks, and generalisation to other forms of conservation; (b) was more problematical. The possible divergence in propositional attitudes between conservers and nonconservers was assessed by three criteria. Firstly, it was reasoned that, if the nonconserver's attitude to his judgment is pragmatic-subjective, then which of the two *nonconservation* answers is adopted will be determined by social factors such as which child is more determined to get his own way, that is, by something like dominance. In this case it would be as if the children had been given a task such as deciding on a number between 1 and 10. Given sufficient motivation towards the task, one would expect the dominant child to impose his choice of number on his partner. However, in the conserver/nonconserver pairings the conserver should often win the day, irrespective of whether or not he is dominant, because he regards his answer as *true* and his partner's as being *false*. Secondly, if a child regards his own answer as true and his partner's as false he should tend to counter his partner's judgment and win by virtue of this countering. The main index of countering used here was that of the frequency of giving judgments opposite to the partner's judgment. Finally, a child who regards his answer as true and logically so should tend to produce more rule-bound justifications for it. However, if a child's orientation to his judgment is pragmatic-subjective he should produce fewer justifications, and what he does produce should be of a social and situational nature.

Typically the conserver's answer was adopted; thus replicating comparable nonconserver-conserver dyad studies such as those by Miller and Brownwell (1975) and Silverman and Litman (1979). In those few cases where nonconserver pairs did produce conservation answers, this was due to one of the children spontaneously judging conservation *before* the partner had made his judgment. Overall, the evidence for perspective coordination was practically nonexistent, and the degree of post-test gain and generalisation after the nonconserver pairings was very slight indeed compared to that of the conserver/nonconserver pairings (see Russell, in press (a) for full details). although it is difficult to make unqualified statements on the basis of these kinds of data, it is fair to say that cognitive change was not facilitated in the nonconserver dyads.

Turning to the criteria for propositional attitude it could be seen that this lack of facilitation was due to the fact that nonconservation dyad members did not appreciate the fact of cognitive conflict. The child whose incorrect answer was adopted in nonconservation dyads tended ($p < .05$) to be the child who had instructed his partner more on the Etch-a-Sketch task, whereas no such relation was found when it was a conserver whose answer was adopted. This latter (conserver + nonconserver) finding replicated Miller and Brownwell 1975. However, only in the case of the conserver/nonconserver dyads did the winner (i.e. conserver) give more opposing judgments than his partner. This seems paradoxical: how could the 'dominant' child have had his answer adopted in the nonconservation pairings if he did not tend to oppose his partner's judgment? The paradox is resolved by the fact that, as more detailed analysis of the checklists showed, it was not that the *dominant* child won by what he did but rathe than the more *compliant* child gave in without any opposition. Quite frequently one saw sequences such as: 'That one's bigger', then hesitation by the partner before he says, 'OK then'; or 'That one', 'That one', 'That one. . . oh we'll take yours'. As regards justifications, these were far less frequent in nonconservers than in conservers. More significantly *all* conservation justifications were in terms of rule-bound principles (reversibility, irrelevance of movement etc.); whereas 10 of the total 24 nonconservation justifications were by reference to pragmatic-situational factors (e.g. 'My brother is good at these and he told me. . .'; 'I got this right when I did it at school'). Indeed some of the nonconservers actually used phenomenal and perspective arguments in *support* of their answers. Two children said 'It *looks* bigger' as a justification. Two said something of the kind. . . .'that one's bigger to you and that one's bigger to me' with the implication being: 'as there is no right answer we may as well pick mine'.

Our data *are* highly interpreted. However, it does not demand much interpretive skill to justify the following claim on the basis of these data: children regard their nonconservation judgments as pragmatic and subjective relative to the way conserving children regard their judgments. But can this notion explain why some nonconservers adopt the conservation answer after mere exposure to it in a session that may last less than 20 seconds and go on to maintain it throughout three post-tests over five weeks? To explain this we would require the additional assumption that the transitional nonconserver is aware that his judgment is subjective-perceptual but that he regards logico-mathematical judgments that are not thus perspective-relative as inherently preferable. Exposure to the correct judgment makes him aware that *it is possible to make objective judgments about length relations.* The speculation is that changes in propositional attitude set the scene for, or canalise, changes in what actual propositions come to be expressed.

Spatial Egocentrism

It is in the field of spatial judgments that the cognitive conflict view of dyadic interaction carries most force, because it is here that perspective clashes may be quite literal. Not surprisingly it is spatial tasks that Doise and his associates (Doise *et al.*, 1975, Doise and Mugny 1979, Mugny and Doise 1978) have employed to elaborate the conflict of centration model. What motivated our study of allocentric placement was again a deep scepticism about the view that in a situation where two children from the preoperational age range are manoeuvred into adopting different perspectives we have the conditions for conflict-fuelled cognitive change. The important difference between the logic of this and the conservation study was that incorrect responses were not verbal judgments about physical properties but placements (or judgments about placements) of items. Moreover, the claim was not being pressed that these placements actually reflect the subjective-pragmatic propositional attitude itself. The assumption was that, as preoperational thought is as it is because of the child's inability to frame the right kind of propositions, then any preoperational phenomenon that does not involve the child in framing propositions is either produced by faulty intepretation of the instructions or by 'performance' errors. (See the review by Helene Borke (1978) for studies showing allocentric abilities in very young children.) This claim will become clearer when the data are discussed. The general relevance of this study to the issue of propositional attitudes was in predicting that reciprocal egocentrism which engenders conflicts of centration does *not* characterise dyadic interaction in spatial tasks between children from the preoperational age range.

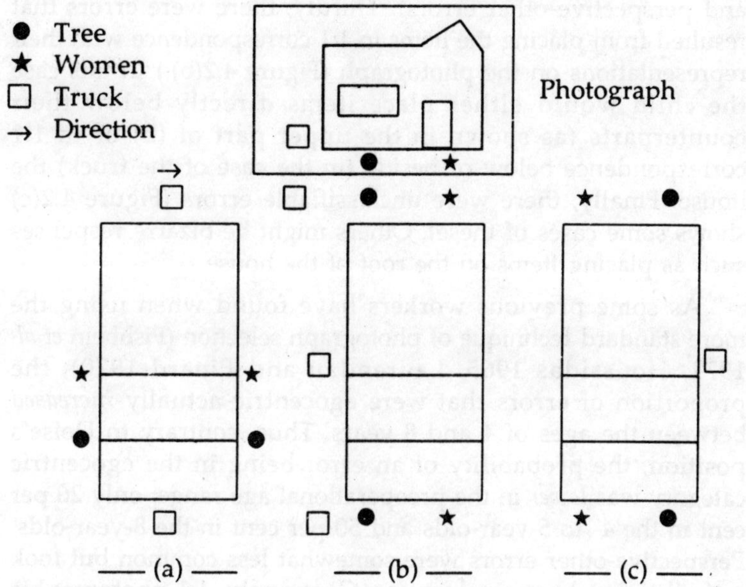

Fig. 4.2. Schematic diagram of the allocentric placement task in the lower portion are three cases of the house facing the child on the left.

Figure 4.2 illustrates the task. As before, the children sat across from each other at the table. To one side was a photograph representing a lego house with a lego woman and tree stationed in front and a toy truck parked at the side. Before the children on the table were all the pictured items. The house was turned to face one of the children. In the lower portions of the figure the house is facing the child on the left. The children were then told to cooperate in placing the three items (truck, woman, tree) in the same positions that they were in on the photograph. When they had done that the experimenter returned and reoriented the house to face the *other* child and instructed them as previously. Four possible kinds of error were framed on the basis of a pilot study. First there was the standard egocentric error where the child places the items as if the house were facing himself rather than facing his partner.

Secondly, there was the reverse case of the child placing the items vis-à-vis his partner when the house faces himself—called here 'perspective-other' errors (see Figure 4.2(a) for egocentric and perspective-other errors). Thirdly, there were errors that resulted from placing the items in 1:1 correspondence with their representations on the photograph (Figure 4.2(b).) In this case the child would either place items directly below their counterparts (as shown in the upper part of (b) or in 1:1 correspondence below or beside (in the case of the truck) the house. Finally, there were unclassifiable errors (Figure 4.2(c) shows some cases of these). Others might be bizarre responses such as placing items on the roof of the house.

As some previous workers have found when using the more standard technique of photograph selection (Fishbein *et al.* 1972, Houssidas 1965, Laurendau and Pinard 1970), the proportion of errors that were egocentric actually *increased* between the ages of 4 and 8 years. Thus, contrary to Doise's position, the probability of an error being in the egocentric category was *lower* in the preoperational age range: only 26 per cent in the 4- to 5-year-olds and 50 per cent in the 8-year-olds. Perspective-other errors were somewhat less common but took a similar developmental course. Conversely, 1:1 photographic errors became less frequent with age (from 35 per cent of total errors to 6 per cent). Unclassifiable errors were infrequent overall but somewhat more common in the youngest children.

Not only were egocentric errors only one kind among others, but they were explicable as errors of *performance* rather than as indices of a deep epistemic egocentrism. The picture which emerges from considering the relative frequency of the actual placements in the egocentric category was that of children trying to do the right kind of thing but not doing it well enough. They rarely made what is the most obvious egocentric error, that of placing the woman or tree on their own side of the house when it was facing their partner. In the five cases, where this error was made it was very clear from the child's conversation with his partner that he thought the experimenter expected them to ignore the house's direction. Secondly, what of the substantial proportion of perspective-other errors? Surely the parsimonious interpretation of both kinds of perspective error ('egocentric' errors could be referred to as 'perspective-self') would be the claim that they simply reflect tendencies to put the truck the wrong side of the house, to reverse woman and tree etc., which happen to be somewhat more pronounced when the house is facing away from the error-maker. We did not test anyone over the age of 9 years, but I am sure that such errors would not be unknown in an adult population. Additionally, the dyads seem to believe—despite what we said to them—that speed was of the essence, thus creating the perfect conditions for performance errors.

Conflict of centration was assessed by recording the incidence of one child countering a placement or judgment of his partner and the resistance of this counter by the child. The resulting profile was not that of two spatially egocentric children coming into conflict over placements. Quite simply the egocentric responder did not contest his placement: he passively accepted counters of it and rarely countered correct allocentric placements. But the picture was entirely different for the children who made 1:1 photographic errors. Counters of these *were* resisted—sometimes hotly—in 50 per cent of cases. Here at least the children seemed to have been adopting a radically different construal of the task from the allocentric construal. Indeed these children may have been adopting a topological conception of spatial location in terms of proximity and spatial succession (see Piaget and Inhelder 1956).

In fact some primitive tendency towards 1:1 correspondence may be responsible for the apparently 'egocentric' errors in the three-mountains task where the child selects his own photograph when asked to find that of what another can see: here the child is selecting a photograph where the items are in 1:1 correspondence with the modelled items. As to why egocentric errors proportionally increase with age, it is possible to consider this, as I have argued elsewhere (Russell, in press (b)), as a form of 'growth error' determined by the second phase of rapid development of the frontal cortex during this age period (Luria 1973), given that the frontal cortex may control egocentric responding in primates (Pohl 1973).

But explaining how the errors come to be made is not our major concern here. What relevance to the issue of propositional attitudes is there in the finding that the child's spatial judgments vis-à-vis another child's perspective were essentially allocentric, apart from an early tendency towards a topological interpretation of the instructions? The relevance arises from the consideration that, if the child's orientation to his judgments is, let us say, subjective in the sense of being perspective-relative, this not only fails to exclude the possibility that he should be able to appreciate other perspectives, but actually suggests that this appreciation of perspectives is part and parcel of the kind of propositional attitude which we have been considering. His problem, on the present account, is that he is *too ready* to accept 'perspectivism' and believes that 'objective' facts about the physical world should indeed be judged on the perspectivist pattern. Of course, such a view may appear needlessly paradoxical and even to go directly against the tide of developmental studies which have plotted the slow and painful increment in 'perspective-taking' abilities with age as related to moral development (Fehr 1978), individual differences (Light 1979) and general cognitive level (Asher 1979). I merely wish to state—because I do not have space to argue the proposition—that perspective-taking studies may well be measuring something other than the ability to, as it were, 'get inside another's head'. There is, after all, another theoretical framework which regards the child as developing away from a primordial self-other empathy (Hoffman 1976) and fusion with the other's consciousness (Werner and Kaplan 1963).

Transitivity

The previous studies both demonstrated that the incorrect child is less certain of his judgment than the correct child (c.f. Scott Miller's copious studies of certainty in conservation, e.g. Miller 1973) and will typically not contest his judgment against the correct one nor justify it logically. The first of our dyadic studies of transitivity reinforced this finding as a kind of spin-off from its main aim, which was to examine the issue of premise memory (see Russell 1981). In this task dyads cooperated on a transitive measurement problem (A>B, B=C, ∴ A>C). The room contained a tower of small lego bricks on the floor (A) and one of large wooden bricks on a table (C); and the dyad was given a stick (B) the same height as the table tower with which to measure. The incorrectly (C >A) inferring children were less likely to justify their answers spontaneously, and almost inevitably gave way when their partners produced the correct answer. However, other factors suggested that the incorrect answer was not a mere performance slip. First, a separate study had shown that a third of incorrect inferrers will, when asked, justify their incorrect inference by reference to the *correct* premises; and in the present study 15 per cent of incorrect inferrers spontaneously did likewise (though mostly to the experimenter). Moreover, nearly 70 per cent of the incorrect children who were challenged by their correct partners reiterated their answers. 'All this makes it difficult to extract any conclusions about the incorrect inferrer's propositional attitude. On the one hand, he is uncertain of the judgment relative to the correct inferrer [other studies have shown the logical necessity with which the transitive inferrer regards his judgment (Miller *et al.* 1977; Somerville *et al.* 1979)]. But on the other hand, it appears that incorrect *strategies* have to be implicated in some way. The terms 'subjective' and 'pragmatic' are too strong to describe the apparent propositional attitude, and yet it does not appear that the child regards his as *the* answer in the way that the transitive inferrer typically does.

We carried out a further study of transitivity in an effort directly to encourage perspective clashes. Here, as before, two children faced each other across a table on which there was a large cardboard sheet this time. Before each child was a black, vertical (to his view) line, one of which was a little longer than the other. They were instructed to cooperate in the drawing (with a pen on a piece of paper stuck temporarily to the cardboard) of a line intermediate in length between the two lines. Each was told to 'make sure the line is longer/shorter than the line on your own side of the table'. To aid them they were given a cardboard strip on which they could mark the extent of each line as well as rule the to-be-drawn line.

At present the checklists have yet to be analysed in any systematic way. But one conclusion is clear: there were a number of ways in which children failed (drawing a line before measuring the original lines, drawing a line equal to one of them, inappropriate marking on the strip etc.) but none of them involved an 'egocentric' mismatch. By this I mean a situation in which each child tries to draw a long or short line merely to ensure that he has fulfilled his part of the instruction. For this reason there were no perspective clashes. There were cases where children happily drew *two* lines in this way but none in which they tried to end up with one line on this principle. The only clashes we witnessed were tugs-of-war over the felt-tip marker. There was, however, evidence of what could be described as a pragmatic orientation to the task on the part of the younger children. They tended first to draw a line, sometimes freehand, that they estimated to be somewhere between the two lengths, then make some rough comparisons with each of the original lines, and finally add to or scribble out a little from the drawn line. Unlike the older children who could not extract the correct measurement procedure, they were perfectly happy with their productions. The younger ones did not appear to be distinguishing between rough estimation and an accuracy that was founded on an appropriate procedure. The older children who failed did appreciate this difference and they were dissatisfied. This is comparable with the finding of Harris and Singleton (1977) that 4-year-old children will rely on their own perceptual *estimations* of the relative size of towers sufficiently separated as to make such estimates unreliable, whereas 6-year-olds will either say nothing or that they are unable to judge. Harris also showed that the younger children do nevertheless realise that side-by-side comparisons are more accurate. There is a tenuous analogy here with our finding that incorrect inferrers will tend to adopt the correct inference when presented with it.

Class Inclusion

In this final dyadic task our aim was not to pair children whose strategies were likely to be both wrong in order to see if this produced perspective coordination via cognitive conflict. Instead, the rationale was to pair children whose approach to the problem was preoperational but in a situation in which they could both be *partially correct*. Would this partial correctness lead to complete correctness through a kind of coordination that did not necessarily involve conflict, or would the dyad adopt some infralogical strategy as a pragmatic compromise (rather as the younger children had done on the previous task)?

The problem was one of class inclusion. Six pencils were placed before the dyad: three yellow and three green (Russell, in press (c)). Each child was instructed in turn. One was told to 'take more yellow pencils than [the partner]'. The other child was told to 'take more pencils altogether than [the partner]'. Thus, the first child should finish up with two yellow pencils and the second with one yellow and three green. To produce jointly a correct solution here neither child need understand the class inclusion principle (as the term is employed by Piaget at least). The 'more yellow' child has to focus exclusively on the subclass and there is no need to cognise the relation of subclass of yellow pencils to the total class. Conversely the child choosing 'more altogether' need pay no attention to the 2 subclasses: he has to ensure that he ends up with at least 4 pencils, by focussing on the class. However, we did perhaps have a somewhat uneven division of labour in that there is only one way in which the 'more yellow' child can succeed, but a number of ways in which the 'more altogether' child can do so. Success must therefore come through negotiation but with the 'more yellow' child being more responsible for this success. Clashes of perspective could come about either by the 'more altogether' child ignoring the other child's demands, or by the 'more yellow' child wanting *all* the yellow pencils.

I shall only mention data for the children who failed the class-inclusion pre-test. As regards success of outcome first of all, the equal sharing of the pencils was very much the predominant strategy of the younger children: all the yellows for one child and all the greens for the other. Two-thirds of the 4.5 to 5.5 years age-group did this and (as in the drawing task) with evident confidence in their correctness. Of the oldest children (in the 7.6 to 8.5 year age-group) 44 per cent of dyads shared the pencils. Although there was a steady increase in correct outcomes throughout the age range, equal sharing was the predominant outcome overall. The propositional attitude which might have been producing such an outcome is again that of satisfaction with something that is just about right and not particularly unfair to either partner, which we saw in the drawing task. 'Pragmatism' is again an appropriate term.

Turning to the question of inter-child conflict, there were no cases of the 'more altogether' child just picking more pencils irrespective of their colour. He or she invariably 'took perspective' sufficiently to take all the greens, at least initially. Conflict was engendered through the 'more yellow' child wanting to have *all* the yellow pencils, and much less frequently by the 'more altogether' child pressing the third yellow pencil on his partner. Thus, conflict was not a function of the adoption of what could be called different perspectives, but rather of the consistency with which children pursued the half-each strategy. Within 'conflictual behaviour' we included (a) countering, (b) snatching a pencil, and (c) resisting the attempt to take a pencil. Twenty-eight per cent of children showed some form of this; and it was over twice as pronounced in the 'more yellow' children.

However, the notion of pragmatic propositional attitude does not fit terribly well with the conflict data. The 'more yellow' child's insistence on having all the yellow pencils often resulted in some veritable battles, and we cannot lightly dismiss the charge that 'more' may have meant 'equal' (as well as 'less'!) for some children—and this despite the care that was taken with the instructions (each child had to repeat his instructions correctly before the trial began).

What of the 38 per cent of these class inclusion *failers* who ended up with the correct division? Do we not here have evidence for something like the Doise viewpoint that two heads are better than one if the two heads are located at different logical perspectives? In order to answer this question we tested children *individually* on the same kind of task. They were presented with a model policeman and a model fireman either side of a table with six plastic bricks between them, three of which were yellow and three green. The instructions were to give more yellow bricks to the policeman and more bricks altogether to the fireman. Twenty-seven per cent of the group (who had been distributed in similar age-groupings to dyads in the 4-8 year age range) succeeded. If we compare dyads with individuals there was a slight overall superiority on dyadic performance, but it was one which fell well short of statistical significance. As before, the predominant incorrect strategy was equal sharing, and again the younger the child the more likely it was that he or she would respond swiftly and with evident certainty. Almost all the children in the oldest group who were incorrect knew they were incorrect and yet did not know what they could do about it.

Understanding Logical Distinctions

The dyad studies provide some suggestive support for the notion that preoperational thought expresses subjective, pragmatic. . . etc. propositional attitudes. But the question has yet to be tackled of how the child is able to change his propositional attitude towards 'concrete operational' judgments to one that is objective, necessary, general and stable. In order to work towards a solution to this problem I would want to make the working assumptions that the child *potentially appreciates* something about how necessity and objectivity grow out of the conceptual system, and that interaction with others brings him round to the application of necessary and objective propositional attitudes to his own logico-mathematical judgments. Such a change is a necessary condition for the acquisition of what Vygotsky called the 'scientific concepts'.

But where does this appreciation of necessity come from in the first place? Actually, I do not have to answer this to make the point about propositional attitude change. But I might say that we can regard [with Vygotsky (1934) and Baldwin (1908)] the child's notion of necessity as emerging from his being led to 'reflect' on the structure of the conceptual system as expressed in language, as an alternative to the Piagetian viewpoint that the notion of necessity is a *result* of the process of equilibration.

We were searching, therefore, for a basic level of competence in cognising the logical characteristics which distinguish between "preoperational' and 'concrete operational' modes of thinking. It is this basic competence of which the child becomes progressively more aware. The criterion we used to assess this competence was teachability; in fact, we asked whether a child understands what an adult is talking about when the adult tells the child that some judgments must be true no matter what whereas some only *may* be true. I want here to briefly mention three teaching studies which we carried out: (a) on necessarily true versus contingent judgments; (b) on absolute versus relative, general versus particular, objective versus subjective, casual versus intentional judgments; and (c) on necessarily *false* versus contingent judgments.

The rationale and procedures for all three studies were identical. Thirty pairs of sentences were presented to the child (e.g. 'That rose is a flower' plus 'That rose is a present'), one of the sentences was repeated, and then the child had to make the appropriate response for either necessity or contingency. We then plotted errors and trials to criterion (9 out of 10 correct in a run, or 30 trials) in the usual manner. In order to study the efficacy of teaching the principles on which these distinctions rested, we compared the performance of a 'teaching' group with that of a 'non-teaching' group. Also, in order to make the situation as game-like as possible the sentences were spoken by a 'talking teddy'; that is, they were recorded on a cassette and played through a speaker in the bear's head. The child sat in front of the bear and between them (in addition to the experimenter) was a response box on the table. This consisted of a metal box with a light on top and a lever at each side which could be depressed. The child's task was to respond by depressing either the left or the right-hand lever, depending on which sentence had been repeated. A correct choice made the light come on and a chime sound in the box. On all studies the children were grouped into three age levels; 5- to 6-year-olds; 7- to 8-year-olds; 9- to 10-year-olds.

In the non-teaching condition the child was told that his task was to find which sentence worked which of the levers, and that he had to find the 'clue' about the difference. The child had to repeat both sentences after the pair had been presented, and was then asked how he thought they were different. When one was repeated by the bear and the child had responded, the experimenter drew his attention to its being a 'left' or 'right' kind of sentence. In the teaching condition of the necessary/ contingent experiment the child was told that it was a game about finding the difference between 'things that must always/ had to be true and things which may or may not be true'. The child was also told which lever was for the necessary and which lever was for the contingent sentences. After each pair was presented the child was asked which one he thought had to be true and which he thought did not. One of the sentences was repeated and the experimenter told the child to respond appropriately. Then, irrespective of his choice, the experimenter explained why he had been correct or incorrect with reference to the actual sentences.

We separated the necessary/contingent sentences into five relatively distinct sets of 30 pairs as follows: (1) *definitionally necessary* sentences were those in which the predicate held by virtue of the subject's definition (e.g. 'John's dad is a man' versus 'John's dad is a farmer'); (2) *situationally necessary* sentences were those where a description of a situation had to be true (e.g. 'There are people in the crowd' versus 'There are children in the crowd'); (3) *relationally necessary* sentences were those within which two terms necessarily had to be related in the way expressed (e.g. 'My green shirt is the same colour as my green tie' versus 'My green shirt is the same material as my green tie'); (4) *informationally empty* sentences were similar to the definitional ones, except that the necessity was less strong because it was possible though unlikely for the negation to hold (e.g. 'That zebra has stripes' versus 'That zebra has babies'); (5) *negated tautologies* were those where the predicate was the equivalent in negative form of the characterising adjective in the subject (e.g. 'The fat man is not thin' vesus 'The fat man is not well').

The main findings of this study were that even the youngest group (mean age 5.10 years) clearly benefited from the teaching; and that what improved with age was the ability to benefit from teaching rather than the ability to find the 'clue' about the difference (a significant interaction between age levels and teaching/non-teaching). As regards necessity versus contingency, therefore, the child in the late preoperational age range at least (4-year-olds did not adapt to the experimental procedure) seems to possess a basic competence in cognising such distinctions as elaborated in speech. There was a very steep increment in performance in the teaching group between the first two age levels and hardly any improvement between the latter two (a 'floor' effect may have been operating for some subgroups). Thus the ability to benefit from such instruction appears to be something that improves during the preoperational/concrete operational transition period. Moreover, although the discernment of when a necessary or tautologous truth as implied *by an instruction* may not be manifest until adolescence (Osherson and Markman 1978), the cognising of a speaker's description of this logical property seems to be present long before then.

However, to distinguish preoperational from operational propositional attitudes on the ground of necessity/contingency alone is somewhat crude because these distinctions subsume and, to some extent, grow out of others. We studied these finer-grain distinctions next. I hope the descriptions carry their justifications: (1) *objective-subjective* (e.g. 'That liquorice sweet is my last' versus 'That liquorice sweet is my favourite'); (2) *general-particular* (e.g. 'Zebras have legs' versus 'Zebras have stripes'); (3) *absolute-relative* (e.g. 'The bat is a wooden one' versus 'The bat is a long one'); (4) *casual-intentional* (e.g. 'The rain made us wet' versus 'The rain made us stay home'). The only difference in procedure between this and the previous experiment was that there was no real attempt to describe the general demands of the task in the teaching condition before presentation began. Subjects were different children in the same age groupings.

The results also were similar. Teaching was highly successful even in the youngest age group, and what improved with age (between the first two age levels at least) was the ability to benefit from teaching rather than to extract the basis of the distinction without teaching. In contrast to the necessary/contingent subgroups some distinctions were much easier to teach than others: teaching of causal/intentional and general/particular was more successful than that of the other two types. This was, to some extent, because the other two distinctions were more difficult to put into words; but then the difficulty of teaching is not likely to be *contingently* related to that of learning. For it is well to consider that in some languages there is a single word for both learning and teaching. Sutton (1979) has shown how the lack of such a differentiation in the Russian language must bear on our reading of Vygotsky.

Our final study using this methodology was an exact parallel to the first, except that it was sentences that were all necessarily *false* rather than necessarily true which were contrasted with the contingent ones. Here are some examples in the same five groupings as before: 'The cat is an insect' versus 'The cat is a mother'; 'The man in the car is walking' vesus 'The man in the car is waving'; 'The boy who is six is younger than the boy who is two' versus 'The boy who is six is fairer than the boy who is two'; 'These cups of tea are to eat' vesus 'These cups of tea are for sale'; 'This water is not wet' versus 'This water is not dirty'.

The same story can be told about the results except that this was a far easier task overall than the other two. Children's perception of a priori nonsense is very good indeed. But is this not what we would expect, given that the child is far more likely to focus on what is verbally funny than what is verbally obvious? Very often the children would laugh at the sentences, although this laughter was by no means a guarantee of successful discrimination. We are dealing here with a very primitive competence: the ability to discriminate between what is conceptually inappropriate and conceptually appropriate with the corresponding propositional attitudes of the playful and the serious. Here is a typical example of the early appearance of this ability. Chukovsky (1976) tells how at 23 months his daughter came up to him 'looking mischievous and embarassed at the same time. . . . She cried to me even when she was at some distance from where I sat: 'Daddy, doggie-miaow'—that is she reported to me the sensational and to her incorrect view that doggie, instead of barking, miaows. And she burst out into somewhat encouraging, somewhat artificial laughter, inviting me, too, to laugh at this invention' (601). Piaget's (1951) famous observations show still earlier forms of incongruity humour in object play.

Reluctant as I am to burden the world with yet another theory of the cognitive function of humour (and being still more reluctant to claim any originality for it), might it not be that, by appreciating the conceptually inappropriate via that most distinctive propositional attitude of the humorous, the child—maybe even from the time of his first peekaboos—is led to construct the category of the appropriate and eventually that of the objectively true? At least one theorist of humour (Rothbart 1977) has claimed that jokes share the property of suggesting incongruity.

So by a peculiar detour we are brought back to our starting point: that of conflict models of cognitive development. For implicit in the preceding analysis is the view that the child has to appreciate the contradictory, indeed conflictual, nature of the relationships between certain propositional attitudes—that the child must see the basic opposition, for example, between the necessary and contingent, the objective and the subjective. And out of this realisation of conflict should evolve the higher knowledge that notions can be located somewhere on a continuum between these two extremes (e.g. 'Was it a *good* film?'). I am suggesting that the child's sense of humour and playfulness is the first move in a process whereby conceptual congruity is sculpted by the chisel of conceptual incongruity.

Of course Piaget's conflict of centration model is hardly uninfluenced by the Hegelian dialectic, and the previous remarks on the importance of the sense of contradiction in cognitive development express the same source. (See Lawler 1975 for an informative analysis of the relationship between Hegelian contradiction and Piagetian theory.) But the sense of contradiction which is here being emphasised is not that between propositions but between attitudes to these propositions.

5

Language and Cognition

Language and cognition have been investigated in many ways but it can be aruged that they are most intimately connected in tasks which require two children to communicate and cooperate in solving a problem. This technique has been used by a number of workers including Doise (1978), Flavell *et al.* (1979), Greenfield and Dent (1979), Miller and Brownell (1975) and Russell (1979).

Although the emphasis may vary, this research field is united in taking a social constructivist approach to intellectual development (see Russell, this volume) and in seeing awareness of one's own cognitive capacities as a significant factor in cognitive growth, (see especially Flavell *et al.* 1979, Markman, 1977, 1979). Another factor common to some, if not all, of these studies is a concern with the context in which cognition takes place, and, in particular, the move towards increasingly decontextualised modes of cognition, (see also Donaldson 1978, Walkerdine and Sinha 1978). Above all, communication itself is seen as the pivot on which these processes turn. Greenfield and Dent (1979, 34) put it as follows:

> Developmental study of this problem is important because determining something of the progressive growth of the ability to comprehend and communicate can help elucidate some central problems in the study of language and cognition. More specifically, it is possible to learn of the developmental interaction of the perceptual/cognitive system with the way in which language is used in context to communicate. A first step is to identify the relevant contextual variables and the cognitive abilities required to make use of linguistic and nonlinguistic elements in order to achieve effective communication.

The studies to be described in this chapter take the first step that is mentioned by Greenfield and Dent. It also happens coincidentally that the task chosen for investigation in this work and that of Greenfield and Dent is seriation.

In contrast to Greenfield and Dent's study, and most of the work cited, the present investigation was conducted with preschool children. If one is interested in the development of purposeful communication between peers, it seems necessary to examine the behaviour at or near its origins. The sparsity, if not lack, of studies of this sort with preschool children seems to be due to the baleful influence of Piaget's theory of egocentrism. Although Piaget's (1926) studies of commuication were carried out many years ago, he seems never to have revised his view that preoperational children are severely handicapped in their ability to talk to one another. As late as 1969 he is found writing (with Inhelder):

> The fact is that the speech of subjects between four and six (observed in situations in which children work, play, and speak freely) is not intended to provide information, ask questions, etc. (that is, it is not socialised language), but consists rather of monologues or 'collective monologues' in the course of which everyone talks to himself without listening to the others (that is, egocentric language). (Piaget and Inhelder 1969, 120).

Piaget's influence in this area is undoubtedly on the wane (see for instance Shantz 1975, Donaldson 1978 and Light 1979), yet there are features of his method which are considered too valuable to discard, especially when compared to the standard referential communication paradigm pioneered by Glucksberg and Krauss (1967).

One of the merits of Piaget's original study, in which one child explained the workings of a household object such as a tap, is that an instruction or teaching function is built into the task. The task has, therefore, a purpose or goal. In this way it is superior to the Glucksberg and Krauss task—in which the listener is asked to identify one of a series of objects or pictures from a description provided by the speaker—where the motive is less apparent. Naturalistic studies (Shields 1978, Dore 1977, Core *et al.* 1979) have shown that children do like telling each other about events that have happened, about how things work and about how to play games. Piaget's choice of somewhat obscure stories and mechanical functions has certainly much to do with the restricted abilities he found. But tasks do not have to be so far removed from the child's experience. Instead we can try to build on the sort of skills which we know that the child brings to his cooperative play (Garvey 1977).

The study to be presented here has borrowed from the approaches discussed in an attempt to include the naturalism that is the hallmark of Piagetian studies at their best, while retaining the degree of control necessary to examine the influence of subject and material variables. At the same time analysis has gone beyond frequency counts of simple behaviour measures to look at the pragmatics involved. The style and content of communication tells us much about the underlying cognitive abilities and limitations which govern performance.

The studies to be described, therefore, required one child to learn a task—putting blocks of varying size on a peg or in a line in order of size—and then to teach the task to another child who was not familiar with the 'game'. The method has the following features.

(1) The use of a set of discrete referents that were related but different. This allowed one to gauge the sensitivity of the participants to the referent non-referent array. In talking about one particular block did they take account of the perceived altenatives?

(2) Speaker and listener faced each other across a table in which they were talking about identical sets of material. The subjects could see one another but the material was hidden from the other by low screens. This procedure allowed one to see clearly the contributions of speaker and listener and the extent to which they took account of each other in their communications—for example, the listener indicating inadequacy of descriptions and the speaker modifying his message accordingly.

(3) The instructional context already referred to ensured that the goal of the exercises was explicit—to seriate a set of blocks or sticks. This, in turn, gave the participants clear

motives: one child to teach another how to carry out a task he himself had acquired earlier; one to learn that task from his peer, well enough to be able to teach it himself.

Aims

An indication of the purpose of the study has already been given. What follows is a more explicit statement of the main aims.

(1) To test the still widely held view that preschool children are unable to engage purposively in an enteprise in which successful communication is critical to success.

(2) To examine the utility of the communication technique for the investigation of a concept like seriation, an operation which Piaget has shown is critically involved in the understanding of numbers. Further, it was hoped that the technique might have applications more widely in the field of cognitive development as described by Greenfield and Dent. Is it the case that children doing *and* talking about something tells us more about the nature of concept development than children who are only 'doing'?

(3) To ascertain if the process of learning from another child (or, indeed, teaching another child) is a significant educational experience. There are a number of possibilities. Children in both roles may gain an understanding of the task that is denied them in the usual educational context. Children in one of the roles may benefit but not the other. For example, the child teaching may gain insights into the problem he did not have before, while the learning child finds the experience of no value. It is also conceivable that the exercise is of value to neither participant though educational benefits need not be the only gain. The experience may be useful as a piece of social interaction and role-taking, leading indirectly to important advances in communication skill.

Study I

SUBJECTS

The sample of ten children—four boys, six girls, with an age range from 3;11 to 5;2 (mean age 4;6)—were split into five groups of two to provide the communication pairs.

MATERIALS

There were two identifical sets of six square blocks, with a uniform thickness of 1.8 cm but increasing in length and breadth by equivalent amounts of 2 cm from the smallest, 3.4 cm, up to 13.4 cm. Each block had a centrally drilled hole of 1.2 cm for stacking on a peg set vertically in a wooden base. To facilitate verbal description each block had a familiar object painted on it, each picture taking up an equivalent proportion (about 10 per cent) of the block. In order of ascendance the pictures were: *ball, flower, car, telephone, key, dog*. There were also two small screens, 16 cm high and 60 cm wide.

PROCEDURE

Before the experiment all the subjects were individually shown the pictures to be used on the blocks to ensure they could identify them.

Preliminary session. In a preliminary session one member of each of the five pairs was presented with a model of a completed seriation and asked to produce the same arrangement from an identical set. Care was taken that the adult did not provide a model in communication terms; apart from pointing out that sticks went in order from big to little, nothing was mentioned. In the familiarisation session the children were required to learn ordering in only one direction, but in the communication session they seriated in the order learned and the reverse order. The preliminary session was concluded when one correct seriation, large to small, had been achieved.

Communication task. In the communication session, the experienced subject (ES) was taken into the experimental room first and told that they were going to play the same game as before, but that this time he must tell a friend of his how to do it. As a reminder the blocks in the finished position were briefly shown to the child, and then taken off and scrambled on the table. The naive subject (NS) was then fetched and the following instructions were given.

'We are going to play with these blocks and this stick today. *(The blocks are lying in random order on the table.)* ES has seen them before. We had a game with them before, and ES will tell you what to do. Can you see the pictures on them? Tell me what they are.' *(The experimenter ascertains that NS knows the names. As NS identifies the blocks, to points out the same blocks in the other child's array.)* Small screens were then put in front of each child's materials so that they were not visible to the other subject.

(To NS). 'Now you've both got the same blocks, haven't you? Now will you listen carefully to ES, because he is going to tell you how to put your blocks on the stick.'

(To ES). 'Now will you tell NS what to do. Make the same thing you made before for me, so that you both have the same blocks on the stick.'

At the completion of a trial, usually when all blocks were on the peg but also if subjects indicated they had finished, the screens were removed so that a comparison of seriations could be made. The experimenter asked if the series were just the same and, if they were not, for the subjects to indicate the differences. ES invariably supplied this information.

When ES had successfully transmitted instructions about seriating in the order learned, the new subject took a turn as speaker and instructed the experienced subject. After this ES again assumed the role of speaker and was this time asked to build up the blocks in the reverse order, from little to big. If this was achieved successfully NS attempted the same task. A summary of the experimental design is given in Table 5.1. All sessions were videotaped.

Results and Discussion

The sample used in these studies is specialised, in the sense that the children knew each other and the experimenter well. This is seen to be a strength of the work, however, since effective communication is less likely if the children are drawn in some random manner from the population. At the same time the sample is also small and the procedure is deliberately not rigorously defined. Accordingly, findings are presented in the form of broad, and sometimes tentative, inferences. These are based on an analysis of the complete behavioural records from videotape.

Table 5.1: Experimental Design of Study I in Seriation

Part One *Order Learned* *(Big—Little)*				*Part Two* *Reverse Order* *(Little—Big)*			
Trial 1		Trial 2		Trial 3		Trial 4	
Speaker	Listener	Speaker	Listener	Speaker	Listener	Speaker	Listener
ES	NS	NS	ES	ES	NS	NS	ES

The first point to note is the general competence of the subjects. This was first apparent in the preliminary session when one member of each pair was given the opportunity to 'practise' the seriation task. Three out of the five carried out the operation successfully first time, and another subject achieved this on her second trial. Only one subject had serious difficulty, but she worked her way through by trial and error to a correct solution on her fourth attempt.

Table 5.2 summarises performances in the communication session. The most noticeable statistic is that 15 seriations are completed in a total of 21 trials, that is 6 of the trials contain error. But, since some of these mistakes are corrected spontaneously by the speaker, a more realistic figure is 4 incorrect trials, a failure rate of only 19 per cent. These figures are based only on the speakers' performances, in other words the verbal report. But because both subjects play both roles, the experienced and naive subjects are represented. It is only experienced subjects, in fact, who make errors, but this is partly due to their playing a bigger part in the process.

So, it can be said that when they act as speakers, naive subjects perform creditably. Their rate of success is remarkable considering it is based on one exposure to the correct solution by way of verbal instructions from a peer. They have first created the correct assembly in response to their partner's description, and are subsequently able to reproduce this seriation accurately when asked to begin again with the blocks scrambled. It seems unlikely that this is a feat of rote learning. Some sort of cognitive rule must be hypothesised, though whether it is based on imagery, language or some other symbolic form is not clear.

Table 5.2: Number of Successful and Unsuccessful and Unsuccessful Seriations by Speakers in Communication Situation (Study I)

Speaker	Order Learned Big — Little		Reverse Order Little — Big		
	Correct	Incorrect	Correct	Incorrect	Total
Experienced Subject	5	4	4	2	15
Naive subject	4	0	2	0	6
Total	9	4	6	2	21

In the more demanding reverse order seriation, where there was no direct experience on which to draw, subjects again performed very capably, there being no significant difference in terms of error rate. An estimation of the performances showed that there was initially some hesitation but that once the seriation was under way it proceeded without difficulty. A real understanding of the principle of serial order must be assumed if only in this limited context.

The speaker-listener relationship. Miller and Brownell (1975) reported the effect of dominance on children's performance in joint solutions to conservation problems. They found that although conservers held sway over non-conservers in discussion, a control study showed that this was not a function of general dominance in argument. In this study it transpired that the experienced subject had leadership (if not greatness) thrust upon him. This was appropriate when ES was speaker and therefore instructor, but it was occasionally less satisfactory when ES was listener since it led to the speaker's teaching role being undermined. Here, briefly, are three examples of the sort of behaviour that was observed.

(1) The ES as listener assumes control, taking over the role of speaker even though NS is performing competently.

(2) ES ignores incorrect or inadequate information on the part of the speaker and operates independently, making no attempt to provide feedback for the speaker.

(3) In one pairing a strong element of competition entered the situation. The participants vied with one another to be first to announce the correct block. Communication did not cease; but, rather than being informative, it tended to be challenging, with the leadership of the dyad perhaps being at stake.

THE DYNAMICS OF THE COMMUNICATION SITUATION

Constructing and interpreting messages: The experiment provided some information about the young child's speech and thought processes durig cognitive activity. It was noticeable that children did not usually communicate information until *they* were satisfied as to its correctness. In this task, when the speaker was uncertain about the block he had selected he would first assess the choice, check it against what had gone and what remained in the pool, and if he decided to discard it there would be no mention of it. Only the blocks that actually went on the stick were spoken about. This demonstrates a high degree of speech inhibition and, of course, greatly increases the communication effectiveness. It may be that a task such as this, which is stretching four-year-olds mentally, would as a consequence tend to eliminate unnecessary speech, because processing capacity is already being fully utilised.

This speech inhibition was also seen in error correcting situations with rather less beneficial results. When a subject put a block (or blocks) in the wrong order, and subsequently noticed it, he would either decide to remedy the fault immediately, or remark on it but nevertheless continue to the end giving an incorrect solution. It is the error correcting behaviour which is relevant at this point. What happens is that the speaker communicates what is a wrong block choice as it is put on the stick, then notices the error. At this point he will remedy the situation, often saying 'Oh' or 'No' and effect a change—frequently a transposition—*but will not inform the listener of the change.* It is as if the extra concentration demanded to correct a fault precludes the ability to comment on the behaviour. Such behaviour is, of course, detrimental to the success of the communication operation. An example will illustrate the point.

The following extract gives the verbal record only, which largely represents the information available to the listener:

Speaker: *Telephone.*
Listener: *Telephone.*
Speaker: No, *Car.*
Listener: *Car?*

When this is amplified by the rest of the behavioural record, the nature of the confusion becomes apparent.

Speaker: *Telephone* (puts it on the stick)

Listener: *Telephone* (puts it on the stick)

Speaker: (Picks up *flower,* puts it on top of the stick briefly, but quickly sees it is the wrong choice) No. (picks up the *car* and puts it on) *Car.*

Listener: *Car?* (Takes off *telephone* and picks up *car).*

Here we have examples of the two types of speech inhibition, one adaptive, the other maladaptive. The listener, not surprisingly, connects the speaker's 'No' with the previous instruction, 'telephone', and accordingly makes the adjustment on his stick. Confusion would also have arisen if the speaker had said *'flower'* when he handled that block, and the suppression of verbal comment about this is a positive aid to communication efficiency.

The effect of nonverbal cues. Although it was stated that the verbal record is the main source of information to the participants, there are important additional aids. The speaker, for example, comes to expect the small cues which tell him that the listener has responded to his message. This is often a repetition of the message—a sort of acknowledgement—or merely the *sound* of the block going on the stick which many speakers wait for. Although they cannot see the block being put on the stick, they can tell by the listener's actions whether or not he is putting a block on the stick, and this is another cue they quickly come to use.

The material itself also provides clues. The experienced participant, particularly, can use these to good effect on occasions, compensating for confusions in the instructions provided by the speaker.

Taking account of the other. Listeners are not always experienced, however, and the general pattern is that they take a passive role. The listener tends to act on the data given by the speaker as though it were sufficient to allow him to make a decision. In the present study a one-word message is sufficient to allow a choice to be made. Its efficiency is dependent on the speaker's understanding of ordering blocks according to size.

This study does suggest that speakers, especially experienced ones, do have some consideration for the listener. In this sense, awareness of the two-way interaction of the communication situation is present. This awareness showed itself in the form of questions ('Have you got the motorcar, Alan?') and repetitions.

An example of the latter follows:

S: And this time it's with (picks up *key)* the *key* (putting it on stick).

L: (No response — looks at E).

S: (realising L has made no choice). It's the *key*.

L: (giggles — puts on *key)*.

If the speaker had been behaving in an egocentric fashion he would not be concerned as to whether the listener had heard and carried out his instruction. Even less would be give an unsolicited repetition of the message. This lack of egocentrism may have something to do with the prior exposure to the materials for some subjects, giving them knowledge to which their partners did not have access. This may have motivated them in some sense to transmit this knowledge to their partner. To reiterate this point, the experienced subjects have two concrete reasons for feeling in an advantageous position *a propos* the naive children. They have played the game before and they *know* how to play it. Not only are they familiar with the materials but they are aware that they have properly constructed the 'castle'.

This real degree of confidence may be an important factor in good communication. Equally so might be the task itself. There may be something inherent in these materials which facilitated seriation, and this is what Piaget has argued. A further study with different materials would be required to ascertain this information.

Varieties of strategy. As well as the materials themselves, the act of describing the behaviour necessary to carry out the task may also facilitate the process. Certainly Piagetian theory and Russian work (e.g. Luria 1959) suggests that speech needs to be describing an *active* process if it is to be successful. This is demonstrated in an incident occurring in the first trial of a female-male pair (Elizabeth/Gregory). The speaker (Elizabeth) begins to seriate but does not make use of the attached labels to transmit messages. Her first message is 'the big block' and she adds two further blocks without communication. The listener is not clear about his role and the experimenter suggests to the speaker that she tells Gregory what she has done. She finds this very difficult. The accurate reporting of an event that has already happened, even when the results are clearly available, does seem to present problems for young children. Part of the difficulty may be the need to use temporal phrases such as 'first', 'next' and 'then'. But it seems that the speaker needs to be describing the action as she is carrying it out to be effective.

Markman (1977) has suggested that the active mental monitoring of the component steps to a problem is an important feature of metacognition and a capacity not generally available to preschool children. Elizabeth's behaviour suggests that the monitoring has to be facilitated by explicit verbalisation. This example also illustrates the problems the task would present when easily-recognised labels for the items are not present, a fact of which Piaget seems strangely unaware in his investigation of seriation in *The grasp of consciousness* (1977).

In contrast to Elizabeth there is the exceptional performance of another child, who starts to tell the listener what she should do without carrying out the actions herself. Since she has been exposed to the task and materials only once before, and then for a very brief period, it seems that knowledge of how to perform the task is present as a plan or scheme. Having carried out the task once previously in a sensori-motor fashion, the necessary information has been assimilated and a strategy formed. Presumably it is this on which the child draws to predict the operation verbally. She is helped by the materials before her, but these only represent the building blocks of the finished structure in a random order and do not, in themselves, indicate how this structure should be created. When it was explained that she may carry out the task manually, her performance (including the reverse order) was very competent, suggesting that the cognitive operation enabling seriation, at this level at least, is present.

Study II

The considerable success that was achieved in the first seriation experiment encouraged a further study with materials used in the standard Piagetian task (Piaget 1952), i.e. graded sticks. It would then be possible to see whether the results obtained in the first study were a function of the material. If it proved to be the case that material which could be said to achieve a 'good' form led to very much greater success in ordering objects, then it would suggest that material properties and perceptual factors in general have an even stronger influence at this stage of development than perhaps Piaget has emphasised. The configurations made by the completed series are shown in Figure 5.1. The outline made by (1) seems, intuitively, to be more 'powerful', but why this should be is open to debate. Whether it is a matter of gestalt laws of perception or simply a question of greater familiarity with one form rather than another, or again a question of experience in actively constructing such shapes, will to some extent depend on one's theoretical preferences.

Method

Subjects. The sample consisted of ten children, four boys, six girl, seven of whom had taken part in Experiment I (see comment below). The age range was from 3;10 to 5;2, giving a mean of 4;5. The sample was divided into five pairs for the communication sessions.

Materials. These consisted of two identical sets of six sticks, 2.4 cm square and varying in height by equivalent amounts of 1.5 cm from the smallest, 7.5 cm, up to the largest, 15 cm, the intervals used in Elkind (1964). Each stick had a familiar object painted on it for identification purposes. These were, in order of ascendence: *chair, cup, fish, house, train, cat.*

Procedure. The procedure was identical to that followed in the first seriation experiment, with a preliminary session for half the subjects followed by communication sessions in which both experienced and naive subjects took the roles of speaker and listener. Seriations were carried out in the order learned and afterwards in the reverse order.

Results and Discussion

Table 5.3 shows the number of correct and incorrect seriations achieved by all children as a function of their previous experience. Clearly, experienced subjects are much more successful than naive ones, obtaining a correct proportion of 79 per cent. In contrast naive subjects get the majority of their solutions incorrect, having a success rate of only 36 per cent. But these figures tell us nothing about the effect which one child is having on the other, nor the effect of the speaker/listener variable. Do ES errors all happen when NS is speaker, for instance? Is NS successful on his own account or only when acting as listener? If the latter, then does this support the notion that young children can be successful teachers?

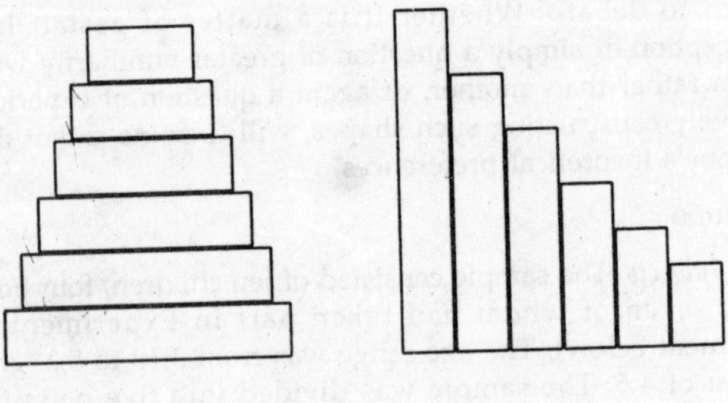

Figure 5.1.

Table 5.3. Number of Correct and Incorrect Solutions in Seriation Task (Study II)

	Correct	*Incorrect*	*Total*
Experienced Subject	19 (79 per cent)	5 (21 per cent)	24*
Naive Subject	9 (36 per cent)	16 (64 per cent)	25

*One short as NS did not complete a trial.

Table 5.4 shows that, of the five errors, two occur when they are speakers and three when they are listeners. Thus incorrect ES solutions are not entirely the fault of naive partners. Nevertheless, it bears repeating that the number of errors made by experienced subjects is very small. As for NSs, their successes occur most often when they are listeners. Table 5.4 shows that there is only *one* correct NS solution as speaker, whereas 8 correct solutions out of 16 results when NS is listener.

Table 5.4: Number of Correct and Incorrect Descriptions or Solutions in the Solution Task

	Order Learned			*Reverse Order*		
Descriptions/Solutions	*Correct*	*Incorrect*		*Correct*	*Incorrect*	
Experienced Speakers	8	2	10	6	0	6
Naive Listeners	5	5	10	3	3	6
Naive Speakers	1	7	8		1	1
Experienced Listeners	5	2	7		1	1

This result shows more clearly in Table 5.5, where the 50 per cent success rate suggests that ESs are surprisingly successful as instructors considering the complexity of the task involved. Table 5.5 also shows that the lesson is not learnt well enough for naive subjects, in their turn, to become successful instructors. As speakers naive subjects appear to be totally ineffectual, achieving no mutually correct solutions.

Table 5.5: Percentage of Trials Ending in Correct Solutions for Both Subjects, as a Function of Prior Exposure to the Task. (All Figures Refer to Subjects as Speakers)

Order Learned		*Reverse Order*	
Experienced Subject	Naive Subject	Experienced Subject	Naive Subject
5/10	0/8	3/6	0/11

The data also show (Table 5.4) how consistently correct the experienced subjects were when carrying out seriation in the reverse order. One further point to note from this table is the sparcity of data in the bottom right quadrant. This is because the experiment was carried out in one session and most of the subjects were thought to be either too tired or too disinclined to complete a trial as naive speaker.

Task Demands

Before considering the factors which give rise to communication failure, it is worth looking first more closely at the task involved. There are some important differences between Studies I and II which are illustrated by the opening dialogue of one of the communication sessions. This highlights a major problem for subjects in this second study.

> *Alan (speaker):* 'Put them . . . stand them up like . . . the big one . . . then a we . . . little bit right up to the big one's shoulder . . . and I think . . . next one is it? Yes. Now measure that . . . then that one, the *fish*.'

Faced with a number of sticks and a verbal message like that above, anyone would be hard pressed to produce something constructive. Because Alan's nonverbal behaviour is omitted, the record is almost bare of information content—and yet that is the record on which the listener must rely, since she cannot observe the manipulation of the material. The excerpt above takes place over a period of 30 seconds, and in that time Alan erects four sticks. Only when he comes to the fourth, however, does he give a meaningful message—*fish*—and this is said largely to himself.

A description of Alan's motor behaviour would put some flesh on the bones of the verbal record. It would then reveal his words for what they were—an aid to himself. For Alan was just talking to himself as he engaged in a problem which demanded a large degree of concentration. His words are not instructions directed to an attentive listener. This seems to be a key concept in understanding the performances in this experiment. Although Alan was sufficiently familiar with the communication situation to know what his role was in it, it appeared that the task was such as to cause him to forget or ignore the duties of that role. Seriation in this form, apparently, is not the simple exercise it was in the earlier experiment. The preview session showed that the majority of the subjects handled the task competently. But they needed to bring to it a measure of attention unnecessary in the blocks-on-rod task. Because of this, the additional burden of communicating the actions to a dependent listener becomes a problem. It overtaxes the system; and, as a result it is either left out or its effectiveness is seriously weakened.

Causes of communication breakdown

At this point a brief diagnosis of communication breakdown can be provided. Sufficient records are available to allow some conclusions to be drawn as to the factors which signal breakdown (see Table 5.6).

In quantitive terms, of the 18 trials which fail to lead to seriation by *both* subjects, in only five could the experienced speaker be said to be a major cause of failure, and three of these five occasions are perpetrated by one subject (Sally) who indicated she had not grasped the seriation concept.

The picture emerges that, given an accomplished listener, four of the experienced subjects would always communicate successfully—i.e. communication failure is seldom due to shortcomings on the part of the experienced speaker. As a listener the experienced subject can be helpful, but there are instances where his superior knowledge adversely affects the naive speaker. For example, under the heading 'inappropriate verbal comment' in Table 8.6, it is remarks by the experienced listener such as 'I've done it already', 'I'm doing it right', and laughter at the naive speaker's errors which largely contribute to communicative breakdown.

Table 5.6: Causes of Communication Breakdown and Their Frequency in Unsuccessful Trials as a Function of Role and Previous Experience of Task

Speaker			*Listener*		
	Exp.	*Naive*		*Exp.*	*Naive*
Stops verbal communication (absorbed in task)	0	2	Not attending distracted	1	3
Selection errors	2	4	Inappropriate verbal comment	1	1
Inadequate communication	1	0	Independent functioning	0	3
Total	3	6		2	7

Other limiting factors contributed by both naive and experienced subjects include task errors, that is, mistakes in seriating and failures of attention. The latter is betrayed by comments like 'I can build a castle', 'You can't see where you're going with your peak [cap] down there', 'Smell my perfume', 'I can do it louder than her' and task-irrelevant activity of which knocking over the sticks was a much favoured instance.

It is self-evident that if a speaker does not provide the necessary information then a naive listener is not going to be able to achieve the desired goal. But even if the speaker does carry out his part of the contract efficiently, success is not guaranteed. The operation can break down because of some inadequacy on the part of the listener. Although his role is passive—he has simply to do what he is told—it is this very passivity that is his undoing. A child is most successful in a cognitive task when he is actively involved. When the task appears to offer no scope for action, the child may very well initiate some himself. For example, in a dyad where Lee is the speaker and Paul the listener, a successful outcome would result if Paul simply complied with the speaker's instructions. But he seems to feel a need to make a contribution. In the first trial he says 'I haven't got my *fish* up' just before Lee instructs him to place the *fish* in line. Preoccupation with his own concerns causes him to miss this message and an incorrect solution results. In trial two he tries to go his own way when in response to the message '*train*', he says 'Well I'm going to put the *cup* up'. Both Alan (see p. 20) as speaker, and Paul as listener, illustrates how the communication set-up can break down if the subject fails to take account of his partner.

Egocentrism as a cause of communication failure. The Piagetian explanation for communication failure in the areas that have been mentioned would be egocentrism. There would seem to be two points to consider. First, is egocentrism a useful term to use? Should we not try to be more exact in explaining behaviour that is said to fall into this category? Secondly, however defined, is egocentrism always the explanation for such behaviour? In the area of behaviour under consideration, is a 'failure to consider the other's point of view' a satisfactory explanation for breakdown in communication in young children? There are, for instance, sound reasons for thinking that in some cases breakdowns are due to a lack of comprehension on the part of the participants. In other cases, a failure to involve the child seems to be a contributory factor (see Lloyd and Beveridge 1981, Light 1979). The Piagetian notion of centration certainly plays a part in this process, but it is perhaps better regarded as one aspect of attention and one of a number of attentional factors that ought to be defined as precisely as possible.

We need to know if the cues in a particular situation are perceived as identical by speaker and listener, experienced and naive subject. This is highly unlikely. To give one example, even when speaker and listener are equally familiar with the material, the speaker is put in a special position by being instructed to choose an object and communicate his choice to the listener. As soon as he has selected an item, the speaker's task is facilitated by having the number of competing cues diminished. He can then describe that object without relating it to any other members of the array. If the description is full enough it will be adequate. The listener, however, is subject to all the cues, and his choice, though supposed to be a function of the message he receives from the speaker, may equally be dependent on the salience which the objects have for him. Even if he does systematically narrow down his focus using the verbal messages sent to him, his interpretation of the message is liable to distortion either because of linguistic incompetence, that is being unable to relate word to referent, or through the compelling influence of perceptual cues, outweighing the power of the speaker's communication (see Donaldson and Lloyd 1974). What this amounts to is that he is told to select one item but chooses another because its size, colour, texture or whatever captures his attention.

It would seem, therefore, that the relative failure of the naive subject and the subject as listener might be explained by attentional factors, comprehension dificulties and lack of active involvement. According to Piaget, egocentrism is a pervasive feature of the behaviour of preoperational children. 'It is only when the child reaches the stage of concrete operations (7 to 8 years) . . . he acquires skill in interindividual relations in a cooperative framework. Further, the acquisition of social cooperation and the structuring of cognitive operations can be seen as two aspects of the same developmental process' (Fraisse and Piaget 1963).

When the performance of the children in the communication task is examined in the light of this statement, many examples counter to Piaget's hypothesis appear. Perhaps the most overwhelming evidence is that four of the five experienced children in this study successfully communicated the method of completing the seriation task such that the outcome was a mutually correct solution. So it is maintained that the degree of cooperation required and achieved for success, in what must be considered a fairly complex task, does much to weaken the Piagetian argument concerning egocentrism.

In conclusion consider the behaviour of Lee as speaker, describing seriation in the reverse order (chair, cup, fish, house, train, cat) to Paul after a number of trails in the other direction, big-little. Paul is rather slow at assembling the sticks, and after announcing the third stick and observing a fair amount of activity on Paul's part. Lee says, 'He's getting mixed up 'cos I put the *cat* first before, eh?' This seems to show not only a remarkably mature assessment of the seriation problem, but also behaviour far from egocentric. Lee has recognised that the change in order could lead to difficulties for the other child and as such has demonstrated a degree of percetion much more sophisticated than the theory of egocentrism would predict. Later in the trial the dialogue is as follows:

Lee: Now the *train* (stands it in line)
Paul: (Puts the *train* in line)
Lee: Have you got the *train* up?
Paul: I've put it up.

Once again Lee is showing a concern for the other child, a degree of cooperation not generally thought to be within the compass of egocentric children.

Evaluation of Aims

To what extent have these studies achieved the aims expounded earlier? The main objective was to determine if preschool children were able to combine productively in a task requiring purposive communication. The results provide unqualified rejection of the view that egocentrism severely hinders communication at this age. In the first study the overall failure rate was only 19 per cent though it increased to 42 per cent in the more demanding sticks task. This points up the more productive way of seeing children's communicative capacity, namely as a function of specific task demands.

The second aim concerned the suitability of the communication paradigm for investigating conceptual development. The signs are promising. The work showed, for instance, that ordering skills are much more severely tested when a child has to specify the location of an item as well as determine its position in an ordered sequence. I have argued elsewhere, (Lloyd and Beveridge 1981) that children will adapt to the level of utility appropriate to the situation. In his recent study of seriation, Piaget (1977) maintains that an understanding of this operation is only present when a child can explicitly state a rule in the form: 'Start with the smallest one and then add successively those that remain.' In these studies (and those of Greenfield and Dent) young children can get their peers to order in terms of size with descriptions like 'put the red one on, then the blue, then the green', etc. This is not to say that one instruction does not represent a sounder grasp of the concept than the other, but that level of understanding, along with materials and goals, must be sensitive to the needs and experience of the participants. A more extended justification of this approach to cognitive development can be found in Lloyd and Beveridge 1981 and also Russell (this volume).

What, finally, is the educational significance of this work? While in principle it is possible to discuss this question, in practice it is made difficult by the fact that the children involved were not yet part of the formal education system. Nevertheless, there are some general points to be made. Children appeared to take their teaching duties seriously, showing concern for the inadequacies of their 'pupils' and using a systematic step-by-step method of instruction. A number of examples have been given to support this claim. Experienced subjects were able to teach the first task sufficiently well for the pupils to become successful teachers in their turn. As soon as the task became more complex we saw a deterioration in the performance of the naive children. This was not because the instructors made any less effort but rather that carrying out the necessary discriminations and providing information about where to locate items proved too large a cognitive load.

As to whether the experienced or naive subjects gained more from the exercise, the objective evidence is equivocal. Inspection of the protocols reinforced the belief that the children given prior experience responded very positively to the teaching role. Steinberg and Cazden (1979) have argued that such experiences raise the self-esteem of the child, an observation these studies support. It is less clear what benefits the tutee derives, though he clearly acquires the ability to carry out the first task.

Without further and better controlled studies it is not possible to make any strong claims. But there is reason to believe that children teaching children can represent an important contribution in schools, a contribution that undoubtedly is apparent to some teachers. Children may use unorthodox methods in instructing their peers but they may have one great advantage over adults as teachers. They eschew the formalism that pedagogues tend to adopt by operating in what Donaldson (1978) has called the embedded mode of thinking. Providing that that mode is not totally idiosyncratic it may be more effective in gaining and sustaining the interest of a peer, despite many obvious imperfections. At the same time the teacher may gain new perspectives on familiar problems and a greater awareness of children's capacities and limitations. At the very least this technique deserves further systematic study.

6

Word Learning

Below are eight words. Each word can stand alone, or all can be put together in a combination known as a sentence.

March	Wednesday	last
in	came	like
lion	a	

With these words a number of sentences can be made. Here is one of them: Last Wednesday, March came in like a lion.

Now the words have become eight units cooperating to make a larger unit, a sentence. As a unit in the sentence each word has a number of qualities or attributes. Even when standing alone, as in the listing above, each word has some of those qualities, but it possesses additional ones when a member of a sentence group. All these qualities are influential. A knowledge of item equips a person to use words effectively.

Of the varied attributes or characteristics, at least twenty-four are important in teaching language arts. Those appear on the chart in Figure 6.1 Teachers and pupils pay attention to the more obvious ones as a matter of course but neglect some that are important. All of the characteristics operate daily in pupils' speech, listening, writing and reading.

All twenty-four attributes deserve attention in the grades because a pupil acquainted with them has a notable start toward successful use of words and toward the pleasures which arise from sensitivity to the qualities of words.

OBJECTIVES IN TEACHING WORDS

In every elementary grade, children know something about each of the twenty-four aspects of words. Their daily experiences with words guarantee that. Steadily their knowledge can be extended, cumulatively building toward systematic study in the upper grades.

Pupil growth in each of those aspects is desirable and possible. Ways to achieve such growth are suggested here. Discussions of certain facets fit naturally into the chapters on speech, spelling, structure and usage, constructing ideas with language, poetry, and imaginative expression. Those facets receive less attention in this chapter.

Certain aspects require direct, sustained instruction; others develop through casual mention. Spelling is a conspicuous example of the former; rhythmic values, phonetic effects, and figurative meanings illustrate the latter.

PUPILS' DAILY EXPERIENCES WITH WORDS

A child in the grades, if up at 7:30 a.m. and asleep by 8:30 p.m., has thirteen hours of active life each day. He spends most of that time hearing or using words. Classroom hours are a continuum of contacts with thousands of words through listening, reading, writing, and sporadic talking. Outside of class he talks a great deal. The author observed that a nine-year-old boy who was being instructed in bowling spoke 101 words in five minutes. A twelve-year-old boy spoke 294 words while eating breakfast, between 7:30 and 8:00 a.m.—one of his relatively "quiet" periods of the day. Anyone apt at rapid counting or equipped with a taperecorder can discover, in fifteen minutes, that a day's total must run high in the thousands.

Through diverse experiences boys and girls become acquainted in varying degrees with all twenty-four of the characteristics named in the chart.

Definition and Spelling. Children work with the definition and spelling aspects of words early and often. "What does that mean?" they ask regarding many words long before they start school. They experience the frustration of being unable to make another person understand some of their words in spite of insistent repetitions. In school there is constant pressure to learn the meanings of more words, particularly in music, art, science, and arithmetic.

Spelling, too, antedates the systematic efforts which start when pupils begin to write in school. Children make preschool inquiries about "how to spell" or "how to write" certain words needed in a letter to a grandparent, parent, aunt, uncle, or playmate. They also see words spelled on billboards, in magazine advertisements, on television, and in preschool books. In the first grade they observe words being spelled on experience charts and chalkboards. Through such viewings come impressions of another characteristic of words—shapes on a page. In the first grade some instruction in reading depends on this characteristic.

Inflections and Interplay. Also apparent to children are three other attributes met in daily usage: Word forms are changed to show change in meaning; words often can be moved from one position to another in a statement, thereby changing to a greater or lesser degree the meaning and the rhythm of the statement; and word meanings usually are established by the presence of other words in the sentence. In their private linguistic playfulness children toy with all three of those aspects. They pick up a phrase or sentence and ring all the changes on it, randomly changing word forms, phrasal rhythms, and meanings.

Literary Values. Almost every story or poem that children hear or read embodies a cluster of attributes, notably connotation, patness, figurative meanings, concreteness, specificality, and capacity to suggest action. In daily life, too, connotation operates when children become excited as they hear words like *picnic, snow,* or *holiday.* Figures of speech are met in many catchy sayings and slang expressions popular among young people. Overuse of such popular words and phrases leads to flatness and tedium, a weakened state of words that pupils recognise by calling an expression "old stuff" or "corny".

Acceptability. Very early a child gets impressions about the acceptability of words. Somebody admonishes him, "Don't say what you just said; that's not nice" or "People don't say such words." In school he hears much about the suitability of certain expressions for thanking someone and for answering the doorbell and telephone.

Historical Changes in Meaning. Old ballads and stories, and particularly the dialogues in them, are likely places where children meet words whose meanings have changed over a period of years. Quotations from diaries, records, or other documents printed in history books or biographies are probable places too, together with early translations of the Bible. And there is always a chance of hearing a parent or grandparent remark that a certain word "used to mean" something different "years ago" or "when I was young."

Shortening and Fusing. The shortening of some words and the fusing of others are known to children. Common words like *TV, phone, plane,* and *taxi* show pupils that long words, if used often, are likely to be abbreviated. Children shorten personal names, too. As for fused words, pupils meet them during reading and spelling lessons. *Into, almost, maybe, steamboat, afternoon, bookcase, viewpoint,* and *nevertheless* are examples known to all. Experiences with fusion are extended by mishearing, because children often hear two or more separate words as one word. Eventually they discover their mistake and unscramble the combinaton.

Stories behind Words. The histories behind the present meanings of words may come to a child's attention through the names of local towns, lakes, streams, roads, or mountains. *Tug Hill* might be a local name with a story, or perhaps *Long Sault, Haycock Mountain, Dead Mule Gulcb,* or *Old Mill Street.* A little later pupils hear about the origins of words like *thermometer, barometer, equator, radar,* or *Telstar* because teachers use derivations as one of the best ways of making large technical terms understandable to a class.

Word Classes and Functions. Three attributes of words seem to infiltrate a child's linguistic life without making him aware of their arrival. Children realise that words have certain kinds of functions in sentences, that there are several kinds or classes of words (roughly equivalent to "parts of speech"), and that any word, when used in a statement, has certain values only because it belongs to a particular class and serves a particular function in that statement. Those realisations, even if they be somewhat vague, operate in everyday language experiences. Developed, they help pupils understand syntax, parts of speech, and the functional shift whereby a word which in one sentence happens of serve as a noun may appear in another sentence as a verb or adjective.

Pedagogical Advantage. Thus all twenty-four attributes come within the normal daily experiences of school children. This is advantageous for the teacher. It also suggests a richer programme of word study than is commonly offered.

VOCABULARY DEVELOPMENT

Both direct and incidental teaching belong in a vocabulary programme. Direct teaching is particularly necessary for pupils of average and below-average ability. Incidental teaching of words develops from a variety of activities. Each area of the curriculum offers words which are new to children. Visits to farms, the post office, stores, factories, and museums add many more. Words associated with a particular industry, such as mining, forestry, fishing, or space flight soon produce a large cluster of terms. "Show and tell" periods, during which children display and explain objects that their classmates are not likely to know, open new words through words. The same is true of stories and poems, whether heard or read.

Through Affixes and Roots. Much can be done through study of prefixes, suffixes, and word roots. If the items are selected well, the results can be widely helpful. Fifteen prefixes, Stauffer found, supply 82 per cent of all prefixes in Thorndike's *Teacher's Word Book of 20,000 Words.* Giving added significance to this count is the fact that prefixes are present in 24 per cent of the words on the Thorndike list. Once knowing the dominant prefixes, children recognise old acquaintances in new words—an advantage which becomes even greater after discovering that certain prefixes recur in slightly differing forms in different words but with the same meanings.

Suffixes are relatively easy to teach because they are few in number and because most of them are understood by children in the earliest grades.

Word roots provide a lifelong motif for extension of vocabulary. Those of English origin, such as *steam* and *boat* in *steamboat,* and *snow* and *man* in *snowman,* usually are self-explanatory, but those borrowed from Greek and Latin require study. Fortunately, there is an approach to such study through borrowed word roots which children use quite often. Examples are *tele, aqua, hydra, dict, meter, micro, cosma,* and *phone.* These become springboards for explorations of other non-English roots. Also, pupils learn that many words, all having family resemblances, are based on one of such much-used roots.

Through Current Events. New words come in through current events. Some of them are old words, new to many pupils; others are newly coined. When the latter come along, children are likely to understand them readily. Thus the words *astronaut* and *cosmodrome* were fairly easy to interpret; and the satellite name *Tiros* was recognised as a word made up in the same manner as *radar,* being built from the beginnings ("edges", whence the type name acronym) of several words.

Through Context. Context as a key to learning the meanings of new words has greater uses than are practised. Children have used it all their lives, when trying to figure out what people mean by remarks not fully understood. Most pupils apparently could be twice as efficient as they are. The situation suggests that teachers should describe specific techniques for inferring word meanings from contexts.

Through Instructional Aids. Pupil activities and various charts (such as suggested later in this chapter under the headings "Pupil Activities" and "Viewpoints to Emphasise through Teaching Aids") have been useful in many classrooms. Picture dictionaries and word boxes speed up word learning in the first grade. A taperecorder helps a teacher analyse pupils' word recognition and skill in approaching new words.

Vocabulary Size. Teachers wonder how much a child's vocabulary increases from year to year, but answers cannot be definite. Children and adults have several vocabularies: words they use for speech, those which they command for writing, those which they understand when listening, and those which they recognise when reading. These vocabularies differ in size. The reading vocabulary catches up to the speaking vocabulary by the third or fourth grade, and thereafter remains in the lead.

Seashore estimated 17,000 to 25,000 as the number of words that the average child in the first grade understands. Mary K. Smith found that in the first grade the average child knew more than 23,000 words, and in the sixth grade, 51,000 words. Those numbers seem huge, being much larger then estimates made fifteen or twenty years ago, but the procedures used in recent studies appear to be more reliable than those followed previously. A general revision upward seems to be in order. Perhaps some expansion is to be expected in these decades, when children learn great numbers of words outside of school, and when the total English vocabulary—which was approximately 37,000 words in King Alfred's time, 60,000 in Chaucer's day, and 140,000 in the Shakespearean period—is now well beyond a half-million words.

UNDERSTANDING THE COMPLEXITY OF WORDS

A word seems more complex to a pupil of twelve than it appeared to him at six. Through instruction and experience during the interim he has discovered intricacies that he had not suspected earlier. He may even have come to think of a word figuratively as a galaxy, a nebula, or a seashell full of strange echoes.

In this situation the classroom has a peculiar role. Its instruction did much deliberately to bring on this awareness of word complexity. If, as is very likely, the pupil has become somewhat bewildered by it all, the classroom has the responsibility of reducing the confusion which it has helped cause.

But reduction of confusion is only part of the classroom objective. More significantly the instruction aims to give a pupil command of those very characteristics which make a word complex. Such command strengthens the child's vocabulary power.

Eleven or twelve facets deserve study in such a programme.

Respect for Definitions

Pupils ought to make a practice of learning enough about a word to avoid mere verbalising when speaking or writing it. They should be able to use or interpret a word in accordance with its generally accepted meaning. And they should begin to understand the nature of a definition, so that when they want to define a term they will follow the pattern suggested.

Both direct and incidental teaching help increase the respect for definitions. In every subject that the pupils study there are terms to be defined and definitions to learn. If, as often happens, a child starts a definition with a phrasing like "A square is where. . . .," direct discussion about correct ways of stating a definition would be desirable.

Incidental comments help children understand that specific meanings of words must be widely accepted in order that verbal messages can pass from one person to many others. Further, a person must respect those accepted meanings; he cannot give new meanings to a word at his own whim if he hopes to be understood. Pupils will discover that word meanings change, but also that those changes usually occur slowly.

Influence of Context. To this matter of definitions there is a corollary which pupils should understand as early as possible. A word, by itself, usually has no clear-cut definition. The word *walk*, for example, may mean any one of a number of things; the word *snow* has fewer possibilities, but still could have several meanings. A word must be part of a sentence in order to have its meaning made clear. Then the linguistic structure of the sentence, together with the other words in the statement, fixes the word's meaning. Thus a word like *run*, having more than one hundred possible meanings, is pinned down to a specific definition in the sentence "The train made the hundred-mile run in record time." Here the linguistic structure, through the position of the word *run*, and with the help of voice intonations when spoken, shows that *run* is a noun, not a verb or adjective. The other words in the statement show that *run*, which may have various meanings as a noun, here means a distance or a number of miles to be travelled.

Children, who like to see how things work, are perceptive enough to understand this interplay. They meet many examples daily. Once clear on what happens, they are wiser in the realm of words and are prepared to understand how words may change their function when used in different sentences.

Symbols or Labels only. There is another significant interrelationship between words and definition—an important one for teachers to know as background information, but one which gets taught only to a few more perceptive pupils. It is this: A word, actually, is a segment of utterance—a segment of the continuum of sound known as speech—having dynamic features such as pitch, stress, volume, and length. Usually it is made up of smaller phonetic components and, in turn, is embedded in a larger structure, such as a sentence, which does much to establish its meaning. The word itself, considered as a unit of sound, has no meaning, but is a symbol of something. Thought of this way, a word is merely a label. Possible exceptions are words like *buzz, bum, crackle,* and *splash* whose sounds suggest what they name.

Associated Meanings. Children respond strongly to the power of connotation in words that they hear or read. They rarely need help in this, except to catch the full meanings of words that are new to them. But regarding their flow of communication to others children have much to learn, as they are not generally aware that words which they speak or write have overtones for their hearers or readers. Here is where a teacher can contribute much to the pupils' growth in daily communication. She can also improve their ability to choose words for original prose and verse.

Instruction can start with a pupil's personal responses to words. The pupil will recognise that words like *snow, beach, doll, lullaby, buzz,* and *Yellowstone National Park* mean many things to him in addition to what a dictionary gives as the definitions. He meets many such words in poems, songs, and stories. These extra meanings, he can discover, come mostly from his personal experiences with the things named by the word. Those personal experiences may be real or vicarious. Sometimes a word's sound, in itself, evokes part of the response.

Noting their personal feelings regarding certain words, children can understand how words carry special meanings for other people, too. A class can discuss this problem intelligently. They see why certain greetings and remarks are much more courteous or kind than others. Some can recall occasions when they were surprised because other persons did not seem to like what they had said, even though the remarks were intended in the best of spirit. Pupils will notice that a word may mean sharply different things to various members of the class, and that a line of verse is likely to please some members much more than others. When they discuss the "fitness" or "patness" of a particular word for a particular time and place they may conclude that much of that appropriateness is due to associated meanings. Certainly any discussion of a word's acceptability or unacceptability turns on the word's overtones of meaning.

Uncertainty of Connotations. On one point both pupils and teacher will always be somewhat unsure: they cannot know for certain what connotations a given word may carry for other people. From general usage they can make a fair estimate of what the word connotes normally among people of a particular social or educational group. Dictionaries usually indicate when a word carries derogatory or unpleasant overtones. But there still remains an uncertainty about a word's connotations for one specific person, unless the speaker or writer knows that person exceptionally well. In addition the problem is complicated by a speaker's or writer's tendency to choose words according to the bias of the connotations which he, himself, holds.

With such uncertainties prevailing, the best a teacher can do is alert her pupils to the nimbus that surrounds a dictionary definition. Perhaps she can transfer to children some of Laird's observations:

"Thus words have no fixed meanings; they have the power of designating referents and of stimulating awareness of meaning in individuals. We use words as though they were dippers, the same dippers for everybody, but the stuff that is dipped up with the dipper depends upon the body of stuff from which it is dipped.

Interactions among words. Children gradually discover how strongly words influence each other in sentences. Opportunities for both incidental and direct teaching of these interword relationships come every day in every grade. Flannel boards and chalkboards are practical. In the middle and upper grades children see the interplay operating when they revise sentences which they have composed. Upon replacing one word with another, they may find that the new word will not work well with the remainder of the original phrasing. They must change all or parts of that phrasing to accommodate the new word.

Qualified Meanings, Phonetics, and Rhythms. A class might hear or see the word *walk.* As long as that word is alone the pupils are uncertain what it means. It could mean any one of many things. But when they have the sentence "I took a walk" they know that *walk* refers to travel by foot. Through the process called "interinanimation" the other words and the grammatical structure have pinned down the word that formerly had been elusive.

Next the class might consider three more sentences:

I took a long walk.
I took a long walk up the canyon.
I took a long walk up the rough canyon.

In them they see that the word *long* affects the meaning of *walk,* that *up the canyon* changes the nature of *a long walk,* and that *rough* makes the *long walk* seem longer.

This interplay extends to phonetic and rhythmic effects, too. The word *bee,* alone, has certain phonetic values, but little rhythm, if any. However *a bee, a busy bee, a busy brown bee* show a progression of new phonetic effects and stronger rhythms. Alertness to these influences is a great help to pupils in composing prose as well as verse. It also opens the way to enjoyment of rhythmic and phonetic pleasures in literature.

"Words are slippery customers," Cherry says. "The full meaning of a word does not appear until it is placed in its context, and the context may serve an extremely subtle function—as with puns or double entendre." Gradually a class can see that what is important is not the word alone but the word in relation to other words. Pupils may be helped by observing similar interplay in art and music, where one colour or one note gains significance by being close to other tones.

Multiple Meanings. The 200 English words repeated most often in print have 14,500 discriminated meanings. The Technology Press of the Lloyd and Warfel. The word *run,* used very much by children, has 104 meanings in the *American College Dictionary.* Sixty-three of these relate to its service as a verb (35 as an intransitive verb, 28 as transitive), 39 to its use as a noun, and two to its use as an adjective. For other much-used words there are large spreads of meaning, too: *turn,* 93; *strike,* 67; *take,* 76; *set,* 67; *round,* 83.

Such multiplicity may confuse children in the early grades. Words that had been considered familiar acquaintances suddenly turn up with new, unexpected meanings. The best cure for such confusion is a discussion of examples well-known to the pupils. Helpful in the discussion are the observations (made in the previous topic) about relationships between the meaning of a word, the word's position in the sentence structure, and the presence of other words in the statement. In speech the vocal intonations help identify the meaning.

It would be impractical to teach children all the meanings of many words but it is possible to alert children to the mutiplicity which exists.

Functional Shift of Words

The functional shift of words is one of the more troublesome items for students of grammar. The word *walk,* for example, is likely to appear as noun and subject in one sentence; as verb and predicate in another; as noun and object in another, and, in the *-ing* form, as a modifier in one sentence but a noun and subject in another:

The *walk* was pleasant.
I can *walk* there.
We enjoyed the *walk.*

A crow is a *walking* bird.
Walking along the shore is fun.

Position. Although elementary school children cannot be expected to master all the subtleties of functional shifts, they can begin to see what is happening. They observe that the function or work of a word is established by the position which th word has in the sentence structure and by the intonation given to the word when the statement is spoken. The interplay with other words in the sentence, as discussed in preceding pages, is a factor.

Observations on this behaviour of words help build up grammar readiness for junior and senior high school. They also yield immediate returns by giving pupils some idea of what happens in sentences.

Classes of Words: Having heard or spoken hundreds of thousands of sentences containing millions of words, children have certain impressions about words serving particular functions in sentences. They have one set of impressions, for instance, in connection with the words *apple, fence, dogs, yard, Jane,* and *picture* in the sentences:

The apple rolled under the fence.
Three dogs ran into the back-yard.
Jane likes the funny picture.

They gain another type of impression regarding *rolled, ran,* and *likes,* and yet another in connection with *three, back,* and *big*. They have a more vague feeling about *the, under,* and *into*.

Impressions gained through sentences are reinforced by experiences with single words (spoken and heard) used as labels for objects *(snow, orange),* qualities *(black),* or actions *(swim, shoot).*

Though unacquainted with the terms "noun" and "verb", children have a feeling for the "nounness" and "verbness" of words belonging to those classes, especially when nouns are concrete and verbs suggest action. These impressions have practical use, even when they happen to be too vague for a pupil to state clearly. They can be refined by incidental and direct instruction, thus establshing a readiness for understanding all the parts of speech.

Mobility. The mobility of words is one basis for the flexibility of language within the structure of English sentences. A class committee might phrase part of its request to visit an airport in various ways: "We should like to visit the airport next Tuesday, if convenient to you"; "If convenient to you we should like to visit the airport next Tuesday"; or "Next Tuesday, if convenient to you, we should like to visit the airport". Many pupils have used the following variants when welcoming visitors into the classroom: "Will you please come into the room?" "Will you come into the room, please?" and "Please, will you come into the room?"

The mobility of words gives language great artistic potential, and the discovery of its possibilities is a major achievement in any person's expressional life. It opens the way to niceties of style and rhythm as well as to subtleties of meaning. It also is a key to clarity because most ambiguous statements can be made clear by a shift of certain words, phrases, or clauses to different positions in the sentence.

More experiments related to this highly rewarding objective are in the next chapter, "Constructing Ideas with Language". Pedagogically the movability of words is pleasant and easy to work with.

Broadened Perceptions of Words

Through connotations words leap beyond the circles of their dictionary definitions. Through figures of speech they spring even further—sometimes almost beyond themselves. With these leaps they arrive near or within the boundaries of literature.

Young pupils' minds follow them quite regularly. But keeping the minds agile through upper grades and high school may require a bit of mental gymnastics if broad perceptions of words are to be maintained. Experiences with nonliteral items in language arts and other arts support the agility, as do observations on the nature of what is concrete and specific.

Figurative Statements. In relation to figurative uses of words the objective is to retain and strengthen a response that exists already rather than to originate something new. A pupil in the earliest grades is almost certain to interpret and enjoy any nonliteral statement that is based on something within the scope of his experiences. One in the upper grades may be slower in "seeing the point" or "knowing what it means". The problems are how to extend the perceptivity which children bring with them and how to avoid the flattening of the response into a sort of metaphorical deafness which often begins at about eleven or twelve years of age.

The Opie book on *The Lore and Language of School Children* abounds in evidence of young people's mastery of the figurative. Many children's remarks which adults call "cute" owe their appeal to figurative elements. For the later decline of insight into the nonliteral a number of reasons have been given, most of them seemingly valid. But whether the operation of suspected factor is inexorable may be doubted.

A programme of imaginative expression appears to be one of the best insurances against decline. Spirited handling of stories, poems, and plays, with full preservation of poetic values, whether in verse or prose, is further support. In no case should the fruit of bold imagination be downgraded as "silly" or "trifling".

Strong support for enjoyment of the figurative can come from subjects allied to language arts. Children's experiences in painting, clay, dancing, and music abound in the nonliteral. Those related experiences give cooperating teachers of the several areas a chance to reinforce each other's instruction.

Concrete and Abstract Words: It is easy to encourage children to use concrete words instead of abstract ones because children naturally think in terms of what is concrete. Physical observations made during an experience are what children remember. Words relating to something seen, heard, tasted, smelled, or felt are the ones they recall.

Other favouring influences are the poems and stories that children enjoy and the figures of speech which catch attention. Both literature and figures of speech depend heavily on words that are concrete.

As pupils become older they acquire abstract words and generalise their observations. Then they need to be reminded that concrete words still are preferable for many purposes. If the nature of a topic requires relatively abstract words, the pupil can nevertheless search for ones that are as concrete as seem applicable to the situation.

Any discussion or report, oral or written, may prompt observations on these relative qualities of words. Children readily see, for example, that *Rover* or *collie* would be preferable, in many situations, to *dog, pet,* or *animal.* The first two call up more definite images of a certain dog than do the last three. So, likewise, *redwood* and *aspen* have advantages over *tree, plant,* or *vegetation.*

When pupils attempt imaginative expression the quest for concrete words is paramount. Much of the energy and discussion devoted to revising a poem or story concerns the search for words that evoke images and memories of sensuous impressions.

Pupils discover that "concrete" and "abstract" are relative terms. Sometimes they are uncertain whether a particular word belongs under one classification or the other. Though *flashlight* and *candle* seem definitely concrete and *illumination* quite abstract, there are intermediate words like *lamp, flare, light, incandescence,* and *rediance* whose abstractness or concreteness is a matter of degree. Each may be concrete in relation to certain words and abstract in comparison with others. Altogether the range of words from *flashlight* to *illumination* makes a spectrum band between the very concrete and the very abstract rather than a series of individual absolutes.

Corresponding relativity exists among verbs in their ability to suggest action—the verbal quivalent of what concrete nouns achieve. *Dished, sprinted, ran fast, moved fast, hastened, hurried, went swiftly, traversed rapidly* might be considered a spectrum band from the dynamic, action-suggesting *dashed* and *sprinted* to the relatively static mental image caused by *traversed rapidly.*

Specific and General Words: Pupils see a parallel between the abstract-concrete contrasts and the specific-general relationships.

Each pair represents a relativity. Also a concrete word is almost certain to be a specifi one because it points out a very particular item. Thus *Rover* designates a specific dog, a *flashlight* a specific kind of illumination, *sprinting* a specific kind of movement.

But the reverse is not necessarily always true. All specific words are not concrete. It realms of the abstract there are specific words which still are abstract. *Realism* is specific in naming a type of art, and *pragmatism* and *rationalism* are specific in designating two viewpoints in philosophy, but all three terms tend to be abstract rather than concrete. The same is true of the word *capitalism* in the area of economics.

The specific noun or verb is preferred to a general and vague one. Literature and imaginative expression favour the specific word just as they favour the concrete.

HISTORIES AND DERIVATIONS OF WORDS

When using a dictionary, an increasing number of people read the word derivation along with the definition. A few read the derivation first. Both groups have established one of the most fruitful of all habits for both enlarging their vocabularies and having fun with words.

They discover, for example, that a peninsula, in terms of the derivation of its name, means "almost an island" and that *quotient* means "how many". *Passive* comes from origins signifying "to suffer" or "to endure" and is related to the word *passion* in *Passion Week*—the week of suffering. An *acronym* is a name made from "the edges of words". A *satellite* is "an attendant" or "a companion" and a *candidate* originally was a person dressed in a white toga. *Tragedy* meant "goat song", *scene* meant "tent", and *curfew* is a combination of two words which together signified "cover the fire". A *nasturtium* is a "nose-twister", a *dinosaur* a "terrible lizard".

Information of that kind provides knowledge in depth beyond that which definitions along can offer. Equally important for pupils, it often "makes sense" out of words that at first seem like a combination of nonsense syllables. The words *peninsula* and *quotient* are examples, and in the upper grades the term *passive,* very difficult for many students of grammar, becomes relatively clear through its etymological meaning. The word *hemisphere* may seem huge and troublesome for pupils in geography but the discovery that the big term is made up of two words, one meaning "half" and the other "ball", changes the situation. Children, of course, do not know the Greek originals, but the discovery of the meaning of those original illuminates the word.

Children can start early. Always there are local place names, river, creek, hill, and mountain names with stories (some fanciful and apocryphal) behind them. Geographic names of Indian origin, having specific meanings in the original, are mentioned in every classroom. The names of the days of the week have histories. Also there are myths and legends explaining how certain stars and constellations got their names. And there always will be words newly coined, such as *radar, sonar, cosmonaut,* and *cosmodrome,* whose origins are part of current news.

As soon as technical terms come into classroom discussions the teacher should see whether derivations might help make them clear. In science, arithmetic, music, art, health, and geography there are scores of terms which can be illuminated. Through those terms and from studying foreign languages the young learners may discover that many words in different languages resemble each other because they came from the same source. This is especially true of words in Indo-European languages, as sampled in Figure 6.3.

---

boat (bot), *n.* **[ME.** *boot, bote;* **AS.** *bat;* akin to **G.** *boot;* **IE.** base **bheidb-,* to split: in the sense "hollowed-out tree trunk"; cf. FISSURE], 1. a small, open vessel or water craft propelled by oars, sails, or engine. 2. a large vessel; ship: landsman's term applied especially to river steamers. Abbreviated bt. 3. any similar craft: as, a flying *boat.* 4. a boat-shaped dish: as, a gravy *boat.* ***v.t.*** to lay or carry in the boat: as, *boat* the oars, ***v.i.*** to go in a boat; row, sail or cruise.

in the same boat, in the same situation; running similar risks.

can·di·date (kan'de-dat', kan'de-dit), ***n.*** [**L.** *candidatus,* white-robed < *candidus,* white: those who sought office in Rome wore white gowns], 1. a person who seeks, or has been proposed for, an office, an award, etc. 2. a person apparently destined to come to a certain end: as, a *candidate* for a mental institution.

ra'dar (ra-där), ***n.*** [*ra*dio *de*tecting *a*nd *r*anging], a radio detecting instrument consisting of a transmitter that sends out high-frequency radio waves and a receiver that picks them up after they have been reflected by a land mass, ship, etc.: it indicates the direction and distance of the reflecting object.

Fig. 6.2. Information and fun in derivation entries of dictionaries. These entries represent three important kinds of word origin: native English, Latin, and formation from parts of several words. *(From: Webster's New World Dictionary of the American Language, College Edition, copyright 1962 by the World Publishing Company.)*

A "derivation box" or "word-origin box" is a practical reference source in the classroom. Each card in the box carries the derivational story or meaning of a word. Key words from all subjects being studied are included. Also some words are put in "just for fun" or because the stories behind them are especially interesting, though not related to any curriculum subject. For some words the story can be told through drawings. In addition to dictionaries, a number of books give information on word origins.

Dictionaries intended for elementary grades rarely give etymologies. This is a shortcoming of the dictionaries and a handicap in word study. But any child mature enough to use encyclopedias in a library can also locate derivations in large dictionaries.

Lat.	molae, molina	Dan.	mølle	ChSl.	zrunuvi, zruny
It.	mulino	Sw.	kvarn	SCr.	mlin
Fr.	moulin	OE	cweorn, mylen	Boh.	mlyn
Sp.	molino	ME	mylne, mille	Pol.	mlyn
Rum.	moara	NE	mill	Russ.	mel' nica
Ir.	brao, muleen	Du.	molen		
NIr.	muileann	OHG	muli(n)		
W.	melin	MGH	mül(e)		
Br.	milin	NHG	mühle		

Fig. 6.3. Word resemblances among Indo-European languages as shown in the word *mill*. Pupil's discover that some words in different languages resemble each other. Bilingual children and those learning

a non-English language are especially likely to observe such resemblances.

The columns above show that the word for *mill* is recognizable in many languages of the Indo-European family. Most of the words are related because they developed from an original Indo-European word root, **mel*, which meant "crush" or "grind". Three of the listed words (Swedish, Old English, and Church Slavic) resemble each other because their common ancestor was an Indo-European root, **gwer*, meaning "heavy" and "upper millstone". This root survives in the names, not listed here, for *handmill* in about a dozen languages.

Sanskrit, a prominent member of the Indo-European family, adopted a word unrelated to the root **mel*. *(From: Carl Darling Buck, A Dictionary of Selected Synonyms in the Principal Indo-European Languages, The University of Chicago Press, Chicago, 1949. Cpyright 1949 by the University of Chicago.)*

In a dictionary entry the etymological information usually is enclosed in brackets or parentheses. To the average reader this arrangement is an invitation to skip whatever is thus set apart. Dictionary users, young and old, may need encouragement to overcome the handicap of this printing arrangement.

All activity in word origins should be tempered by caution. Derivations of some words are uncertain; of others, unknown. There always is a temptation to make a good story out of the situation. Folk explanations of local geographical names are likely to be more or less fictitious. Consequently a certain amount of skepticism is desirable. There is no harm in enjoying a good yarn about a name or term, but it should be enjoyed as a yarn, not as supposed fact.

USE OF A DICTIONARY

A pupil who has reached the level of the third grade in reading and spelling is considered ready to use an elementary dictionary. Some children in third grade, therefore, and most in fourth grade, can be expected to consult dictionaries successfully.

Familiarity with the alphabet is necessary for efficient use of a dictionary. Children can acquire it in the early grades by working with "word boxes" or "dictionary boxes" in which cards are arranged alphabetically according to the one word written and explained on each card. It is furthered also when children use telephone directories, help make up the class roll, or see how quickly they can arrange themselves in line according to the alphabetic letters of their last names. As soon as pupils begin using encyclopedias and atlases they have more experience with the alphabet.

In primary grades children are expected to alphabetise according to the first letters of words; in intermediate grades, according to the first two letters, and possibly according to the first three.

Knowing the alphabet well, a pupil can develop skill in opening a dictionary to a page reasonably near the one needed. Thus if the word he is looking up starts with *e* he can open the dictionary in the first third of the book; if the word begins with *t* he can open it in the last third. This, combined with alert use of guide words at the tops of the pages, speeds up his finding the word.

Finally, for efficiency, the pupil must know what kinds of information are in the dictonary that he is using. Too often he thinks of pronunciation, spelling, and definition only. When opportunities occur the teacher can introduce him to other useful items: the breakdown of the word into syllables, what part or parts of speech the word can function as in a sentence, how many different meanings it can represent, other words that have meanings much like it or approximately opposite to it, the plural form of the noun, some forms of the verb, special idioms or expressions in which the word is used, and cross references to other words. The pupils learns that his dictionary informs him also on prefixes, suffixes, word roots, contractions, homonyms, and heteronyms. In larger dictionaries pupils find additional information, notably a greater number of meanings, possible uses, and derivations.

As for the abbreviations used in the dictionary, children are likely to learn the ones that they meet often. Drill on the others and familiarity with the page that lists all abbreviations are time-savers.

Children see the abbreviations *n., v., adj.*, and other indications of parts of speech in the entries for many words. A bit of instruction on these may reduce confusion. An *n.*, for instance, in the entry for *walk* does not imply that walk always is a noun. It merely signifies that when the word *walk* is used as a noun in a sentene, then its meaning is that which is given after the *n. Walk,* like hundreds of other words, may serve as several parts of speech, depending on its position, context, and intonation in the sentence.

ASSURING GROWTH IN THE USE OF WORDS

Development of word-study objectives is cumulative. All pupils will have a start toward those objectives by the end of grade 6. They can be expected to be further along by the end of grade 11. Those who go to college will still be accumulating more knowledge and skill when they are graduated. At no time in life can anyone say, "Now I've mastered all there is to know regarding words".

Because all twenty-four facets are within a child's experience, all twenty-four can be taught. But they also can be mistaught. If motifs and materials are remote from the children's world, or if instruction is pedantic or pedestrian, little will be accomplished. Success is achieved when the teacher knows much about all aspects of words and is ready to introduce information, experiments, and problems that are timely.

These twenty-four facets of words constitute part of the language resources which students of English discover. They contribute to the fun which people find in working with language as a medium. They function both in the everyday craftsmanship of constructing ideas and in the art of literature.

PUPIL ACTIVITIES

1. One person likes to hear the words *murmur, broom, coconut, bollow,* and *swallow.* She says she enjoys their sounds and the rhythms. The words seem musical to her.

Another person is fond of *window, prancing, melon, lily, water,* and *lawn* for the same reasons.

Are there some words that you enjoy especially because of their sounds and rhythms? Do your friends like the same words?

2. We say "the bee buzzed", "the cat meowed", "the cow mooed", and "the dog barked". Try shifting the last word around: "the bee barked", "the dog buzzed". What seems wrong with the words then? Of course, they no longer match the meaning the dictionary says they have, but do you notice some other reasons why they do not seem to fit when shifted?

3. If you start with the word *boat,* you can think of words like *oar, rudder, prow, skipper, schooner, hull, anchor, boatswain.* All those words name things connected with boats.

How many seconds of time do you need to think of ten words connected with *iron mine?* Your first word might be *ore.*

Next try the word *fruit* and see how many seconds you need to think of twenty words connected with it.

4. Which of these two sentences helps your imagination see the more vivid picture of what happened? Why?

(a) Going around the curve too fast, the car bumped into a tree.

(b) Going around the curve too fast, the car bumped into an oak tree.

Let a few of your classmates try the same experiment.

Compare these sentences in the same way:

(a) I have an appetite for food.

(b) I am hungry for a hamburger.

Here are seven words. Which of them bring to your mind more vivid pictures? Why? The words are: *separate, cut, hew, chop, back, bite, split.*

5. Copy a short poem that you like, then decide which words in it help you see pictures of things named or described. Which words do not bring many pictures to your mind? Perhaps some words suggest no pictures at all.

Draw a red line under the words that help you see pictures and a blue line under words that do not bring many pictures to your mind.

Try the same experiment with a few lines of prose from a story that you enjoy.

6. Some words make us feel cheerful; some seem to make us feel sad. Write a list of eight words that make you feel cheerful.

7. When you are talking with somebody and happen to say a word that you never have used before, are you a little surprised at yourself?

Are you less surprised the second time you use it? Does it seem easy and natural after about the third time?

8. Ask two of your friends to guess how many new words they are likely to meet during the usual day: in school, travelling to and from school, reading advertisements and signs, and watching television. Then for two or three days days each of you keep a count of the words that are new. Compare your numbers with the guesses you made.

9. Find an object that is different from anything that a few of your friends have ever seen. It may be a new gadget or a curio from years ago or from a foreign country. Show it to those friends and ask each to give a name to it.

Can you tell why your friends decided on the names which they gave it?

10. It has been said that making a definition is like drawing a large circle, then drawing a smaller one inside of it. Sometimes there has to be a third one, smaller still, inside of the second one.

When we define the word *quadruped,* we say, "A quadruped is an animal having four feet". When we say "is an animal" we are drawing the big circule which contains all animals. When we say "having four feet" we draw the smaller circle inside the large one. This smaller circle includes only those animals that have four feet.

Try a definition of the word *pebble.* Do your friends agree with your definition? How many "circles" do you draw when making the definition?

Perhaps your friends will be willing to try to define *hat* or *tripod.*

11. Have you practiced opening a dictionary at about the right place even when the book has no index tabs? Suppose you want to find the word *tremor.* Do you think of opening the dictionary near the back instead of in the front or near the middle?

Try your skill at opening the dictionary near the words *hard* and *isle.*

12. Get six or seven of your friends to join you in an alphabet game. See how many seconds you need to arrange yourselves in line alphabetically according to the first letter of your last names. Use the second or third letters of the last names if first letters are alike.

13. Ask six of your friends how they use the guide words at the top of dictionary pages to help them find a word they are looking for. How many of them forget to use these guides?

14. When a word stands alone, you may not be sure what it means. Take the word *run* as an example. When it is alone you cannot tell whether it means going fast, an exercise, a command, or a distance covered. But as soon as it is with other words you know which meaning fits.

They run too fast for me.
The daily run gave him good exercise.
Run as far as the park.
The train made the run in twenty minutes.

See how uncertain you are about the word *will* when it is alone. How many different meanings can you give it by putting other words with it in a complete sentence? Also try the word *fly* in the same way.

15. A piece of green paper next to red paper looks very green. The same green paper, if put next to orange paper, will

look less green and somewhat bluish. The way a colour looks depends much on the colours that are around it.

Have you noticed that words affect each other the way colours do? The meaning of a word depends partly on other words around it. Notice what happens in these two sentences:

I saw the car bounce down the street.
I saw the old car bounce down the rough street.

When the words *old* and *rough* are added, they affect the meanings of other words. How do they make some change in the meanings of *car, bounce,* and *street?*

16. Cut a paragraph from a discarded newspaper or magazine. In that clipping blot out every fifth word. Then see whether your classmates can guess what the blotted words were. Can they at least tell what kind of word (name of something, word telling what is being done, connecting word, describing word) was in each place? Why can they tell?

Try with another clipping in which you blot every fourth word, or even every third word.

17. Find out why your home town, village, township, or city was given the name that it has. What is the story behind the name of your state? Behind the name of the road or street along which you live?

STUDY ACTIVITIES FOR TEACHERS

1. "I never saw his *like,*" "I never saw his *equal.*"
"She was a *sight.*" "She was a *vision.*"
"He is *strong-minded.*" "He is strongheaded."
"He had a great *overview* of the situation." "He had a great *oversight* of the situation."

How can we account for the differences of meaning between the two sentences of each pair? Can we explain them mainly by differences in dictionary definitions of the italicised words? By differences in the connotations of those words?

2. The rose is in bloom.
The peach tree is in bloom.
The desert is in bloom.

All the words in these sentences are the same except *rose, peach tree,* and *desert*. Each of the repeated words serves the same role in each of the three sentences. Also all the new words are alike in being nouns and subjects of a sentence.

But the meanings of the repeated words differ from sentence to sentence. These different shades of meaning result from the influence of the particular words that are new: *rose, peach tree, desert*. The differences are conspicuous in *bloom,* but are noticeable even in *is* and *in*.

This phenomenon, in which the meaning of a word is shaped by the presence of other words, is often called *interinanimation*. Why does this name seem suitable?

3. Suppose we list the following:

(a) The names of two cities and two countries that we never have seen but we would like to visit.

(b) The names of two cities and two countries that we never have seen but which we would not particularly care to visit.

(c) The names of two bodies of water (rivers, lakes, oceans) which we never have seen but on which we would like to sail.

(d) The kinds of trees and flowers that we would like to see along the shores.

Studying our list, can we account for our choices? Was connotation a large factor? Connotations of the sound of the name? Connotations based on memories of impressions we picked up from various sources?

4. In montage, as commonly met in movies, painting, and music, one image or one sound is either superimposed on another or placed close beside it, in contrast. The close association intensifies the effects of each individually and of the two collectively. Two plus two seems to equal more than four.

Can we think of some figures of speech, notably simile and metaphor, as montage? In them, are denotations and connotations of one word piled on the denotations and connotations of another word?

Is it montage that produces such lightning flashes of language as "now cracks a noble heart"? (The plain sunray of language would be "a great man is dying now.") Is there montage in "Kind Arthur was the king who rode down history on a harpstring"? Little, if any, in "Kind Arthur has continued for centuries to be popular as a theme in a song and story"?

5. "Concrete, specific nouns unveil panoramas from our memories. Action-suggesting verbs set those panoramas in motion."

Test the truth of the above statement by comparing the effects of sensory words with the effects of abstract nouns and of static verbs.

Where is the greatest concentration of concrete nouns and action-suggesting verbs: in prose stories? in poems? in factual prose?

6. Although abstract nouns do not generally evoke many mental images or serve well in poetry and narrative prose, they have been powerful instruments in the advancement of civilisation, in so far as civilisation moves ahead on abstract, theoretical thinking. Could we say that one of the great moments in human evolution occurred when for the first time a person used a noun *abstractly* and someone else understood what he was talking about?

7. *Hoidy, kukes, tolatol,* and *malek* when heard or read in isolation seem like the nonsense words which they are. But if we put them in a sequence, along with the noun-making signal *the,* they acquire a degree of significance:

The hoidy tolatol kukes the malek.

The puzzling words, still meaningless, have gained two elements:

(a) Each word has taken on the role of a class of words (part of speech): adjective, noun, verb. This acquisition, alone, gives each word a kind of significance, a partial intelligibility. We know that *malek,* for example, is the name of a person, place, thing, or idea, and we have a special point of view toward nouns.

(b) Each word takes on the functions of a specific role in a sentence: subject, predicate, modifier.

This also gives each word a degree of meaning.

How does the preceding example illustrate the following statements?

"A word is made by the sentence which it helps to build. It lives on what it helps bring into being."

"In an English sentence, structure determines meaning more than meaning determines structure."

8. Russell Stauffer identified the word prefixes appearing frequently in E. L. Thorndike's word list. Thorndike identified the most frequent suffixes. These lists of suffixes and prefixes are in Betts's *Foundations of Reading Instruction*.

With a knowledge of those affixes and of forty to fifty word roots we could make reasonably safe guesses about the meanings of words like the following, were the words to come into use: *multist, theoful, audier, pseudophonic, circumvert, intragraphic, ultratotian.*

9. Suppose scientists, mathematicians, grammarians, psychologists, and philsophers had had no Greek or Latin words to draw on for technical terms. Then they would have made many words from native English, after the pattern of *airlift, wheelbarrow,* and *rainbow.* What might have been their words in place of *telegraph, television, locomotive, library, calendar, interrogative, dictionary, equinox, schizophrenia, reflex,* and *monarchy?*

10. In the parentheses within the sentences below are some ideas not presently covered by any single words in our language. Invent words for those ideas. Use only *one* word to designate the whole idea that is givn within one set of parentheses.

The (night half of) (every flying house) (did and did not) (bow diagonally sidewise) whenever it was (counting the number of windows) in (other flying houses).

In (a country located near the equator of Mars) the (people who have three eyes) have worked out a mathematical system that starts its numeration with (a whole number that is less than one) and accepts the concept of (a half is nevertheless a complete whole).

Having coined new words, speculate on how they would be pronounced and spelled after about forty years of frequent use by many people.

11. Checking through our teaching of science, social studies, arithmetic, health, art, music, and language arts we may find dozens of terms that seem strange, almost foreign, to our pupils. How can we use derivations to help children understand such words?

Here are some words whose derivations illuminate the meanings: *torrid, equator, Antarctic, Orient, Occident, hemisphere, peninsula, delta, inaugurate, tariff, parliament, veto, barometer, isotherm, telescope, equinox, petrified, volcano, compound, parasite, capillary, diameter, subtract, quotient, triangle, interrogative, imperative, alphabet, passive, staccato, fresco, silbouette, mural, symmetric, octave.*

12. The word history of *quisling* throws a spotlight on world events of the 1940s. So do the histories of the words *radar, sonar, atomic, supersonic,* and *cold war.*

We might speculate: If we wrote the history of certain selected words would we thereby be writing a history of civilisation? And if the answer is affirmative, what words would be on the list? Would we need 125 words or only about seventy?

A start on that list might be: *tragedy, personality, orchestra, barbarian, alchemy, metaphysics, humanism, leviathan, Sabbath, pecuniary, manuscript, hydrant, stoic, cosmos, renaissance, Gothic, beef, nirvana, clixir, jongleur, journal, ostracise, plebiscite, candidate.*

What twenty-five additional words can you add in ten minutes?

VIEWPOINTS TO EMPHASISE THROUGH TEACHING AIDS

1. *Words are tags or labels for things, events, ideas, etc.*

(a) A picture or drawing of a pen or cage in a zoo. On the fence is a label telling the name of the animal. On the same poster or bulletin board is a picture of an airplane, with the word *airplane* beneath it. The caption says that words are handy labels.

(b) On the desk or shelf is an object that the children have not seen before. They do not know its name. When talking about it, they experience the need of a conveninent label for it.

2. *A dictionary helps us quickly if we know what we can find in it and where to look for what we want.*

An enlarged facsimile of a dictonary page, with marginal comments and lines leading to the parts commented on.

3. *A definition is stated according to a definite plan.*

(a) On a poster or with a projector show:

A pebble is:	A house is:
(Drawing of three concentric circles demonstrating how a definition starts with a large class of things, then narrows down to smaller and smaller classes. Illustrate it with the definition: A pebble is a small rounded stone worn by action of water.)	(Drawing of one large circle. Questions: How many circles are needed? What would you put in each circle?)

(b) A poster showing both a correctly stated definition and a poorly phrased one. The lettering in the second is blurred. Caption of the latter: How can you tune this one into focus?

4. *A word is likely to have meanings in addition to its dictionary meaning. Words make us remember things that we saw, heard, tasted, felt, smelled, or experienced in some other way.*

(a) Animated-cartoon type of drawings, picturing the thoughts that might come to the mind of a person hearing the word *jungle, desert, poem, rainbow, jewel,* or *story.* Some of those memories of experiences and ideas seem to have little direct connection with the dictionary definition of the word.

(b) A poster, chalkboard, or overhead projector sketch showing a word. A definition of the word is written beneath it, and some associated meanings are written around it, radially, like a corona.

(c) A poster based on the idea that some words are like tightly packed parcels. When opened, they are found to contain much.

5. *Occasinally a word is used in such a way that it means something very different from what it usually means.*

Poster or chalkboard presentation:

The parakeet *flew* out of the cage.
He *flew* into a rage of anger when he heard the news.
I was *petrified* when I saw the bear coming.
On the trip we saw a *petrified* tree.

6. *Words can be interesting, considered from the viewpoint of sound only.*

(a) Tape recordings and phonograph recordings of prose and verse, listened to a number of times. Listeners concentrate on the sound rather than on the meaning—a kind of concentration which becomes easier with practice and after two or three rehearings.

(b) Tape recordings or direct speaking of words put together in meaningless combinations. Included are some large words unfamiliar to the pupils. After two or three rehearings, pupils can concentrate on the sounds.

(c) Phonograph records of French, German, Italian, or other language not known by a majority of the pupils. Attention readily goes to the sounds.

(d) Words heard from phonograph records, but with the volume turned down so far that pupils hear a flow of sound rather than distinct words.

(e) Speech heard indistinctly through the walls of a room.

7. *Often a word needs other words with it before we can tell its exact meaning.*

(a) On poster, chalkboard, or projector, present the word *strike*. Then follow with a series of sentences, each sentence giving *strike* a different fixed meaning. This fixing of meaning is done by the words that go with *strike*.

Sample sentences:

Strike the iron.
The clock will strike.
They hope to strike oil.
It is strike three.

On a poster the sentences can be covered with individual flaps that may be raised as needed. Only the word *strike* is seen at first.

(b) A word and sentences such as *(a)*, above, can be drawn through an opaque projector in sequence, in the manner of a ribbon sign.

8. *Words influence each other. A word is likely to affect the meaning of words close to it and vice versa.*

(a) By projector or chalkboard present: He drove as fast as he could along the . . . . . street. Then in the blank space add the word *rough*. Discuss how the presence of *rough* influences the meanings of *drove, fast,* and *street*.

(b) Also present:

He had a rough
- street to drive on.
- draft of the letter.
- voyage.
- voice.
- time of it while sick.

Pupils notice how *rough* has its meaning influenced by the word or words following it.

9. *Many words are made up of two or more parts.*

(a) On chalkboard, projector, or poster give some words broken into parts, together with the question and words below:

steam	boat	tele	vision
thermo	meter	sun	flower
bak	er	air	plane

Can you find the parts in these?

automobile	triangle
telephone	speedometer
earthquake	intake

(b) Pupils dramatise the combining of parts into words. Each child represents one part (*meter, tri, er,* for instance), and two or three children stand together to form a word.

10. *Some parts of words appear in a number of different words but always have about the same meaning. If we learn the meaning of those parts we will know them whenever we meet them, even in words new to us.*

(a) Various types of charts: pinwheel, word-tree, hand-shaped (with basic word part in palm and other word parts which go with it recorded on the fingers).

(b) A poster naming some important word parts. Caption: You'll meet these often. Better make them your friends.

(c) On the chalkboard is a word part that the children know. Beneath it is a word new to the class generally, but containing this known part. Caption: *(The known word part)* is an old friend. Now guess what this word means: *(the new word).*

11. *Prefixes and suffixes are word parts that help us make many words.*

(a) Common prefixes and suffixes are on separate slips of paper or cardboard. They may therefore be placed before or after words and word parts with which they combine. This can be done on chalkboard, flannel board, or posters.

(b) Pupils dramatise the adding of prefixes and suffixes to words. A child representing a prefix or suffix stands with another child to form a word.

(c) Animated-cartoon types of drawings that show the meaning of a word and then illustrate how the meaning becomes changed: when *-er* comes along and joins *bake,* or when *-ette* comes to join *kitchen*. Likewise, what happens to words when a prefix is added: *annually, semiannually.*

12. *Some words have derivations that are very interesting.*

(a) Sketchy drawings showing the origins or earlier meanings of words which children use in their schoolwork or meet frequently elsewhere. For example: *map, climate, peninsula, capricorn, equinox, equator, radar, cathedral, hydrant, candidate, arena, circus, hippopotamus.*

(b) Dramatic skits by pupils, portraying the origins or earlier meanings of words such as those named above.

13. *In English we have words borrowed from many languages.*

(a) Outline maps of the world, with borrowed words written in the areas of the countries from which they were borrowed.

(b) A map of Europe, with borrowed words writen in the neighbouring ocean areas and with lines leading from the words to the countries from which they came.

(c) An international party of words. American and English words are present, as are words from many national languages of the world. Children represent the words. National costumes are a possibility.

14. *People tire of hearing some words or groups of words over and over.*

Tape recordings of conversations. Several conversations illustrate natural, lively use of language. Several others use some words or phrases too often. Excessive use of slang may be present, too. Hear the tapes a number of times, until the repeated expressions become tedious.

15. *There are different kinds or classes of words in our language, and each class has its special job in a sentence.*

On poster or projector present these sentences, showing each kind or class of word in a different colour:

Red birds chirped and sang.

They sang gaily.

(Each of the words *red, birds, and, they,* and *gaily* is in a different colour. *Chirped* and *sang* are in the same colour, though different from the colours of the other words.)

INQUIRIES AND PROBLEMS FOR STUDENTS

1. How can children's eagerness to see new things and learn about them be used to promote word study? Try out the possibilities with a child whom you know.

2. Have fun with words the way children do. Play with phonics, distort syllables, exaggerate rhythms, roll the words off your tongue, try them out.

3. Look into the Opie volume, *The Lore and Language of School Children.* What can you discover there regarding children's vocabularies and the ways children use words?

4. In Alastair Reid's *Ounce, Dice, Trice* playful things are done with words. How do your observations there compare with what you find people doing with words in real life?

5. List fifteen words that are in your passive vocabulary but not in your active one. Experiment with various ways of getting them into your active vocabulary.

6. Children know many words which are not on "controlled vocabulary" lists. What contemporary influences might cause this? To what extent do such lists get out of date quickly now?

7. Reflect on the twenty-four word characteristics shown in Figure 6.1. How many of them are influential in the daily lives of children in a grade which you have visited? How many could be discussed satisfactorily in that grade?

8. "The connections in which a word occurs, the situation with respect to which we use it, are the word's *meaning.*"

This quotation is from page 61 of Robert A. Hall's *Linguistics and Your Language.* Illustrate it with familiar words that potentially have a number of meanings.

9. Could one say that denotations really are connotations—but connotations which people in general agree on in connection with a particular word?

10. Find the derivations of five important terms used in social studies, five in geography, five in arithmetic, and five in music. How many of those derivations could help children understand the meanings of the respective terms?

11. How many of your classmates make a practice of reading the derivations of words which they look up in a dictionary? What reasons for omission are given by those who do not read them?

12. Study the cutting from Buck's *Dictionary of Selected Synonyms in the Principal Indo-European Languages,* reproduced in Figure 6.3. What does it tell you about words, the evolution of words, and the relations between English and other Indo-European languages?

7

Development of Ideas

A pupil wants to tell about his experiences with dandelion fluff—the fun he had in blowing it, his surprise, at the way the downy bits flew, and this observation of how far the seeds were scattered. Three elements influence his report: what he wants to tell, the type of person to whom he speaks or writes, and his knowledge of the English language. The first, the marshaling of facts, calls for both logic and knowledge of the topic; the second requires acquaintance with the ways and interests of human beings; the thirds draws on those resources of the English language which he knows at the time. All three elements are interrelated.

The third one—handling the resources of the English language—is so influential that it calls for separate attention Good composing is more than merely speaking or writing something intelligibly; more than just using grammar which is correct. At its best, composing goes beyond intelligibility and correctness; it uses the resources of language to state ideas accurately and in pleasing style.

Composing a talk or write-up on "Catching Rainwater" or "A Recipe for Cookies" can be a matter of careful attention, employing considerable skill approximating art. The present chapter concentrates on such composing and on how a teacher can help children improve their use of the resources mentioned in the preceding chapters on structure, usage and words.

It is commonly held that a pupil's ideas and the language forms in which the states them are conceived together. But even if ideas and language arrive simulataneously there are valid reasons for teaching pupils more about resources of language.

A compelling reason is this: A person cannot state an idea in words or language patterns that he does not already know. If he is acquainted with better patterns, he might use them to express his ideas more effectively. The more words and patterns a person is acquainted with, the more he has to choose from—however automatically or unconsciously—when he thinks and talks about ideas. Behind good composing there is good thinking, but there is also considerable knowledge of how to use the resources of language. There is know-how in language, just as there is in working with colours, forms, and lines or with sounds, rhythms and harmonies.

OBJECTIVES IN TEACHING COMPOSING

While in the grades, children can understand at least eight to ten practical aspects of using compositional resources. Though these aspects are down-to-earth the handling of them need not be pedestrian, as they lead beyond utilitarianism and point in the direction of art. Because they border on art they can never be mastered fully; always a pupil or an adult can practice them a little more skillfully. At the same time their use can be free of ornateness which might reduce the clarity of a statement.

In each grade a teacher can hope to attaincertain stages in developing these eight to ten aspects. Kindergarten and first grade take up instruction at whatever stage the child is in following his preschool experiences with language. After that, development is a continuance throughout the grades.

Each objective discussed below is an important compositional resource. All except the one relating to paragraphs can be considered in every grade. A sensible policy for a teacher to follow is to being working toward watch objective as early as possible.

COMPOSITIONAL RESOURCES

For pupils the inventory of resources works somewhat like this. Suppose that the language offers four expressional patterns (types of sentences, perhaps) in which the pupil's idea could be stated. Then the pupil has a choice, but only within the number of those patterns that he knows. Suppose that he knows two of the four and chooses one of those two. Probably the teacher ought to accept whichever of the two the pupil chooses, if it seems reasonably satisfactory. She may use this opportunity, though, to have the pupil compare the effects of his chosen pattern with those of the other pattern which he knew, by having him use it for the same idea. The teacher might then consider it timely to introduce the other two patterns from which the pupil had been unable to choose because he had not known them. If the sentence in question is part of a paragraph, the structures of the preceding and following sentences must be considered in making a choice.

It is a lifelong enterprise to become acquainted with expressional possibilities Much can be accomplished, though, by the end of the sixth grade. Explorations in speech, phonics, writing, imaginative expression, descriptive grammar, words, and literature help build up the inventory.

Speaking or writing, a person choose words, phrasal patterns, sentence patterns, and punctuation from the inventory that he knows. In order to develop style a person must know enough resources to have a choice. Awareness of what can be done with language is, in itself, an inspiration for the pupil to do something with language. It makes the verbal medium exciting to work with.

Sentence Patterns

Children come to school with a mastery of the basic declarative, interrogative, exclamatory, and imperative sentence patterns. A first grader's sentences average about five words in length. Over the next four or five years his sentences gradually become longer. In the middle grades children start composing sentences that have subordinate clauses. They succeed in this when speaking, but they run into two difficulties when they write; they put down long statements in run-on manner and, conversely, they put in periods where they should not, thus producing fragments. These two difficulties are avoided in speech because intonations and pauses show relationships among clauses or phrases. But since children's knowledge of written punctuation lags behind their skill in oral punctuation, fragmentary and run-on sentences result.

In third grade the better pupils can be expected to write complete sentences fairly consistently. After the fourth grade they should begin to avoid run-on constructions, as they become aware of the sentence as a group of words belonging together—a block of utterance contained within some kind of structure and making a unit. They may need a few more years to overcome the tendency to punctuate dependent clauses as if they were independent sentences. Clauses beginning with *when, while, because,* and *if* are especially troublesome.

Instruction speeds up this growth in sentence composing. In early grades the teacher has opportunities to comment on sentences that she writes on experience charts. Continually through the grades in both speech and writing, teachers can heighten the feeling for the sentence as a unit. In middle and upper grades they can analyse the special punctuation problems which develop as soon as pupils begin to write complex sentences. Especially should teachers get children to *listen* repeatedly to well-constructed sentences, both as spoken directly and as recorded on tape.

Sentences on Screen. Watching sentences unfold on a screen, as on a ribbon sign, can be highly instructive. Such unfolding is easily controlled if a teacher writes or pastes sentences on a long strip of paper (from an adding-machine roll, for example) and pulls the strip through an opaque projector. As the words and phrases come progressively onto the screen the class has a chance to observe that a sentence is an organised statement—a neatly packaged parcel—and that it unfolds or reveals itself word by word, phrase by phrase, punctuation mark by punctuation mark.

In the ribbon-sign disclosure of sentences the class can see, too, that certain parts could not stand alone as separate sentences. Alone, those would be only fragments. To reinforce certain points of phrasing, arrangement, or punctuation the teacher can stop the sentence at will or pull it back and repeat selected portions.

Break from Primer Style. When children begin composing variations on the subject-verb-object construction and adding subordinate clauses they not only show a degree of maturity in though and expression but also open the way for varied sentence effects in composing. They are equipped to open their sentences in different ways and to construct various kinds of sentences. Thus they break away from the monotony of "primer" style. Figure 7.1 illustrate a successful break.

Such explorations into possible ways of phrasing sentences prepare the way for high school experiments in style. Eventually the student of English will see that in certain circumstances a single word may be a sentence, or that a group of words which he formerly would have considered "fragmentary" can stand alone. His ultimate surprise—and liberation—will come when he discovers that the concept "sentence" is elusive and virtually indefinable.

The Paragraph

Children may get their first impression of the paragraph easily and naturally when they say or heat two or three closely related sentences about topic or about one aspect of a topic. This is likely to occur during oral sharing of news or personal experiences. Again it may come when they see related sentences on experience charts or when they write a letter of thanks or an invitation.

Impressions of the paragraph deepen when pupils have occasion to discuss two or more aspects of a subject, devoting a few sentences to each aspect. This might happen in the fourth grade when someone is telling about "How to Thread a Loom" or "How to Make a Scarecrow for the Garden." One aspect of the former topic could be told in a total of three or four sentences, making only one paragraph about the subject. But two groups of sentences might be needed: one group telling how to get the loom and materials ready, the other telling about the actual threading. A similar division of grouped sentences might be natural for the topic on scarecrows. For this topic there could be a third group to tell about putting up scarecrows at the most effective locations.

The paragraph (spoken or written) is an extremely important unit around which to teach logical organisation of materials and ideas. It also helps a speaker or writer (and the listener or reader) break the materials of a topic into workable subdivisions.

<table>
<tr>
<td>Each sentence tells a fact clearly.

The thought moves ahead clearly and steadily.

There are words that lead from one sentence to the next and also relate the new sentence to the one just finished.</td>
<td>Our class in Room 21 did many things since school started. First we made a room calendar. Then we learned about seeds in our teacher's yard and garden. After that we built a terrarium. Now we are starting to write.

Next week we will study more about the alphabet. Also we will watch for birds that come to this part of the country in winter. The first time we see a new kind of bird we will write its name and the date on our room calendar.

We call our calendar "Watching and Learning."</td>
<td>Sentence openings are varied.

A fairly long sentence contrasts with shorter sentences, making a change of pace.</td>
</tr>
</table>

To be realistic, a teacher must admit that in much contemporary writing the paragraph has fallen apart. Material that, a generation ago, would have been placed in a single paragraph is now broken into two or three. This fragmenting has been caused by various factors, some journalistic. But the older concept, demanding that a paragraph be large enough to have a kind of development, unity, and self-sufficiency, is still a fruitful one for teachers and pupils to study.

Variety of Conjunctions

The problem of freeing children from overreliance on *and, or, but,* and *because* as conjunctions involves more than merely telling the class that *since, however, although, even if, therefore,* and other exist. It includes instruction regarding meanings, the relationship that each conjunction expresses, and the direction toward which each one points.

One aware that each conjunction expresses a unique relationship between the units which it links, a pupil less how important a conjunction can be. Consequently he understands why he should choose from a range of ten or twelve conjunctions rather than from only three or four.

Sentences on a flannel board or chalkboard, constructed with a variety of conjunctions, become good centres of discussion on this topic. Samples on tape recorders serve well, too. A portion of a sentence such as "she earned the scout badge" followed by a choice of conjunctions—*and, because, although, therefore*— leads to informative discussions (see Figure 7.2). This can be shown on an overhead projector transparency, with overlays for various conjunctions. The ribbon-sign effect obtained with an opaque projector is exceptionally helpful because the unfolding of a sentence may be stopped just before the conjunction appears or just after. Thereby pupils see how influential a conjunction is as a sign indicating the direction which the remainder of the sentence will take. This, in turn, encourages pupils to search for the particular conjunction which will give their expressed thoughts the directions they want them to have.

As pupils gradually develop a feeling for the various ways in which several parts of a statement can be connected they may arrive at another discovery: By skillful use of punctuation and by careful arrangement or sequence of the parts of a statement, they will be able, in some sentences, to do *without* a conjunction. The fewer the conjunctions, the better, provided the statement is clear. The best conjunction, according to many people's judgment, is the one that is implied, not expressed.

Modification of Ideas

The importance of the modification of ideas has been stated by Anderson:

> Through the long history of man's struggle with language there has developed a simple but profoundly important device for refining and clarifying communication, namely, the modification of basic ideas through the use of words and groups of words as modifiers. I do not know the history of this development, but it

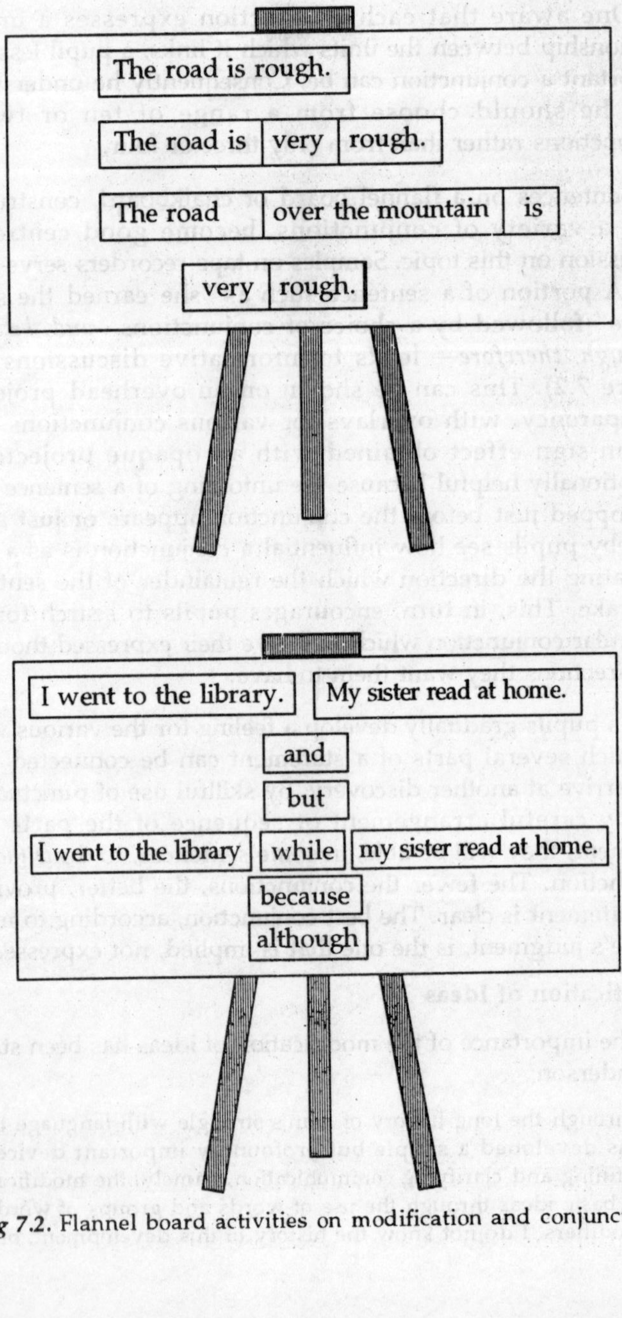

Fig 7.2. Flannel board activities on modification and conjunctions.

> must have been a slow and laborious one. Let me illustrate the principle with a simple sentence which I saw one of my collegues use with a sophomore class in high school. First she wrote on the blackboard this simple sentence: "I saw animals." These words communicate something, but not much. Before a clearer and more definite meaning can be conveyed, the basic idea—"I saw animals"—must be modified, refined. The teacher went on to illustrate her point. "I saw a thousand animals." Then, "I saw more than a thousand animals." "I saw more than a thousand beautiful animals with spiral horns." "I saw more than a thousand beautiful animals with spiral horns bounding across the plain." By adding words and groups of words . . . the basic idea was modified until it conveyed a more precise meaning, and even accompanying feeling tones.
>
> Here is a basic principle of grammer, or of linguistics if you wish—the modification of ideas. It is a grammatical principle capable of being understood. It should be taught as an intellectual matter, not as a matter of drill. Furthermore it is a big idea. It involves perhaps a fourth or more of all the grammar we teach or need to teach. Consider what a unit of instruction in grammar with this as the unitary understanding would involve: an understanding of the function of adjectives, adverbs, prepositions, prepositional phrases, misplaced modifiers, dangling participles, punctuation of consecutive adjectives, punctuation and proper use of appositives, formation and use of possessives, and a number of other items of grammar, usage, spelling, and rhetoric—all integrally and functionally related to the basic concept of modification . . . I submit . . . that such an approach to grammar would promote critical thinking and clarity of expression . . . . This is not grammar for college entrance. This is grammar for communication, grammar for everybody.

Although Anderson refers to high school grammar, the principle of modification can be perceived by pupils in the grades. Chalkboards, flannel boards, and projectors help in presenting samples of modification for observation and discussion. Examples should be simple enough for grade pupils to understand, as in Figure 7.2. Case studies come up, too, when the class members test out various phrasings for public address or assembly announcements, invitations, and thank-you letters.

Modification of ideas is not new to pupils in the grades. It is part of the general language equipment which children acquire before entering school. During school years its use needs extension and refinement. For the teacher, linguistics provides considerable information on the way English statements can be generated and transformed.

Excessive Adjectives. Discussion of modification should caution children against the tendency to overuse adjectives. Samples of strong contemporary prose and poetry demonstrate that adjectives are used sparingly. "A good prose style moves on its nouns and verbs," says Ciardi, adding, "A heavily adjectival style is slovenly because it is badly selected. The adjectives tend to be there only because the author failed to select the right noun in the first place."

Flexibility of Language. The flexibility of the English language exists, whether used or unused. The problem is to make pupils aware of its existence and then use it for their advantage.

If a child wishes to tell about how he went to school he can say, "I went to school quickly." But English idiom will allow him to say it otherwise, if he wishes:

I went quickly to school.
I quickly went to school.
Quickly I went to school.

Less common, but still understandable and usable in certain situations, would be two more variants:

To school I went quickly.
Quickly to school I went.

A class may be surprised to see that the language is flexible enough to allow at least six arrangements of these five words. They can see, also, that each arrangement carries a shade of meaning which differs more or less from the meaning of any of the others. Each gives special emphasis to some word or aspect. Figure 7.3 illustrates another approach to the topic.

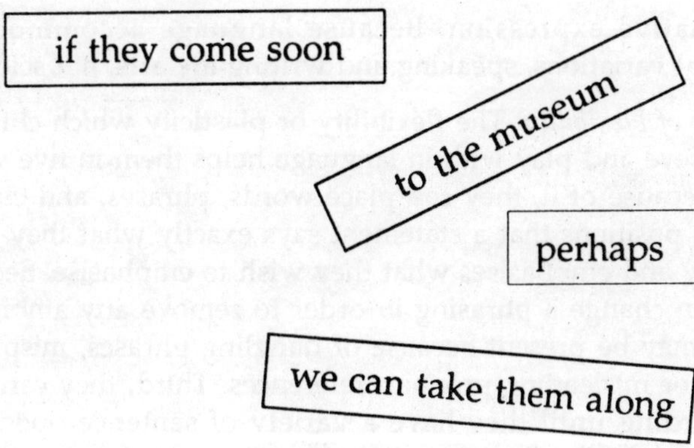

Fig 7.3. Readily movable segments of a sentence. Portions of a sentence on separate slips of paper or cards give pupils a pleasurable way to experiment and learn. Discussions naturally touch on topics like these:

How four or five different arrangements of the portions vary in the ways they present or "package" the contents of the sentence.

How the several arrangements differ in the ways they catch the attention of a listener or reader, or hold the attention.

How movable a word like *perhaps* can be and how each position of that word establishes a unique meaning.

Why certain portions of the sentence cannot stand alone and be sentences.

In longer sentences the variant possibilities are even greater. Punctuation, both oral and written, is a factor introducing even more variants, notably in long sentences.

Classroom experiments in flexibility are interesting and can be exciting because they involve action and tangible things to do. They appeal to boys and girls who are at the age when there is interest in testing out to see what can be done with materials at hand.

This inherent interest is fortunate because the truth about language flexibility is one of the really great discoveries that a user of language can make. Flexibility opens the way to infinite development for anyone who applies it in either factual or imaginative expression. Because language accommodates personal variations, speaking and writing are arts, not sciences.

Use of Flexibility. The flexibility or plasticity which children can obseve and play with in language helps them in five ways. First, because of it, they can place words, phrases, and clauses in such positions that a statement says exactly what they want it to say and emphasises what they wish to emphasise. Second, they can change a phrasing in order to remove any ambiguity which may be present because of dangling phrases, misplaced words, or misleading pronoun references. Third, they can shift the wording until they have a variety of sentence openings, sentence lengths, and sentence types. Fourth, they can avoid awkward combinations of sound or harsh rhythms caused by adjacent words that do not go well together. Fifth, they can link a sentence solidly with the sentence which precedes it and the one following it, thus pacing the thought smoothly from sentence to sentence, paragraph to paragraph. All five potentialities are used to some extent by pupils in the grades. For high school and college students they lead to subtleties of style and expression and nuances in meaning.

Rarely do experiments in flexibility lead to exotic and unidiomatic phrasing. Children have standard English patterns indelibly in mind from their years of listening and speaking. An experimenter's efforts may be noticeably deliberate for a while, until facility comes. But the same is true of anyone—child or adult—learning new techniques in a craft or art.

Precision and Choices. Two supplementary observations grow out of children's experiments. First, although language is flexible, choice of phrasing is limited by the specific idea which pupils want to state. In some cases, only one arrangement of the words they are using says precisely what they want to say. They might be able to say that idea in other phrasing if they started over again, with different words and a different approach.

Second, when a person composes a sentence he can make a series of choices as he builds up the statement. He can choose whether he will start with the subject part of the sentence (*I went home while he . . .*) or some other part *(While he...)*. Then he probably has some choices regarding the particular verb to use and whether or not he shall put in a modifying word or phrase. As he gets near the end of the sentence he has fewer choices left, and finally none at all. He reaches a point of no digression Figure 7.3 illustrates this segment of choices.

Pupils become quite absorbed in the experiment of taking a sentence such as *Cats like to curl up on a rug and go to sleep* and finding places where there would have been choices of expressing the same general idea somewhat differently. After the word *cats* the verb had to be plural, but some verb other than *like* could have been chosen. After *like* the composer could have used *curling* instead of *to curl*. The moment he choose *to* he had to go ahead with a form such as *curl* instead of an *-ing* form. Thus on through the sentence there were possible chocies at certain places. This is evident in Figure 7.4.

▲While▲my sister▲made sandwiches I▲prepared lemonade.

▲Cats▲like to▲curl up▲on a rug and▲go to sleep.

Fig. 7.4. Where the speaker or writer has a choice. Pupils can see that at each of the marked places in the sentences they have a choice as to what to say or write next. At the very beginning there is the choice of how to start—what part of the sentence content to put first. At later places the choice becomes narrower, but pupils can still decide which part of their statement should go next or select the verb or noun that seems best for the occasion.

Sometimes once choice determines what the next words must be, thus removing any choice there. The choices made earlier in the sentence cannot be changed, unless the composer turns back and says or writes the sentence again. This circumstance may remind the children of the situation in Robert Frost's poem called "The Road Not Taken."

Position of a Word or Phrase

The chapter on "Structure and Usage" explained that the place held by a word in an English sentence is important because position has become on of the major signals that the language uses to show meaning. Anyone speaking or writing must heed this situation. Pupils can experiment with the effects of word and phrase positions just as they rest the related linguistic quality of flexibility.

Children entering school have a feeling for the importance of position in the more obvious spots of a sentence. Without further instruction they know the reversals in meaning which result when key words are switched to other positions in sentences like:

Linda gave Phyllis a doll.
Phyllis gave Linda a doll.
The boy hit the ball.
The ball hit the boy.

In a sentence such as *The squirrel ate the sunflower seeds* children would sense the absurdity of meaning resulting from a switch in location of *squirrel and sunflower seeds.*

But pupils need instruction in how position affects some less obvious aspects of meaning. When they phrase a sentence in the manner of *I saw a man walk down the street with a long beard* their remedy is in a knowledge of position—how to shift *with a long beard* to a place which will make the meaning unmistakable. Dangling modifiers of all kinds, unclear references of relative pronounds, ambiguous use of *only* and *alone,* and uncertain references of adjectives all can be cleared up by shifting the relative positions of certain portions of the sentence.

Experiments combined with direct instruction are the best approach to this aspect of constructing ideas. Specimen statements can be spoken, or heard from tape recordings, and shown on chalkboard, flannel board, and projectors.

Who-Whom Test. When compositional difficulties with *who* and *whom* arise, position offers a test of which form is correct in a given statement. If the grammatical structure would permit the use of *he* or *she* at a certain place, then *who* is the correct form to use there. If *him* or *her* fits, *whom* is the one to use.

AUTHORITY OF THE ENGLISH LANGUAGE

When constructing ideas with language a pupil is putting the language code into action. Even as he respects grammar in theory, he should respect it in practice. He must conform to certain basic structural features that change very slowly, if at all. Among these are the subject-verb agreement in person and number; the subject-verb-object sequence; number; tense; verb forms; two case forms in nouns; nominative, possessive, and objective case forms in personal pronouns; gender; and the automatic reference of pronouns.

As structural linguistics makes clear, a person may choose the particular words that he wishes to use but he has little or not freedom in the patterns of structure into which those words fit. The structures are inherited from centuries of speakers and writers of the language. Know and use the resources of the English language, but respect its authority. This is a fruitful viewpoint in every grade.

Yet an ambitious pupil soon discovers that cooperation with the code does not mean regimentation. Though he cannot flout the basic structures of his language he still has elbow room, a tolerance within which to move. He can choose the particular structure that he prefers from the several available structures. If he knows the rich resources of the language he can still be "himself" in the way he says what he wishes to say.

DYNAMIC PUNCTUATION

Punctuation, which is spontaneous in speech, becomes a problem in two situations—when a pupil reads aloud and when he composes in writing. The difficulties were pointed out in earlier chapters; here there is occasion to note that punctuation can be dynamic instrument when pupils construct ideas in language.

The problem of punctuation in writing is stated by Cherry:

> Compared to speech, writing is relatively clumsy, lengthy, and slow. We can introduce great expression and flexibility into our vocal utterances by stressing, speed, pitch, and articulation. (There as a hundred ways of saying "Yes".) It may take a page of finest prose to convey the spine-chilling effect of one piercing scream.

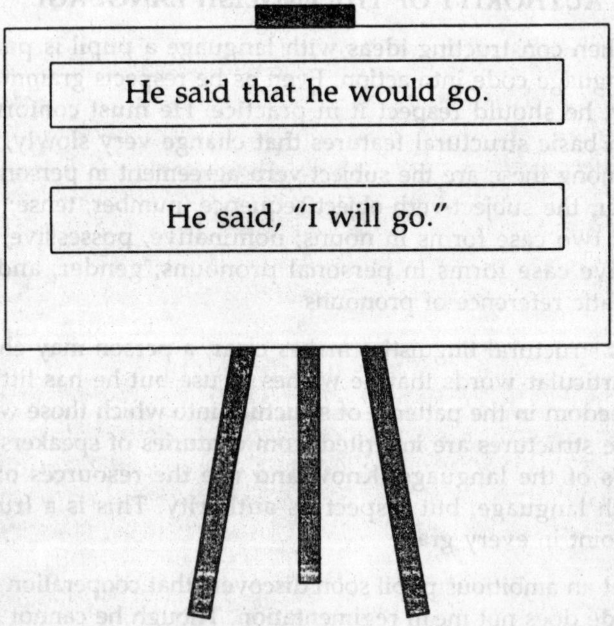

Fig 9.6. The use of a flannel board in teaching punctuation.

Even more subtle and compact are gestures—a shrug, a turn of the head, or a look of despair. There can be words in a wink. In the ballet and the theatre, communication and understanding are as dependent on movement and gesture as upon words and music. When we speak to a friend on the telephone, slight plays no part, and normal gesture reinforcement is lost, which we partly replace by changing out habits of speech. Again, if speech is literally transcribed into writing, a great deal of information is lost; conversations in novels are rarely like real-life talk, but are constructed by the author to convey the right impression.

The difficulties are evident. Elementary school children do not have control of the semicolon, dash, colon, brackets, and parentheses—signals which do much to make sentences and paragraphs "alive". They put commas where periods belongs, thus producing run-on sentences. Conversely they put periods where commas belong when they start using dependent clauses. Also they often omit commas where needed in connection with passages of direct address.

Two things can be done to improve the situation. Pupils can listen to the *sound* of language as a guide to written punctuation; and they can see varied samples of dynamic punctuation. Sentences on long strips of paper drawn through an opaque projector may be stopped at critical points so that pupils can either observe the punctuation which is there or decide what should be there. In the latter case, after the decision is made, the strip can be pulled a little farther, disclosing what punctuation the author had used. Fig. 7.5 shows how a flannel board can demonstrate punctuation.

Getting people actually to listen to the sound of the language as a guide to punctuation is difficult. Fourth, fifth, and sixth graders tend to be better at it, however, than adults, who are more heavily committed to written language. Listening exercises, notably with the use of a tape recorder, increase children's mastery of intonation patterns and thereby improve the background for effective punctuating when children speak or write.

Unfortunately for a writer, there is not quite a one-to-one relationship between a single bar juncture in speech and the need of a comma in writing, or between a double bar juncture and a semicolon.

Pupils could use the exclamation and question marks more frequently than they do in writing if they were better acquainted with them. The same is true, to a lesser extent, of the dash, colon, and parentheses. In speech they use the oral equivalents of all of them. It is doubtful whether textbooks and teachers should be as disinclined as they seem to be to present these instrument frankly and vigorously.

A RELAXED APPROACH TO COMPOSING WRITING

High school and college teachers speak of students "tightening up" when attempting to write. Something like expressional paralysis sets in. The behaviour is the more conspicuous because it often occurs in students who speak quite fluently and composedly.

It may be that the tensions originate in high school more frequently than in elementary grades, but teachers in the grades should try to preclude such developments. The difficulty seems to develop partly from the differences between the processes of writing and speaking, partly from the emotional climate in which writing is done, and partly from meagerness of the writing experiences from grades 7 to 12, especially in grades 10 to 12. College students speak of the labour entailed in revising a written discussion and the greater responsibility they feel when writing than when speaking. If, in addition to all these factors, there is an overformal classroom situation or an overmeticulous insistence on accuracy in spelling, punctuation, or syntax, the situation is almost certain to develop tension.

Discussion of Problem. In any grade, frank discussion of writing problems tends to ease the situation. Harris found this true in a third grade. During discussions the children told her what they did not like about writing. They said they disliked copying things over, and assumed that whatever they composed would be recopied two or three times. Because of that dislike, mainly, they had written very little, keeping their discussions brief. For the same reason they restrained their originality in idea and thought because much originality might result in more recopying, even rethinking. Spelling, punctuation, and "correctness" troubled them, and large numbers of red marks discouraged them.

Harris tried to provide incentives that would help children make the first draft as good as possible, so as to cut recopying to a minimum. As further aid she had the children write the first draft directly on white paper, not on yellow practice sheets, and also write lightly, with generous spacing, so that corrections could be made by erasing and inserting. Little recopying was necessary.

Adjustment to the Occasion. Language Arts for Today's Children suggests that pupils first put on paper the essence of what they wish to say, with major attention to the ideas they want to present. Then they should read it to see whether they need to change the opening, ending, sequence, words, or phrasing to make it clearer and more interesting. This amount of revision should be considered sufficient if the material will be used by the writer only, or if the writer plans to read it to the class. But if others are to read it, three additional steps are recommended: careful revision for form and punctuation; a reading by the teacher, who will suggest improvements for clarity and effectiveness; and recopying for a final draft.

Knowledge of Resources. Through experience the author has found that for writers of all ages, elementary grades through college, an acquaintance with additional resources of the language contributes much to relaxation. In fact, one of the characteristics consistently present in tense writers is a poverty of language resources available. Whether those students know but few resources because they have written little or have written because they know few resources is not clear.

DIFFICULTIES IN TEACHING CONSTRUCTION OF IDEAS WITH LANGUAGE

Difficulties arise from the complexity and subtlety of trying to teach a process which in its plainest form is a craft and as its best is an art. A number were implied in preceding pages: stressing correctness without causing pupils to tighten up from fear of making mistakes or of laborious recopying; getting a child to compose sentences which are free of the primer style, yet are neither too long nor too complex for his age; and introducing a caution about beginning sentences with *and, or,* or *but* without forbidding the practice.

In altogether prohibiting *and, or,* and *but* openings and prepositional endings the teacher is denying the composer one of the resources of the language. The caution against those words as openings has some merit during the early years when pupils tend to put periods where commas belong, but for those years equally strong cases could be made against *when, while,* and *because,* since children make fragmentary sentences from clauses starting with these latter conjunctions, too. No one has legislated against the latter, however, nor have cautions about them hardened into prohibitions.

All six of those words are safe as sentence openings for anybody who can apply the linguistic juncture test, which reveals whether the statement following *and, or, but, when, while,* and *because* can (or is intended to) stand alone.

Overstress on Simple, Compound, and Complex Sentences. It is difficult to direct study of the *simple-compound-complex* classification to sentences without overworking it. This is a danger in the upper grades. Study of this classification may increase the knowledge of grammar but it does relatively little to improve the art of composing. More profitably some of the time could be devoted to experiments and discussions on the effects of the various ways sentences can be phrased: the ways a sentence can be begun; how it can be continued once it is begun in a certain way; how ended; which way is best for emphasising a particular aspect of the sentence content; what other phrasings would emphasise the same aspect; which phrasing seems best to win a hearer's or reader's attention; which fits best with the sentences preceding and following. Such considerations relate to basic matters of long-range importance in the construction of ideas. They strike to the heart of the matter. They point to the future—to high school and college studies in the rhetorical classification of *loose, periodic, parallel,* and *balanced* sentences. The *simple-compound-complex* pursuit contributes little to compositional growth and rather soon reaches a dead end.

Individual Needs. When classes are large a teacher has difficulty developing the opportunities which composing offers for accommodating the range of individual differences among children. Composing is a highly personal achievement. If a teacher is satisfied with the median performance of a group for everybody, she is shortchanging her brilliant pupils and probably frustrating the least able ones. The fault, however, may not be the teacher's, but rather the administration's or the community's, for failing to keep classes small. Or the fault may be due largely to conventional language arts textbooks, which regiment the group rather than serve individual needs.

Fragmentation and Dullness. Another difficulty is attributable largely to textbooks. In many texts the several aspects of composing are subdivided into brief daily lessons. The result is a fragmentation. No large view of the choices and possibilities in language ever comes into focus.

A final problem must be mentioned. Fortunately it is not very common, but when it occurs it probably ranks as the most grievous difficulty of all: The class hours of composing sometimes become pedestrian and dull, even when teacher and pupils are working with what can be an exciting medium of personal expression.

PUPIL ACTIVITIES

1. Take six pieces of paper and put one of these words on each piece: *I, fed, carrots, rabbit, my, only*. Give one piece to each of six classmates and have five of those classmates stand in line so that they make the sentence, "I fed my rabbit carrots."

Next get the person holding the word *only* to join the line. Maybe he will stand at the end. Then the sentence will read, "I fed my rabbit carrots only." After that, have him go to other places in the line.

Talk about different places where he could fit into the line and about how the meaning of the sentence changes when he moves from one place to another.

2. "Anne," said the mailman as he held out a handful of letters, "this must be your birthday."

"This must be your birthday, Anne," said the mailman as he held out a handful of letters.

Said the mailman, "This must be your birthday, Anne," as he held out a handful of letters.

Said the mailman as he held out a handful of letters, "This must be your birthday, Anne."

Here you have four ways of telling about what the mailman said to Anne. Do you like one way better than the others? Why?

Ask your classmates what they think about the four. Can they discover a fifth or sixth way of arranging these ideas and words?

If you were to use one of these four sentences in a story, there might be another sentence in front of it and one after it. Do you think that the way those other sentences are worded would help you decide which of these four to use?

3. Four members of your class will be a committee. They will make up a sentence about a subject that interests the whole class. Their sentence might be about a book, an animal, maps, or space flight. It should be eight or ten words long. The other members of the class will not know what the sentence is.

Suppose the sentence is this: "The hummingbird flew like a flash from blossom to blossom." The committee will list the words on the chalkboard, changing the word order from what it is in the sentence.

The listing might be:

blossom	like
flash	the
a	from
to	hummingbird
flew	blossom

Next, all the class members who were not on the committee will try to put the words together to make a sentence.

How many seconds pass before somebody makes a sentence using all the words? Does anybody happen to put the words together to make the same sentence that the committee had started with? How do some sentence differ from others in meaning, even though all contain the same words?

If the class wishes, the committee could tell what punctuation marks belong in the sentence. There might be a period, question mark, exclamation point, comma, or other punctuation sign.

4. All along the street big crowds watched the parade.
Big crowds, all along the street, watched the parade.

Maybe your can find one or two other ways of restating these sentences. Do you think that each way makes some one item seem important to a person who reads or hears the sentence? What seems most important in the first sentence? In the second one? In the sentences that you made up? Does one way sound better than the others?

Now try the same experiment and questions with these sentences:

Cumulus, nimbus, stratus, and cirrus are four important types of clouds.

Four important types of clouds are cumulus, nimbus, stratus, and cirrus.

There are four important types of clouds: cumulus, nimbus, stratus, and cirrus.

5. When you have a ball of modelling clay you can make many different things from it. Maybe first you make a rabbit. Then you push it into a lump again and make a bird nest and a bird; then an automobile; then a crocodile.

You can do all that with clay because it is flexible, pliable.

Try to do something like that with a sentence. Move the ideas, words, and phrases around so that you give different "shapes" to the sentence. Perhaps you can make two sentences out of a long one, or one sentence out of two short ones.

6. See how you can move these four sentences from place to place in a paragraph. See which sentence you think does best as the first sentence of the paragraph. Which as second. Which as third. Which as the last one.

Here are the sentences:

Everything looked busy and bright that morning.

It was early summer.

A few bees had found a new place to get nectar, and they told the other bees in the hive about it.

Just beyond the woods along the meadow a field of clover had started to bloom.

Try shifting the sentences. How do the effects change? Which arrangements do your classmates like?

7. I will go *and* they will stay.
I will go *if* they will stay.
I will go *but* they will stay.
I will go *though* they will stay.
I will go *because* they will stay.

Words like the ones italicised above have been called sentence "switchmen". You can see that each of those five words sends the thought in its own special direction.

In newspapers and magazines you see many sentences having "switchmen" in them. How many different words of that kind can you find on one page of a magazine or a newspaper?

8. _________the weather is wintry I put bird food out on the window tray. ________I have sunflower seeds I mix them with other things. _______I am quiet, six or eight birds come. ______grossbeaks come, there is a lot of fun, ______ sparrows do more chattering.

Some important connecting words have been omitted in the paragraph above. In each space there could be a connecting word, and you can think about what the word might be.

9. It's fun to try various words in the blanks and notice how the different words change the meaning of a sentence. Can you see why connectives are sometimes called the switchmen of the thoughts in sentences?

10. You will find it interesting to notice how writers begin their sentences, and here is a way to see those beginnings very clearly:

<u>In a newspaper,</u> find a paragraph or two that your like. <u>Draw a line under</u> the first three or four words of each sentence, just as your see the lines drawn in this paragraph. <u>Then the beginnings will</u> stand out clearly and you can compare them easily. <u>Are the openings</u> a little different from each other? <u>Or are they</u> so much alike that they seem tiresome? <u>You can test out</u> the effects especially well by reading aloud just the underlined words, omitting the rest of each sentence.

You might like to try this experiment on some sentences that your have written.

11. In drawing there are a few shapes which you use quite often. Four of them are the circle, oval, rectangle, and triangle. Could different kinds of sentences be thought of as having "shapes" too? Think of examples. How could your describe them?

12. You've watched rugs, carpets, and pictures unroll or unfold. As they unfold you see nice patterns, designs, and colours spread out before you.

Have you ever noticed that sentences unfold or unroll too? They unfold word after word, phrase after phrase, idea after idea.

Sentences unfold for us as we listen or read. When we hear them, they unfold as we listen. When we read them they unfold before our eyes.

Here are four interesting ways of seeing them unfold:

(a) Watch someone write a sentence on the chalkboard. See how it unfolds or grows.

(b) Watch sentences being typed on a typewriter or as they come in on a teletype machine. Teletyping can be seen at a radio station or at some newspaper office or police office.

(c) Watch the "ribbon" kind of electric news bulletin. You see the words, letter by letter, come around the corner. Gradually the sentence is unrolled and finished. Often you wonder how the sentence will be completed.

(d) Type, letter, write, or paste a sentence on a long strip of paper and pull the strip through an opaque projector. On the screen a sentence will unfold the way it does on the ribbon news bulletin.

A strip of paper from a roll such as is used in an adding machine will be handy for this. It will hold more than one sentence, all of it typed, lettered, or written in one long row.

In these experiments you can notice how words and ideas are arranged to make good sentences. Even sentences that you heard or saw before may surprise you when you see them unfold in one of these ways.

13. Start with the sentence "Rain fell". Add words or groups of words to "rain" and notice how the meaning of the sentence changes. Then add something to "fell" and see how the meanings change still more with each addition.

Get your friends to try this experiment with another short sentence.

14. Your home state and the United States have many resources, such as forest, farm land, coal, oil, and water power. Our language, too, has resources for us to use. Words, sounds used when we talk, and punctuation marks for use in writing are three kinds of resources of our language. How many resources can you think of to add to these three? How many more can your friends think of?

STUDY ACTIVITIES FOR TEACHERS

1. We have an item that we want the reader or hearer to surely catch and remember. Should we put it at the end of a sentence? Or at the beginning?

To many people the end of a sentence is the most strategic spot. Others argue for the opening. Do our observations of hundreds of sentences support one or the other?

Most people agree that anything put in the middle of a long sentence is pretty well obscured from the general reader or hearer. Do examples support this view?

2. "A lot of people leave school remembering just two things about writing. First, that sentences should not end with prepositions. Second, that sentences should not begin with *and*, *or*, or *but*. Both are pieces of misinformation."

This was said by a college teacher of English. Is there evidence that it is true? Have cautions regarding these constructions been oversold to pupils and teachers alike?

3. Linguistic science identifies four pitches in English speech (marked 1, 2, 3, 4), four accents (ˋ ˆ ˘ ˊ), and four junctures or breaks in the continuum of sound (+ | || #). These are dynamic factors in speech.

When composing in writing, what punctuation resources do we have for representing oral punctuation? In what ways can punctuation be a dynamic part of written composing?

4.	
Declarative Interrogative Imperative Exclamatory	Here is the classification of sentences as determined by the *purpose or intent of the speaker or writer.*
Simple Complex Compound	This second classification of sentence is based on *grammatical construction.*
Loose Periodic Balanced Parallel	This third classification is rhetorical. It is based on *the pattern or shape in which thought is presented* to a hearer or reader.

Here are three major classifications into which sentences are grouped. The groupings are not mutually exclusive, and any sentence will have one name under each classification.

Why is knowledge of the third classification highly influential in composing? Do those four types include all basic "shapes" in which ideas or information can be packaged? Does the "shape" of a sentence affect the idea which the sentence contains?

5. Any statement produces some kind of effect, good or not so good. Some statements lead to more than one type of effect. Item 10, below ("a statement in active voice") in the first column might lead to the effects numbered 7 and 15 in the second column. Some effects are noticeable in both speech and writing; some primarily in speech, others primarily in writing.

How could we match each of the items in the first column with likely effects in the second column?

Kind of statement	*Effects of statement*
1. Interrogative sentences	1. Emphasising a point
2. Imperative sentences	2. Arousing curiosity
3. Exclamatory sentences	3. Clarifying a point
4. Declarative sentences	4. Prodding the attention
5. Sentences with predicate omitted intentionally	5. A feeling of intensity
6. Sentences with subject omitted intentionally	6. Strong picturing of scenes, objects

7. Simple sentences	7. A sense of action
8. Compound sentences	8. Compactness
9. Complex sentences	9. Informality
10. Active voice	10. Simplicity
11. Passive voice	11. Suspense
12. Unnecessary use of the passive voice	12. Leisurely procedure
13. Loose sentences	13. Stability
14. Balanced sentences	14. Weightiness of style
15. Parallel sentences	15. Force, energy
16. Periodic sentences	16. Change of pace in phrasing
17. Frequent use of participles	17. Conversational informality
18. Long sentences	18. Hard-hitting presentation
19. Short sentences	19. A rhythmic series of waves
20. Sentences that open with other than the subject (opening with a participle, conjunction, verb, adverb, adverbial phrase)	20. Change of pace in something presenting facts or ideas
21. Long paragraphs	21. Carelessness
22. Short paragraphs	22. Awkwardness
23. Sentences containing a number of long words	23. A "solid" page
24. Sentences containing a number of short words	24. Heaviness in pace and rhythm
25. Sentences containing a large proportion of nouns	25. Nimbleness in pace and rhythm
26. Sentences containing a large proportion of verbs	26. Tedium
27. Sentences containing a large proportion of adjectives	27. Weakness, passiveness
28. Sentences having a rhythm that is more nearly regular than the usual rhythm of prose	28. Suggestion of strength in reserve
29. Sentences containing contractions that are common in daily speech	29. Melody, perhaps emotion
30. Words, phrases, or syllables repeated needlessly and crudely	30. A static situation
31. Words, phrases, or syllables repeated purposely	31. Hard reading

VIEWPOINTS TO EMPHASISE THROUGH TEACHING AIDS

1. *Everybody composes many sentences every day.*

(a) A poster having on it statements like:

How Many Words Do You Put Together in Sentences Every Day?

5,000?
7,500?
12,000?

Which number is nearest to yours?

How many sentences do you speak or write in a day?

2. *Usually some words in a sentence can be moved to a different position. Such shifts change the meaning of the sentence.*

(a) With projector show a sentence, then demonstrate that some words, phrases, or clauses can be moved from one place to another in the sentence.

(b) On flannel board, work out several rearrangements of a short sentence. The several versions can stand beneath each other for comparison.

(c) Children dramatise the shifting of words. For example: each of five children carries a card having on it one word from the sentence "We cleaned the playground today." The six stand in line so that their words make a sentence. Then they change places, seeing how many times they can change and still have a good sentence.

(d) On a poster are these seven words: *the, on, were, shadows, curved, black, wall.* They are clustered informally and on a slant in one portion of the poster. Caption: How soon can you put all these together in six ways? Do the six sentences say six different things?

(e) On a table are a lump of modelling clay and a pile of eight slips of paper, each slip having on it one of these words; *now, the, is, shelf, the, yellow, on, doll.* Behind the desk is a sign: "See how easily you can make something with each of these." An arrow leads to the clay; another to the words.

3. *Often two or three sentences can be made into one sentence, or one big sentence can be divided into two or three. To do this a person may have to add or drop a word or two and change a few words.*

(a) On projector or flannel board start with two or three short sentences that are combinable and make one sentence out of them. Also start with a sentence that can be divided and make two or three sentences out of it.

(b) On a poster put two or three short sentences that are so related in idea that they could be combined into one. Caption: How would you make one sentence from these?

4. *The parts of a sentence can be arranged in different ways.*

(a) By chalkboard, posters, or projector, present the following outline:

We can arrange the parts of a sentence:

This way:

I fed the cat and put her in a warm place.

The game started when the rain stopped.

(One thing after another, strung together like links of a chain.)

Or this way:

After I fed the cat I put her in a warm place.

When the rain stopped the game started.

(Everything closely locked together in a kind of climax. The whole sentence must be read or heard before a reader or listener understands the most important part.)

Or this way:

I went swimming but mother shopped.

Winter is cold, summer is hot.

(Two ideas that are very different are put opposite each other. They make a kind of seesaw arrangement.)

Or this way:

I went into town, met my friends, and bought the groceries.

Regularly at eight o'clock I walk to school; at ten I go to the library, and at twelve I eat my lunch.

(Three or more things that are somewhat alike are said in the same way. There is repetition.)

(b) Use lines to help illustrate the four main ways of arranging ideas and facts in a sentence.

Some sentences are like this:

(Hung together loosely.)

Others are like this:

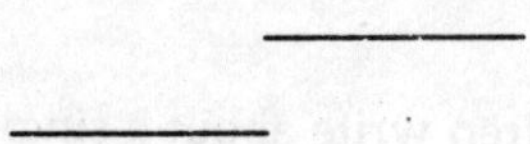

(Build up to the end.)

Others are like this:

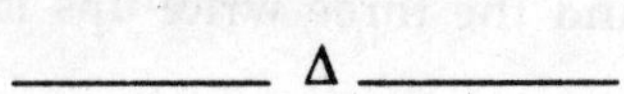

(Like a seesaw.)

Others are like this:

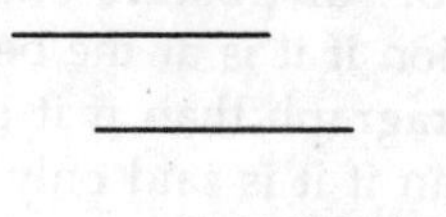

(They repeat.)

5. *The various items used in the English language can be put together in many different ways.*

(a) A poster or actual demonstration to bring out these similarities: Tinkertoy pieces and building blocks can be put together in many different ways.

The same is true of different kinds of words, punctuation, and sentences (long, short, questions, statements, exclamations, and commands).

(b) A poster headed: *Our language gives us these to use.* Beneath are a number of lines, some filled, some blank.

Words	*Periods*
__________	__________
long sentences	
__________	__________
__________	__________
__________	__________

At bottom of poster: Can you name five more?

(c) Start with three equal-size lumps of clay from which three pupils make a rabbit, a human head, and an alligator.

Have three other children write about a single topic that all agree on. Give some basic words that all are to use. How do their statements differ?

The three modellings and the three write-ups make an illuminating exhibit.

6. *A particular idea can be made to seem especially important to someone who hears or reads the sentence or paragraph.*

(a) With chalkboard, projector, or posters show that something gets more attention if it is at the beginning or end of a sentence or paragraph than if it is in the middle; if it is repeated, than if it is said only once; if it stands alone in a short sentence or paragraph than if it is in a sentence or paragraph with other ideas or facts.

(b) By poster, projector, or chalkboard offer this problem:

A reporter wants to tell three facts:

Jane wore a peasant costume.

She was at the Halloween party.
She won first prize for the best costume.

How can he say them in one or two sentences and make the wearing of the costume seem most important to the reader?

How can he say them so as to make the winning of the prize seem most important?

7. *A sentence unfolds or unrolls when we hear or read it. It gives us its meaning word by word, phrase by phrase. Different kinds of sentences unfold in different ways.*

(a) Ribbon signs give superb visual experiences. Word by word the sentence unfolds around the corner or onto the screen. If there is a ribbon-sign news bulletin in the area, the class can observe it from the viewpoint of how sentences unfold. Ribbon signs for advertising purposes are fairly common in banks and other business places. The equivalent appears sometimes on television.

(b) An opaque projector and a long strip of paper make a fine substitute for an actual ribbon sign. Using them, a teacher can control the kinds of sentences that appear.

8. *Connecting words show how ideas or facts in a statement are related. They set the direction of the thought.*

(a) On a poster or projector are two clauses which could be trend to make a sentence: "gold was discovered," "many people rushed but some are not connected, but beneath them is a list of connecting *and, because, when, as.* A transparency and overlay are effective. Caption: Which would you use to connect them?

(b) On a poster are pictures of a boy and an automobile. Beneath is:

from
to
He hurried in the automobile.
with
into

Caption: One little word makes a big difference.

(c) An animated-cartoon type of sketch showing a railroad track. Down the track an idea is coming. Ahead are switches, each labelled with the name of a conjunction, and each leading to its particular track. Caption: Which switch will be thrown?

(d) A poster listing a number of connecting words and showing a track-switching situation resembling that in c, above. Caption: Know your switchmen.

9. *When the words in a sentence are properly arranged the meaning of a sentence is clear.*

A poster shows a statement that is not very clear. (The statement might be taken from current classroom speech or writing.) Caption: How would *you* change this to make it clear? (A good version might be appended, under a flap. After thinking out a revision a pupil could raise the flap and compare his wording with the one offered.)

INQUIRIES AND PROBLEMS FOR STUDENTS

1. There have been estimates that a child of three speaks 7,600 words a day; a child of five, 10,500. Do some observing yourself. Perhaps you can make reasonably accurate counts for short periods that are typical. How many questions does a child of four or five ask in a day?

2. What can a teacher casually point out about composing while she is writing statements on experience charts? While pupils are reading from the charts?

3. List thirty items that are part of the resources provided by the English language. How many of your thirty are used by five-year-old children? By pupils in the fifth grade?

4. Children like to see what can be done with whatever they have at hand; how far a ruler will bend before it breaks; how many ways they can manipulate or reassemble anything that is flexible or that can be taken apart and put together. How can a teacher direct this kind of interest so that pupils will want to see what they can do with lanugage?

5. The English language has been said to be rich in prepositions but relatively poor in conjunctions. What is your opinion on this?

In this regard, how does English compare with other languages that you know?

6. Because a sentence is an organised unit that unfolds or discloses itself word after word, phrase after phrase, clause after clause, superfix after superfix, and closes with an intonation pattern (a certain pitch and a terminal juncture), how does a statement in language resemble statements in other time arts, such as music?

7. Recall Robert Frost's poem "The Road Not Taken". What connections do you perceive between its central idea and one's exercising of choice, wherever choices are possible, in the phrasing of a sentence? Are phrasal choices made early in a sentence irrevocable? And do they influence subsequent choices?

8. "Our gasoline fits any shape of tank you happen to have" was a sales gas. A corollary would be: The shape of the tank affects the shape of the gasoline that you put into it.

Those statements apply to liquids. Are they true for ideas also, when one considers the interactions between ideas and the sentences that state those ideas? Do some ideas fit into sentences of certain "shapes" better than into others? Does the "shape" of a sentence affect the shape of the ideas contained?

9. Part of the charm of good composing comes from variety in sentence patterns. An occasional sentence opens with a participle, adverb, modifying phrase, or subordinate clause. In conventional diagraming of sentences, as practiced in upper grades and high school, such variant sentences, however effective, are reduced to the predominant subject-verb-object pattern, to fit the standard diagram. Because of this, might diagramming tend to overemphasise the conventional sentence pattern and thus suppress pupils' interest in composing other patterns?

10. William Empson, in *Seven Types of Ambiguity,* says that inherent in the English language are at least five conditions that tend to cause ambiguity in statements. How many of the five can receive systematic attention in the first six grades?

The conditions are: (1) extreme flexibility in the meanings of prepositions; (2) indefiniteness in pronoun reference; (3) frequent identity of participle and verb forms; (4) variety of uses of the auxiliary forms; (5) the likelihood that a word may serve as several parts of speech or in several cases.

11. Discover some of the interrelations that exist between the teaching of composing in language and the projects and ideas offered in the chapters on imaginative expression, poetry, stories, dramatics, and "language arts among the arts."

8

Aspects of Literature

Stories, poems, and all forms of dramatics flourish in elementary classrooms. Something from literature will fit into any moment of the day. A poem, story, or playlet may be part of a long-range project. Or it can provide an interlude between social studies and arithmetic, or a profitable use of the four minutes available before recess. It is a natural part of story hours and reading periods. Again, it may celebrate a special event, a holiday, or a day of brilliant sunshine. It may be timely because a pupil brought along a rabbit or a bouquet of daffodils.

Thus literature may be in order at any time. The occasion may be unpredictable but a teacher can be ready. There may be a chance to teach something about literature in connection with rhythmic exercises and music. And the class can draw on literary experiences that happended outside of school.

Literature can be chosen for its own sake. If it links up with current class interest in travel, geography, the stars, the seasons, or daily news, so much the better. But if it does not happen to do this, it is likely to sell itself to children and produce its own justification, if given a fair chance.

In this last respect literature differs from other classroom work. Composing, spelling, reading, grammar, and penmanship have significance in proportion as they relate to a project or problem that the pupil is interested in. But literature can be an end in itself.

OBJECTIVES IN TEACHING LITERATURE

Literature receives glowing testimonials as a source of pleasure, enlightenment, and moral and spiritual vitality. The claims are great, yet nobody argues seriously that they have been exaggerated. Consequently the hopes of what literature should do for children are great.

A Friendly Attitude Toward Literature

One of the most influential objectives is that of maintaining or developing friendly attitudes toward literature. The quality of a pupil's lifetime of reading, playgoing, moviegoing, and television watching may be determined by whatever attitude is established. Generated rather than taught, the attitude usually is a byproduct of the total classroom climate. The teacher thinks she is teaching a certain poem, play, or story. Although she actually is presenting a specific selection, each pupil is acquiring personally a liking or disliking for or indifference to the whole situation. Attitudes are shaped less by the selections than by the tone of the circumstances in which young learners experience literature. Ingredients in that tone are the readiness of the children for the selection, the degree of buoyancy in the teacher's manner, and the play of the teacher's mind over the selection.

Perception in Daily Life

A second objective is to help children obtain from literature many impressions and revelations that supplement the impressions gathered from life firsthand. For example, a child has seen robins and clouds hundreds of times. Then he comes upon a poem or story about them. He enjoys the selection and thereafter looks at robins and clouds with more interest. Waterside animals gain new attractions for the child who knows *Wind in the Willows* and so, too, will taxis, for the class that has heard about taxis rolling along the avenue "like spools of coloured thread."

Understanding the Inner World

Related to the second objective is a third: literature may help pupils understand the *inner* world. Literacy characters, situations, and ideas can do much for a child who is making what Lerner calls a "Journey into the Interior." Children try to understand their families, playmates, social environment, and themselves. They need education in the emotions and should acquire emotional, aesthetic, and spiritual resources for adulthood.

Noting Diverse Viewpoints

A fourth objective is related to both the second and third: through literature a child can discover that on many topics there is more than one way of thinking. Different authors have different thoughts about the same subject. Pupils note this conspicuously in poetry, as they are likely to meet several poems on the subjects of swallows, rain, snow, work, and the stars. Experiences in visual arts can reinforce this discovery because different artists represent similar objects, and sometimes the same object, differently.

Observing the Language

Another point which can be developed throughout the grades is the awareness that poems, stories, and plays are examples of good composing in English—a fine handling of the same language which pupils use when reporting on a social studies topic, planning the day's programme, writing letters, or talking in the corridor. The awareness of this will grow from year to year if teachers mention the fact occasionally in connection with enjoyable prose and verse. The mentioning can be quite casual. It would relate to such language elements as choice of nouns and verbs, concreteness, sentence structure, rhythms, sounds, punctuation, and the position of words, phrases, or clauses in sentences.

Interest in Owning Books

Some teachers urge pupils to collect poems and stories. Such collecting tends to increase interest in literature and to acquaint the collector with many selections. It can be start toward a personal library. One caution is necessary: the collector should be selective. A pupil gains little if he clips, pastes, or files everything that looks like a poem or story.

Growth in Literary Enjoyment

Every teacher hopes that her pupils will progress toward the enjoyment of better and better literature. Children are sensitive to the fitness of things related to rhythms, word choice, figures of speech, plot situations, and the suitability of the general plan of the selection. But they need to extend their responses to more intricate literary forms and more mature topics if they are to avoid arrested development.

Gifted children may be able to progress on their own. They move from books and magazines enjoyed by average pupils of their age to samplings of adult material. Others need guidance to find selections that will help them grow.

An Effort. To extend their response, pupils must apply effort. The fact that literature should be entertaining cannot be used as an argument against stimulating pupils to do some earnest thinking about various aspects of plays, stories, and poems. Quite the opposite. Unless sought and found, many potential pleasures of the complex literary art go unnoticed. Unless children apply some effort their growth in literary enjoyment lags behind their growth in years.

Pupil experiments in original imaginative expression seem to provide the surest and the most pleasant way of extending literary enjoyment. Class discussions of stories, plays, and poems are necessary, too. Discussions should be supported by the teacher's deft comments on enjoyable features of prose and verse. Such comments sometimes are casual, sometimes frankly direct.

The situation requires a fruitful balance between "just enjoying" a piece of literature and giving some attention to the qualities which make the selection enjoyable. This is a delicate balance, and a controversial one. A popular viewpoint holds that adequate enjoyment of an art comes easily and quickly. But many curriculum committees and commissions on liberal education argue that study is necessary. They regret that people who expect pupils to work hard in other subjects suppose that no effort is necessary in literature. In actual practice it appears that the pupils who show the greatest satisfactions in literature (as in any art) go beyond what the average person means when he talks about "just enjoying" a piece of literature.

Appreciation. "Appreciation cannot be taught" is a statement that appears too often and too glibly in writings and lectures on methodology. It is easy to utter but it does not sound sincere. Usually it seems to be said less with a feeling of regret than with a sense of relief at having dismissed a difficult problem.

Research might show that the statement is a half-truth. Appreciation cannot be taught as "appreciation." No knowing teacher would exhort or command pupils: "This is a fine poem. Now appreciate it!" But she might have her pupils exert mental effort to discover certain qualities that can be observed and enjoyed if she believes that these things must be learned or "revealed" before they can be appreciated. In proportion as her pupils recognise additional enjoyable elements they become responsive to those elements, and in this sense she will have taught "appreciation".

PUPIL BACKGROUND FOR STUDYING LITERATURE

A teacher could scarcely hope to have pupils more favourably preconditioned for literature than they are in elementary grades. From daily life children bring memories of countless experiences and also of people, conversations, characterisations, human activities, plants, animals, and the sky. Their imaginations are stretchable, uncurbed by adult restraints of the matter-of-fact. But, like adults, they have dreamed during sleep, and during wakeful life they retain memories of those fantastic experiences.

Intensity is other trait predisposing children to literature. Partly it comes from the shinning freshness of life, partly it is a facet of emotions natural to childhood. It heightens classroom responses to the suggestive power of words, characters, fictional situations, and ideas.

Children also comprehend philosophical and aesthetic ideas associated with literature. These they understand in terms of their personal experiences and vocabulary. Though children have unsophisticated (commonly called "unspoiled") ways of looking at events and situations, they are surprisingly perceptive.

It is revealing to ask people, young and old, to complete this statement. "I began to like literature when. . ." Responses will range from "when my mother read to me," "when I had some books of my own," "when we wrote original poetry," or "when I heard a writer tell about how he composed" to "when I felt a challenge in trying to figure out what the author meant". By implications the answers carry suggestions for pedagogy. Beginnings of literary enjoyment are diverse and unpredictable. Apparently a teacher can find no one sure way; she must trust to many ways.

DIFFICULTIES IN TEACHING LITERATURE

Difficulties in teaching literature have three characteristics. First, they arise from the complex natures of both the literary art and the nurturing of literary appreciation. Second, poor results from teaching literature are less openly revealed than correspondingly poor achievements in spelling, reading, and language usage. Being part of a child's thoughts and imaginings, a meager knowledge of literature may remain hidden except, perhaps, in his conversation and his selection of literary entertainment. Third, the consequences of poor literary development are far-reaching; they affect a person throughout life, always limiting his use of the potentials which literature offers.

Easy Appeal

A difficulty lurks in the almost sure-fire appeal which stories, plays, and poems have for children. This appeal may lull a teacher into negligence. Her pupils listen or read attentively. All seems to be going well. And all *is* going well, as far as it goes. But much more could be done. Only a fraction of what could be developed from the selection is really brought out.

Literacy Craftsmanship

The complexities of teaching literature are increased by a lack of specific knowledge about the craftsmanship of verse, drama, and prose fiction. Without such knowledge any teacher is hampered in developing appreciation. She does not know certain important features to look for and point out in a selection. She is likely to dismiss her responsibility with the cliché, "appreciation can't be taught." Or, if she turns to matters of craftsmanship, she may either emphasise unimportant aspects or overdo mechanical analysis. In the latter situation, instead of accepting the structural skeleton for its basic worth, and then presenting a full-bodied work of prose or verse, she finds and presents nothing more than a skeleton. For corrective she could turn to writing workshops, writers' conferences, and books on how to write stories, poems, and plays.

Museum visitors experience a situation that is analogous to that of pupils in literature class. People view art exhibits in the company of two types of persons: those who are artists, or at least know the craft, and those who never have experimented with the materials of art. Conspicuous differences exist between what the two types of companions observe and comment on. Most visitors have no doubts as to their preference for the former type. Children feel corresponding differences among teachers who accompany them through the art of literature.

A Moral Or "Lesson". Related to a lack of acquaintance with literary craftsmanship is the danger of imposing too much moralising on a class after a selection has been read. A literary experience should be neither a sprint nor a marathon. A few observations or questions almost always help round out the experience, but children in the grades look forward to another selection. Direct moralising should not occupy much time. Literature, like any art, conveys its message by inference rather than by direct statement, and children normally make the inference without much help. Questions such as "Why did the character do that?" or "What would you do if you were in his place?" guide the thinking.

The danger of overworking the "lesson" is particularly great among teachers who know little about literary art. Such teachers see almost nothing to talk about except the "lesson". A moral of some kind is easy to find. So it is seized upon and overstressed.

Dated Selections

The passage of time causes difficulty in choosing stories and poems. Some selections which remain exciting to the teacher may have little meaning to children who know life from the experiences of the current decade only. Although much is said about the immortality of literature, a piece of writing does become dated.

It may become old-fashioned in theme, in viewpoint of the theme, in ways of handling emotional situations, and in craftsmanship. "Every generation or so a certain amount of Eng. Lit. dies," says Clifton Fadiman. Of course, some dated pieces, like any good works from the past, will give much pleasure to student who have acquired enough background to understand the older points of view.

Classics. Emphasis on "classics" is another cause of difficulty related to the passage of time. Most classics were pronounced great by judges who were both specialists and adults. School systems that insist on presenting such classics should be cautious lest the selections baffle pupils, who are neither specialists nor adults. Anthologists and curriculum planners may misjudge pupils' literary interests. Too many selections are retained primarily because they are traditional and revered.

Although a teacher should offer selections that the class can enjoy, her eagerness to do so should never bar literature of such caliber that will stretch pupils' minds and imaginations. A "classic" may be altogether suitable when the teacher knows how to develop it. Perhaps some difficulties arise less from the nature of the classics themselves than from an unreadiness of teachers to reveal the play of mind and art which those classics embody.

LITERATURE AND SKILL IN READING

As soon as a child starts reading independently, an interplay beings between his skill in reading and his experience with literature. That interplay is observable in grades 4, 5, and 6, where reading disabilities occur quite frequently, especially among boys. It becomes more noticeable in upper grades and high school. Reading abilities are related to achievements more closely in literature than in any other area.

Multiple enjoyment. When reading a poem or story a child has many more elements to enjoy—or to miss—than when reading ordinary factual prose. A half dozen literary features may be present, each a potential pleasure. There are characters to be realised through dialogue and actions; scenes and settings to be visualised; aptness of words and phrases to be savoured; humor; the author's plan or sequence of telling the story; the poetic turns of thought in a poem; the rhythmic and phonetic pleasures of the lines; the pattern of the poem; nonliteral statements to interpret; "between-the-lines" implications to catch. To enjoy these ten or twelve elements a pupil needs mental energy, and the more skilled he is in the mechanical and mental techniques of reading, the more energy he has left for finding those literary pleasures.

Rate. In literary reading, certain traits in addition to speed are desirable. Liveliness (even playfulness) of mind and imagination ranks high. It may be more important than speed. In fact, efficient reading of literature may call for rates slower than maximum. This is true especially when a pupil reads poetry. The quality of a child's experiences with a story or poem is more important than the fact that a selection was "done".

Sometimes the pupil should slow his pace to the tempo of oral reading, saying the lines aloud to himself or others, and perhaps repeating choice portions a few times. Oral enjoyment of literature should not end when children can read for themselves. Oral values continue to be just as important during low-maturity and advanced stages of independent reading. Fine passages of poetry or dialogue may deserve several repetitions, some or all aloud: one reading to become generally acquainted with the words and ideas, one to understand the passage better, and one or two more to enjoy elements like sounds, rhythms, and word arrangements.

Appealing Material. Whenever a pupil looks at a page of literary prose or verse many factors go into action, just as when a child reads nonliterary material. Eye span, eye movement, general health, personal interests, environment, degree of intelligence, social and emotional circumstances, and home attitudes regarding books and reading are among those factors. In literature, though, a teacher has one great advantage which may surmount some adverse factors that hamper a child: she is presenting material that has exceptional appeal to the reader. If the school library is well stocked with books and the children are encouraged toward free-flowing spontaneity in reading, pupils often exceed the reading levels they have attained in nonliterary prose. Gifted children in these circumstances have been found to read material much beyond the norm for their grades.

For supplementary and recreational reading, literature provides something richer than the contents of the usual series of basic readers.

STUDY ACTIVITIES FOR TEACHERS

1. When we were of grade-school age certain stories and poems were very popular. They ranked as the "big hits" of the time.

Which of them survived to be popular with our pupils? Which seem to have lost out?

If certain ones have lost out, can we find valid reasons why they have little appeal to children today?

2. Do we find that some stories and poems which eighth and ninth graders liked some years ago are now tedious to these grades but are enjoyed by sixth or seventh graders? If we note drifts of certain literary works down the chronological scale, what might be the reasons for such drifts? Different outlooks or experiences among pupils nowadays? Has the story or poem become part of the popular literary lore of the general public? Did television and the movies accelerate the drift?

3. How often someone commenting on the vividness of a poem or story will say "you can almost hear. . . ," "we can almost see. . .," "you can almost smell. . . !" References might be to horses' hoofs, the ocean, or a hillside of flowers.

Do we tire of that inevitable "almost"? Do we wonder why lively minded people can't *actually* see, hear, or smell what is so vividly represented? Why *almost*?

What remark would be better than "almost" in this situation?

4. At a writer's club called The Inkshed a poet, playwright, story writer, marionettist, and producer of animated cartoons are conversing. They talk about how each can present the need of slum clearance.

We are at an adjoining table. What remarks do we overhear?

5. There must be many unused literary patterns or forms in what we might call the "chamber of unborn literary designs." What might some of them be?

6. Part A, below, lists some occurrences and situations that are frequent in daily life. Part B names aesthetic qualities prominent in literary art and other arts. Reflecting on items in Part A we may decide that most of them are related to one item or more in list B. A wave of the hand, for example, might represent at least three: emphasis, suggestion, and symbolism. Interest in the arrival of mail can embody both suspense and climax.

Matching these lists should strengthen our awareness of connections between life and the aesthetics of literature. Most of the qualities giving power and charm to stories, poems, and plays operate in daily life. Do we find them stronger and purer in literature?

PART A

A wave of the hand.
Great interest in the arrival of the mail.
A wink of the eye.
One person mimics another.
The give and take of a conversation.
Well-arranged store windows.
Interest in a sudden fight on the playground.
A dinner made up of a series of courses.

Someone at a meal says, "No thank you, I don't wish any bread."

A person recalls with some pleasure a very unpleasant experience.

A remark, "It's all clear to me now."

A mother is singing her child to sleep.

Lobbying and "pulling strings" in politics or school affairs.

Dancers change rhythm when the orchestra tempo changes.

Mr. A—tells Mr. B—; Mr. B— tells Mr. C—; Mr. C—tells Mr. D—.

We view a painting too close up.

A woman shopping for a hat says, "A veil is so flattering."

People tire of repetition that is continued too long.

A certain person thinks that snakes are "horrible" but can't help looking at them.

Mr. A—says, "How *generous* you are!" meaning the opposite.

Mr. D—likes to listen to one end of a telephone conversation.

Mr. C—feels impelled to bow, though sitting in the audience, when an actor "takes a bow."

Someone says, "The door won't give."

A store window displays twenty-five packages of the same commodity.

A lawyer is pleading a hard-fought case.

A person phrases a telegram carefully.

A person cites specific details to prove that he really was at a specified place at a specified time.

We give a hint and hope that the other person will "get the point."

Part B

1. Conflict	12. Concreteness
2. Contrast	13. Crisis
3. Emphasis	14. Suspense

4. Pattern
5. Rhythm
6. Psychic distance
7. Selectivity
8. Indirection
9. Suggestion
10. Figurative expression
11. Symbolism
15. Empathy
16. Unity
17. Suspension of disbelief
18. Triteness
19. Variation
20. Instability
21. Coherence
22. Irony

7. Spectators at an ice skaters' ballet may be divided into two kinds—those who know how to skate and those who don't. We would have no doubts as to which group sees more in the ballet and enjoys it better. Those who know how to skate appreciate the skill and achievement in ways that nonskaters cannot begin to approach.

Can we find some analogies between this situation and that of two groups of people listening to or reading literature: those who understand something about how stories, plays, and poems are composed, and those who do not?

VIEWPOINTS TO EMPHASISE THROUGH TEACHING AIDS

The entertainment and publishing worlds are busy offering literary audio-visual experiences to the public. For our pupils and for our educational programmes such experiences can be fruitful. Many of the commercial offerings can even be used at a place and time the teacher chooses, particularly if they are available on films, phonograph records, sound or video tapes, or in print.

To be remembered, also, as potential audio-visual resources in literature, are the pupil's experiences in life: his impressions of his environment, his observations of people and animals, his reflections on experiences. All these give him sensory impressions of the materials from which stories, poems, plays, and biographies are made. Thus they give him points of contact with literature and a yardstick for measuring the truthfulness of literary works.

1. *A hearer or reader should have a lively sense of participation in the actions and thoughts of stories, play, and poems.*

(a) On chalkboard or a poster put two or three lines of a poem, or a sentence or two from a story or play. Choose passages that are rich in meaning or suggestion. Place the lines a little farther apart than normal. Caption: How much can you read between the lines?

(b) On chalkboard or a poster give two or three opening sentences of a story or lines of a poem. Caption: You take it on from here.

(c) On chalkboard, poster, or projector present eight or ten lines from a story or play, but omit one sentence or part of a sentence from within the portion quoted. Caption: What would *you* put in there? or *You* help the author.

(d) After the class has had a field trip, open house for parents, or some other communal experience, choose four or five words that serve to recall memories of lively moments of the occasion. Present those words, listed in a column on a chalkboard, poster, or projector. Caption: How many experiences do these words bring back to you?

(e) Drawings, done in the manner of animated cartoons, of what goes on in the mind of a person who hears or reads a specific story or poem. The pupils can select a poem or story being read currently and draw cartoons suitable for it. If they place their drawings on a long strip of paper they can pull the pictures through a "movie box" while someone reads the selection aloud.

2. *A hearer or reader can visualise a setting or scene in literature.*

(a) Maplike diagrams showing the settings of stories and narrative poems. These can be developed on a chalkboard or overhead projector or shown in finished form on posters or opaque projectors.

(b) Pictorial literary maps of countries and parts of countries.

3. *Literature is so varied that it offers something for everybody and for any mood or wish.*

(a) A poster showing a cafeteria counter full of books and magazines. People of different ages and occupations, and of happy mood or solemn mood, are all finding something satisfying.

(b) The class visits the school library. Each child selects something he or she likes. The whole class takes a moment to observe that such selection was possible and that it happened.

(c) Book jackets in exhibits and on bulletin boards or projectors.

(d) Books shown on television.

4. *Newspapers and magazines give news and opinions about books, plays, poems, and authors.*

(a) Bulletin-board mountings and table displays of magazines and newspapers in which literary sections and items are marked with crayon. Papers can be circulated in the classroom if enough copies are available.

(b) Bulletin-board and projector showings of news clippings and pictures relating to books and authors.

5. *In literature one meets u great variety of characters.*

(a) Cutout figure or drawings representing literary characters. Caption: Live with these in stories, *or* See these in action.

(b) Exhibit of pupils' clay modellings of their favourite characters. Associated with the exhibit can be a game of identifying the characters.

(c) Cutout figures, drawings, or clay modellings of two or more characters from different stories, plays, or poems.

Caption: What might happen if these two (three) met?

(d) Cutout figure, drawings, or dressed dolls of five or more character from one type of literature—plays prose stories, or narrative poems. The assemblage will be marked "a character party" from that type of literature, for instance, "a character party from stories."

(e) A classroom party (imagined or real) for literary characters. Prepare and post the invitation list. Invitation cards can be issued. If another classroom is interested in cooperating, some pupils from that room can come as the guests, each pupil impersonating one of the invited characters.

(f) A character cavalcade, consisting of pupils impersonating characters and stepping out of a large book cover.

(g) Drawings, done in the manner of animated cartoons, of literary characters and their actions.

6. *It is interesting to know how authors did their writing, why they wrote a work, how they composed and revised it.*

(a) Dramatic skits based on what is found out about the authors of *Alice in Wonderland, Winnie the Pooh, Peter Pan,* and other works that were inspired by factors which interest children.

(b) Exhibits of photographs of authors' manuscripts, especially manuscripts showing revisions. For some works, successive versions exist, and can be compared, Opaque projectors show such items well.

7. *Audio-visual suggestions in the next chapter, "Imaginative Expression."*

INQUIRIES AND PROBLEMS FOR STUDENTS

1. Ask twenty-five to thirty people to complete this sentence: "I began to like (or dislike) literature when. . . ." Include people of various age groups and differing educational backgrounds.

2. "Too little solid research has been done in the teaching of literature." Do your explorations support that statement? Identify three aspects that you believe are greatly in need of research.

3. Try to find out specifically what students means when they say that a teacher "picked apart" or "shredded" a story, poem, or play. Ask your classmates who represent various grade and high schools. Do you discover any consensus regarding what "picking apart" means or whether the procedure, in retrospect, is considered undesirable or desirable?

4. What do teachers mean when they talk about having pupils "just enjoy" a story or poem? How many of them imply something that would help pupils enjoy better literature?

5. After the age of three, children normally distinguish between reality and fancy, according to Susan S. Isaacs. Have your observations supported that opinion?

6. Many people believe that activities in imaginative expression provide one of the quickest and surest means of increasing literary appreciation. Do your experiences (or those of your friends) support this view?

7. After finding out the personal attitudes of fifteen children toward literature in general, try to determine whether those attitudes are related to the individual's skill in reading or to home attitudes toward reading and books. Did any child who was a poor reader seem to dislike literature when he had to read it but enjoy it when he could listen to it? Did he like plays when they were staged?

8. What signs of appreciative behaviour can one see while watching a class that is hearing or reading a piece of literature? Which signs are primarily mental? Which primarily physical?

9. What procedures seem best for getting grade children to make good use of the school library?

10. Today's crisis and streamer headline becomes tomorrow's calm article with a one-column headline, and then

next week's statistic. A football game or a flood agitates a populace. Before long it is tabulated data: 3 touchdowns, 126 yards gained; or 18 feet above flood stage.

Does an event told excitingly in literature recede too? Or is there about literature something that tends to perpetuate interest? Can you agree with Ezra Pound's statement that literature is "news that stays news"?

9

Drama and Language Development

There is a Broadway of drama on any street: Somebody waves a greeting to a friend. Someone else, noting the approach of a person he does not wish to meet just now, crosses the street or disappears into a store. Two haberdashery stores stand side by side, each advertising "the lowest prices in town". Five young people meet at the street corner. One of them slyly gives the "high sign" to another without its being noticed by the other three. Above the street a banner exhorts, "Vote Selkirk for Mayor". A billboard insists that you see *Skin of Our Teeth* at a summer playhouse three miles away. A movie theatre advertises *The Song of the Saddle.* A homeward-bound workman and a taxi driver sound their horns and race each other as the traffic light changes. Two women waiting for a bus look for shelter from the heat of the sun.

So drama exists everywhere along the street. More is occurring inside the buildings. Action, pantomime, interplay of rival forces, suspense, give-and-take in personal relationships—all flourish. Every school, classroom, and playground has its drama, too.

These situations are raw materials rather than finished scenes but they represent the stuff from which plays are made. For productions on stage, screen, and television are sub-divisions, aesthetically refined, controlled, and conventionalised, of the larger drama of life. In language arts, pupils and teachers work with the drama of the larger scene as well as that of the theatre. Dramatic play and pantomine of early grades draw their inspiration mainly from the larger scene.

OBJECTIVES IN TEACHING DRAMATICS

Clear enunciation, sufficient volume and inflection of the voice, confident poise before an audience, and naturalness of gesture are among the obvious objectives in school dramatics. Motivation to attain them becomes particularly strong when young actors realise why they should follow the teacher's advice to "speak out so that everybody can hear", "say it the way this character would say it", or "make the voice go up and down, so that it shows what the character means".

In dramatics children discover that they can say things through means other than words—through facial expressions, gestures, bodily movements (including various ways of walking, sitting down, and getting up), pauses in speech and gesture, and even silence. They can discover the importance of mental concentration, too. In imagination they must hear, feel, see, smell, or taste whatever sensory items they speak about or are supposed to experience on the stage. For practice children could be asked to imagine the sound of a power lawnmower, the view of a jet and its vapour trail, the taste of a peach, the smell of a potato that is being baked, or the feel of silk. Also they can attempt intense imagining of physical activities, physical states, emotional states, and the viewpoints of specific animal characters.

Significant in the pedagogy of dramatics is the objective of increasing children's skill in reading plays silently. This skill is somewhat special and it is one which many readers never develop satisfactorily. The silent reader of plays has to supply the stage action, the characters' physical appearances and gestures, and the setting. These he must create and visualise because stage directions of most plays are sketchy. They are not so specific as the running descriptions that children find in prose stories. A pupil experienced in dramatics is prepared to supply what the script merely suggests. He can read between the lines.

PUPIL BACKGROUND FOR STUDYING DRAMATICS

On reaching school age, children have acquired a dramatics background that a teacher can use to advantage. They have heard much conversation and spoken much. They have imitated people and animals and performed innumerable stunts, gyrations, and "tricks"—all the while exhorting people to watch what they were doing and how they did it. They spontaneously combine the spoken word with corresponding gesture. They seem ever ready to join in make-believe action, even though some studies in child psychology suggest that this participation is far less spontaneous than is generally supposed. Repeatedly they have experienced situations which were filled with personal conflicts with people and environment and observed conflicts that involved other people. To those conflicts they responded with strong empathy, projecting themselves freely into the situations of people and animals, real or fictitious.

School drama does its part, also, toward making dramatics natural to children. It meets the child at least half way. Notably it offers children a greater variety of ways to participate than does any other form of literature. Pupils can not only hear and see plays as produced informally in the classroom, but also act in plays, prepare puppet shows, manage the production of plays, read plays silently or aloud, and compose them. What is more, they can be active in dramatics even before they have learned to read.

PUPIL'S DAILY EXPERIENCES WITH DRAMATICS

Six or eight times a day a class in the grades is likely to use some form of dramatics. In one early grade, two pupils acted out portions of their reports in the "show and tell" period, one to show how policemen finally caught a monkey that had escaped to an apartment house roof, the other to demonstrate a way to clean a canary cage. A little later, when the class was interested in a Robin Hood ballad, two casts of three actors took turns in doing informal dramatisations of the story. Soon after that there was discussion of how people mowed grass in 1850, and one of the boys pantomimed the swinging of a scythe. After lunch three girls played the role of telephone operator, trying to observe the courtesies proper for that person. As part of the health lesson the class watched a box movie made by five pupils to show the proper use of a cake of a soap when a person washes his hands.

Such frequency is natural when teachers know the versatility of dramatics and the native fondness that children have for acting. Pantomime, dramatic play, and informal dramatising can be put into action quickly. Out of them come not only fun but also some of the day's best opportunities for improving voice projection, articulation, and platform presence. Transformed by a Robin Hood cap and jerkin a child will peak out and gesticulate with an abandon which he could not command to ordinary life. A similar change occur when he is behind the screen, operating a puppet and speaking for it, or when he is role playing in a personality different from his own.

In these latter achievements, dramatics can be therapeutic. Enthusiasts may have overrated such benefits, and many directors of drama repudiate the use of dramatics for therapy, but certainly some types of experiences in drama can relax personal tensions and increase confidence in speaking.

Exceptionally advantageous are the day-by-day occasions when pupils and teacher can talk naturally about the craftsmanship of plays. These moments come whenever anybody plans an informal dramatisation, a puppet show, or an original skit. There are discussions of how the characters are to be shown; the way the dialogue should open; how the actors should speak, gesticulate, and walk to represent the characters; and what conflicts or struggles the people or animals of the story are experiencing. Such discussions are technical, but under the classroom circumstances they are natural. The situation resembles that of a choral-speaking group deciding how to interpret a poem.

Sometimes activities in dramatics go beyond language arts, involving music, art, industrial art, and the dance.

School dramatics may be influenced by children's experiences with drama outside of school. Most of those experiences come from television and theatre movies and are largely beyond a teacher's control. Teachers attempt to do in dramatics what they do with newspaper "comics"—give the child samplings of something better, hoping that experience with good shows will make the child more selective in what he views.

KINDS OF DRAMATIC ACTIVITIES

The variety of dramatics mentioned below support drama's reputation as the most diversified form of literary enjoyment in school. Ingenuity and talent together are evoked by one type or another.

Pantomime and Dramatic Play

Pantomime and dramatic play predominate in the kindergarten and primary grades. They spring from children's natural interests in body movement, facial expressions, gestures, and pretending. Their inspiration comes from the daily experiences and little dramas of life: playing house, shopping, caring for a baby, delivering mail, directing traffic, packing to go on a trip, picking cotton, planting beans, putting the doll to bed, feeding chickens, making pies, feeding the dog, or imagining one's self to be a bird, cat, or aeroplane. The motif may be anything which children of early grades understand and to which they can respond.

Because it shows thought, feeling, and mood through action alone, pantomime is good training in bodily gesture. Not requiring speech, it gives the timid child an easy approach to performing for a group. It suggests the importance of action in drama and quite naturally leads the way to fuller participation through the addition of such speech as normally would accompany the gestures.

Dramatic play may be thought of as pantomime with words added. Like pantomime it calls for a lively sense of make-believe. The actor must identify himself with the part. The performance may involve a group of children or a single child.

Pupils start with a situation—serving a meal, for example—and carry it through with action, speech, and characterisation. For dialogue or monologue they rely on the spontaneity of the occasion rather than on a prepared script.

Both pantomime and dramatic play may spring up in impromptu manner. Neither requires rehearsing, costuming, or stage properties. Music and dance rhythms may be added, if feasible. For convenience a teacher should always keep available a bit of floor space which is clear or which can be cleared quickly to accommodate the action.

Shadow Plays

In shadow plays, the actors are behind a sheet or sheer curtain which is tacked, on a frame or suspended from a rod. A bright light focused on the sheet from behind defines the shadows of any actors who are between it and the sheet. The spectators watch from the front of the screen. Their view is clearer if the room is darkened.

If words are desired, they can be spoken by the actors, read by a narrator or narrators, or provided by a tape recording. There are no special demands of costuming, because the children are seen as shadows only. Animals can be represented by cardboard cutouts mounted on sticks. Some actions can be shown by movements of the hands alone, throwing shadows on the screen. Action should occur as close to the sheet as feasible, in order that the shadow outlines will be sharp. The screen helps shy and diffident actors overcome their timidity.

Puppets

As many as thirty-four kinds of puppets are listed in some manuals. Kinder groups puppets into six families, as shown in the table on the following page. The large variety is a happy response to children's interest in puppetry and to the benefits they derive from this kind of dramatics.

For early grades the best kinds of puppets are *finger, hand* (or *glove*), *stick* (or *rod*), *shadow*, and *paperbag*. *String* puppets (commonly called marionettes) also serve well in the grades as early as little ones can manipulate them. Single-string puppets are easy to handle but many-stringed ones require expert manipulation. Once introduced to puppetry, a group discovers an endless variety of materials and textures for their creations.

Suggested Grade Placement for Puppetry*

x—Preferred in the grade *xx—Usable in this grade*

	Kgn.	1st	2nd	3rd	4th	5th	6th	7th	8th	9th
Stick figures *(also called Rod)*	x	x	xx							
Paperbag puppets	x	x	x	xx	xx					
Hand puppets										
Simple	x	x	x	x	xx	xx	xx			
Complicated		xx	xx	xx	xx	x	x	x	x	x
Shadow figures										
Still	x	x	x							
Movable				x	x	x	x	x	x	xx
Masks			xx	xx	x	x	x	x	x	x
Marionettes				xx	xx	xx	x	x	x	x

*James S. Kinder, *Audio-Visual Materials and Techniques,* 2nd ed., American Book Company, New York, 1959, p. 510.

Finger Puppets. To make a finger puppet the child draws a picture of the chosen character, then cuts out the picture but leaves a short, narrow strip of paper at each side to serve as a band that can be pasted around the puppeteer's forefinger. Sometimes the character's features are drawn directly on the finger or on part of a nut shell, which can be stuck over the end of the finger.

Hand or Glove Puppets. Though of various kinds, hand or glove puppets are figures that slip over the hand and are operated with the forefigner (which works the head) and the thumb and middle finger (which operate the arms or, in animal puppets, the forelegs). They require the construction of head, arms, hands, and sufficient body to cover the operator's hand and wrist. They serve well when only one or two characters are to perform. A sock is a good choice for the basic material.

Stick or Rod Puppets. These are quite easy to make. Starting with flat cardboard or tag cutouts of the characters needed, the children draw in the features, add whatever colour they desire, and staple the flats to long thin sticks. If greater realism is wanted, two cutouts for front and rear views can be stapled together at the edges, stuffed with a bit of scrap paper, and mounted.

Shawdow Puppets. With a projector light or spotlight played on a screen, white wall, or window shade, or with a light behind a transparent sheet, shadow puppets are possible. Most children love the trick of holding their fingers for a rabbit head shadow with its wiggling ears and quivering mouth. Variations on this produce other animals and characters. Shapes can be made from cutouts. These need no colouring but should have holes to represent eyes. Shadow size varies in relation to distance from the light.

Paperbag Puppets. Either a hand- or a string-operated puppet is successfully made from a paperbag. Horns and ears are easily added by cutting slits, notching, or stapling. If the bag is to be made into a hand puppet the bottom should be rounded by stapling the corners. Then, if the bag is turned inside out, the rounded end makes a smooth area on which hair and facial features can be drawn or painted. Tissue paper or crushed newspaper serves to fill out the head and neck for shaping. A tube of cardboard, or paper rolled to fit around a finger, is placed vertically inside and fastened with a string at the neck so that the puppet fits over the index finger. Holes can be cut at the sides of the bags for the thumb and middle finger. Whatever dress or other clothing is wanted can be painted on the bag.

If the paperbag puppet is intended for strings the initial procedure is much the same as the one described above. The bag should be small, size 6 or 8. After it is inverted, stuffed, and shaped for the head, strips should be cut at the sides for arms. To those strips the arms, made of crushed paper, are fastened with bands of string. The body can be stuffed with soft paper and the legs formed by cutting the lower half in two parts. Joints should be padded lightly, so as to remain flexible. They are established by stapling the paper flat at the knees, elbows, and waist. The dress can be either crepe paper or cloth. Manipulating strings are attached to head, waist, and arms.

To give a paperbag puppet a movable mouth the pupils should cut a traverse slit in the bag at the mouth position. A recessed wedge of paper, possibly with teeth, too, can be fitted into the slit. Then the mouth may be opened and closed for speech motion.

The Puppet Stage. A ready-at-hand puppet stage is very useful in any classroom. Its presence stimulates thoughts of puppet making and puppet plays, just as the mere presence of puppets induces children to make up dialogue for them. With the stage right at hand, an impromptu dramatisation can be started without delay.

A puppet stage can be made out of a carton. Puppets are manipulated from the top opening or, in the case of hand puppets, from openings made in the side or bottom. A 2- or 3-inch border, left when the stage opening is cut, keeps the box strong and gives space or support for a decorative proscenium.

Improvised puppet stages have been made from chairs, card tables, other small tables, and even stools. The piece of furniture is laid on its side, with legs pointed toward the audience and the sides covered with whatever cloth happens to be available.

Pedagogically the puppet stage justifies itself amply. Timid children have the advantage of speaking behind a screen and for the puppets. Occasionally a timid pupil will begin experimenting when alone, particularly if he finds puppets lying at some inconspicuous place in the room. Operators feel that they must speak loudly and distinctly in order to be understood from behind the screen. Puppetry tradition calls for strong inflection of the voices. There is also an inducement to improvise dialogue because a person cannot hold a script and manipulate a puppet at the same time. When the manipulation is exceptionally complicated the lines can be taped ahead of time and played during the performance, so that the operators may give all their attention to handling the puppets.

Children making puppets and puppet stages must solve various problems related to colour, design, measurement, material, and lighting.

Flannel Board

Stories can be dramatised on a flannel board if the class prepares cardboard cutouts to represent the characters and action of a particular story. The cutouts must have a few pieces of flannel attached to the backs, to adhere to the flannel board. As the story is told or read, children put the appropriate cutouts on the board.

Box Movies

A box movie resembles a puppet stage in general design, but instead of accommodating puppets it provides for the unrolling of a scroll on which is a series of drawings or mountings that progressively tell a story. The scroll can be mounted on two vertical dowel sticks, or pulled through two vertical slots, one cut in each side of the box. Like a puppet stage, a box movie proves to be a stimulating piece of equipment to have in the room.

For the "film", there is a long strip of wrapping paper, cut to a height somewhat less than that of the box. On that strip, pupils draw or paste a sequence of actions and scenes, in black and white or in colour. If they wish they can do something roughly equivalent to an animated cartoon. They can find good stories to portray from folklore or history, or use their own invention. Finally, they roll the long strip into scroll form and pull it through the box.

The words may be provided by tape. A favoured procedure is to have each child compose a few sentences to go with the picture which he drew for the film. All the scripts are recorded on a tape, as continuity for the movie.

Informal Dramatisation

From dramatic play and puppetry the transition to informal dramatisation is easy. Most stories that the children enjoy rehearing (*Little Red Riding Hood, Pinocchio, Cinderella, Winnie the Pooh,* fables, narrative poems, etc.) break readily into scenes, action, and dialogue. The idea of acting out certain parts of a story comes altogether naturally.

What happens in good informal dramatisation is far different from the once prevalent procedure of looking around for a readymade play to "put on". Pupils and teacher together plan what scenes should be presented, what episode would make a good opening, how the playlet should end, what each character is supposed to be like, what each character should do and say, whether stage setting and props will be necessary, and how rapidly the action should happen.

When developing a dramatisation a class may start at any point in the story where pupil interest is high and the situation lends itself to being acted out. From this point the class can build both ways, deciding what should happen before this exciting scene and what is needed after. This procedure often is better than starting at the beginning of the story.

Young children make scenes brief and numerous. Older pupils develop scenes more fully, and in about the fifth or six grade they like to prepare a script for actors to follow.

Sometimes a play is done impromptu. After a very brief analysis, or even without one, a story is acted out. Spoken parts and the action are spontaneous. On other occasions the dialogue and action are worked out partially, but the pupils do not fully memorise the lines. Actors speak extemporaneously, filling in portions that they do not remember.

Original Scripts

Occasions for composing original playlets arise in every grade. Somebody wants to do a play about the first Thanksgiving, Captain John Smith, or Columbus. Or it may be a dramatisation of seed dispersal or of weather elements like sun, wind, clouds, cold air, and warm air. The result is usually a fine experience for authors and perhaps for those who present it. For the audience the experience may be either stimulating, mediocre, or dull, depending on the merits of the script.

The production of scripts that are worth the time involved in staging and listening becomes a major problem whenever children attempt original playlets. Some of the aspects involved, together with suggestions for improving the quality of a script, are discussed in the preceding chapter, "Imaginative Expression". When pupils have had very little experience with original scripts some teachers prefer to begin with dramatising a story found in literature because this gives pupils a start with a plot and good characterisation. *The Three Bears,* for example, or *The Pied Piper of Hamelin* provides a well-constructed core for a script.

Pupils' first attempts to compose dramatic sketches of their own should relate to simple, everyday situations, such as a discussion of which of two suggested places should be chosen for a picnic. Working with motifs which they know very well, children can make their first discoveries about creating dialogue and character and setting up a conflict.

Siks suggests that pupils should attempt to answer a number of "planning questions" in order to understand the characters' feelings, appearances, and actions, and also the action of the story, the dialogue, the scene, the setting, conflict and reaction, and the use of space on the stage. By their analytical nature the questions set pupils thinking about fundamental points related to their play. This is illustrated by three questions which Siks would have children think about regarding a tailor, a character in a play: "Once the tailor was just your age. What one thing do you think he must have enjoyed doing when he was a boy? Why? Of all the musical instruments there are, why do you think the tailor chose to play the violin? Why do you think the tailor became a tailor instead of a musician?"

Most scripts can be improved by revision, and the process of revision becomes an educative one for everybody when it is shared by the whole class. A tape recorder is a valuable aid.

ROLE PLAYING, SOCIODRAMA, AND PSYCHODRAMA

Related to educational dramatics are role playing and sociodrama, two specialised types of drama helpful in resolving personal and social problems. Although more therapeutic and instructional than literary, they are being used to increase a pupil's understanding of other people's situations and problems and to alleviate group conflicts.

In role playing a pupil extemporaneously acts out a role and a situation that are assigned to him. The role may be that of a policeman, nurse, mother, motorist, store clerk, or telephone operator, and the situation could be any that would be natural. The action or situation may or may not have any definite social or psychological relationship with the pupil, but as the role player projects himself into someone else's experience he broadens his view of human existence. When playing an adult role he will learn something about the skills or courtesies which the role involves. Consequently role playing is good for practising a skill that is to be learned or for preparing a group for a field trip or educational visit.

Since role playing resembles dramatic play, children take quite naturally to it. The pupils playing the roles need a few minutes for planning their scene, and the audience should be told to expect role playing rather than an ordinary dramatic programme. At the end of the scene or scenes, parts may be repeated, with a change of actors, thus giving a number of children the experience of playing roles new to them.

Sociodrama acts out a social problem: the feelings, prejudices, and sensitivities of a group toward another group, or of an individual toward a group or other individuals. Occasions for its use in the adult world are obvious. In elementary grades it can help a child fit himself into a group working on a play, improve his relationships with people outside his family, learn to await his turn to use the playground swings, be willing to share his toys, or realise that the teacher must give attention to everybody in the class, not exclusively to him.

Sociodrama therefore starts with an unresolved problem. It can be initiated by the telling of a story that ends with a conflict which is not settled. The class then carries the situation forward, playing out the end of the story and resolving the conflict. The unresolved story can be either drawn from an outside source or made up by the teacher to fit some problem situation in the classroom. In the latter case the teacher avoids using the name of any member of the class.

Several groups can play out the end of the story. Afterward the class can compare the solutions and decide which appear to be the more desirable ones.

Related to sociodrama is psychodrama, the dramatising of personal tensions. According to its advocates such dramatisation makes people feel better regarding their personal problems and makes them more willing to receive suggestions. Being both diagnostic and therapeutic, it is welcomed by counsellors of adults. Thus far it has been tried very little in schools, though it offers possibilities in cases of maladjustment and discipline.

Formal Dramatics

Full staging of plays, with costumes, makeup, stage properties, complete memorising of lines, and numerous rehearsals happens rather rarely in elementary grades. It can be done, but teachers generally believe that it demands too much time and energy in proportion to its rewards. Also it has the disadvantage of limiting the experience to a few pupils who in all likelihood need it least.

PUPIL ACTIVITIES

1. Make a play out of a story that you and your friends enjoy. You may be able to take much of the dialogue right from the conversation in the story.

2. By acting, show how to set a dining table. Perhaps you can do it very well without using a table.

Then show how you would receive guests at the door.

3. Stage and act out a street-crossing scene. One or two of you will be wanting to cross the street, on foot or bicycle. Someone will be the policeman, and others will be automobiles coming in opposite directions.

4. You can pantomime people doing the things that are listed below. Are you able to do it so well that your friends can tell whom you are pantomiming?

(a) A clerk wrapping a parcel and receiving the money for the purchase.

(b) A gasoline station attendant.

(c) A person driving a new car.

(d) A person setting a dining-room table.

5. By acting, show how the leafy branches of a tree bend and sway in a strong wind. Also show how the tree bends in the wind. Think of a tree that you often have seen.

6. When you watch plays at school and on television, notice what you can learn about acting and the stage. See:

(a) How actors come on the stage.

(b) How actors stand, sit down, and get up.

(c) How actors go off the stage.

(d) The gestures of the actors.

(e) How actors use their eyes as part of their acting.

(f) The way actors are grouped on the stage when three or more are on at the same time.

(g) How actors speak so that their words will be understood.

7. Think of some exciting experience you had during the last year. Perhaps you can remember one in which you were worried or frightened or were trying to do something that was difficult for you to do. Then plan a play based on what you remember from that experience.

What would you have happen first, when the curtain opens? How would you keep the play interesting as it goes along? How would you end the play?

8. Make a tape recording of a dialogue in which you and a friend imagine that you are George Washington and the officer in charge of food and other supplies at Valley Forge. Talk as well as you can on the things that Washington and his officer might have been talking about in the camp.

Then listen to what you have recorded. See whether you want to change some parts and add anything. After that, make a new recording and play it for your whole class to hear.

You and your classmates will think of many other historic people whom you could represent in a dialogue. In some cases you might have more than two people in imaginary conversation.

9. You and a friend can make a puppet play having two or three characters. If you do not mention the names of the characters your classmates will have the fun of guessing who they are. For the main characters choose people that your classmates have read about. Two or three people from history might be interesting—explorers, early settiers, or leaders in government. There also are interesting men or women whom you heard about in science or health—inventors, experimenters, doctors, and nurses. Or you might choose poets, story writers, or musicians.

10. Think up some happenings that you would like to see on an animated-cartoon film. You can use your imagination more freely than if you were planning something for living actors to perform or for your puppet theatre because an animated-cartoon film can show almost anything that you can think of. If you work out some pictures on a long strip of paper you can pull the strip through a box theatre.

Here are a few samples of what children have said they would enjoy seeing on a film:

(a) A flea is on a dog. The dog's hair is like a forest, and the flea uses a pick and shovel to dig in that forest.

(b) Someone is not listening to another person talking, and the words bounce right off of his ears.

(c) Four woodpeckers are pecking and their pecking makes a musical melody.

(d) Words dance along on telephone or telegraph wires.

11. Also through a box theatre your classmates might like to see "films" which you could make about something studied in school. If your class is interested in plants you could show how sunshine, rain, and warmth work together to make corn or some other plant grow. Or you could show how the roots of a plant work. Or how a blossom opens. If your class studied parasites you could make a good film about some parasite on a plant or animal.

As a special feature you and one or two of your friends might make a tape recording of dialogue or explanation to go with your drawings and play it for your classmates while they watch your film.

12. See how much you can make two or three characters say in only twenty words of dialogue. Have the characters talk as in a play. Make every remark, every word, say something that is important.

STUDY ACTIVITIES FOR TEACHERS

1. If a situation is stable—or at any rate too stable to be an interesting situation on the stage—how can it be made relatively unstable? What factors can be introduced to win the spectators' interest?

Suppose that each of the following situations is stable, in the sense that people and circumstances are calm and free of conflict. What factor or factors can be introduced to upset the stability? Why do some factors lead to more dramatic effects than others?

A party out on a picnic
A man alone in camp
A naval fleet cruising far from land
A Memorial Day parade
Three children going across a farm, on their way home from school
A man playing Santa Claus, in costume, to his family at home
A clear day in the North Temperate zone
Pupils in a classroom

2. Occasions for making personal decisions and meeting conflicts—even crises—arise in actual life every day. If we kept a tally of them, what might the total be over a twenty-four-hour span? How does the number that we face in two hours compare with the number present in two hours of average stage drama? In two hours of a movie?

3. Here are some events, circumstances, and remarks from everyday life, contemporary and earlier. Which of them contain such dramatic elements as conflict of forces, struggle, and crisis? Is there evidence that life and history are full of the essence of drama?

The longbow appears in battle for the first time.

Someone asks, "But is that *true*?"

People vote for reform in the city government.

Travellers in Arizona search for water.

A man restrains himself from knocking someone else down, even though he knows very well that he *could* knock him down.

Man's intelligence clears up a mystery and thereby frees man from a superstition previously related to something unknown.

Colonial peoples act to free themselves from exploitation by imperialistic governments.

Two electronics companies submit competing proposals to supply the control system for a rocket making a trip to the moon.

Travel time from the Pacific coast to the Atlantic is reduced from five days to a few hours.

An owner of a 5,000-acre ranch in North Dakota grows wheat, and so does the owner of a huge ranch in Argentina.

Man discovers that the earth is not the centre of the universe.

"Gold! Gold!"

"It never was done that way before!"

Two department stores buy advertising space on adjacent pages of a newspaper.

"I wish I were back home."

"Each minute seemed like an hour."

How many minutes does it take us to think of a dozen additional items?

4. By means of a tape recorder or shorthand we can obtain full records of ordinary daily conversations as they flourish when two, three, or four friends are together. Probably the recording can be made without the conversationalists being aware of it.

Listening to the recording we can note how talk in daily life differs from talk on the stage. We are likely to find differences in the extent to which dialogue stays on a particular topic, in the importance of what is said, in the degree to which every word counts, and in the pacing, probing, or progression of the talk toward some definite objective.

Would people be likely to pay to hear the conversation which was recorded? To rehear it several times?

5. We are on a hilltop. From there we see what is happening in the valley: people at work, children racing, cars on the highway, an impending crash of two cars at a sharp curve. What similarities of situation and feelings can we think of between such a hilltop view and seeing a play or movie in a theatre or on television?

6. One evening in a theatre we see a tragedy that emphasises the greatness and excellence of human beings as embodied in two characters, a man and a woman. The characters on the stage or film stand out in heroic dimensions.

The next morning we see men and women in the bus on which we are riding. Do we ever wonder whether those people around us and the ones on the stage the night before belong to the same species? Do the contrasts, if we note any, suggest some of the differences between art and life?

7. Could a history of 2,000 years of the theatre be written by telling the derivations and histories of thirty to forty words or names? Perhaps. At any rate, speculation on the possibility would be profitable.

Here is a suggested list of twenty-seven terms. We might want to make a few substitutions. The etymologies are good starting points for the histories of a majority of the words.

orchestra	Columbine	Blackfriars
tragedy	Punchinello	Haymarket
comedy	Harlequin	melodrama
chorus	masque	Savoyard
scene	farce	klieg (lights)
dramatis personae	*deus ex machina*	Mickey Mouse
amphitheater	*commedia dell' arte*	fade-out
Thespian	apron	iconoscope
prologue	limelight	kinescope

VIEWPOINTS TO EMPHASISE THROUGH TEACHING AIDS

1. *Dialogue in drama has special qualities.*

(a) A tape recording of dramatic dialogue from radio or television, or a phonograph record of a drama. Listen to it several times.

(b) Catch on tape some samples of ordinary conversations by two or three people. Listen to it several times, noticing how everyday talk and stage dialogue tend to differ on point like saying much in a few words and concentrating on one topic. How could the conversation samplings be changed to be good for use in a play? What parts would need to be omitted? What could be added?

(c) On a poster or chalkboard put a brief passage of good dialogue. Caption: Every word counts.

(d) Have drawings or cutout figures of two or three people—literary characters whom the children know, or a type such as policeman, nurse, farmer, store clerk, baseball player, or baseball umpire. Question: What might they say? *or* Can you give them one minute's talk? (Efforts to build up a suitable dialogue can be taped if pupils assume the roles of the several characters.)

(e) Observe good dialogue in puppet plays and informal dramatisation.

2. *A play is carefully organised.*

(a) On a poster or chalkboard, mention some story that could be dramatised and that the pupils know quite well: an episode from local history or some event in the history of exploration, science, transportation, or invention. Captions: How would you start a play on this? What would be your opening lines? How many senes would you have? What would be the last scene?

(b) Poster or chalkboard presentation of a plot for a play—probably a plot based on one of the motifs named in *(a)*, above. Caption: Your play has ten minutes on the programme. How will you make every minute count?

(c) Phonograph or tape recordings of plays which demonstrate that a struggle or conflict appears soon after the play begins and that some kind of conflict or tense situation is present almost everywhere in the play.

3. *There is enjoyment in plays that are based on struggles of the mind and spirit rather than on physical action alone.*

(a) Phonograph or tape recordings of scenes in which characters are worried and have hard decisions to make.

(b) A poster having two pictures, one showing two characters in physical struggle, the other showing one person trying to make a difficult choice. Caption under the second picture: He's (or she's) struggling, too.

4. *Gestures are important on the stage.*

(a) The line of a puppet play are taped. They are played back twice: the first time, the puppets are held in place but given little or no action; the second time, the puppets are given full gestures.

5. A *person can read a play silently and yet experience it strongly.*

(a) A poster or chalkboard having some lines from a play. The lines can be placed a little farther apart than normal. Caption: How would this be on the stage? or *You* add the action and setting.

(b) Read a play. Then see that play staged. Then read the play again. Notice how much action and setting we must supply in our minds when reading a script.

6. *The actor is very important in the production of a play.*

(a) Poster showing actors and a few lines which they speak. Caption: They make the lines live.

(b) Phonograph, sound or video tape recordings of a scene as done by different actors. The different effects achieved by different actors become evident.

7. *There are fine things to be enjoyed in movies and television.*

(a) View a short film or part of a film several times. Discuss what things are discovered or become more pleasing in the second or third viewing. What things become less interesting?

(b) With video tape a programme from television can be recorded, repeated, and judged in the manner of a film in (a), above.

(c) A poster with illustrations suitable for the caption: We choose our books carefully. Do we select our movies and television programmes with care?

INQUIRIES AND PROBLEMS FOR STUDENTS

1. After rereading the opening page of this chapter, keep a record of everyday "drama" that you experience personally or observe during a half day.

2. Note the importance and prominence of pantomime in daily life and at social gatherings.

3. Choose a story that children could dramatise. Phrase ten planning questions which would help children understand the characters' feelings, appearances, and actions.

4. Observe the total situation when pupils and the teacher are analysing a story preparatory to dramatising it. Do pupils lose interest in the story or cease enjoying it because of the analysis? Might an equal amount of analysis, done under other circumstances, be more likely to lead to complaints and tedium?

5. Attend several dramatic skits which children staged from scripts that they wrote. Could you suggest improvements in the dialogue? In maintaining the conflict? In developing the possibilities of a situation?

See whether you can offer additional suggestions after checking through the discussion of "Imaginative Expression."

6. The theme "world peace" is to be presented in various dramatic forms. Five people undertake to prepare the presentation: a writer for the regular stage; a scenarist for motion pictures; a puppeteer; a designer of animated cartoons for motion pictures; a writer for television. Each person wants to get his ideas across to the public and, at the same time, entertain his spectators.

What advantages does each of the five have in relation to the other four in achieving those two objectives through his particular medium? What disadvantages?

10
Prose and Language Development

"Once upon a time," a magic phrase, works in prospect and in retrospect. In prospect it makes a hearer or reader receptive to a story. The receptivity which it creates is always spiced with expectancy, a touch of excitement resembling that of the moment in the theatre when lights dim and the curtain starts rising.

In retrospect "once upon a time" recalls memories of stories previously experienced. Memories cascade from people's infancy to old age, eloquent with implications for teachers because they reflect the associations which stories and story teaching establish in human lives.

Anyone can sample those associations by asking people of all ages to tell what they think about first upon hearing the expression "once upon a time." Responses will come readily and have a wide range: being put to bed at night," "my father's knee," "a magic lamp," Goldilocks," and "my first teacher" to "the reading hour," "Friday afternoons," "graduation exercises," "How long ago was 'once upon a time'?" and "Now he's getting ready to fib like the truth." The range of responses will be wide but the tenor quite consistent. Soon the interviewer will see that children's stories touch human lives pleasantly at many points.

OBJECTIVES IN TEACHING STORIES

Practically all children are friendly in their attitude toward stories, and teachers in early grades hope to perpetuate those attitudes through the enchantment of stories told or read aloud. In middle and upper grades teachers try to extend the range and depth of enjoyment. They have several specific objectives.

Taste in Choosing Stories

Linked with efforts to help each child find stories that he likes is the hope that pupils' taste in prose fiction will mature with their age. Such maturing should carry the pupil through and beyond "the funnies." Brilliant pupils and skilled readers push ahead on their own initiative if they have a variety of books and magazines. Other pupils need guidance which introduced then to new areas and qualities in fiction. Such guidance requires some personal attention to each child, since general recommendations to a class will not stimulate everybody. It also calls for patience. Teachers succeed best by accepting, without belittling remarks, whatever material a child is reading at the beginning of the term. They start with such selections as he can enjoy and advance his tastes through a gradually ascent rather than by a jolt. Taste requires time to evolve.

The Art of Story Telling

Teachers look toward a literary subjective. They want pupils to notice how authors tell their stories and what elements make a story good. This objective is reasonably easy to achieve. Many stories deal with situations, type of people, and feelings that children know through personal experience. In such stories pupils can see how the author selected, arranged, and presented material so as to make characters seem alive through talk and action. Also it is easy to note that authors do not merely *say* that the characters had thought about something or had done something. The characters themselves talk and act, as in Figure 10.1. As for the dialogue, children can see that it makes a situation alive by dramatising it, and that in good dialogue every word counts for something. The events, also, reveal the skill of story tellers. The opening and closing items are carefully chosen. In addition to all these elements an author occasionally puts in interesting, somewhat incidental, observations or remarks as the story goes along.

George and Robert spent half an hour this afternoon making jack-o'-labterns. Each made one. They made them from yellow pumpkins. While cutting out the features they talked about the shapes and sizes of the eyes, nose, and mouth.

"Your pumpkin is bigger than mine," said Robert.

"Yes," answered George, "but yours is yellower and has a better shape."

"May be. Anyhow. I'm making the eyes a little smaller than you made yours. And I'm cutting them diamond-shaped because my knife is too big to cut them round."

"There, one of my eyes is done. I wonder how it would be to have a lantern with only one eye."

"Might try it sometime. Say, how big should the nose be? Twice as big as the eye?"

About, but a different shape. I'll make mine wide at the bottom. Last year I cut a very long, narrow nose. Everybody liked it, though. They thought it was funny, and said it looked like somebody they knew."

Both boys were quiet for a few minutes, too busy to talk. There were sounds of cutting and scraping.

"Now for the mouth," said George, after finishing the nose. "I want to give him teeth."

"That's hard," replied Robert. "You must cut notches to look like teeth and if you aren't careful the mouth gets too big."

"Or crooked, maybe. My knife isn't very sharp, but here goes! Oh! I cut too far down making that notch. Boy, he's going to have a big mouth! Maybe somehow I can fasten the piece on again."

"That's the clock striking," interrupted George. "We said we'd have these ready by four."

Again they were too busy to talk. Sounds of scraping and cutting were more industrious than ever.

"Done!" exclaimed Robert. He picked up his lantern and blew a strong puff to clear away bits of carvings. George held his pumpkin upside down and shook the loose pieces out.

"The only thing left to cut is the hole at the bottom for the candle," said George. "That I can do on the way home."

"Let's go," suggested Robert. "Say, I wonder if anybody ever cut ears on a jack-o-lantern. Or may be stuck something on the outside for ears."

They started home, swinging their lanterns and looking at them every few steps.

Fig. 10.1. Summarising *versus* dramatising situation. Dialogue, action, and careful arrangement of sequence make a situation come alive. They dramatise events by showing people or animals doing things and feeling happy, sad, or excited.

Summarising statements merely say that certain things happened or were said. Pupils meet them in newspapers and conventional classroom reports.

Such features of a good narrative can be pointed out without hazarding the enjoyment of a story. There rarely are complaints about a teacher having "picked apart" or "shredded" a prose story. "Grim analysis" is alleged far less frequently in connection with stories than with poems.

Enjoyment of Environment

Another personal development may be expected: A child is likely to see more in his surroundings and experiences after having read what authors have observed in people, animals, events, situations, and environment. To promote this objective, teachers select stories containing such observations and encourage class discussion of what the author has observed. They can emphasise those observations by playing down the plot. To do this they select one page or part of a page (not the opening) of a story which the class has not read. The pupils do not yet know the plot and therefore can more readily notice other elements, particularly what the author says on one page alone about the sky, for example, or about birds, roads, books, or houses; about people's gestures, clothes, or manner of walking. During their first or second venture pupils are puzzled. They feel lost, not knowing the thread of the story and lacking the customary interest in plot. But after a few trials they understand the purpose of the activity and enjoy what the author has perceived. They also are starting toward the mature discovery that many stories have much to offer in addition to plot.

Skill in General Reading

Teachers also hope that strong interest in story reading will improve a pupil's skill in general reading. Such improvement is likely to occur more through the momentum supplied by interest in the subject than through training in the mechanics of eye span, eye movement, word recognition, or suppression of vocalisation.

Factual Reports

Having observed the effectiveness of story tellers, gifted pupils may decide to use some narrative techniques in their factual reporting. Occasional reports in science, current events, or social studies would be strengthened if the reporter used dialogue and showed characters (or other elements) in action. This could be done without reducing the accuracy of the report.

PUPIL BACKGROUND FOR STUDYING STORIES

In the realm of short stories a teacher starts with a great reservoir of pupil good will. Children come to school predisposed to listen to stories, to tell them, and to read them. Quickly responding to a suspenseful situation involving people or animals, they wonder what will happen next and how the conflict will end. In addition they have a growing interest in places, things, and people, far and near, and in adventure, real and vicarious.

Children also hear about spectacular events reported in daily news. These events may rival fiction in excitement and heroism, but they nevertheless are assets for the teacher because they stretch pupils' minds to big dimensions, making them ready for the play of fiction.

Children are sensitive to personality and character. This sensitivity comes from their years of meeting people, watching them, and being dominated or otherwise influenced by them. It evolves through four stages, according to Watts. First is the black-and-white stage, wherein each person is clearly labelled good or bad, kind or unkind, beautiful or ugly. Next comes a pattern-of-traits impression of people. Each person seems to be a cluster of characteristics that work together. The third stage recognises the existence of flaws or defects of character in otherwise admirable persons; bad and good exist side by side. Finally, there is recognition of an "individualised portrait." At this stage the observer sees the subtleties of a personality and the great complexity of motives in any individual who is constantly interacting with his environment.

A pupil's understanding of literary characters evolves through similar stages. In literary appreciation he responds to characterisation that is within the scope of his current viewpoint toward people.

PUPILS' DAILY EXPERIENCES WITH STORIES

School days abound in occasions for stories. A class studying ships is ready for stories of sailors, waterways, and the sea. If a pupil reports on a television programme about a Swiss valley, stories on life in Switzerland are timely. A class that reserves a period called *The Story Hour* is on the lookout for any storybooks which the school has provided.

Whether the topic be travel, transportation, animals, insects, the weather, explorers, the United States, a foreign land or people, or the American Revolution, the great stock of stories in print offers something to match the subject. Stories also are of various lengths and various degrees of difficulty, thereby fitting into many occasions of the day.

A story generally requires more time than a poem for reading. Also it usually cannot be introduced quite so casually as a poem can be. Yet it has practical advantages. The reception of a story is less dependent on the mood or spirit of the classroom than is the reception of a poem. The phrase "once upon a time" or its equivalent strikes favour in almost any situation. Also stories tend to be so interesting that even a bungling pedagogy does not destroy the appeal. Suspense builds up from unstable situations, and conflicts work their ways to solutions, while pupils are mesmerised by hypnotic words and convincing details.

Furthermore, prose fiction is a literary form which is easily approachable. It conforms closely to the contours of daily life—

to realistic events known to children and to the life of the imagination, also familiar. Stories have points of craftsmanship to be recognised and enjoyed, of course, but these are fewer and simpler than the ones in poetry.

Yet another advantage helps stories fit into the school day: pupils can read them silently with much satisfaction, whereas a poem or play loses some effect when not spoken. Many stories gain by being heard, but generally the loss through silence is not so great as in drama and poetry.

In daily life children experience three kinds of activities which are akin to prose fiction: thinking about situations, people, and animals which could be used as material for composing original stories; reflecting on personal experiences which contain the story elements of conflict, action, dialogue, and interplay of characters; and hearing about other people's experiences. Those activities increase enjoyment of prose fiction.

SELECTION OF STORIES

Anthologies and libraries reveals the great choice of stories available to pupils and teachers. There is something for any grade, any topical interest, any reading ability. One finds folklore of past and present, animal fiction, fantasy, realism. Through translations, stories come from many lands.

Traditional Selections

Anthologies generally print stories considered standard, traditional, and likely to please many teachers. The collections are useful even though limited to short narratives.

Before complacently accepting traditional selections a teacher should look into Novell's *What Boys and Girls Like to Read*. This study of responses from 1,200 teachers and 24,000 children in New York State maintains that many stories (and poems) recur in anthologies because they seemingly have "stood the test of time," though they are not really popular with children. It also refutes the frequently stated opinion that children ultimately determine which selections shall be put into anthologies. Norvell says that "adults have decreed" the choices. The contents of anthologies, he believes, are too often determined by authoritarian writers, educators, and editors.

Norvell's observations deserve thought. Even those recommendations which, to some readers, may seem iconoclastic raise issues that need to be brought into the open. That is evident in the samples of his statements on "Guidance in the Programme of Reading and Literature (a Summary)" which follow:

Children well know what they like even though they can't tell why.

Make frequent investigations of what children enjoy and keep a cumulative record.

There are lessons to be learned from comic books and comic strips: the importance of (1) illustrations, (2) continuous action, (3) ease of reading, (4) ease of access.

When appraising discussions of children's reading recall: facts often are dull; the false often glitters.

Beware of advice from guides who are sentimental about children and sentimental about literature.

Mental development requires interest.

It requires stamina to adhere in practice to a rule all writers on children's literature acclaim: no selection is good for children unless they enjoy it.

Old poems and old stories are new to children.

When children of *all ages* are considered, humor is the most enjoyed characteristic of reading materials.

Many selections, particularly those classified as juvenile, increase in interest to a high point and then decline. Present each selection at its most favourable time.

Aesop's Fables and fairy tales are especially popular in grades 3 to 5. Myths, legends, and hero and folk tales are most popular in grades 5 to 7.

Girls enjoy many boys' books, but boys reject almost all girls' books.

Violent struggle is an unfavourable factor in reading for girls; favourable for boys.

Children approve and disapprove *individual selections* regardless of authorship.

Do not reject a book because it is one of a series. Judge each series book by the same standards used for other books.

When told as adventure, biography is popular with boys and girls.

Keep in mind the important differences between fairy stories (popular with young children) and fairy verse (unpopular).

When assessing new reading material for children, recall that in the past authorities have labelled as dangerous or trashy: *Tom Sawyer, Huckleberry Finn, Treasure Island,* the Waverly novels, Dickens in toto, and dozens of other startlingly new works of genius—they didn't conform to accepted canons. The same will, of course, happen again.

Reject completely the advice, "Consult your own taste," and enjoy the selection through the pleasure of boys and girls.

After more than twenty-five years of continued, careful research, a conclusion: Ultimately investigation will supersede divination in the field of children's interests.

Fairy Stories

Are fairy stories harmful for children? Do they contain too much cruelty and terror? Fairy stories survive those perennial questions. Criticism seems to exaggerate children's reactions to the "old witch," "big bad wolf," and "cruel stepmother." When transposed to pictures in movies and television such characters appear more terrifying than in a book or in oral narration. In the classroom situation a fairy story must be judged according to the psychology of the young listener or reader, not from exaggerated pictorial effects of television or movies or from the outlook of adults.

Fairy stories should not be mixed with science; but confusion is unlikely because pupils are beyond the fairy-tale age by the time they study much elementary science.

Animal Stories

Animal stories deserve their popularity. Emotional interest in an animal or insect is as acceptable as interest in any other type of fictional character. But scientists insist on one qualification: the characterisation of an animal should conform reasonably well to the biological facts of the animal's species. A story should not condemn the grasshopper for improvidence because he does not store up supplies in the manner of an ant or bee. Granted that a grasshopper's late-summer unconcern for future supplies may not be a good model for human beings to follow in temperate and frigid zones, such unconcern cannot be labelled profligacy of lack of wisdom. By late summer the grasshopper is on the retired list, according to his life cycle. He has been pensioned off!

Stories about other creatures deserve judgment in terms of instincts and life cycle. Whether human beings should follow the examples of those characters is a matter apart from whether animals should be condemned or praised for what they do.

A teacher can avoid stories which err in their point of view and still find plenty of animal fiction, some allegorical, some symbolical, some realistic. There are stories for people of every age, and they include some of the world's most cherished narratives.

Science has a fiction of its own, indigenous to the present decades. Science itself, with its breathtaking achievements, not only sets patterns for science fiction but also at times becomes more spectacular than its fiction.

DIFFICULTIES IN TEACHING STORIES

Although stories sell themselves to children, some activities can hamper rather than help the enjoyment. Luckily, ordinary shortcomings are easily remedied, and the difficulties in teaching stories are not very great.

Shortcomings may relate to classroom or library equipment or to poor planning of the day's programme. Those are remediable. When they arise from a teacher's lack of knowledge of what constitutes a good story, the deficiency can be remedied more easily than corresponding ignorance regarding the craftsmanship of verse.

Some children have little opportunity to discover the wide range of stories available. This may be due to a lack of books in the school library or to an oversight by the teacher. For the same reasons, pupils may lack stories that would fit into their classroom units or personal interests.

There can be difficulty in bringing boys and girls beyond "the funnies." This may be due to either a child's inability to read well or his lack of acquaintance with better stories. Classroom experiences suggest that children who have had happy contacts with standard stories are not very likely to spend excessive time on comics and crude accounts of violent emotions and crime. The best way to carry a young reader through the period when he might become addicted to substandard material is to have him enjoy something better.

Probably comics seem more stirring and less stupid to children than to adults because children bring great vividness of interpretation. That vividness supplements meagerness by putting something on the page when not much is actually there.

Opinion vary regarding abridged "children's editions" of books like *Don Quixote, Robinson Crusoe, and Gulliver's Travels.* Such editions lack the quality of the originals. Also there is the likelihood that children, under the impression that they once read the works, may never turn to the full text.

A critical time in story activity comes just after a child finishes a story. It is even more critical when a whole class completes the same story. A number of safe and profitable things can be done then, such as recalling the pleasures derived from the story, comparing this story with other stories, noting how the events were arranged, and thinking how the story could be dramatised. Occasionally it is best to do nothing at all. Sometimes wrong things are done—a wrong kind of book report, for example, assigned in the middle or upper grades, or some other project that is ill timed. An activity which is very satisfactory following a story in one situation might be very wrong after another story, or even after the same story, in different circumstances.

PUPIL ACTIVITIES

1. A girl from a fifth grade saw an unusual event on her way home from school. A pet monkey had escaped from the house of its owner and had climbed into a maple tree. From that tree it was able to reach the roof of an apartment house. There is dashed from ledge to ledge, seeming to have much fun with a policeman and three other men who were trying to catch it. After about half an hour it was caught in a net that was thrown over it while it was on a television antenna.

During the next five or six days the girl told her family and friends about the monkey. After five or six tellings her story seemed to hold people's attention better than the first few times she told it. She still told the truth about what had happened as she had seen it, but now her account was more interesting to listen to. Can you think of three reasons why it was more interesting?

2. In a newspaper we often find a new items that could be made into a play or story. The things which are reported in the item seem to be just the kind that we like to read about in literature.

Watch for a news item like that. When you find one, think what changes would have to be made in the way the news reporter told it if it were to be turned into a story.

3. Here are five ways of saying that the house was cold. You will find each of the ways used in stories. Do you think that some ways are better than others?

The house was very cold that morning.

The temperature was down to 42° in the house that morning.

The thermometer dropped to 42° in the house that morning.

"B-rrr! Did the fire go out last night?" Exclaimed Jane that morning.

That morning everyone wore his overcoat to breakfast.

Jane tried eating with her mittens on, too.

You can have fun thinking of some more ways of telling that the house was cold.

4. Turn to one page of a story. It need not be the opening page. Most likely some of the lines will be made up of conversation. These will be shown by quotation marks. Other lines will not have any direct talking in them.

Count the number of lines having conversation in them and the number of lines that contain no conversation.

Do the same experiment with four pages from several other stories. Do you find more talking in some stories than in others? Do you like the talking parts especially well?

5. Here are eight ways that authors show what a person is like in a story or play.

What the person says
What the person does
What the person thinks
What somebody says about the person
How people behave when they are near the person
The person's nickname
How the person arranges his or her desk, room, or house
What the author says directly about the person

How many of those eight do we use in real life to decide what kind of person a new acquaintance is?

Can you think of a ninth or tenth way to add to the list above?

6. Compare the ways that several different stories start. What kinds of openings do you like especially well? Some stories open with characters talking. Many begin with something happening. Others start with a description of the people, the characters, or the place or time of the event.

7. George is falling out of the boat.
His friends are rescuing him.
Now they have him on the beach.
Now they're reviving him.

Here are four things that happened. But the four sentences telling about them do not, by themselves, make an interesting story.

How would you change the way of telling about those happenings if you were making a story out of the accident? What things might you add?

Where would you start the story? Would you start with George falling out of the boat? With something else?

8. Have one of your friends write a list of happenings that could be put together to make one story. Six or seven items should be enough, and each item can be written as one short, separate sentence. But your friend will not arrange them in an order necessary to make a story. Instead he will mix them.

Then you try to find an arrangement that seems good for a story. Which happening ought to go first? Which next? Which would make a good ending?

Does your friend like your arrangement?

9. Get a classmate to find two stories that are short and then ask him to make a brief list of the things that happen in each story. Have him write each happening in one short sentence, each on a separate slip of paper.

Next have him mix the items from the two stories, so that you will have the happenings from the two stories jumbled.

Now you can try to separate the two lists. Can you tell which happenings belong to one story and which to the other?

You can go further and try to put the items from each story into an arrangement that you think is good.

10. You and your classmates have some favourites among the characters you met in stories. Some of them may be people; some, animals. Suppose those characters were to come to your school or home as real people or real animals. Do you think that they would seem like regular people or animals? What might they do? What would happen if they went among to a circus of fair?

11. Your school is going to have an open house programme for parents and friends. For this special event your class wants to have an exhibit of pictures that illustrate the stories which the class enjoyed since the beginning of the year. A committee

gives you a chance to draw these pictures that will show the characters and events in the story that you liked best.

What characters or scenes will be in your pictures? Do you think your pictures would be good ones for a publisher to put in a book, along with the story?

12. Watch the players in a game of baseball, basketball, tennis, or football. Notice how players behave when the game is very tense and close. Do you think that in those tense moments each player shows something about what kind of person he is? Does he show his sportsmanship? How he can plate with other people? His disposition?

Do characters in stories sometimes show what they are like in the same way? They are in trouble or in some other kind of tense situation. Does what they do in a tense situation show us much about what kind of people they are?

13. You and your friends sometimes tell each other about the books you have read. Here is something that you might try in order to make the reports more interesting:

Find a number of different ways to introduce the book or to start your talk about it. Perhaps too many of your classmates start by saying "The title of my book is. . .," "My book is. . .," or "The author of my book is. . . ." You probably are tired of those kinds of openings.

Might you start with something that happens in the story? Or perhaps you could begin with a character. One girl stated with this: "Would you like to meet. . .?" She named the chief character of the story. She could have said it this way: "Here's where you meet . . . ."

You can think of other pleasant ways.

Sometime, before you have finished your report, your classmates will want to know the title and author of your book.

STUDY ACTIVITIES FOR TEACHERS

1. What four reasons could be given to explain why a crowd gathers when a fight happens on a street? Do people enjoy an unstable situation in life as well as in fiction?

2. Stability and instability weave their way through athletic games as well as through novels and short stories. In tennis, for example, there is the major instability regarding who will win the series of sets making up the match. There are secondary instabilities connected with the playing of each set, each games, and each point in each game.

Specifically, why are baseball, football, basketball, hockey, and chess interesting as illustrations of stability and instability, and of struggle in a crisis?

3. If we count the number of conflicts, major and minor, which we have to face during each of a number of days we may be surprised at the total. How many of the conflicts are impromptu, arising from unexpected telephone calls or quick requests from someone? How many are long-term ones, allowing more time for deliberation? To what extent do decisions represent our character? Establish our character? Establish people's estimate of our character?

Do we ever seem to be more truly "ourselves" in our impromptu decisions than in our more deliberate ones?

4. "A night watchman at the textile plant was robbed this morning while reading a crime story in a pulp magazine."

There we have a summarising statement of an incident. It merely reports what happened.

How could we make the event come alive by embodying it in dialogue, action, objects, and sense impressions?

Of many possible ways, one might be:

"The saffron-haired woman stealthily pulled a dagger from her purse just as . . . ." These words Mr. Griffin was reading in a mystery story. Mr. Griffin is night watchman in the Ledgeworth Textile building. The clock had struck one in the morning. The light was dim, and Mr. Griffin adjusted his spectacles.

"Just don't move," growled a voice from behind. Mr. Griffin's spectacles dropped to the floor as he saw three masked men encircling him.

How could the following summarising statements be dramatised, each in a few sentences?

Janie and Harry, youngsters in their early teens, had a lot of fun decorating the Christmas tree.

Spring had arrived by the time we returned to the farm.

Two men were injured in the automobile accident at the corner of Fifth and Fairway Streets.

The man called again and again for water.

5. The named characters in Charles Dickens's novels are said to total 2,084. In addition there is the unnamed peddler in *Oliver Twist*.

Can one comprehend the creative energy required to originate so many characters?

6. Pupils and adults complain about "long, tedious descriptions." What are their reasons for the dislike?

Do movies, television, and picture magazines give everybody so many visual impressions of various places and types of settings from all over the world that readers no longer need elaborate descriptions, especially not the once common "set pieces" to establish the scene? Are nouns, verbs, and perhaps a few adjectives all that are needed to summon up mental images of most places?

Could it be that some readers who complain have not yet discovered that a description can be pleasurable in itself? Have they not yet been weaned from stories that consist primarily of physical action?

7. Here are remarks heard quite often:

"It was a good story after I got into it."

"The book was slow reading at first, but then it got going."

Is the trouble with the reader (lack of background for the story, addiction to "thrillers," unwillingness to accommodate himself of the fact that stories written years ago tended to have leisurely openings) or with the author (who devoted too many pages to preliminaries)?

VIEWPOINTS TO EMPHASISE THROUGH TEACHING AIDS

1. *Stories are fun.*

(a) Tape recordings of comments from people who have enjoyed stories. These comments can be from children and from adults who are interviewed about their memories of childhood reading.

(b) A poster having on it the opening sentence of an actual story. ("Once upon a time. . ." will do.) Caption: The author takes us on from here, *or* There's fun beyond those words.

2. *There is pleasure in watching the struggles or conflicts that happen in stories.*

(a) Poster, chalkboard, or overhead projector diagram showing a character (well known to pupils) being pulled in two or three directions by different wishes, worries, duties, or other forces.

(b) A tug-of-war drawing, showing conflicting characters of a story pulling in different directions. Caption: Who will win?

(c) A tug-of-war drawing to represent a mental struggle going on in a character's mind. Caption: There can be a tug-of-war in the mind, too.

(d) A picture of a person or a group of people in a quiet, calm situation—three people sitting on the bank of a stream, or two people walking carefree along the street. Caption on poster: What might happen that would start a story?

3. *Dialogue helps make a story lively and different from an ordinary report of an event or from a news article on something that happens.*

(a) A tape recording of an ordinary report about how one of the children became aware that a pet was lost and how he found it. A recording of the same event, this time told partly with the dialogue that happened when the child realised that the pet was lost and when he and others were hunting for it. Such recordings, heard several times, reveal the enlivening power of dialogue.

(b) A poster giving (1) a summarising statement (like a plain news report) of a brief event and (2) a dramatised presentation of the same event, now enlivened by dialogue and action. Caption: Which is ready to go into a story?

(c) A poster, stating:

We can just report that something happened: "Philip and . . . ." (A plain statement of an incident.)

We can tell or show it the way it happened. (A dramatised statement of the incident, enlivened by dialogue and action.)

(d) Opaque projector showing of a page from a story. Discussion of how the dialogue helps tell the story interestingly.

4. *In many stories we can find interesting things on each page, in addition to enjoying the plot.*

(a) On a chalkboard or poster, or with an opaque projector, present a portion (a sentence or two, a paragraph, or even a whole page) from a story which the children do not know. If the selection has been chosen wisely, the pupils will find something pleasant and interesting in the passage as it stands alone, without knowing of the plot as a whole. The interest may be in something the characters say, *how* something is said, the words used, what is said about an animal or the weather, how a character or situation is described, a conflict or struggle that in going on, or some other element that can make a portion of a story enjoyable in itself. Experiences like this help the child become a more perceptive reader, enjoying the fine touches which a good writer puts on every page.

(b) A poster mounting of passages like those mentioned just above. Items that make a passage enjoyable in itself are marked with crayon. Marginal comments can be added to point up the interests.

(c) A phonograph or tape recording of a story. Listen to a chosen portion of it. Hear it several times and discuss, as in (a), above.

(d) Poster with caption: It's nice to see how the story comes out—but we may as well have fun along the way.

5. *Increasing pupils' acquaintance with story characters.*

(a) Drawings and pictures of characters, shown through an opaque projector.

(b) Children vote for their favourite literary characters: the one they would like to have visit the classroom; the one they would like to take along to a baseball game; the one they would like to take to the country fair; the one they would like to have come to the school assembly; the one they would like to interview for the school newspaper; etc. A pictural graph can be made showing the results of the votings.

(c) On an overhead projector, draw sketches of characters—human and animal. Can the pupils identify the characters?

INQUIRIES AND PROBLEMS FOR STUDENTS

1. "Children may be missing something if they never read their generation's equivalent of Alger or Bobbsey Twins books, but if they read *nothing but that kind* of book they are missing a lot more." What are your opinions on that statement?

2. Do your friends regard comic strips and comic books as actually "funny"? Do they consider them cartoons? Serial stories? "Shorthand novels"?

3. Make a study of various ways in which pupils give oral book reports. What features mark the most successful reports? How would you help pupils avoid the tedious "and then . . . and then" sequence?

4. Obtain an anecdote that is new to you and tell it to your friends. Is your fifth telling more effective than your first? If it

is, why? What does this experience suggest regarding the importance of craftsmanship in story telling?

5. Survey the contents of one or two anthologies of children's literature. Which stories would seem to be most suitable for the particular classroom that you know best? Knowing the class rather well, could you recommend for it some stories not in the anthology?

6. Record on tape a juvenile story that you either tell or read. As you listen to the recording notice your timing, tempo, and voice inflections.

7. What were your two favourite prose stories when you were in the fourth or fifth grade? Are those stories still popular among today's children in those grades?

8. Ask twenty-five people to tell you their first thoughts upon hearing you say. "Once upon a time."

9. Discuss this: "A triple task is the teacher's: to know what books are available, to know children, and to bring children and books together."

11
Poetry and Language Development

A good poem is a snug parcel, skillfully packaged. When it is opened in a classroom a teacher and her pupils find numerous features to look at and think about. The contents prove interesting and likewise the wrappings.

All teachers and pupils do not see the same things. Some discover a cluster of delights. Some overlook pleasurable qualities. Others exaggerate the importance of one or two details. And some try to find things that are not there.

Suppose a number of classes heard or read these lines, composed and submitted anonymously by a college student and entitled "Baby Seeds":

In a milkweed cradle
    Snug and warm
Baby seeds are hiding,
    Safe from harm.
Open wide the cradle;
    Hold it high!
Come, Mr. Wind,
    Help them fly.

It presented in fifty classrooms by fifty teachers this composition would have a varied history. It might be read aloud or silently. It might be read aloud once, twice, or three times, then left without comment. Many classes would talk about the poet's idea of calling the seedpod a cradle. Some would notice that the writer speaks to the wind, and speaks to it as if it were a person, calling it *Mr.* and giving it a capital *W* in writing. A good many groups would notice that certain words sound alike, and some probably would say that the kinds of words used by the writer make them "see" a milkweed stalk with its pods and flying seeds. Somebody might add that the author says much in those few lines and words. And a few teachers or pupils might note how the piece looks on the page, particularly its appearance as compared with that to prose or of some other poem such as "The Wind", "Taxis," and "Wynken, Blynken, and Nod."

Discussion of seek dispersal would be likely to arise in a majority of the classes. Indeed, a special class interest in that subject might have been the reason why the teacher or a pupil introduced the poem. Or the poem might have been the opener for a study of seeds. A few groups, one might expect, would straightway concentrate on seed dispersal and neglect to say anything at all about the poem *as a poem*.

We can imagine a corresponding variety of findings by fifty groups reading the following verse, likewise composed by a student.

Shadows of tree
cut the snowy walk
into thirty pieces.

Each flake of snow
shines brightly with
its own fire.

The sky is as far as
the silver moon
caught in the maple.

Here pupils and teacher would not how the poet saw the path cut into pieces, the snowflake fire shining, the nearby sky and the moon caught in the maple. Something might be said about the "picture" words and the many things suggested in the few lines. There would be no occasion for remarks about words rhyming, but the absence of rhyme might be noted. There would be less likelihood of comment on rhythm than in "Baby Seeds." If both poems happen to be seen somebody might note differences in appearance and in grouping of lines.

This poem, like the other, might be read and enjoyed without any comment. Because it offers little occasion for moralising or for factual discussion on anything equivalent to the seed-dispersal motif of the first, no one would be likely to take off on a matter-of-fact digression that would neglect attention to the poem *as a poem*.

Popular poems meet similar diversity in different classrooms. It is the common experience of such selections as Elizabeth Coatsworth's "The Mouse," Robert Frost's "The Pasture," John Kendrick Bangs' "The Little Elfman," Mary F. Butts's "Dewdrops," Emily Dickinson's "A Bird," Dorothy Aldis's "In the Barnyard," Edna St. Vincent Millay's "Afternoon on the Hill," and Christina Georgina Rossetti's "Who Has Seen the Wind?"

Diversity is to be expected in connection with class enjoyment of any work of art. In poetry it can be profitable, but there is one point beyond which it should not go. It should not remove the poem from the category of poetry; it must not reduce a poem to something nonpoetic—to being handled as if it were a prose treatise, moral essay, or prose sermon.

A meritorious poem can stand with its own strength, and should so stand. It can communicate as a poem and is to be enjoyed as such. When made into a pack-horse it no longer is a poem. Most of its delights have vanished. A poem has its glory as a poem, in its own right.

OBJECTIVES IN TEACHING POETRY

Maintaining children's native responsiveness and maturing their poetic understanding to keep it abreast of their chronological age are worthy long-range objectives in teaching poetry. Between the two, the balance is delicate; there is danger of strangling the former through fumbling efforts at the latter.

The preservation of reponsiveness is a delicate undertaking influenced by diverse factors, some deriving from the complexity of poetic art, some due to marginal circumstances which superficially might seem only slightly related to liking or disliking poetry. More than any other form of literature, poetry is sensitive to influences which prevail around the edges of a classroom lesson. The teacher believes that she is teaching one thing. She actually may be teaching it, but at the same time, because of manner, attitudes, and the classroom climate, she, unawares, teaches something else. That something else may either enhance or eclipse what she thought she was teaching.

The project of maturing a child's understanding of poetry hinges on discovering more and more in the snug package of a poem. This becomes of great consequence in junior and senior high school years. The understanding of poetry needs to grow apace with the pupil's progress in other subjects. His understanding should be as grown up in relation to poetry as to science or social studies. If comprehension is in the young adolescent stage in those latter studies but still infantile in approaching verse, the pupil can be expected to dismiss poetry as childish or irrelevant. If maturation keeps pace with chronological age, the young person can interpret poems appropriate to his grade and in them find delight and wisdom.

The seven features to enjoy in poetry, discussed below and illustrated in Figure 11.1, are rational points in a plan for maturing poetic enjoymens. They must be development deftly, feelingly, lest a grim, mechanical analysis destroy the responsiveness. Through them a child develops an acquaintance with the nature of poetry. He might conclude that a poem differs from prose mainly in possessing these seven qualities in greater degree.

The Tantalising Mr. Jet

Why all that zooming, Mr. Jet,
When a fleeting glimpse
Is all we get?

Coy and gleaming
You tantalise
As off you race
Into space.

Why can't you

Ideas that stand apart from the commonplace and ordinary: a plane being spoken to as if it were a person; a tree acting as a traffic officer.

Nouns that name specific things and verbs that suggest action: Mr. Jet, space, pace, trees, arms, ice, traffic, wind, zooming, tantalise, race, directing.

A definite pattern: lines repeated; lines grouped; rhyme.	Slow your pace For just one time, Mr. Jet?	Rhythm that is more nearly regular than the rhythm of normal prose.
Compactness: much said in a few words; only 18 words in "Winter Trees".	***Winter Trees*** Trees, Arms in air And, except for ice, Of cover bare. Trees, Directing the traffic Of the wind.	Ideas put together unexpectedly: trees and traffic officers.

Fig. 11.1. Poetry that children enjoy.

PUPILS' DAILY EXPERIENCES WITH POETRY

In daily life children have three types of poetic experience: They hear, speak, read silently, or compose poems; they think about poetic ideas without developing them into poems; and they meet poetic ideas in plays, songs, instrumental music, movies, art, the architecture of fine buildings, or some other embodiment apart from verse. Experiences with the first type are most likely to happen in school; those with the second and third types may occur anywhere and at any time, but wherever they happen they can be a part of a school's poetry programme.

The school day accommodates a number of selections because poems fit into so many situations. There are poems for any mood or subject, and any length of time available. Thus, poem might be apropos when the class is interested in farm life or transportation. It could add just the right touch to Arbor Day or Halloween, or the day of a big snowstorm, or to the morning when a child brings a bird or rabbit to school. Being short, the poem is not likely to sidetrack other activities. Rather, if well chosen, it will stimulate them.

Poems fit the more readily into a school day because children can experience them in a number of different ways. Pupils may listen to them, read them aloud, read them silently, memorise them, speak them in choral groups, sing them, and compose them.

Occasionally a day brings poetic liabilities instead of assets. Pupils and teachers sometimes hear poetry misused. For instance, a speaker in assembly or elsewhere wants to reinforce a moralising point in his speech. He draws on "poetry" to support his idea. "I want to quote a few lines of poetry," he says, or "I would like to give you a little poetry at this point," or "As the poet says. . . ." Then he quotes fragments (often from the end of a poem) which may be fine enough when read as part of the complete work, but mere moralising bits and almost entirely unpoetic when out of context. Isolated, the lines become only versified essays. And they are quoted for purposes that have nothing to do with poetry.

This is a misfortune for teachers and pupils. Hearing much of this sort of distortion, they may develop incorrect notions of what poetry is. At best, it the teacher has been trying to develop the idea that poetry is a kind of expression to be enjoyed in its own right, the pupils may be confused. Were less of this kind of quoting heard, there might be fewer teachers and pupils, in high school as well as in the grades, reducing a poem to a prose precis.

FEATURES TO ENJOY

In the first two children can hear poems, speak them, and sometimes act them out or dance to their rhythms. There can be a few deft, casual observations about the unusual idea or point of view that the poem states, how the words sound, how some sounds are repeated, how the lines seem to sing, and the shape of the poem on the page or chalkboard. Such observations must be done with a light touch, free of any suggestions of "picking apart" or "grim analysis," and they need to be undertaken if pupils are to grow in poetry as they grow in other mental and aesthetic aspects of their lives.

Like any form of art, literary or nonliterary, poetry requires a pupil's thought, even study. There is much to discover, and discovery requires effort. What is never perceived is never enjoyed, and unless pupils see enough in poetry they will dismiss it as unconsequential. Indifference and hostility toward poetry in junior and senior high school develop from such lack of discovery. Young people's understanding of poetry has not matured as fully as their general mentality. With poetry lagging behind their chronological development, pupils do not see enough in it to make it appear worth their attention. They consider it silly or meaningless. What really happens is a thwarting or arresting of development.

Happily there are school activities through which pupils discover special features of poetry without being unpleasantly aware of the effort. Two of them are choral speaking of poems and original composing of verse. Each induces pupils to analyse the content and structure of poetry; each is an oblique approach to technical knowledge.

Unusual Turn of Thought

A bed becomes a wooden-shoe boat that sails the skies in Eugene Field's "Wynken, Blynken, and Nod"; a mouse talks in Elizabeth Coatsworth's "The Mouse"; a river tells about its journey from the highland to the sea in Sidney Lanier's "Song of the Chattahoochee." In Ralph Waldo Emerson's "Fable" a mountain and a squirrel argue; Mary F. Butt's "Dewdrops" personifies dewdrops, and in George Macdonald's "Little White Lily" a lily speaks.

This play of perceptive imagination, frequently called poesy, is one of the joys of children's poetry, as it is of adult poetry. It yields ideas and observations that are noticeably different from the commonplace and matter-of-fact content of normal prose. It gives pupils the best opportunity in the whole curriculum to become acquainted with and interpret nonliteral statements. It also challenges pupils to match the imagination of the poet.

Having become acquainted with this quality in poetry, children see that a major reason why many versified and "singing" commercials are tediously dull is the absence of poesy—a poetic turn of thought.

Sounds in Lines and Words

This pleasure of sounds comes sometimes from whole lines, sometimes from a word or two. Often it is helped by two or more words that sound alike, as in rhyme, alliteration, or assonance. Some words sound like the things they name. Some poems are so melodic that hearing them is like listening to music.

Sounds are conspicuous features in Mary McB. Green's "Aeroplane," Vachel Lindsay's "A Dirge for a Righteous Kitten," Leroy Jackson's "Hippity Hop to Bed," Robert Louis Stevenson's "The Wind," J. A. Lomax's "A Home on the Range," and Dorothy Baruch's "Cat."

English sounds available to poets are likened to those of a symphony orchestra in Robson's chart.

Rhythms

In some poems the rhythm is more nearly regular than in others, but in almost every poem it is more nearly regular than in normal prose. Pupils respond to it with a readiness that in quite willing to break into a dance. This is notable when they read poems like Lewis Carroll's "The Lobster Quadrille," Edward Lear's "The Owl and the Pussycat," Rachel Field's "Taxis," William Blake's "The Piper," Christina Rossetti's "Who Has Seen the Wind?" Langston Hughes's "Mother to Son," or Mary F. Butts's "Water Jewels."

It is easy for children to see that the order or arrangement of words has much to do with the rhythm. If some words are moved about in a line, the line may be rough instead of rhythmic. Easily understood discussions of rhythm, with examples, are in Hughes's *First Book of Rhythms* and on the companion Folkways phonograph record, *Rhythm of the World.* The book and record carry the subject of rhythm beyond language into music and visual art.

One caution ought to be observed. Pupils should not be misled into inferring that rhythm exists in poetry only. There is danger of such confusion when children hear people talk glibly about rhythm being a characteristic of poetry. Prose has rhythm too, although the rhythm of normal prose is less regular than that of poetry. Once clear regarding this fact, pupils are better prepared to understand the natures of both poetry and prose.

Concrete Words

Words in poems are of the kind that make a hearer or reader see, feel, smell, taste, or hear something. Many of the best words are nouns and verbs. They are concrete rather than abstract, specific rather than general. Such words are more numerous in a poem than in a passage of normal prose of equal length.

Much in a Few Words

A poem is like a tightly bound package. A few words or a line or two make a person think of many things. The class can see how true that is if the teacher writes a phrase, line, or two lines (with extra space between the lines) on the chalkboard and then records the many things which the short quotation leads the pupils to think of. Few equally short passages from normal prose would evoke so much. That is a major reason why poetry is the quickest way of saying something.

Almost any standard poem illustrates this compactness. Familiar examples from poems that children enjoy are Robert Frost's "The Pasture," Carl Sandburg's "Splinter" and "Fog," Emily Dickinson's "A Bird," and Edna St. Vincent Millay's "Afternoon on a Hill."

A Plan or Pattern

Each poem is put together carefully, according to some plan. Pupils see that lines sometimes are grouped into stanzas, each stanza having the same number of lines. Or the lines are grouped, but not into clusters of equal size. Frequently all the lines are in one group with no stanza divisions. Lines may be long or short. In one poem all lines may be of equal length, or some may be shorter than others. In many poems certain lines are repeated two or three times, according to a pattern. Rhyme, too, when present, usually follows a plan.

Children easily see the plan or arrangement when they look at a poem in a book or on the chalkboard, if their attention is directed to it. The design, itself, is fun to examine. Its pattern can be made especially clear if the teacher draws straight lines on the chalkboard to represent the poem's lines, making the drawn lines correspond in length and grouping to those of the poem. Coloured crayons can show which lines rhyme. Another way of nothing the physical design is by looking toward a light through the back of a page containing a poem. Then one sees the poem's layout very clearly. In some cases, there is added interest if the paper is held upside down.

Pupils who have observed the plans of a number of poems like to guess the arrangement of lines in a new poem just from hearing it read, without looking at it.

Patterns are conspicuous in most poems that children hear or read. Easily observed examples are in "Hickory, Dickory, Dock." Eugene Field's "Wynken, Blynken, and Nod," Lewis Carroll's "The Lobster Quadrille," Abram Bunn Ross's "Two in Bed," William Blake's "The Lamb," Mary F. Butt's "Wild-Birds," George Macdonald's "Little White Lily," Mary McB. Green's "Aeroplane," A. A. Milne's "Puppy and I," and Robert Frost's "Stopping by Woods on a Snowy Evening."

Indirect Statement of a Message

Most of the enduring poems put their points across by hints, suggestions, or figures of speech, not by outright declaration. The poet does not declare bluntly, "This is what I mean," or "This is the lesson." Instead he as much as says to his readers: "Here is something. Now you get a meaning out of it." Sir Philip Sidney believed that great poets "teach by a divine delightfulness." Many poems, of course, are not intended to convey a lesson or moral.

A number of nineteenth-century pieces state their lessons very directly, usualy in the last stanzas. But in so doing they break away from the tradition of poetry and become essentially nonpoetic, presenting versified sermons or essays. Thereby they also confuse both pupils and teachers regarding what poetry really is. The danger is reduced when a teacher touches but lightly on the moralising lines or ignores them. It disappears entirely if there is a discussion of how these poems differ from normal poetry in their statement of a moral.

Indirect statement of a moral or theme is notable in Edna St. Vincent Millay's "Afternoon on a Hill," Seumas

O' Sullivan's "A Piper," Ralph Waldo Emerson's "Fable," John Kendrick Bang's "The Little Elfman," and Elizabeth Coatsworth's poem beginning " 'Who are *you?'* asked the cat of the bear."

SELECTION OF POEMS

The Subject Index to Poetry for Children and Young People reveals the great number of poems available. Indexed according to subject, the poem titles fill 582 closely printed double columns.

Anthologies have listed poems according to the several grades but any list can be only suggestive because all children in a grade are not at the same stage of maturity. Neither are all pupils in the same mood at a given time of day, nor is any classroom of pupils, considered as a unit, in the same mood throughout a day.

For a particular grade, then, or for a specific day or quarter hour of a day, a poem's suitability may depend on how imaginative or fanciful it is; whether it contains a story; whether it is humorous, gay, or serious; the strength of its rhythmic swing; whether it has much rhyme, little rhyme, or none; whether it provides the children with an opportunity for bodily action while listening or reciting it; whether it has some lines repeated in playful refrains.

Likewise poets cannot be assigned to grades. Many writers known primarily for adult poems composed a few pieces that children enjoy. Also there are some authors not renowned for high literary quality who wrote poems that are popular among children.

A teacher's acquaintance with many poems and sensitivity to children's point of view seem to be the best equipment for selecting poetry. A teacher cannot foretell precisely when a particular poem will be suitable, but she can be ready with a promising selection, sometimes introducing it casually, slyly even, as Robert Frost has remarked, bringing it in "waywardly" or "wantonly."

CHORAL SPEAKING

Choral speaking of verse acquires its popularity justly. Poetry is at its best, for both speakers and hearers, when read aloud. The inevitable discussions of the thought and structure of a poem and the judging of varied readings develop appreciation of poetry. In addition there are the benefits to speech.

Types

Four types of choral speaking work best in the elementary grades: unison, refrain, antiphonal, and a-line-a-child.

Unison

Unison reading serves well when a poem contains little change of mood and no dialogue. Mary Austin's "Prairie-Dog Town," Robert P. Tristram Coffin's "The Skunk," Eleanor Farjeon's "A Kitten," and Olive Beaupré Miller's "The Circus Parade" could be spoken in unison. All pupils read together, and if the group has given any thought to "light" voices (the more delicate, high-pitched ones) and "heavy" or "dark" voices (lower-pitched and heavier), it tries to blend both kinds of voices in a suitable rhythm, volume, and tone. Unison is almost always the best type for a class that has little experience in choral speech.

Refrain

Refrain reading is natural for a poem that contains refrain. It is suitable for pieces like "Hickory, Dickory, Dock," Rose Fyleman's "Bingo Has an Enemy," or Vachel Lindsay's "The Mysterious Cat." Usually the whole group says the refrain and one person (a pupil or the teacher) speaks the other lines. Other arrangements can be tried out. Several persons can say the lines together; or the group can speak the lines, and one or two people the refrain.

Antiphonal

Antiphonal reading brings light and heavy voices into play against each other. It dramatises a poem that contains dialogue, questions and answers, or other elements giving contrasts. Elizabeth Coatsworth's poem beginning " 'Who are *you*?' asked the cat of the bear" suggests this kind of presentation, as also do Laura E. Richards's "Talents Differ" and A. A. Milne's "Puppy and I." From the nature of the poem the class can decide which lines should be spoken by heavy voices, which by light.

A-line-a-child

In a-line-a-child reading, a number of lines are read in solo manner, each by a different child. Chosen parts of the poem are spoken by the group in unison. Each child having a solo part must watch his cue, as in dramatics, so as to speak his line promptly when his turn comes. The a-line-a-child method works well with poems in which three or more characters speak, as in Maude Burham's "The Barnyard" and Walter de la Mare's "Bunch of Grapes."

New Groups

If her class has had little or no experience with choral speaking, the teacher usually begins with speaking in unison. Later, in connection with a suitable poem, she suggests that the reading might he divided. Pupils will soon discover that in certain poems such divisions bring out meaning and feeling, if the division is made suitable and the speakers do their parts well. There may be interest in trying some types of choral reading other than the four mentioned above.

A group new to choral speaking might well be started on relatively quiet poems and then advanced to louder ones. If started on poems which encourage loudness, the group may have trouble in suppressing its tendency toward loudness when soft, delicate effects are needed.

If a new group needs to develop more response to rhythm, nursery rhymes or other poems strong in rhythm are practical. Well-defined rhythms also help children stay together when reading.

Some poems give especially good training in sounding the vowels; others, the consonants. "Hey Diddle Diddle" and

"Hickory, Dickory, Dock" play up consonants, and Robert Frost's "Dust of Snow" and Elizabeth Coatsworth's "The Kangaroo" emphasise vowels. Such phonetic practice should include listening to playbacks on a tape recorder.

Phonograph recordings done by choral groups, professional and amateur, give impressions of how poems are interpreted elsewhere.

Approaching a Poem

When deciding how a poem should be spoken, the class is obliged to consider the poem's meaning, mood, phonetic effects, and over-all plan or structure. Most of those features are matters of craftsmanship and are more or less technical. But motivated by interest in reading the selection, a class looks into these features willingly and naturally. There need be little danger of anybody feeling that the poem is being "shredded" or "picked apart". This happy approach to studying the craftmanship of poetry is one of the great rewards of choral speech. Also, before the realise it, the class will have memorised several poems.

Lists of thirty-two poems suitable for choral speaking in lower grades and forty-seven poems recommended for upper grades are in Ogilvie's *Speech in the Elementary School.* The poems are grouped according to topics: animals, cars, family and home, Christmas, play, weather, folk tales and ballads, Halloween, humorous verse, out-of-doors, and miscellaneous.

DIFFICULTIES IN TEACHING POETRY

In the early grades the difficulties of teaching poetry are relatively few for teachers who understand the nature of poetry and its craftsmanship. Those teachers give poetry a fair change in the classroom. And given a fair change, poetry wins favour for itself.

But the situation is different when a teacher has only random and confused information about poetry. Difficulties show up in considerable number.

From Lack of Knowledge

Teachers lacking a stabilising knowledge of poetry give children distorted impressions of poetic art. When presenting a poem, such teachers may be afraid of it, smother it with emotion, love it to death, hold it sacrosanct, crush it into an essay, laboriously dissect it, or use it as a take-off for a flight into personal interpretation of "what the author means."

Correspondingly their pupils develop confused notions about what poetry is or is supposed to be. Young people become uncertain whether a poem is a packhorse for social studies, ethics, and philosophy; a mechanical fabrication; an intellectual and aesthetic puzzle; a study in vocabulary; something that needs to be converted into prose; a work of art; an occasion for "busywork"; an object for grim analysis; a potion of intoxicating hashish; something sissy, concerned excessively with what is "fancy" or "pretty"; a vague mistiness; or a bejeweled gossamer, untouchable.

Reduction of a Poem to Prose

In some classrooms a poem, after having been read, is straightway reduced to a prose statement of its theme or "lesson." This statement thenceforth is accepted as if it were the poem. It is presented for what it is not. It is no more the poem than a half-spoonful of sweet liquid is the ball of spun candy at the county fair. The procedure supports the quip of the child who defined poetry as a "thing you make prose out of."

Search for "Hidden Meanings"

Some teachers are obsessed with the notion that every poem has a hidden meaning or lesson. They never are satisfied with face value of a poem. They hunt for edifying meanings in selections that apparently were composed without intent of a "moral." This quest confuses children. It also distracts children from enjoying the poem as a poem.

Solemnity and Awe

Poetry sometimes is presented too solemnly, even grimly. This solemnity (not to be confused with earnstness) occurs most frequently among teachers who know relatively little about poetry. The limited knowledge tends to make the teacher solemn, probably out of self-defense. Unsure of herself, the teacher is afraid to let her mind be playful, ardent, or whimsical as the poem might suggest.

An aura of awe and mystery prevails in some presentations of poetry. A breathless tone or manner of speech usually is part of this situation. Accompanying it is an attitude of "touch it not."

Such procedure may be all right for hearers who already understand poetry as poetry. It is all right for any hearer, once in a while. But if this is the only way a class gets to know poetry, there is no firm basis for growth in appreciation. To many children poetry will become remote, baffling, even silly. By junior high school years the pupil concludes, "Poetry is not for me."

Underanalysis or Overanalysis

There are dangers of operating in two opposite extremes—presenting all poems without comment, on the theory that they are to be "just enjoyed," and overanalysing poems, with heavy emphasis on mechanical aspects of poetry. The former, whether arising from ignorance of anything to say or an honest conviction that a no-comment policy is best, can result in arrested development, because in every art there are elements to be discovered and learned, and learned best through guidance. The latter—overanalysis—usually overworks some obvious aspect like rhyme or meter. Here again lack of information is partly to blame. A teacher who knows poetry well finds additional elements for a class to experiment with or talk about. Her handling of mechanical aspects is not mechanical. She is also less grim. She knows enough about the craftsmanship of verse to be confidently relaxed when discussing it.

Excessive Attention to Rhyme

The importance of rhyme is much overstressed. Elementary textbooks in language commonly err in this. They give the child a verse couplet with the second rhyming word omitted, as in:

Bright and wide and very high
A rainbow spreads across the . . . .

Pupils are asked to fill in the bland. Not only does the quest for the altogether obvious word offer no mental challenge, it provides no literary or vocabulary growth either, for the same reason of obviousness. Moreover, the exercise focuses attention on rhyme, and particularly on rhyme in short-line couplet form—a form that is little used today in standard contemporary poetry, except in humorous verse. Thus the exercise wastes time and misdirects pupils.

A simple change would improve the exercise. An internal word, not the rhyming word, could be the one omitted:

Bright and wide and very high
A rainbow . . . . across the sky—

The rhyme, being supplied, would not draw undue attention to itself. Pupils could explore the possibilities of various words to fill the blank: *stretched, spread, arched, rose, leaped, sprang, shone, blazed, hung*—these and others might be tried for suitability. There would be plenty of mental challenge. Matters of rhythm, word length, sound, imagination, meaning, and poetic idea would come up for discussion. The two-line exercises, transformed, would be a *literary* experience.

From Neglect of Allied Arts

Too often poetry activities are conducted without knowledge of how the pupils' experiences with poems might be illuminated by their experiences with painting, drawing, rhythmic exercises, and music. The latter experiences give children impressions of rhythm, repetition, pattern, imaginative and figurative statements of ideas, and the way ideas are stated by suggestion rather than by direct telling.

PUPIL ACTIVITIES

1. "The Mysterious Cat" by Vachel Lindsay, "Aeroplane" by Mary McB. Green, and "The Wind" by Robert Louis Stevenson are poems containing sounds much like the sounds made by a cat, an airplane, and the wind. You notice this when you read the poems aloud.

One group of the children enjoyed these poems so much that they began talking about subjects that might be used for other poems which could have special sounds in their lines and words. They thought that these subjects would be good: footsteps, old cars, snoring, school lockers, rain on a roof, vacuum cleaners.

Can you think of three or four more subjects for such poems?

2. Eugene Field's poem "Wynken, Blynken, and Nod" says that going to sleep is like going on a voyage with a bed as a boat. Carl Sandburg's "Fog" says that fog behaves like a cat. In Sidney Lanier's "Song of the Chattahoochee" a river talks, telling about its journey from the mountains to the sea.

Many poems contain imaginative ideas like those. In each the poet thought about something in a way that was different from the way people usually think about that subject.

What special imaginative ideas do you find in the poems named below?

"Taxis" by Rachel Field
"My Shadow" by Robert Louis Stevenson
"October's Party" by George Cooper
"Moon Song" by Hilda Conkling
"The Moon's the North Wind's Cooky" by Vachel Lindsay

3. You can tell poetry from prose when you see it on a page. A poem looks different from a prose sentence or paragraph.

Have you ever noticed the shapes of particular poems as they appear on the page? See how interesting the designs of these poems are:

Edward Lear's "The Owl and the Pussycat"
Eugene Field's "Wynken, Blynken, and Nod"
Mary Austin's "Texas Trains and Trails"
Dorothy Baruch's "Stop-Go"
Rachel Field's "Taxis"
William Blake's "The Lamb"

Some lines are short; others are long. Lines are grouped in stanzas of different sizes.

When you see the shape of a poem, can you guess something about what the poem is like, even before you have read it?

If you hear somebody read a poem that you have not seen, can you imagine what that poem looks like on the page?

4. Get one of your classmates to find a poem that has a definite shape or pattern which is easy to notice on the page. Perhaps the stanzas make the pattern, or maybe there is some other special arrangement of lines.

Then have your classmate show you just a part of that poem—perhaps one-third or one half of it. After you have looked at that part carefully, and have read it, try to guess what the rest of the poem looks like.

5. Ask a friend to show you a poem that he likes. Have him tell you which lines he thinks are especially enjoyable. Then you make a guess as to what he likes about those lines. Is your guess right?

You may need to read the lines several times. Your friend might like a line because of the nice idea that it states, or because of its sound or its rhythm, or because the words in it make him think or see so many things.

6. Tell a classmate to choose a poem and copy five or six lines of it, but have him write it in such a way that it looks like a passage of prose. He is to put the lines in a paragraph and use capital letters for nothing but proper names and beginnings of sentences. Next ask him to copy a few lines of prose from a book or magazine. Then he will give you both items that he had copied. Can you tell which item is the prose and which is the poetry in disguise?

For this experiment to be interesting, your friend should copy from a poem that you do not already know.

You could prepare the same kind of experiment for him while he is copying the passages for you.

7. Get one of your friends to copy two or three lines from a poem which you have not heard or read. Then have him copy

those lines again, making a few changes in them. Tell him to put in a word or a few words of his own in place of a word or words in the original poem. After that he will give you both copies, and you are to see whether you can tell which is the original.

While your friend is preparing the copies for you, you could write out the same kind of experiment for him.

8. Ask a friend to copy two or three lines from a poem and omit one word (or perhaps two) in one of the lines. After he gives you his copy you can try to decide what the omitted word (or words) might be. Or maybe you can think of a word that is even better than the one the poet used.

This experiment will be most interesting if your friend takes lines from a poem that you have not read or heard. Also, if the lines rhyme, he should omit some words other than the last word of a line, because you would not have much fun just thinking of a word that rhymes.

For example, suppose your friend chose these lines, from Alfred Tennyson's "The Eagle":

He watches from his mountain walls,
And like a thunderbolt he falls.

The word *thunderbolt* would be a good one to omit. Then you would think what word or words to put in the space between *a* and *he*. You would have much less fun if he omitted the word *falls*, because then you merely would have to think of a word of rhyme with *walls*.

9. Most likely you have used (or at least have heard) a metronome in your music activities. Once, when talking about poetry, a girl in the fourth grade said, "The beats of the words are like a metronome for the poem."

What do you think she meant by that statement?

10. Get a phonograph record of a poem and listen to it a number of times. Some people like to listen for different things as they rehear it. Once they listen for the thought of the poem, then for the music of the sounds and rhythm, then for the

mood or feeling, then to see whether they can imagine how the poem's shape of pattern looks on the page. You might think of other things to listen for, too.

11. You have seen and heard many poems, but did you ever think of how many different *kinds* of poems there are?

Page through three or four books of poems and make a note of each different kind of poem. You will find long poems, short poems, poems with lines grouped in stanzas, poems without stanzas, poems with short lines, poems with long lines poems with lines that rhyme, poems without rhyme, poems having lines with regular beat or rhythm, poems with less regular rhythms, serious poems, and funny poems.

How many different kinds have you noted by the time you have paged through the books? All those kinds belong under the name "poetry." The word *poetry* is somewhat like the word *tree* or *dog*. There are many kinds of trees and dogs. Each of the three words includes a big variety.

STUDY ACTIVITIES FOR TEACHERS

1. School and athletic cheers often make interesting patterns when in print. Can we recognise the patterns when we hear the cheers?

Some cheers are composed mainly of meaningless syllables. Are such cheers somewhat equivalent to poems composed of sound only?

2. A child, rocking in bed, began chanting as she rocked: "You don't get up early on Easy Street." Soon she tries a number of variations, her first two being "You don't go to school on Easy Street" and "You don't wash your clothes on Easy Street."

How could these lines (or lines like them) be used as refrains of a poems, at either the ends or beginnings of stanzas?

3. Children like poems containing refrains, and many poems in collections for children have refrains as part of their patterns. Such refrains, we are told, do these things:

Produce musical effects

Build up emotion through repetition

Break the poem into units that are easy to understand and remember

Help establish a structural form for the poem

Give the hearer or reader a number of relaxing pauses in the pacing of the thought

Do you agree? Can we add a sixth or even a seventh?

4. If we get someone to choose seven or eight lines of blank verse and write or type them in paragraph form so that the passage looks like prose, we may have the experience of seeing whether we can tell where the successive lines of verse end.

A similar experiment can be tried with a stanza or two of stanzaic poetry.

Does the problem become much more difficult if the lines come from a free-verse poem?

5. Are we aware of the poetic qualities in proverbs? "Fear has big eyes." "He who rides a tiger fears to dismount." "A rolling stone gathers no moss." "He that swallows a stake cannot bend." "One beats the bush, another catches the bird."

How much of the poetic spirit can we see in them? How much concreteness? Compactness? Rhythm? Figurative nature? Do proverbs tend to state their point indirectly, by inference, rather than by direct assertion?

Do these qualities explain why proverbs are enjoyed by many people and are easily remembered?

6. Could we argue, whimsically, that the great poet is one who *leaves off the last stanza?* The concluding lines of most poems that the world has cherished are free of obvious moralising. Does the moralising kind of ending, common in nineteenth-century poetry, seem like a needless appendage?

7. The Arabs are said to call poetry "lawful magic." How many reasons can we think of to justify that description?

8. "If I hear both sides of a telephone conversation, that's prose. If I hear only one side, that's poetry."

A college student ventured this statement whimsically in connection with the observation that poetry tends to be compact and economical of words. A lively argument followed. What might the comments have been?

9. Alliteration, rhyme, and assonance, conspicuous in poetry, flourish, too, in prose. We hear examples every day.

What special phonetic effects are in the following?

crisscross	sooth to say	leave in the lurch
rate race	technical terms	self-sacrifice
knickknack	self-seeding	dead as a doornail
hubbub	wrack and ruin	hearth and home
whatnot	hugger-mugger	farm and fireside
road hog	deaf and dumb	a price rise
whole hog	hurly-burly	a wage raise

We say "men and women" and "ladies and gentlemen," not "women and men" or "gentlemen and ladies." But we say either "boys and girls" or "girls and boys." Does rhythm influence the sequences?

VIEWPOINTS TO EMPHASISE THROUGH TEACHING AIDS

1. *There are interesting things to hear and see in poems.*

(a) Phonograph and tape recording of individuals and verse-speaking groups enable pupils to hear successive readings of poems.

(b) Television or video tape presentations. These have the advantage of being able to show the reader some or all of the lines as they are being read.

(c) A slide or filmstrip showing of a poem. Looking at the poem on the screen, children have a chance to discover what is interesting in the poem's ideas, words, and pattern.

(d) A poem mounted on a poster. Caption: Can you find two (or more) interesting features in this poem?

The interesting points can be named on the poster, but covered with a flap. Pupils then can raise the flap to check whether they have found the correct features.

2. *Unusual kinds of ideas make poetry enjoyable.*

(a) A poem mounted on a poster or bulletin board. The words or lines containing poetic ideas or turns of thought are underlined, coloured, or shown in some other way.

(b) On poster, chalkboard, or projector present four or five separate sentences about the same topic—about "echoes," for example, or about "spider webs." The first statement is matter-of-fact, prosaic. The second is a little more imaginative; the third, more so; and any additional ones are quite poetic in idea, even though stated in a prose sentence.

Caption: Which of these could be put into a poem?

(c) On a poster list seven or eight short sentences, some being imaginative and poetic in idea; others, matter-of-fact and prosaic. Each sentence can be about a different topic, or two or more sentences can be about one topic.

Caption: There are at least three (or four) ideas for poems among these. Can you find them?

(d) On a poster, picture of jet plane in flight. Beneath the picture are these statements:

To many people it's just a jet plane or a plane that goes very fast.

To a poet it might be:
An air-slicer
A scooter-bug of the sky
A skilled ventriloquist
A dot leading a line
A fly crawling on a blue ceiling

Caption: What can you add?

3. *A word that is "just right" helps make a line of poetry enjoyable.*

(a) On a projector, poster, or chalkboard:

1. A line (or two) from a poem, and two or three variations of the original. The variations are less effective than the original because in them the teacher has substituted a few words or phrases not quite so good as the original. The differences may be in rhythm, sound, or fitness of meaning.

2. A line or two or poetry, with especially suitable word or words underlined or otherwise marked. Caption: Why does this word (do these words) fit so well?

3. A line or two of poetry. Caption: Which word is (words are) especially fine?

(b) On a poster or chalkboard, a line or two of poetry with a word omitted. Caption: What word would you supply?

4. *Poets use the sounds of the English language effectively.*

5. *Poets revise their poems in order to make them better.*

Show facsimiles of manuscripts which contain revisions made by the author. Successive versions are particularly interesting.

6. *Various revisions can improve a line or lines of verse.*

On a poster or chalkboard, three or more versions of an original line of verse. Caption: Which do you like best? *or* Which do you wish you had written?

7. *Poems have enjoyable patterns or designs.*

(a) Show part of a poem. Looking thoughtfully at the portion shown, pupils guess what the remainder of the poem looks like.

(b) On a poster, a poem is mounted, but part of the poem is covered with a flap. Pupils guess what the covered part looks like, then check with what is under the cover.

(c) Project poems of various patterns.

(d) Suggest rapid pagings through books of poetry, with main attention on appearances of the poems.

(e) Pupils listen to a poem, probably more than once. They make guesses about the shape of the poem as it appears on the page. (Choir readings of a poem suggest the structure of the composition.)

(f) Show poems that are well planned. Elements that hold a poem together (groupings of lines into stanzas; repetition of words, ideas, or refrains; rhyme; rhythms) are indicated with coloured crayons.

8. *The rhythms of poetry tend to be more nearly regular than the rhythms of prose.*

On a chalkboard or poster there are a few lines of a fairly rhythmic poem and two or three sentences of normal prose. Pupils read the lines and the sentences aloud and see whether they could jump rope or skip to one set more readily than to the other.

9. *The name "poetry" includes many different kinds of compositions.*

(a) Show different kinds of poems—long, short, with stanzas, without stanzas, with rhyme, without rhyme, with regular rhythm, with irregular rhythm, humorous, not humorous, some that tell a story, some that do not, with long lines, with short lines, with both long and short lines.

(b) A poster showing several kinds of birds (or trees) and several kinds of poems. Caption: There are many kinds of birds (trees). There also are many kinds of poems.

INQUIRIES AND PROBLEMS FOR STUDENTS

1. Talk with a number of pupils from a second or third grade and also with some high school students from grade 10 or 11. Try to find out their attitudes towards poetry. Do you discover any consistent differences in attitude between the two group?

2. As you examine Iona and Peter Opie's *Lore and Language of Schoolchildren,* reflect on what the rhymes, chants, and riddles indicate regarding children's imagination, mental playfulness, and interest in rhythm.

3. Popular opinion holds that poetry is abstract. People well acquainted with poetry say that poems are the most concrete form of language expression. Arrive at a decision for yourself by determining the proportion of concrete nouns and action-suggesting verbs in several short poems and in passages of normal prose containing the same number of words. Consider also the relative number of metaphors, similes, personifications, and other concrete types of figures of speech.

4. George Russell Harrison, in *What Man May Be,* page 214, says, "Instead of painting a picture which tells more than a thousand words, the poet tries to make one word invoke a thousand pictures." What is your opinion on this statement?

5. Do you find that your viewpoint regarding certain poems has changed during the last five years? If so, what might have been the reasons for the change? Do those reasons suggest any implications for a teacher of poetry?

6. Be on the lookout for occasions when unpoetic lines of verse are quoted for unpoetic, didactic purposes. How can such quotations complicate the task of a teacher of poetry?

7. Examine the poetry units in several English language series intended for the grades. Do you approve of the way of ways they handle the matter of rhyme?

8. In *Adventures into Poetry* Flora J. Arnstein presents many poems composed by her pupils and describes the classroom situations in which some of the verse came into being. Read about the creative activities and the accompanying discussions, and speculate on whether those experiences gave the children exceptionally good backgrounds for appreciating poetry written by other authors.

12

Oral Communication

Speech is one type of composing in language—a type that is swift, complicated, frequent, and primary. Its swiftness is twofold: the swift, unpremeditated manner in which oral phrasing, facial expression, gestures, and other bodily motions follow the origination of a thought; and the swiftness with which it reaches the listener's mind. All happen so quickly that the processes of thinking, uttering, and hearing seem fused into one.

Speech is complicated. In some respects it is more complicated than writing. Though not demanding the kind of muscular coordination needed in writing, or the skills of spelling and written punctuation, it requires coordination of breathing, tongue and lip movements, facial expression, and gesture. It may also entail emotional strain when the speaker is before an audience or in some other situation that causes tension. Thought, breathing, articulation, and neurons must coordinate.

Speech is conspicuous for its frequency, too. People surprise themselves when they note how often they speak and listen in several hours of a normal day. Children, in school or out, maintain a perpetual flow of talk and gesture. A teacher's problem is less one of finding opportunities for children to speak or listen than of discovering how to use the abundant occasions wisely.

Speech is the primary form of verbal language. In each pupil it dates from the first half year of life when, as an infant, he began to babble a variety of sounds (in patterns that apparently are stereotyped among infants the world around).

Then gradually he learned the thirty-six or forty phonemes employed in his parents' language and put those phonemes into combinations and sequences meaning something in the English code. As a listener he responded first to intonation signals rather than to words—to speech rhythms, stress patterns, and tones of people around him. His personal use of recognisable words came some months later. It has been estimated that even for a two-year-old child there is a lag of several months from the child's first hearing of a word until his first meaningful use of it—two or seven months being needed to make neural records of the concept named and of the word, and to establish an automatic reflex connection between the two. When his speech has become well developed and he has mastered the basic phonemic and grammatical patterns of English, the child's first experiences in writing are still to come.

So, too, speech antedated writing in the history of the human race, and the differences between the spoken, or primary, form of language, and written language, a secondary, derived form, are key items for teachers to remember when planning their pedagogy. Speech, as Cherry says, "is not spoken writing"; it is "bound to the time continuum; we must receive it as it comes, instant by instant." It is, as viewed in structural linguistics, a stream or continuum of organised sound that is punctuated (one could say *orchestrated*) by breaks or junctures of various lengths, stresses, pitches, and gestures. Teachers who understand this basic fact are prepared to teach more than merely "speech"; they can teach spoken language.

OBJECTIVES IN TEACHING ORAL COMMUNICATION

Refinement of the growing oral expression that started in infancy is a sensible objective for early years. This becomes a normal progression, except for temporary confusion in articulation while front teeth are missing. Refinement should be in the directions of courtesy, fluency, posture, and freedom from distracting mannerisms. Additional resources of oral language may need development. Courteous listening is something new in a pupil's speech behaviour, but only through it can pre-school tendencies toward monologue be displaced by the niceties of conversation.

If stammering exists, a teacher must try to establish a relaxed situation and obtain the help of therapists. If a pupil is bilingual, the alert teacher has a double objective, best attained through the businesslike approach provided by linguistics: to help the child make a transition from his native tongue to English and to use whatever contributions a pupil who knows another language can make to the classroom programme in language arts.

PUPIL BACKGROUND FOR STUDYING ORAL COMMUNICATION

From the moment in infancy when he first heard a voice, a child develops a background for schoolwork in oral communication. Early, he notices that various intonations, facial expressions, and bodily gestures have specific meanings. He becomes aware of certain patterns of sounds, words, and intonations and imitates them. Meanwhile he babbles a large range of sounds, some of which he later discards because they are not used in English speech.

After having learned some speech patterns and sorted out the sounds needed in English, he gives himself a great amount of practice articulating them. From television and radio he gains further speech impressions, and at an early age gives much interest to the telephone. All along, of course, he has had instruction and correction from older people.

If he has been a normal child, his total experiences in the several aspects of oral communication have become vast by the time he enters kindergarten. He has progressed from random exclamations to rational statements, from sporadic hearing to relatively sustained listening.

Through this cumulative experience he gains several impressions which a teacher finds pedagogically advantageous. He senses that people's manners of talking and listening affect the way other people respond and that oral communication is immensely important in life, and he concludes that a person's speech behaviour constitutes a large part of that individual's personality.

All told, a normal child comes to school with a large background of speech in the language with which he has grown up.

PUPILS' DAILY EXPERIENCES WITH ORAL COMMUNICATION

Each wakeful hour contributes to a pupil's daily experiences in oral communication. In school and out there are continual demonstrations of the importance of speaking and listening as means of survival. Daily, young people experience moments of sensitivity regarding performance in all aspects of speech. Consciously or unconsciously they rate other people on performance and are quite sensitive to any evidence that someone else is rating their own quality.

In-school experiences are, naturally, more systematic than those outside of school. The major ones take the following forms.

Taking Part in Discussions

Class and group discussions are so natural, frequent, and influential that Ogilvie calls them "an integral part of the classroom living." Continuing, she says:

> All day long children talk about questions of common interest. They plan their work. They prepare to go on a trip; they talk about it afterwards. They decide on a story to tell with puppets; they make arrangements for putting on the show before the school. They are findings answers to their own inquiries. This habit of discussion is an important fact in most elementary school classrooms. The spirit of inquiry, brought about by a willingness to talk things over freely, accounts in many cases for the successful management of a classroom.

In an early grade, discussions usually are quite informal. They might be about the arrangement of furniture in the room or how to keep the room and corridors more tidy. In grade 5 or 6 the planning of a class newspaper or a discussion of "Different Kinds of Weather East and West of the Rocky Mountains" could be informal too, or it might be headed by a chairman and a group of four or five other pupils who follow a somewhat formal procedure.

Pupils' ability to state their opinions and their reasons for holding them improves in the middle grades. Watts observes that seven years is about the age when children begin to give reasons to support what they say. Increasingly, thereafter, they argue by means of thought and reason instead of quarreling verbally. But when discussing a problem type of topic, children in any grade need help in identifying the problem and discovering the key issues to be considered.

In every class the teacher must encourage quiet pupils to join the discussion, help timid ones (who represent a kind of discipline problem in reverse) gain the feeling that they can contribute worthily to the situation, and get talkative ones to defer to others in the group. "Let's see what the others think about this," "Everybody should have a turn at talking about the subject," and "You name who shall answer" (addressed to pupils who volunteer too often) are constructive comments.

A tradition of having everybody take part can be built up if the group regularly talks about the success or failure of its discussions. "Everybody had a chance," "Each took a turn," "We heard everybody's ideas," "Each listened well," and "We kept the discussion on the topic" are comments that establish an idea of what is a good discussion.

Sociometric diagrams of pupil relationships and flow charts of class discussions help teachers improve the situation. Such charts reveal the group dynamics of the classroom. They show interplays of personalities, individuals whose opinions carry greatest influence, pupils to whom remarks and questions are directed, isolates who need to be "brought out," and pupils who tend to monopolise the time. Reassignment or rotation of chairmanships or of other responsibilities may be indicated, and perhaps some changes in the seating or physical arrangement of the discussion group. Isolates revealed by sociograms often come into active participation if they are given opportunities to do things for the group—arranging the chairs, for example, stacking books, copying words on the chalkboard, or leading the class in the march to assembly. Samples of classroom sociograms, together with interpretations of them, are available in various textbooks.

Sharing Experiences

The sharing of experiences deserves the considerable time allotted to it in many class programmes. In addition to offering good motivations for speaking and listening, it strengthens the feeling of oneness of the group and gives the teacher insights into the personal traits of each child and his relationships to other children and to the group. It also stimulates the types of observation, reflection, and reporting needed in imaginative expression.

The sharing hour brings a miscellany. One snowy morning a first-grade girl said she noticed two doves standing on the same piece of bread in the street and eating from it in friendly manner. A girl in a second grade told of having entered her Maltese cat in a pet show. A boy from the sixth grade shared the feelings he had experienced 1,900 feet down in a lead mine. Another boy from the same group related the excitement of telephoning for firemen when a neighbour's rubbish fire spread to a grassy field. One fifth grader told of her visit to Bryce Canyon; another reported his surprise at reading about the derivations of the words *curfew* and *peninsula*. A fourth-grade girl described her visit with an elderly lady who knits scarves to sell as birthday and Christmas gifts.

In experience sharing, as in any other type of speech situation, there are standards to be upheld if performances are not to deteriorate into a waste of time. How many details shall I tell? Which details will be most valuable? In what order shall I tell the items? What experiences have my hearers had that I can refer to, so that they will better understand what I tell? How can I avoid repeating the tedious "and then . . . and then"? Skill gained by applying such standards is a life-long asset.

Conversing and Telephoning

Objectives of instruction in conversation and the use of the telephone are easy to establish. In conversation they are truthfulness: courtesy; considerations of time, place, and topic; willingness to let other people have chances to talk; avoidance of mannerisms; a pleasant voice; attentive listening; awareness that conversing is a two-way transaction; ability to express disagreement courteously; tactfulness in interrupting someone, changing the topic, and breaking away from a conversing group; and spontaneity.

Althouggh these objectives are widely approved, and children understand their values, classroom life provides few situations in which they can be taught naturally.

The difficulty is that conversation, the type of speech which pupils will use most frequently and find very educative throughout life, is hard to develop spontaneously in school. Genuine conversation—sometimes called "the poetry of the learned"—happens there once in a while, and when it occurs all participants realise that they are experiencing something fine. It may be about new kinds of dolls and doll dresses, television programmes that occur on Saturday afternoons, or a recent hailstorm. After it is over, the participants remember it with pleasure and would welcome more experiences of that kind. But there is no sure control of the time when such successful conversations can happen again. An entire class makes too large a group for genuine conversation, and there is something artificial about selecting a smaller group and suggesting that they "have a conversation about . . . ." Informal occasions such as receptions for parents, an open house for another grade, and a rock exhibit are likely to generate some conversation, but those situations are largely beyond the teacher's immediate control. Discussion of the niceties of conversation can be held prior to such events, and the results can be judged in retrospect.

Talk in the kindergarten is mainly egocentric. Until they reach the third grade, children speak almost entirely about personal experience associated with home, play, parties, and pets. Gradually, in later grades, conversation can include broader interests and ideas on current affairs.

Instruction in the use of the telephone emphasises consideration for other people who might want to use the phone. Special attention is given clarity and expressiveness of speech because facial expressions and other gestures cannot help convey the message. This last point is especially necessary for any child whose speech tends to be slovenly. When telephoning he must convey everything with his voice alone, and, what is more, with a voice which is reduced and distorted somewhat by the mechanism.

Already at six years of age some children can dial a number, and practically all children enjoy speaking over a phone. Classroom instruction is limited by the fact that children do most of their telephoning outside of school. There is some in-school calling, however. One pupil might telephone to the town historian to arrange an interview. Another might call the local newspaper office about a school news item. A class planning a trip to a zoo, museum, post office, or fire station usually has occasion to telephone.

Making Announcements

Classrooms, school assemblies, the school's public address system, closed-circuit television, and tape recorders are the main places and media associated with oral announcements. If a sixth grade wants to invite each fourth- and fifth-grade room to contribute two news items and an anecdote to the newspaper that it is preparing, it might send a classmate to each of the fourth- and fifth-grade rooms. If an entire elementary school is invited to watch the fifth-grade dramatise the life of Samuel F. B. Morse in the assembly hall, a pupil might announce the time and place over the public address system. If a fourth-grade room is sponsoring a pet show for all fourth grades, it might send somebody to each room to announce the rules of the show and delegate another member to announce the event in assembly.

When preparing to make announcements, pupils expect the teacher to emphasise clear articulation of words and a moderate rate of speech. Those two items of advice are essential, but several additional and less obvious considerations are practical. The first one or two sentences of the prepared announcement should be short rather than long. If the announcer happens to be nervous or tense, the short sentences will give him a chance to get his bearings and also will be less likely than long ones to reveal the speaker's nervousness. In addition, short sentences make it easier for the audience to become accustomed to the appearance of a new speaker, a new voice, and a new topic.

As a further aid to hearers, announcers sometimes avoid stating key information (like the time and place) in the first sentences unless they intend to repeat it later. The audience is likely to give only partial attention to what the speaker says when it is preoccupied with adjusting itself to the new person and the new voice. For the same reason announcers might do well to speak especially slowly at the outset and to pause briefly between their appearance (on the stage, in the classroom, or on television) and their first sentence.

Voice projection is helped when the announcer looks at people near the back of the room rather than at those in front rows, because a speaker's voice tends to adjust its volume to reach the people at whom he is looking.

Tape recordings give pupils the great advantage of hearing and revising their announcements beforehand. The invitation committee in a fifth-grade phrased its invitation to a choral-speaking programme three ways, taped all three, and then chose the one that seemed best for its purpose. Some groups send the tapes to another room, the assembly, or the school's public address centre to broadcast the announcement.

Introducing People

Although opportunities to introduce people occur on special occasions rather than during the usual classroom day, they happen a fair number of times each year. Someone's cousin comes along to school for a day; a member of the class has a neighbour who moved to the area in mid-December and who starts school right after New Year's Day; parents and friends attend a Halloween party; or there is an open house so that parents and others may visit the new school building.

Children need practice in speaking names more slowly and in pronouncing them more distinctly and more completely. Boys especially require guidance in this. Thought must be given to the other side of the introduction situation too—what the pupil should do and say when he is the one being introduced, and how to break away graciously, following a brief conversation with a person or group to whom he had been introduced.

Interviewing

A commercial artist in the school town makes block prints, and a pupil visits his studio to learn how he obtained the excellent colouring on a certain card which had been extensively bought as a Christmas greeting. A man at the trout hatchery stocks streams and lakes with fish and therefore has much information that interests a fourth-grade studying conservation. A sixth grade asks two of its girls to interview a neighbourhood woman who weaves small rugs and sells them to a Denver gift shop. In a group studying fruit growing, someone thought of visiting a local man who sprays orange trees. A third-grade boy learned about diving apparatus and techniques from a man who goes skindiving for lobsters.

Such projects become quite frequent when the teacher and pupils use community resources. Each interview entails a series of experiences in oral expression: opening the topic with the interviewee; phrasing questions in such manner that they will bring out full explanations rather than a mere "yes" or "no"; introducing new aspects of the subject as the interview develops; adapting the inquiries to new or unexpected turns in the developing interview; listening efficiently; and being tactful and courteous throughout. An interview may involve writing also, as explained in, "Newspapers and Magazines in the Classroom".

Preplanning is therefore necessary. The child should learn about the topic and the person whom he will interview. Particularly he should think of what to say first when he meets the person, so as to introduce himself and explain his purpose. This problem of getting started may be resolved partly through written or telephoned arrangements before the visit. In any case, the interviewer should be prepared to use something better than certain types of openings that are blurted out all too frequently: "Our teacher wants us to . . . ," "I have to . . .," or "We must . . . ."

Each interview with someone outside of the school constitutes a bit of public relations for the school and the class. The public's estimate of both the school and the interviewer's classmates is affected by the degree of preplanning and the tact of the interviewer. Tape recordings of good interviews are both interesting and instructive as models.

Reporting and Explaining

Here the elementary teacher contributes much to a young person's preparation for high school and college, where lucid explanations and convincing reports are necessary for success. She contributes by training pupils to study a subject well before attempting to report on it, to think carefully about the subject, and to develop a well-organised plan for presenting the material.

To establish a favourable climate for reporting, a teacher can do at least three things: encourage pupils to choose topics which will give them a chance to feel that they really are informing their hearers, provide attentive listeners, and insist that a reporter explain his topic fully enough to be understood by people who know little about it.

Certain skills and procedures are basic to good reporting and explaining. The seven discussed briefly below can be introduced in elementary grades. They serve pupils well in written reports as well as in oral ones.

Development and Organisation: Although untrained in formal logic, elementary school children recognise what "makes sense" in a situation or discussion. On that native childhood feeling for the fitness of things a teacher builds toward habits of logical thinking.

Pupils in early grades often lose themselves in a few details of a topic or detour too far in one subdivision of it. They need help in limiting the topic to workable scope, seeing the topic as a whole, and thinking a straight course through the material. When talking about "How the Weather Affects Farm Crops in Our State," for example, or "How the Weather Affects" the Clothing Business," a pupil or a discussion group may require guidance if the coverage and logic are to be reasonably good. Without guidance, the discussion probably would go off in the direction of one particular storm or one type of weather and never return to the main theme. Also pupils are likely to make illogical inferences and confuse cause and effect.

Already in the first grade a teacher can point out the logical order of the items that she puts on an experience chart. In any grade, after a successful presentation of a topic, class time is well spent in noticing how the material has been arranged. The effects of different sequences can be shown pictorially (Figure 3.1).

Topics like "The Way Books Are Arranged in the Library," "How the Streets of Our Town Are Laid Out," and "How to Go from the School to the Airport" suggest, by their nature, a logical organisation for a reporter to follow. So, also, do subjects like "How to Plan and Care for a Window Flower Box," "How to Care for African Violets," and "Some Differences between Poetry and Prose."

As soon as children begin composing paragraphs the teacher has a fine instrument for encouraging good organisation because the nature of a paragraph requires pupils to bring related ideas together.

Interest in organising material on a topic encourages a search for more information on that topic. Pupils soon realise that the more they know about a subject the better they can work out a good plan for presenting it. A typical experience was that of a boy who wanted to tell his class about magnets. He planned a short talk on the subject. Then he read more about the topic and also experimented with two magnets that were in the classroom. Soon he changed his plan for the talk because his reading and experiments suggested a better way to introduce and develop his topic.

One class made a poster to illustrate the importance of organisation. The poster showed someone trying in vain to catch six small items that were tossed to him all at once. In contrast was another person catching easily a single parcel. That parcel contained six small items snugly combined in one package.

Outlines. An outline provides a map or blueprint of one's materials and trend of thought on a topic. At a glance it shows the extent to which the pupil's material covers the subject and

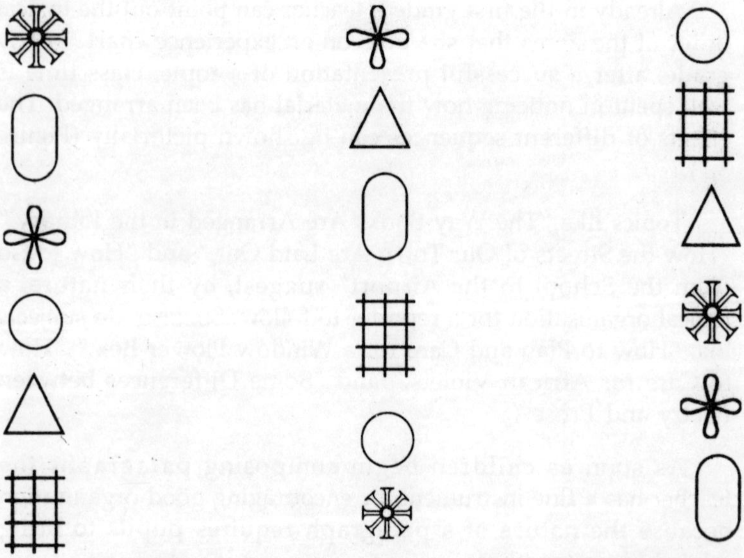

Fig. 3.1 The importance of arrangement. Arranged in three different sequences, the six shapes produce three different effects. The differences are easy to see.

Six ideas arranged in three different orders in an oral or written report also produce three different effects. Instead of shapes, the pupil might have these six items to present:

 = pupils who were winners in the contest

 = where the contest happened

 = what prizes were won

 = when the contest happened

 = prizes won by pupils in the local school

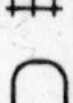 = main events in the contest

Those six items could be arranged and rearranged just as truly as the shapes. Each arrangement would have its particular effects. Listeners or readers would notice the differences.

whether his thinking proceeds in a logical way. Therefore the earlier a pupil learns how to make and use outlines, the better.

When a class happens to be working on a topic such as "Three Kinds of Information in Dictionaries," "Three Kinds of Industry in Our Area," "Four Important Fruits Grown in Our State," or "Uses of the Corn Plant," the situation is ideal for guidance in outline making. For such topics the major divisions of an outline suggest themselves at once and a few sub-items come readily to mind. Simple topical statements of main divisions, with equally simple statements of sub-items, are sufficient for introducing the technique. Gradually the class can proceed to more detailed outlines and more complicated subjects.

Outlines built up on a flannel board or overhead projector while the pupils plan them and watch them develop are usually well worth the time they require. Having seen two outlines take shape, one child said, "Such maps keep our thoughts going where we want them to go."

Illustrations and Generalisations. A third grade experimented one spring with several methods of causing seeds to sprout: putting the seeds in moist soil, laying them on a wet blotter, immersing them in water, and providing various conditions of temperature and light. Each pupil tried the experiment with one kind of seed and with one set of conditions for sprouting the seeds. The project extended through four weeks and led to many observations and comments on the sprouting of corn, beans, wheat, peas, cabbage, and tomato seeds.

Repeatedly during discussion of the experiment the teacher found a pupil making general statements implying that germination of any seed or of all seeds would occur under the conditions observed for the sprouting of one kind of seed, particularly under the conditions which caused his seeds to sprout. Another pupil, having seen different conditions germinate a different kind of seed, would take issue with his classmate but, in turn, would be just about as ready to generalise on the basis of his personal observations.

Then the teacher began to ask questions and redirect pupil thinking. Do all seeds require moisture for sprouting? Do all need warmth? Light? A covering of soil? A period of eight days? From the ensuing discussions the class identified several conditions that appeared to be true of all germinations. They also concluded that all kinds of seeds will not sprout under the same circumstances, and that the conditions which one pupil had provided for sprouting beans, for example, were not the only ones which could cause beans to sprout.

Through their reporting on this experiment the pupils began to distinguish between a sample (or a few samples) and a generalised situation. They had an early lesson in the phase of logic which cautions against jumping to broad conclusions on the evidence of a few examples. To explain and report well, pupils in oral communication must learn that lesson.

Several weeks after the discussion on seed germination the same class found itself generalising to hastily again, this time about pupils' conduct on the playground. But the teacher's questions corrected the situation in a few minutes because the class had benefited from its discussion in the seed experiment.

Definitions: Nobody under forty years of age, it has been said, is really interested in definitions, because young people are too busy *living* the meanings of words, not defining them. That may be one reason why definitions and definition making are somewhat difficult to teach in the grades, but any pupil continuing into the upper grades and high school needs to know something about the nature of a definition.

Fully developed, the conventional definition, based on types or identities of things, first locates the subject in the large class (genus) to which it belongs, then narrows the classification step by step (through species and differentia) until final identification is achieved. The process resembles the drawing of concentric circles (as in figure 3.2) with the smallest circle identifying the subject only: "A square is a plane figure of four sides having all its sides equal and all its angles right angles." "Hail is precipitation in the form of pellets of ice." Thus a definition shows where one thing stands in relation to everything else. As people sometimes say, to define is to confine.

A toward correct defining is necessary in elementary grades if reporting and explaining are to be done satisfactorily. Perhaps progress toward formal definitions will go little further than drawing the first circle ("A tiger is an animal . . ." or "Brass is an alloy metal . . ."), but even that first step is a corrective for mental slovenliness, and it eliminates the all too common "is where" or "is where you have" ("A square is where . . ."). Children can understand also that a definition should not contain the name of the thing being defined and that whenever possible a definition should be stated in the affirmative rather than the negative.

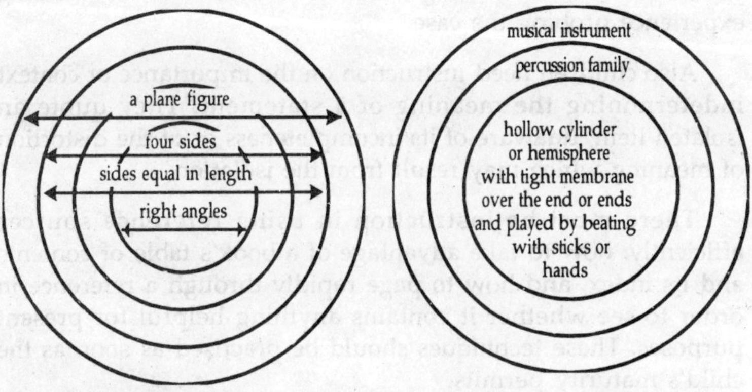

Fig. 3.2: Diagram of a definition. Concentric circles help children understand how to state definitions. The largest circle represents the general class or type to which the item being defined belongs. Smaller circles narrow the area, step by step, to the specific details which characterise that item.

A few additional guides on teaching definitions appear in the discussion of "Words".

Library Usage

A class discussion of the weather led to a mention of the *chinook*. Then a boy said his father told of experiences with the *williwaws* in the Aleutians. This raised the question of the other widely known winds of certain parts of the world, and this, in turn, made the children realise that they needed the library or some equivalent source for information. Soon they found out about three additional winds: *foehn, mistral,* and *tehuantepec.*

Children have little background for judging the reliability of sources of information or opinion. But a beginning can be made early. Intermediate grade children should have the experience of comparing the different information found on a given topic in news articles, magazines, advertisements, and encyclopaedias. Sometimes an opportunity develops from differences between texts. For instance, if two articles or books disagree on the size or population of a country or on the number of bales of cotton raised in the United States in a stated year, the class encountering such variance can have a rewarding experience probing the case.

Also children need instruction on the importance of context indetermining the meaning of a statement. They quote an isolated item, unaware of its incompleteness or of the distortion of meaning which may result from the isolation.

There must be instruction in using reference sources efficiently: how to take advantage of a book's table of contents and its index, and how to page rapidly through a reference in order to see whether it contains anything helpful for present purposes. These techniques should be practised as soon as the child's maturity permits.

Children will discover that they save time by copying ample material when doing reference work. Full notation of an author's name, the book or article title, the publisher, the date of publication, page references, and any other data that might be needed will reduce the likelihood that the pupil must go back later to get bits of information which he had not recorded during his first search.

Crediting the Sources

As soon as children begin to draw information from libraries or other sources, they encounter the problem of giving credit to authors and publications. Elaborate entries are not to be expected, but some attention to crediting in the grades will prepare pupils for correct handling of footnotes and bibliographies in high school and college, where documentation is very important.

Several good methods of indicating authors, titles, dates, and publishers in a written report are in standard use. But unless guided, pupils almost always fumble along with confused, inefficient arrangements. Yet an acceptable method is as easy for a child to follow as an unacceptable one. Much is gained if the method is followed by the whole room, and even more if it is adopted by the entire school.

Sources are credited for two reasons: A speaker or writer, out of honesty, must tell where he obtained material; and hearers or readers like to know the sources. Some readers may want to go to the sources for further information. Children can understand both reasons.

Graphs

In a sixth grade a girl was to tell about cotton growing in her home state. As part of her report she wanted to show some changes in the size of the cotton crop since 1900, especially as reflected in the production figures for the years 1900, 1920, 1940, and 1960. Knowing something about how to make pictorial graphs, and having a flannel board in the room, she set up a row of cutouts (designed to look like bales of cotton) for each of the four years. Each cutout represented 1 million bales. Thus she improved her report with a pictorial graph that communicated its data quickly and tangibly.

A graph is a form of written communication, efficient in oral or written reports. Pupils can use graphs profitably if they know how to make them. Reports on grain or fruit crops, the output or consumption of manufactured goods, the production of oil or minerals, the number of each of the major kinds of trees along the village streets, the amount of traffic at different hours at several streets—all these can be brightened with graphs made on flannel board, chalkboard, or paper. A member of a weather club graphed the club's records of 30 days: 18 days of sunshine, 3 days that were cloudy all day, 9 days that were partly cloudy, and 6 days on which rain fell. The travel club of a school prepared a pictorial graph showing the travel times from Los Angeles to New York City in 1880, 1900, 1920, 1940, and the present.

Pupils should choose the type of graph (pictorial, "pie," or line) which best portrays the kind of data that they want to present.

Experience shows that pupils in the second grade are able to read bar graphs and pictorial graphs. A simple bar graph is somewhat the easier of the two because it does not require a key or a numerical ratio of symbols to data.

Conducting Business Meetings

Occasions for experience in conducting a business meeting range from an informal session of a committee that is planning an Arbor Day project to the more formal procedures of a well-established space club. But in every case such parliamentary procedures as can be understood by a given grade should be employed because the regulations encourage efficiency and courtesy. As Ogilvie says:

> Parliamentary procedure is logical; it applies common sense to getting business transacted easily and quickly. When a child learns the rules of parliamentary procedure as he needs them he sees why they make sense. They are logical, for their purpose is to expedite business. For example, all argument must relate to the motion on the floor. If a member introduces extraneous matter, he is ruled out of order. Because the members attack one subject at a time, they must organise their thinking around one topic. The orderliness of the procedure aids them in getting problems solved more efficiently.
>
> In addition, parliamentary procedure provides for the full and fair democratic expression of the opinions of every member of the assemblage. Advocates of both sides of an issue have a chance to make their choices of action known and to give their reasons for their judgments.

Ogilvie considers the third grade a proper time to introduce parliamentary practices in earnest and believes that children who continue to use them in their meetings from the third grade on will be able to handle all the standard kinds of motions by the time they reach eighth-grade.

Reading Orally

When a pupil speaks extemporaneously, the patterns of his thought set the patterns and intonations of his sentences. When he reads aloud, the process is reversed; the sentence patterns are on the page, and he must discover the thought patterns that the author intended, re-create them, and project them. His role resembles that of a phonograph, which picks up the recorded signals and recreates the original.

Therefore preparation for oral reading requires effort and assistance. The average pupil does not complete the preparation. That is why so many children who speak interestingly without a manuscript seem transformed into other persons when reading orally. Their voices become expressionless; their faces, deadpan. They no longer project to their audiences.

If the child has written the script himself, he can attain a communicative reading more readily, but there is still danger of monotony. Reading well orally is much more difficult than people generally suppose.

Tape recordings help greatly in alerting pupils to the problems of oral reading. A child records what he plans to read, listens to it, records again and listens, and persists until he achieves an expressive reading. Facial expression and its effectiveness can be checked with a mirror.

Choral Speaking

Choral speaking supports the oral communication programme in several ways. It improves enunciation, articulation, voice quality, and speech intonation. It increases the courage of a timid child as he is caught up in the dynamics of unison speech. It tones down the overbold pupil, who realises that he must coordinate his speech with the group. The returns are large enough to encourage the development of many choral-speaking groups (usually on an informal basis).

Listening

Two facts emerge from teachers' experiences with listening: Pupils' listening is inefficient, and it can be improved through training. Some estimates rate the efficiency as low as 25 per cent. Improvement is especially urgent for a generation which receives so much of its information orally.

Professional literature on the nature and importance of listening is both extensive and widely available. Everybody agrees that skills of listening should be taught. Yet classroom instruction in those skills seems to lag.

Experiments using mechanical speed-up devices show that the mind is able to receive spoken language even faster than speakers can produce it.

Standards for Listening: A list of qualities to listen for stimulates good listening. The process of deciding what items should be listed is profitable in itself if it involves class discussions. Lists differ according to whether the listening is to be primarily analytical, informative, or appreciative, but they give everybody a standard and they help solve problems that arise from pupils who would rather talk or who withdraw within themselves and cease to listen.

Linguistics is an influence for acute listening. Mainly it alerts people to sounds and intonations as clues to what someone wants to say. But anyone listening for signals will be heeding the meaning also.

Selective Listening: Teachers justifiably approach listening with at least one reservation. They do not aim to have a child listen intently to *everything* that is audible at a given time. Adults more or less consciously avoid paying attention to some things, setting up a kind of auditory insulation against excessive impingement. A person who listened intently to every sound that assaults the modern ear might become a sonic wreck; his identity would erode in a riptide of noise.

But all teachers try to develop discriminatory listening. They know that their pupils will have lifelong exposure to tricky dialectics and verbal chicanery as well as to the sincere and true.

Experiences in Listening: Occasions for improving listening arise every day. There are directions, explanations, and reports, together with show-and-tell and experience-sharing periods. Special activities to develop listening are easy to plan. They should include opportunities for speaking because pupils like to be listened to, and their awareness of satisfaction in receiving attention may increase their willingness to listen to others.

Activities related to listening can be interesting, as the following examples show:

Pupils listen as announcements are being read over the school's public address system. Then they compare what they remember. Finally they get the copy from which the announcer read and check how well they have listened.

After school assembly the class talks about how much they remember from the announcements that were made.

Two classrooms (or two groups in the same room) exchange tape recordings on interesting and informative topics. A copy of the script is sent along too. After a group has heard the tape that it received, it checks its listening against the script.

A conversation is recorded on tape. Pupils who have not heard the original conversation listen to the tape and see whether they can follow the thread of thought.

Discussions, some good and some not so good, are taped and then listened to analytically. Pupils notice how an idea develops a discussion and where illogical items come in. They compare well-organised discussions with confused ones.

Someone familiar with puppetry tells the class four things to remember when making a puppet. Did all pupils catch all four?

Children listen to a television programme but do not look at it. How much can they picture imaginatively from what they hear? (A similar experience can be obtained from a radio, but there is no way of checking against an actual picture.)

The teacher reads a description of a landscape. After the reading she asks the children to draw the landscape from their memories of its description.

Pupils and teacher list all the aural impressions that they can detect at a certain time from any source whatever: speech, motion, machinery, traffic, weather, etc.

A sequence of sounds is recorded on tape. Children listen to the sounds and decide what may have caused them. The sequence might be made up of such sounds as those of a doorbell, policeman's whistle, or cash register; rain, the opening and closing of a door, crunching of paper, or sharpening of a pencil; removing a telephone receiver from a hook, starting a car, or the rattle of dishes.

Pupils listen to a tape recording of a speech. The tape is stopped at a certain point. Pupils, having kept up with the speaker's development of thought, try to think ahead and guess what the speaker will say next. Then the hearing of the tape is resumed.

A stimulating series of "44 Things to Do" is offered by Nichols and Stevens in *Are You Listening?*

BILINGUAL CHILDREN

The linguistic approach to teaching bilingual children is businesslike and realistic. As explained linguistics analyses the structure and idioms of languages, the phonetic systems, and the placement of tongue and lips in forming language sounds. The teacher is encouraged to learn the linguistic facts of any non-English language spoken by pupils in her class. Particularly, she should examine the nature of any consonant or vowel sounds or any phonetic combinations which are not used in English. She will find it valuable to study diagrams showing how the positions of the tongue and lips differ for the formation of specific phonemes in other languages. (Placements for making the sound represented by *r*, for example, differ considerably from language to language.) She may have available a motion picture film which presents in slow motion an X-ray picture of the jaw, tongue, and lip movements used and also a stretch-out of the sounds uttered when a certain phoneme is spoken in English and other languages spoken by her bilingual pupils.

With this linguistic information a teacher knows which English phonetic items are difficult for bilingual children. She should notice, too, the word order and sentence patterns of the other language; where the accents occur in words, phrases, and sentences; and how the speaker's voice rises and falls.

Equipped with such knowledge, a teacher knows how to analyse the bilingual child's difficulties. She is in command of a situation that, were she without the information, would almost certainly be a fumbling confusion of trial and error.

A certain English phonetic item may trouble a bilingual child, not because of the nature of the sound but because of the position of the sound in the English word—that sound being at the beginning or end of the word, for example, or next to another sound that must be pronounced in combination with it. Thus the child may pronounce easily the sound represented by the phonetic symbol *dz* when it occurs, as it might in his language, at the beginning of a word but have difficulty if, in English, the sound comes at the end or in the middle of a word. Or perhaps he can articulate the sound spelled *ts* in some native combination like *tseth* but not in an English terminal like *-ats;* or the native sound represented as *tsh* but not the English one written as *sh.* Likewise the sound represented by *mb,* occurring rather frequently at the beginning of words in some languages, may be troublsome terminally in an English word like *dumb.*

In schools having foregn language instruction in the grades, the teacher of bilingual children has an advantageous start because teachers and pupils are already thinking in terms of comparative language—sounds, placement of tongue and lips, grammatical structure, and phrasal idioms. Such thinking, though it may have originated in the school programme of French or German, opens the way for solving bilingual problems in any language, be it Polish, Spanish, Hungarian, or Japanese.

Respect for Other Languages: It is important that the non-English language be treated respectfully. Such respect can be accorded in full linguistic honesty because in linguistics there is no thought of one language being superior to another; every language, however "primitive," is adequate for communicating in its native culture and is actually quite complete and sophisticated as a structured code for exchange of ideas and information. Certainly English can make no valid claim of being superior to other languages. A foreign language may seem strange to a member of any linguistic group, but no language can truthfully be called "funny" in a derogatory sense.

The attitude of the pupil's family toward their non-English language is influential. It may need bolstering. Too often they suppress that language in the belief that it is socially disadvantageous.

ASSURING GROWTH IN THE USE OF ORAL COMMUNICATION

Pupils, like adults, consider their speech a highly personal facet of themselves. They hold this viewpoint toward what they say and particularly toward how they say it. Naturally, then, they tend to be both sensitive and interested when a teacher suggests improvements in manner of substance of speech.

The effects of a teacher's criticisms depend on several factors: the maturity of the pupil, the number of people, present at the time, the nature of the occasion, and the relationship between pupil and teacher. Each situation should be handled according to its circumstances, and the teacher ought to know whether the child is emotionally normal or shows evidence of tenseness or proclivity to speech disorder.

Usually a pupil should not be interrupted while speaking, although some situations ought to receive attention immediately. The transitory nature of speech requires that attention be given rather soon because what has been said has been said, and the original speech situation cannot be recalled fully, even through a tape recording.

Four types of growth in oral communication are practical in elementary years. They relate to the quality of what the pupil says, the pupil's thoughtfulness of his hearers, his command of certain physical aspects of speaking, and the quality of the syntax and vocabulary which he uses. An urgency hovers about all of them because a person's performance in speech is on display constantly in daily life and is much more steadily revealed than his accomplishments in writing, arithmetic, or social studies.

The Quality of What is Said

Classroom discussions and reports should show that the pupils' minds have taken hold of their topics. Mental vigour deserves nurturing because ideas, opinions, and facts are the motivations, presumably, for speaking. It is the message—something worth saying, and satisfactorily organised—that is supposed to be served by the skills of speech. By using some energy to think about what he is going to say, a pupil makes listening worthwhile for his classmates; by organising his material well, he increases the probability that his communication will be clear.

The quality of what pupils say is a consideration in all the types of speech mentioned in this chapter. In the first few grades, concentration on a topic is brief, but during those few minutes the pupil can avoid flitting capriciously around the subject. In grades 4 to 6 the attention span lengthens. But in any grade, kindergarten to six, children can be stimulated to venture perceptive observations and ideas. Talks and discussions in classrooms can reflect a lively mentality, whether the topic be "Fair Use of Our Playground Swing," "How to Set a Table for Dinner," "Collecting Stamps," "Poetry Lines That I Like," or "What We Know about the Moon." Further possibilities of children's mental play over subject-matter appear in "Imaginative Expression".

This pursuit of quality does not demand that everything which is spoken be profound. Some topics and occasions do not call for profundity, but even they benefit from the play of mind working at its best.

Revising the content and organisation of oral projects is easier in one respect than revising written material. Or at least it seems easier, as it requires no extensive recopying. Speaking a paragraph or two several times is far less laborious than rewriting the same words.

In another respect, though, revising a speech is difficult: there is no tangible version to examine objectively and revise. If a speech is given on a trial basis it ceases to exist as a speech after it has been spoken. The speaker cannot hear himself. The best he can hope for is to receive constructive comments from listeners, if anyone heard him. A tape recorder is a fairly good solution to this problem. With it the speaker, hearing and rehearing himself, can check on the quality of the content and organisation of what he says.

Thoughtfulness of Hearers

Who will be my hearers? What are their interests? How can I interest them in my topic? What have they done or heard about that I can refer to and use as a link between them and my subject? How can I be courteous to them in what I say and do?

Those are fundamental questions for anyone planning a talk. They cannot be carried very far in early grades as long as children are notably egocentric, but there are possibilities in intermediate grades. The idea of courtesy in speech and manner is known to most children through their experiences in conversing, telephoning, receiving guests at classroom parties, and introducing people to each other. The other problem—linking a topic with the hearer's interest—is newer to pupils, and also more difficult. Every child practices such linking though, usually on a person-to-person basis, when trying to win favours from relatives or friends.

This problem becomes quite stimulating in class. Pupils can decide what openings would link certain topics with the experiences of specific audiences. For instance, if the topic is "Fruits That I Like," the speaker can be sure that his hearers, too, have their favourite fruits and often shop at fruit stands, and right in those two circumstances the speaker has a bridge between his topic and his audience. Or if the subject is "Some Ways That Seeds Are Scattered," the speaker might asume that most hearers have stepped on mushroom puffballs and seen the spores fly like dust, or have plucked burrs of seeds from their skirts or trousers, or have found elm or maple seeds lodged in their hats. In each instance the hearers helped scatter seeds, and with that fact the speaker can draw his audience into his subject.

A talk on "Kinds of Cloth" could open with people's experiences with various types of cloth found in the clothing they wear, and one on "Clay Modelling" might start with the hearers' memories of working with dough or of making mudpies.

The quest is for a common demominator with the audience. After the linkage is established at the opening it should be maintained throughout the speech. Pupils tend to neglect the linkage after the opening. Too often they drift away from that point of contact, thereby losing the interest of their audience.

The purpose of this kind of growth in speaking is simple, but the application is somewhat complex and requires a teacher's guidance. Too many speeches seem to be presented in an attitude of "here's my material; take it or leave it." The cause of such mishandling, though, seems to be less in deliberate intent than in the speaker's thoughtlessness and in the subtlety of the problem.

Standard of Syntax and Vocabulary

A double reward comes from improving English usage in speech. First, the improvement makes communication more effective; second, improvement in oral usage seems to be the best route (some people think it is the only route) to language improvement in writing. The greater effectiveness in communication occurs partly because it pleases listeners, partly because it conveys the message more surely, since it conforms more accurately to the English code.

Relationships between oral and written usages are discussed further in Part III, "Language." Linguistics gives primary status to spoken language, and most teachers imply a belief in speech as the standard when they urge children to test the correctness of an expression (written or oral) by the criterion, "Does it sound right?" or "How does it sound?" In urging that test the teacher has the responsibility of seeing that usages which actually are respectable "sound right" to the pupil.

Studies in children's speech patterns show that often in early grades the pupils assume their teacher's manner of speech and in middle grades imitate their classmates also. Whatever the pupil's age, the environment exerts strong influence. The school, with its mere six or seven hours a day and five days a week, may have little success in counteracting the effects of all the remaining hours which some children spend in the presence of substandard English.

Children are likely to employ four types of speech in a day: the speech prevailing in the informality of their homes; that employed at home when visitors are present; that which is natural amid the excitement of the playground; and that of the classroom. The types differ in precision of articulation, voice modulation, speech courtesies, tempo, and vocabulary. The attentiveness of the listening which accompanies them varies too.

Mechanics of Oral Communication

Speech requires a number of physical skills associated with control of the tongue and lips, breathing, resonance, posture, and gesture. Those skills are primarily mechanical even though they have relationships. Therefore they are discussed in, "Mechanics of Communication".

PUPIL ACTIVITIES

1. "This pond may look quiet but there's very much life in it."

Say this sentence a number of times. Each time you say it, put the main accent on a different word or group of words. How does the meaning change when you shift the accent?

Anybody who hears you will notice differences, too, when you pause a little at various places in the sentence, or when you say some parts faster or slower than others.

Try these sentences in the same ways:

"I waited while they talked."

"Go now."

"Guess who."

"When are they coming?"

2. A boy told his friends that he could speak the word *yes* in different ways. He said that by speaking it in these ways he could make it have five different meanings. He could even make *yes* mean *no,* he said.

How many different meanings can you give *yes* by saying it in various ways?

3. Get two or three of your friends to make up a little dialogue and write it out for you. The dialogue might be

between a mailman and someone from a family that is new in the neighbourhood, or between a store clerk and a customer who wants to buy a hat.

Then read the dialogue to your friends who wrote it. Do they think you have read it in such a way as to bring out the meaning and make the dialogue sound natural? Do they suggest any changes in your reading?

Let one of them read it aloud to you. Perhaps you can get another friend to join your group and read it while all of you listen.

4. Read to your classmates a part of a story that contains some dialogue. Can your listeners tell where there are quotation marks? Where there are commas? Where there are periods?

5. Take two stories that are short, one funny and the other serious. Read both of them aloud while you stand in front of the mirror.

Does your face show that the stories are different? Or do you "freeze" your face when you read aloud?

6. Open a book or magazine to a page that you have not yet read. At once red the page aloud. Then try it aloud again, noticing how much better you can read it this time.

Read it aloud six or seven times. When did you feel that you read it well enough to read to your classmates? At the fifth time? At the seventh? Or did you need even more readings?

7. Try to obtain a tape recording of a talk or conversation by a person or people whom you do not know and have not heard before. By listening, what can you tell about the speaker or speakers? Is the speaker excited? Angry? Happy? A boy? A girl? A man? A woman? Does he or she speak clearly? Would you have any advice for improvement of that person's speech?

8. Often you see people talk when they are too far away for you to understand what they are saying. But you can see their gestures and the expressions of their faces. What can you tell about their talk by watching them?

9. Listen a number of times to a poem that is recorded on

a tape or phonograph record. After hearing it often, start speaking the poem along with the recorded voice. Imitate the inflections, accents, and pauses. After you have practiced a while, get your friends to try to tell whether they are listening to you or to the recording. Do this by starting to speak along with the recording, then turning down the volume of the phonograph or tape recorder. Your friends should not be looking at you during this experiment.

10. A certain radio announcer sometimes signs off with this statement: "This is your station announcer saying good-bye and telling you that a good buy is always to be found in our city." He says it so well that the difference between "good-bye" and "good buy" is always clear.

How many times do you and your friends have to try that sentence until you have decided on a good way to say it?

11. You and three or four others from your class could make a "business-meeting team." You would learn to conduct business meetings by practising how to lead discussions, make motions, vote on motions, and take up items of business.

Then you might offer your services to other classrooms, explaining that you would be happy to visit them and help them with their business meetings. You could do the same for school clubs and other organisations.

12. When you give a report to your class, look first at the people farthest away, then at the ones near you. Notice what happens. Do you find that you are likely to change the loudness of your voice without thinking about changing it? Do you believe that a person tends to make his voice carry to the people at whom he is looking?

13. People reporting on a party or trip sometimes say "Oh, it was wonderful!" or "We had a grand time," but give no illustrations to prove that it was "wonderful" or "grand".

Try to tell about a trip, picnic, or party without saying "I had a grand time" or "it was wonderful." See whether you can give five or six examples of what happened or of what you did. Then maybe your hearers will know that the affair was "wonderful" and "grand" without your saying that it was.

14. Tell your classmates that you are going to read something that is well planned. Explain that it is so nicely organised that they should be able to tell when the discussion turns from one point to the next point. Also ask your listeners to make a mark on a piece of paper as soon as they can tell that the discussion is going from one point to another.

Then read the piece to them. While reading, watch your listeners to see whether they are putting down marks at the right times.

You might write the piece yourself or take a selection from a book, newspaper, or magazine.

15. You and a friend choose a story that all or most of your classmates know quite well. Record it on tape but make a few small changes in it when you record it. Then play it back for the class and see how many of your classmates notice the changes that you made.

16. How many minutes or hours a day do people spend listening to you? See whether you can find a way to count the time. Every minute during which you talk and somebody listens should be counted. Then estimate the amount of time that people hear you talk during a week, a month, a year.

STUDY ACTIVITIES FOR TEACHERS

1. "Here is your topic for a fifteen-minute talk: 'Selecting Wall-paper for a Living Room.' What humour could you draw from the subject itself, so that you wouldn't have to bring in any outside jokes? You have five minutes now to think of such humour."

Might occasional challenges like that one inspire speakers to search their topics instead of jokebooks for something to enliven their talks?

2. By moving away from a radio or tuning down the volume a person can notice which vowel and consonant sounds or combinations of sounds are first to fade out or become blurred; which next; which carry farthest.

One can make a similar test by moving away from a person who is speaking or by listening to speech that is occurring in an adjoining room.

Such experiments reveal also the extent to which audibility depends on the sounding of vowels and enunciation depends on the clear-cut utterance of consonants.

3. Much is said about the bad English spoken on playgrounds and in corridors. Teachers hear the shouts, exclamations, and excited exchanges, but usually don't see what is going on.

Perhaps full view of the situation would change the opinion. One would see the accompanying gestures, facial expressions, and general animation. Words, syntax, manner of speech, gesture, and the excitement of the moment might appear as a harmonious unit. Could it be that to someone who does not actually see the situation, the English of playgrounds and corridors sounds worse than it really is?

4. Many people who habitually groped for words or used fill-in sounds like *uh, ah, er-r,* or *and-uh* have developed fluency by exercises of this type:

They take a familiar idea like "tree," and then, with all the speed they can force themselves to muster, they name, in swift succession, whatever objects they associate with "tree"; *bark, bough, root, leaf, twig, sap, wind, nest, bird,* etc. They press for greater and greater speed.

The idea "road" is another good motif for the purpose.

5. Using a tape recorder, one can experiment with the three kinds of accent. In *stress* accent one portion of the word is spoken with more force than another. In *time* accent a sound is held longer than others, though it is not necessarily given special stress or pitch. In *pitch* (or *musical*) accent a portion of the word or phrase is spoken in a pitch that differs from the pitch of other portions, though it is not necessarily given special stress or length.

How many of these three types of accent do people use when exclaiming "Who, me?" or when chiding somebody with "You'll be sorry"? To what extent are time and pitch accent more noticeable in the Italian and Swedish languages than in English?

6. How can a teacher use song or instrumental music to help children:

Give adequate values to the sounds of *n* and *ng* at ends of words?

Pronounce all syllables of words?

Cure nasality?

Correct a tendency to transpose sounds?

Overcome monotonous ways of reading aloud?

Overcome incorrect word grouping?

7. What procedures seem best for training a person to concentrate on:

One particular sound among the various sounds in a noisy room or street.

One instrument in a chamber-music group, band, or orchestra.

The programme from one radio when two radios in the same room are tuned in on different programmes.

8. Faculty meetings illustrate group dynamics in action. Would flow charts of discussions at several meetings reveal definite patterns?

9. Here are some things associated with a summer wind-and-rain storm, named in a familiar sequence of occurrence: the sky becomes overcast, clouds thicken, a few large raindrops fall, wind increases, rainfall turns to a downpour, clothes and shoes get wet, people scurry to shelter, paths and pavements are watery, rain rattles on windows and roof, rain and wind roar in the trees, there is full flow in gutters and ditches, water spills from eaves and drainpipes, water drips through leaky roofs, the wind lessens, the rain slackens, there is a sudden but brief renewal of rain, the sky clears gradually, people return outdoors, the moist earth and vegetation give fragrance to the air.

But when thinking about summer storms, would most people recall those items in a different sequence? Might wet shoes and clothes be their first thought? Or flooded gutters and ditches, and the rattle of rain on windows and roof? Or the fragrance of moist earth and vegetation?

The latter type of sequence, following associational or emotional logic rather than strictly intellectual logic, is common in poems and stories. Does it have its uses in factual speaking and writing, too? Might it be the better way to win a hearer's or reader's interest? Using it, might people reporting on trips and conventions avoid the tedious "Next we . . . Then we . . . Next we . . ."?

VIEWPOINTS TO EMPHASISE THROUGH TEACHING AIDS

1. *Speaking is like radio or television broadcasting: there are transmitters and receivers.*

(a) A poster or overhead projector showing drawings of a person talking and a person (or people) listening. Also there are sketched-in lines indicating that the person talking is television station Speaker and that the broadcasting is through Channel 1. The listener is pictured as a receiving set. Caption: We must send the message correctly if it is to be received correctly.

2. *People "tune in" and "tune out" on speakers, according to whether or not the speaker presents his material well.*

(a) Cartoon sketches showing listeners tuning in and tuning out of speeches and conversations.

(b) A poster having on it:

I listened to the report because:

-- *(What would*

-- *you say*

-- *here?)*

I lost interest in the report because:

—————————————— *(What would*

—————————————— *you say*

—————————————— *here?)*

(c) Tape recordings and kinescopes of talks. Listening to them, pupils note when they either give up listening interested or begin to listen with even greater interest.

3. The speaker's voice should continue in good volume to the end of a sentence.

(a) Tape recordings of sentences properly carried through and of ones that fade out.

(b) Poster cartoon showing a landscape with part of a sentence sagging (and therefore dropping out of sight) below the horizon. A caption can be added.

4. A speaker's voice should go up and down somewhat to show the meanings of what is said and to give variety to speech.

(a) Tape recordings of speeches and conversations, some varied in pitch, some monotonous.

(b) Pictures of oscillographs of speaking voices.

(c) A poster showing a modulated oscillograph line and also a monotonous one. Caption: Which is your speech profile?

5. We should pronounce enough of a word to make the word clear to our hearers.

(a) Tape recordings (video, if possible) and phonograph recordings (including choral-speaking records) of words well spoken. Also samples containing words that are vexingly obscure in the recording—obscure because they were not fully pronounced.

(b) Poster having on it five or six words that commonly do not get pronounced fully. (*February, library, going, government,* for example.) Captions: Do you put lazy spots in these? Broadcast the whole word.

6. Accent is important to make a word clear and to show the meaning.

Animated-cartoon drawings (which can be pulled through a box theatre) showing Mr. Accent moving about among words and jumping from syllable to syllable in individual words. When he hits the wrong syllable of a word he sometimes disguises the word, or at least makes it confusing to understand. When he moves from syllable to syllable in a word like *address* or *entrance* he changes the meaning of the word.

Mr. Accent can be assisted by one or two Little Accents, who hit the lesser accents of long words. If there are two Little Accents, one can be somewhat smaller than the other.

7. Group discussions are best when many pupils take part, the group keeps to its intended subject, and the thinking is logical.

(a) Tape recordings of group discussions.

(b) Tape recordings of discussions held in other rooms or in former years.

8. When listening to discussions and speeches a person should be attentive and thoughtful.

(a) Animated-cartoon drawings showing what goes on in the mind of a good listener.

(b) A poster or a projector card giving questions that a listener should keep in mind. Questions can be placed so as to fan out ardially from the head of a listener.

9. A person must get enough facts in order to give a good report.

(a) Tape recordings of two reports, one rich in facts, the other deficient in them. Listening to the recordings, pupils note the contrast and the reasons for it.

(b) A poster: Facts are strong. Give them a chance.

(c) A poster showing cross sections of two barrels or tanks connected by a pipeline. The barrel at the left is scarcely half full and is marked as containing only a few facts about cotton harvesting. The one at the right, just beginning to fill from the pipeline, is marked "The hearer's or reader's needs." Beneath the tanks are a caption and two arrows, one arrow pointing to each tank: Caption: This one will never fill this one.

10. The ends of lines of poetry can be spoken in different ways, with differing effects.

(a) Tape and phonograph recordings illustrating various ways of reading the ends of lines—voice sustained to the end, voice dropped, voice raised slightly, last syllable held a bit longer, last syllable given normal length, etc.

11. *Parliamentary rules keep a meeting orderly and help it do business efficiently.*

(a) Tape recordings of club and class meetings that were well conducted.

(b) A poster diagram presenting a few elementary (but basic) facts about how to conduct meetings, state motions, and act on motions.

INQUIRIES AND PROBLEMS FOR STUDENTS

1. Observe the speaking, gesturing, and listening habits of a nine-year-old boy or girl during several ten-minute periods. Kep a record of everything the child does in matters related to oral communication. What percentage of the child's active hours do you find devoted to some kind of verbal communication? Might that percentage be valid for adult Americans? What seems to be the frequency of listening, speaking, and gesturing among your fellow students?

2. Here is the schedule of an intermediate grade class. Think about the number of occasions a boy or girl in this grade has each day for speaking, gesturing, and listening:

8:30–8:50	Opening activities
8:50–9:00	Sharing news and planning
9:00–9:30	Arithmetic
9:30–10:00	Reading and related activities
10:00–10:30	Spelling and word study
10:30–10:45	Intermission
10:45–11:30	Social Studies
11:30–11:50	Handwriting
Noon recess for lunch in school cafeteria.	
1:00–1:30	Science
1:30–2:00	Language (oral, written, usage, etc.)
2:00–2:30	Health and recreation
2:30–2:50	Art
2:50–3:30	Music

3. Notice how school groups speak the words associated with the salute to the flag. How could their renditions become good examples of choral speaking?

4. Is a dead-level speech profile an indication of a dead-level, pedestrian mind?

5. Keep a record of how many kinemorphs you identify in fifteen minutes spent at a public meeting, on a street, or in a dining room. Beforehand, read about kinesics and paralinguistic elements of oral communication.

6. Analyse the group dynamics in one of your discussion-type classes and also in a student committee meeting. Identify the factors which shape the activities and attitudes of individuals and of the group. Make a flow chart of the discussions. If you can obtain or make a sociogram of the class or committee, see what relationships exist between the sociogram and the flow chart. Prescott's chapter on "Analysing Group Dynamics" in *The Child in the Educative Process,* with its explanation of sociograms, might help you make the analysis.

7. Experiement with various ways of helping discussion groups identify their problems or issues. Then see whether you can help a group concentrate on the topic that it is supposed to discuss.

8. With as much objectivity as you can command, observe your mental processes as you solve a problem. What do you say to yourself? When the problem is primarily mental, is your process very different from when the problem is largely physical or mechanical?

Then note how children's minds work in problem solving. What do children say to each other in the process? To themselves? Do they try alternative means of solving a problem?

9. Although the conventional Aristotelian pattern for phrasing a definition (genus, species, differentiation) is satisfactory for most purposes, it has recognisable limitations, especially when the item to be defined is changing or relative in nature or is highly individual. The conventional definition,

being based on identities, does not accommodate everything which one might wish to define. With it you can define "a man," for example, but not "John," a particular man. Do you see why? Black's *Problems of Analysis* points out details of those limitations.

10. Suppose that your performance in making an oral report were to be criticised by your classmates or teacher. In what manner and at what time would you prefer to have the criticism offered?

11. What impressions do you have regarding the efficiency of listening by your classmates? How do you manage to listen effectively when distracting sounds compete for attention?

12. If you know a second language, identify any characteristics of lip and tongue placement or other aspects of sound formation and articulation which are present in that language but not in English. Also identify two features of the grammar, word order, or sentence pattern wherein that language differs from English. How would you proceed in helping a speaker of that language learn English?

13. Observe how assembly and after-dinner speakers obtain humour in their speeches. How many find humour within the topic itself? How many depend on imported humour that is more or less extraneous to the topic? What happens among audiences when the latter type of speaker follows his irrelevant joke with the remark, "Now to be serious again"?

13

Written Communication

Writing is a symbolisation of speech. And because speech, the primary form of language, is a symbolisation of what the speaker had in mind to say, writing becomes a symbolisation of a symbolisation.

Writing, being a derived form of language, is therefore communication twice removed from the original thought. It is not written speech; because of the contrasting natures of speech and writing it cannot be. Much more happens in oral communication than can be shown with standard symbols on the written or printed page. These differences create problems for pupils; they also complicate the teacher's pedagogy.

Written communication demands skill and pedagogy not required in speech. The child must learn the set of marks (graphemes) which his society uses to represent the elements of spoken language. To make these marks and perform the act of writing, he needs a degree of muscular coordination. Then he faces the complexities of spelling and the even greater difficulties of trying to represent, with written punctuation, the pauses, intonations, and kinesics which he uses as eloquent signals in his speech. Also there are the conventions of a printed page: spacing, letter and line alignment, and capitals.

In addition, the pupil needs the capacity to work at writing and to work alone: to work, because writing, with revisions and recopying, is more laborious than speaking; to work alone, because writing lacks the social stimulus (as well as the spontaneity) of speech; it is an individual, solitary, and deliberate enterprise.

Each of those circumstances is important in the pedagogy of written communication.

OBJECTIVES IN TEACHING WRITTEN COMMUNICATION

The big undertaking of teaching written communication takes on a stimulating tenor if approached from the viewpoint of discovering and using the resources which the English language offers to anyone who writes. Such discovery and use constitute the principal objective in written communication, regardless of whether a teacher takes advantage of them as a strategic approach.

The process requires the development of numerous skills. A skill like muscular control for handwriting may be mainly physical, but those needed for written punctuation, planning the format of the page, and spelling are both physical and mental.

A hope constitutes one very important objective. It is the hope that when boys and girls write something for social studies, science, or any other subject, they will write as well as they do in language arts. It is one of the heartbreaks of English teachers, through all grades and into college, to receive handsome papers and then see careless writing done by the same pupils in other subjects.

PUPIL BACKGROUND FOR STUDYING WRITTEN COMMUNICATION

Compared with his background in speech, a pupil brings relatively little to his classroom lessons in writing. He has scrawled with crayon and pencil, and may have written his name and a few words, especially when a letter was being prepared for a grandparent or aunt. He may have impressions of capitals and lower-case letters, but of punctuation he knows nothing except for a vague idea that a dot belongs at the end of a string of words.

The child sees writing, though, as something that he would like to learn and should learn. His personal interest is high. But ahead are the tasks of learning to spell and developing muscular control for shaping alphabetic letters, manuscript and cursive.

PUPILS DAILY EXPERIENCES WITH WRITTEN COMMUNICATION

Occasions for classroom writing are as varied as school needs and pupils' experiences because writing is a key form of communication in academic life. The samplings below give an idea of where motifs for writing can come from and of how certain typical motifs developed in specific grades. Writings associated with imaginative expression are illustrated only briefly here.

Kindergarten: After having mailed Valentine greetings, one kindergarten class visited the local post office and learned how mail left and arrived in the town. Upon returning to their room the pupils composed a thank-you letter to be sent to the post office employees. The teacher copied the letter on the blackboard for everybody to see before she wrote it in actual letter form.

Grade 1: When the class wanted to visit the village fire station, it composed a letter asking permission to make the visit. The teacher wrote the letter, which was mailed. After the visit the pupils talked about their observations and told the teacher what to record on the chalkboard. The class also composed a thank-you note which the teacher then wrote in letter form.

In another first-grade room the children maintained a yearlong interest in making a combined calendar and record of events. The teacher and pupils divided the writing. The teacher put the record on experience charts after the class had chosen and talked about the events which should be recorded. (These included the class experiences of caring for a rabbit and observing robins that built a nest in a spruce tree near the school.) Pupils wrote most of the entries on the calendar and weather chart: the temperature record and seasonal changes in the leaves, flowers, fruits, birdlife, and appearance of the sky.

Grade 2: "How Do We Get Our Milk?" was a study made by a second grade in a large city. Associated with the study were these items of writing: letters explaining the project to parents, group observations and records of the trip, and thank-you notes to the milk company and the bottling plant guide. Children did most of the writing, aided considerably by the teacher. Several pupils also wrote imaginative stories as a result of the experience.

One second-grade classroom organised itself as a Good Citizen's Club. Writing came into the project during the preparation of three letters that were sent when the members wanted to buy inexpensive pins for themselves. Pupils wrote the letters and the whole class talked about the importance of margins, neatness, and good handwriting.

During the morning "news" period in another second grade someone reported having seen bluets near a melting snowbank. This led to a flower-observing trip and then to extended discussions on why wild flowers are not more plentiful. As an outgrowth of the discussion the class composed a letter to the department of conservation of the state. The class chose one of the girls to write the letter.

Grade 3: The "daily news" periods of one classroom did much to teach skills of language. Each day's record began with an entry of the date and date. Thus the pupils learned to spell and write the names of the days of the week and of the months. Each day the news items remained on the blackboard until late in the afternoon and were referred to several times during the day. On some days the children made copies to take home. Sentence building, word arrangement, spelling, use of capital letters, punctuation, and penmanship developed from the activity. The class occasionally closed its school day with a final reading of its "daily news".

Another third grade was obliged to fill out an application blank in order to obtain a free exhibit on paper making and the various grades of paper. The blank called for information about the class and school.

An early June walk by another class brought up the question of whether white colour helps keep things cool. (The group had met an ice cream vendor in the city park, and one of the girls asked him why his suit and wagon were white.) A classroom experiment began: two tin cans, equal in size, were covered with paper, one white, the other black. Next, water and an ice cube were put in each. After the cans had stood in the sun a while the children observed that the ice in the white can had melted more slowly than that in the black. Then the class worked together on a write-up of the experiment, telling about the successive steps and the final observations. Everybody copied the write-up from the blackboard. Three boys who knew the vendor were chosen to tell him about the experiment.

A "jack-and-the-bean-stalk" seed had been planted beneath the bedroom window of a pupil from another third grade. When the plant had grown to the top of the window, the boy told the class about it. This brought on a discussion of how seeds sprout, how plants grow, and what nourishment plants require. There was a request for a rereading of the "Jack and the Bean Stalk" story, and the class wrote up what they had observed and read about the sprouting of seeds and the care of growing plants.

Grade 4: The importance of careful wording and phrasing developed when a fourth-grade arithmetic class was making up its own mathematical problems. Both the choice of word and the position of words and groups of words in a sentence had to be exact if the statements of the problems were to mean what the class intended. When writing one problem, the pupils noticed how radically they could change the meaning of a sentence by changing the punctuation.

Industrial arts activity related to airplanes led another fourth grade into discussions of international mail routes and world trade. Explanations of how mail is handled on planes and on ships and summaries of shipping news as published in the newspapers of a port city were written up carefully. The write-ups became part of the room's display called "Our Most Interesting Explorations of the Year." The search for information and the writing were divided among individuals and groups.

One fourth-grade's extended study of Tanganyika and neighbouring areas of East Africa called for much writing. Items included letters to travel companies, steamship lines, and consulates, requesting maps and folders regarding East Africa; records of animal and plant life there; descriptions of people, crops, and handcrafts; suggestions for a tour of the area; explanations of the weather; and preparation of a travel folder designed to interst people in visiting that portion of Africa. Margins, spacing, neatness, and clear handwriting were considered especially important in the letters and travel folder.

Grade 5: Playground rules posted on a school's bulletin boards confused pupils on several matters because the statements were ambiguous. A fifth grade cleared up the points by rephrasing the rules so that the meaning was unmistakable. But the process of rephrasing was neither brief nor easy, though it held the enthusiasm of the group. Oral discussions preceded the writng. Punctuation and the best position for certain words and phrases proved to be extremely important.

Parks (national and state) and public camping grounds within the home state engaged the interest of a fifth-grade class in Maine. Finally each child designed a tourist folder for his favourite park or camp-ground, and the class cooperatively prepared a larger folder for the whole state. Spacing, punctuation, and legibility received much attention.

Grade 6: John Ruskin's *The King of the Golden River* struck the fancy of a class whose school was on a river and near mountains. The location, weather, and classroom situation were just right for the story to come alive. As a result the class collected and recorded facts and legends related to the local river and foothills.

After enjoying Stephen Foster songs, one sixth grade prepared a classroom television show on Foster's life and song writing. Selection of characters to appear on the programme, the order of events, and the preparation of dialogue were decided largely on the basis of: "How can we make the best use of the fifteen minutes that we have for the show?" Pupils wrote a legible, well-spaced copy of the script for each character of the show.

A pupil's oral report on the reading of a book called *What Time Is It?* started a sixth grade on a study of old and new methods of telling time. In addition to oral explanations and some written reports, there was a write-up of an interview that two of the children had with a watch repairman in a nearby village.

In a small school the sixth grade had joined the fifth for the year's activities in art and music. Early in April the pupils reviewed some things that they had learned about pictures, colours, lines, shapes, designs, clay modelling, songs, tunes, chords, and pitch. When they saw how numerous those items were, and how interesting, somebody thought that elements like colours, lines, tunes, chords, and pitch could be personified as characters in a story or play. The class members soon found themselves personifying the various items, talking about themselves (in character) and about each other. Only the more elementary and simple aspects of art and music were developed, but dialogue was written out and the play became part of a May Day programme. Afterward, when the class was talking about the venture, the teacher suggested that sometime they might try a playlet in which they, as characters, would represent various kinds of words, accents, groups of words, sentences, capitals, and punctuation marks.

A PROGRESSION THROUGH THE GRADES

In kindergarten and first grade the teacher does most of the writing, using a chalkboard or a mounted experience chart. At first she writes in her own words the information or ideas that her pupils tell her about. Soon she records the words that the pupils suggest should be written. Late in the first grade and in the second grade most pupils begin to write for themselves, although a few children start in the next grade if slow in developing the muscular coordination needed for writing.

During the transition period, children at first copy what the teacher has written on the chalkboard but feel free to make changes or additions as they copy. Next, in many classrooms, there is a stage in which pupils write as the teacher dictates. Soon thereafter the pupils do both the composing and the writing. The teacher gives much help at first, but tries to make the young writes progressively more independent.

Even while still using a chalkboard or experience chart, a teacher introduces techniques of writing. Sometimes by direct comment (often rather casually) she draws attention to format, spelling, handwriting, punctuation, organisation of material, and sentence construction. For example, she takes occasion to say, "I'll leave space at each side, so that what I write will stand out nicely," or "I'll put a mark here to show that this is the end of the sentence." Likewise she can explain her use of quotation marks, question marks, or other signals important in writing. She might bring up the idea of organisation by suggesting that "this sentence seems to fit best after that one" or "these ideas go well together."

Time and patience are necessary. Writing, a complex skill, requires sustained effort to be learned, just as speaking had taken intensive apprenticeship during the pupils' first three or four years of life. In contrast to speaking, writing is still a new venture for most children in the first grade, few pupils having advanced beyond scrawling their names and brief messages on slips of paper for enclosure in letters to relatives or playmates.

Sentences and Paragraphs: As written by first and second graders, sentences are short and the discussion of the topic is brief—probably not more than three sentences. The material is not likely to be arranged in paragraph form. Yet no composition is too brief to deserve some attention to how the content should be stated.

In grades 3 and 4, sentences and discussions become longer. Three, four, and possibly five sentences on a topic can be expected in the third grade, and one or two additional sentences in the fourth. Paragraph arrangement of the sentences can be started in the third grade and required in the fourth.

Having reached grades 5 and 6, pupils can be expected to compose two or three short paragraphs or one paragraph of five to seven sentences. Also they begin writing sentences that contain subordinate clauses, and this innovation brings on considerable trouble with punctuation of the clauses.

Organisation: From grade to grade there is progress likewise in organising material, forming a good opening sentence, following logical sequences of items, and being thoughtful of the person or persons to whom the writing is directed. Those aspects of communication are as important in writing as the preceding chapter showed them to be in speech. They must have attention along with skills of handwriting, written punctuation, format, and spelling. Fortunately for economy of time and effort, what a pupil learns about them in speech is usable in writing, and vice versa.

Attention to organisation and sequence begins with experience-chart writing. By the fourth grade, children can make a list of the important points related to a topic. In the next grade they draw up an outline having main heads and subheads. In the sixth grade most pupils should be able to make an outline that is fairly complete. Whenever any grade prepares a record of a trip, meeting, or experiment, there can be experiences in deciding what items are most important and how they should be organised.

Graphs: Graphs, already noted as aids for a speaker, are equally (and perhaps even more) useful for a writer. They are a form of writing. Compact and pictorial, they present in little space a set of data which might require several paragraphs of prose. In addition they usually surpass prose in showing data clearly and in such form as to be quickly understood by a reader.

LETTERS

A teacher approaches letter writing with notable advantages. Her pupils, even before starting school, have had considerable experience at home with letters that arrived or were mailed. In the past many of them "wrote" notes to aunts, cousins, or friends. In every grade they normally have warm pleasant feelings toward the whole matter of receiving and writing letters.

In school, letter writing serves natural functions. There are dozens of occasions when letters should be written. Thank-you letters must be sent to postmen, farmers, firemen, or others whom the pupils visited. Get-well notes are mailed to sick classmates. Invitations for school parties go out to parents and friends. Information is requested from chambers of commerce, consulates, and travel agencies. Letters are exchanged with children in a foreign country or in some region of the United States. When writing such messages, children understand what their letters are supposed to do, and therefore they see why qualities like neatness, legibility, and general good form are practical and worth attaining.

Letter writing becomes fully realistic when the situation calls for the actual mailing of a letter. Use of a mere classroom "post office" may lead to pointless note writing.

In the first grade, letters usually are composed by the class, and the teacher is satisfied if a letter is only one or two sentences long. In the second grade, some children write their own letters, through group composing continues. The length is likely to increase to three or four sentences. In the third grade, letter writing is an enterprise for everybody.

Business letters usually represent the interests of the whole class and therefore can profitably be composed by the group. Effective models can be selected from letters received or written in the school office. From such models, better than from textbook reprints, the pupils understand the practical values of the heading, inside address, and other items that are standard in business-letter forms. Further, the samples convince the pupils that the forms recommended in class are really being used in daily life.

It is interesting for pupils to interview people who receive and send many letters. Reports of such interviews help the class think realistically about letter writing.

A letter-testing scale for each classroom is practical. To establish one, pupils and teacher assemble letters from various sources then mount them under such heading as "very good," "good," and "not good enough."

Instruction in letter writing includes instruction in punctuation, capitalisation, neatness, format, handwriting, spelling, sentence structure, and the courtesies of a writer toward a reader. Thus the influences of teaching letter writing extend beyond the writing of letters.

PUPIL ACTIVITIES

1. When you mail a letter you are sending something to talk for you. It is your delegate. Explain that fact to several of your classmates and ask them what they would want their letters to be like, as their delegates.

2. Interview seven or eight people who receive many business letters. These might be secretaries or officials in banks, stores, schools, or newspaper offices. Get their opinions on what they like or dislike about letters that come to them. Talk about what the letters say and about the form in which they are set up. Perhaps someone will give you samples of good letters and of poor ones.

3. In a library try to find some friendly letters written by Hans Christian Andersen and Theodore Roosevelt. You and your classmates will enjoy what the writers said.

4. Write two letters that say the same things in the same words. Make one letter very neat and in excellent format but do the other one carelessly. Show them to a number of people and find out how those people would feel toward the sender of each letter. Would they be as willing to answer the untidy letter as the neat one?

5. Except on Halloween you wouldn't like to go visiting when there is a black smudge on your face. Neither would you think well of anyone who came to your door that way.

Look at the papers that are handed in to the teacher and at letters that people send. Also look at notices on the bulletin board. How often do you see a paper, notice, or letter that is as unattractive as a person would be with a smudge on his face?

"The papers you hand in and the letters you send are you," someone said, "and it pays to have them well groomed."

6. The statues around your school are on pedestals. They are not standing directly on the floor or lying on the ground. They are on some special mounting so that they stand out with plenty of space around them.

Paintings and other pictures are in frames and are hanging or standing somewhere where they can be seen easily and also seen alone. They are not lying on tables or hanging on top of each other.

When we write, we must think about space and appearance too. A number of things help our writing stand out nicely so that it may be seen easily on the paper. See how important margins are for this. Also notice the value of space between words and between the letters in a word.

Why is it pleasant to have special spacing around poems that are written or printed?

7. "The Growth and Marketing of Coffee"
   "How Coffee is Grown and Marketed"
   "From Coffee Plantation to Supermarket"
   "From Coffee Plant to Kitchen Table"
   "From Coffee Plant to Cup"
   "From Coffee Plant to Market Shelves"
   "From Plantation to Percolator"

Which of the titles named above do you like better than others? Which ones do you think would be best to attract readers? Why?

Also think of good ways to word titles on each of the topics below. Ask your friends for their opinions.

Erosion of Topsoil ("Topsoil on a One-way Ride to the Sea" was one pupil's wording for it.)

How to Tell Directions When in a Forest

Stars and Constellations

Electric Eyes for Counting Traffic

Weather Contrasts: June 21, December 21

How Our Alphabet Developed

Different Shades of Green in Nature

How to Tell the Direction and Velocity of the Wind

STUDY ACTIVITIES FOR TEACHERS

1. What opinions on this quotation from Stuart Chase can you gather from your friends?

Talking came eons ago, writing just the other day. All normal children teach themselves to talk by imitating their elders and they work hard at it. But many children have trouble with reading and writing—perhaps because the business is so recent, perhaps because it is badly taught, perhaps both.

Writing, however, has one great virtue; it stays put. Nobody (unless he has total recall) can remember exactly what he heard even an hour later, as any judge can bear witness. But what Confucius said thousands of years ago is there on the page exactly as his scribes wrote it.

2. A teacher in the upper grades wrote two factual articles for an educational magazine. That was her first experience in preparing something for public print.

Later she remarked: "Ever since I did those articles I've had more sympathy for my pupils. When children wrote I used to think of their job from the reader's point of view—as an outsider. Now I think of it from the writer's viewpoint. There's a big difference. I know of difficulties and problems that I hadn't realised before."

3. A person is to write a factual discussion of the monarch butterfly. To inform himself on the subject he observes monarch butterflies and reads about them in reference sources.

But such knowledge alone is likely to remain rather formal. Perhaps there are informal impressions which would be helpful. Some people believe that there are. They would think about butterflies in the fashion suggested by the questions below. These questions are fanciful, they realise, but they say that such imaginative thinking helps them know their subject with a fullness not possible through factual study alone. Then, supported by the additional impressions, their minds play with the topic, thinking about butterflies in a friendly, informal, yet factual, way.

Here are samples of questions they think about:

What would be a suitable nickname for the monarch butterfly?

What are adult human beings likely to say when they see a monarch butterfly? What do small children say?

If I were designing jewellery, how could I use this butterfly as a motif for a design?

What might the butterfly think of an exceedingly hot day in summer? Of a very early frost? Of a thunderstorm?

What do birds say when they see a monarch butterfly?

What do these butterflies say when they see a human being?

What ideas or circumstances could a monarch butterfly symbolise?

How might a monarch butterfly costume itself for a masquerade party?

What holidays does the butterfly society observe?

If no monarch butterfly had evolved in the world, would mankind's environment have been the poorer?

How might the creator of an animated cartoon use a monarch butterfly in his film?

What does a tree look like to a butterfly?

If a monarch butterfly wrote its autobiography, how many divisions would his book have? What would be the headings of those divisions? The title of the book?

Give the names of two monarch butterfly social clubs. The name of the butterfly protective society. What name do monarch butterflies use for their own species?

Arrange the menu for a banquet held during its larva stage.

What is the attitude of monarch butterflies toward other species of butterflies?

If I were buying shoes for a monarch butterfly, how many pairs would I buy?

What advice do the older adults give to the newly arrived butterflies? What do the younger ones say to the older?

When two butterflies meet in the morning, what is the nature of their salutation?

Similar questions have been asked in classrooms, too. They were asked, of course, with the assurance that pupils would not confuse fiction and fact.

A fifth-grade class, for example, might supplement what it finds in history books and encyclopedias about Christopher Columbus. Pupils could speculate on:

What might Columbus enjoy seeing in my home town?

If Columbus were to walk into our school dressed in a fifteenth-century costume, would we recognise him?

If our class took Columbus to the county (or state) fair, how much guiding and explaining would be necessary?

If Columbus visited San Francisco, what would he say about ocean liners? About the Pacific Ocean?

VIEWPOINTS TO EMPHASISE THROUGH TEACHING AIDS

1. *We need facts and ideas when we write. To compose something worth reading we must have something worth writing.*

(a) A poster or opaque projector sheet presenting only certain conjunctions, definite and indefinite articles, and punctuation marks across the lines of a page. Big spaces are between the given items. All words having to do with facts or ideas are omitted or deleted. (A magazine or newspaper clipping can be used with the main words blotted out.) Caption: Something is needed to fill in.

(b) Drawings done in the manner of animated cartoons, showing ideas starting and growing in someone's mind. After a while the person is ready to write about the ideas.

2. *The opening sentences should make a reader want to continue reading.*

(a) Tape recordings or projections of the beginnings of several reports. One or two of the beginnings should be distinctly more effective than the others. All could be on the same topic. Take a class poll as to which report the pupils would prefer to hear or read.

(b) Poster mountings of the opening paragraphs from two reports on the same topic. One opening is more effective than the other. Caption: Which is the better "How do you do?" *or* Which makes you want to keep on reading?

3. Doing a report can be fun because there are interesting things to work with.

A series of posters and captions showing pupils' activities when preparing and giving a report. (1) Learning about the subject (the fun of hunting and finding); (2) Selecting the facts or ideas (the fun of choosing those which are most useful for my purpose); (3) Thinking of different ways the facts or ideas could be presented (the fun of finding a good way, answering questions like: What shall I start with? What shall I make seem most important? Can I use graphs and pictures? What shall I end with?); (4) Working with the English language (the fun of choosing words and kinds of sentences so that the language says what I want to say); (5) Thinking about the hearers or readers (the fun of deciding how I can get them to pay attention to what I say).

4. When writing facts we can use the best kinds of sentences and paragraphs that we know how to compose.

(Useful for this viewpoint are the audio-visual suggestions in, "Constructing Ideas with Language.")

5. Letters tell people much about the writer.

(a) A series of drawings, in the manner of animated cartoons, showing what happens in a reader's mind when opening and reading a good letter; when opening and reading a crudely written letter. If these drawings are on a continuous strip they can be pulled through a movie-theatre box.

(b) A poster showing someone reading a letter. Caption: Thus he judges you.

(c) A letter is mounted on a poster. Caption: This is your "How do you do?"

(d) Satisfactory letters, social and business, are on a bulletin board or poster. Beneath is the statement:

Your letters are your delegates. Be represented well.

(e) Using a disk or tape recorder, a class prepares a "talking letter" and sends the disk or tape to other rooms, other schools, or other countries.

INQUIRIES AND PROBLEMS FOR STUDENTS

1. Notice what teachers say as they write experience charts. What points regarding punctuation, format, and organising ideas do they comment on while making the chart?

2. "When you are present before your hearers your speech is your personality, next to your appearance. When you are absent from your readers—especially if your readers have never met you—your writing is *all* your personality."

What is your opinion of that statement?

3. Think about various relationships existing between the factors and the teaching of written communication.

4. Try to observe a pupil writing letters under each of these circumstances:

(a) The letter is merely as an "exercise" or assignment.

(b) The letter is one that the pupil wants very much to write for a practical purpose.

Compare the situations as to the pupil's inclination to learn more about letter writing and the quality of letter produced.

5. Use a pictorial graph the next time you prepare a report or term paper containing considerable data. Notice (a) how the graphic representation cuts down the amount of prose you need to write, and (b) how pleasantly surprised your instructor is to find a student using this efficient method of presenting information.

6. Think of three topics that, because of the way they naturally break into two, three, or four sub-divisions, would be practical to use in teaching a fourth-grade class how to outline and organise material.

7. Do you, in general, write your papers in science, social studies, and psychology as carefully and with as much attention to style as those you prepare for a course in English? Why?

8. To what extent do you find that your prose style is better and your composing less likely to contain errors in grammar when you know your topic very well? Can you note whether grade school pupils have similar experiences?

When faculty members say that a student "doesn't know how to write," might the real trouble be that the student didn't know the subject he attempted to write about?

9. Robert Hall believes that the traditional approach to punctuation "neglects the fact that most, although not all, of our English punctuation reflects intonation patterns." He is convinced that "punctuation can be taught much more quickly, easily, and effectively if the teacher knows how to analyse intonation, how to make its patterns clear to the pupils, and how to point out to them the ways in which intonation is reflected in punctuation."

Keep this statement in mind when you observe various teachers. Also try out Hall's method yourself.

10. Are readers generally less tolerant of flaws in someone's writing than in his speech? To what extent is this because an oral fumble vanishes with the sound and may soon be forgotten, but a blunder in writing remains on the record for anyone to see?

14
Newspapers and Magazines in the Classroom

Newspapers have been called "literature in a hurry." That designation may be appropriate; news columns are produced rapidly, and Ezra Pound has said that literature is "news that stays news."

Pressured by various factors, the products of journalism are topical and transient. But this circumstance does not prevent issues of newspapers and magazines from being influential during their moments of living. Neither is it a valid reason for ignoring them in the classrooms or for being reluctant to sponsor newspapers written by pupils of a room or school.

With or without benefit of school guidance, children read journalistic products during school years and after. Already in early and middle grades pupils hear about newspapers, look at the comics, notice headlines, read some articles, scan the columns about television and motion pictures, and clip items for notebooks and bulletin boards. In adult years many of them will choose newspapers and magazines as their principal reading.

It is realistic, therefore, to accept both commercial and school newspapers and magazines as curriculum material. They can be used for their merits, and their shortcomings can be recognised and countered. Classroom guidance may lead to adult readers who are able to understand the "pressures of the press" and the merciless impact of the newspaper page.

PUPILS' DAILY EXPERIENCES WITH NEWSPAPERS AND MAGAZINES

Even a kindergartner has impressions of newspapers. To a child who has not yet learned to read, a newspaper is something that comes regularly to the house and on which grownups spends considerable time. In it he may find several pictures to look at, along with some "funnies" which he either deciphers or wants somebody to read to him. He is likely to notice a few advertisements, and if there is unusually large type in the advertisements or headlines he may try to name some of the letters.

A child hears people talk about what is in the newspaper: "I see by the paper . . . ," "The paper says . . . ," "The meeting is tonight at eight, according to the paper" are common remarks in family conversation. Once in a while he hears one person says to another, "Well, I saw your name in the paper" or "I saw your picture in the paper yesterday." As a result he concludes that being mentioned or pictured in a newspaper is important and influential.

But he also gets impressions which suggest that a newspaper is not valuable very long. He sees it tossed about carelessly. Nobody reads it any more, after the first or second day. It is spoken of as the "old" paper or "yesterday's" paper, and what is in it is considered "stale" news.

In a day or two the paper meets any one of a number of undignified ends: it may be used to kindle a fire, wrap a parcel, make papiermâchinè, hold garbage, or stuff into an empty space that needs filling. Perhaps it becomes something for children to step on just inside the house door when rubbers or shoes are muddy. It may be thrust into the ashcan or stacked up with other papers for removal with the rubbish.

It is lies around several months is turns yellowish and brittle. An occasional clipping pasted in a book or filed in an envelope begins to look old too, and even the contents of clippings seem less interesting with the passing of time. All told, the newspaper is taken as part of the general environment, along with radio, television, and milk bottles.

To thousands of boys a newspaper has special connotations—the connotations of a commodity. These boys sell and deliver newspapers. But to newsboys the dominant associations with newspapers probably are financial rather than journalistic.

Magazines seem a little more valuable than newspapers but less permanent than books. A magazine usually survives longer than a newspaper, and its pages don't turn yellow and brittle so soon. But it can be cut up, and eventually it is burned or thrown away.

USE OF NEWSPAPERS AND MAGAZINES

Since newspapers and magazines are inexpensive and readily available, teachers and pupils use them variously. Some uses are obvious. They are a source of clippings and pictures for personal or group projects, a training ground for skills in reading, and a means of extending pupils' vocabularies. They give examples for firsthand study of their various parts or sections. They offer model news articles and interviews to guide the staff members of classroom or school newspapers. They provide current information that has not yet appeared in textbooks. They help in the preparation of a class for visits to editorial and printing offices. Their news coverage can be compared to that of radio and television.

Less obvious, but very relevant to language arts, are four additional uses. First, magazines and newspapers show a pupil that margins, spacing, neatness, and other elements of planned layouts are pleasing to readers and also practical. Second, their columns give speakers and writers examples of how writers win attention at the openings of articles and then proceed in a manner which continues to hold readers' attention. Third, articles and headlines reflect current usages in spelling, vocabulary, and syntax. Well-edited publications have a style and standard of usage that pupils could adopt for factual speaking and writing. Some newspapers, of course, display journalistic style at its worst, and cannot be taken as models.

As a fourth less obvious service, newspapers and magazines offer raw material adaptable for plots, characters, and settings in imaginative expression. To a pupil seeking such suggestions a glance through a newspaper is like having a mezzanine seat overlooking the lobby or corridor of the world. He sees news reports of rescues, fires, floods, expeditions, elections, sports contests, rocket space flights, legends, lost treasure, and mysterious disappearances; items about cats, dogs, deer, monkeys, birds, and the zoo; and interviews with aviators, inventors, fashion designers, sailors, sports champions, actors and actresses, musicians, and authors.

In Imaginative Expression: Two circumstances aid pupils who use these news items as motifs for imaginative expression: the materials in the articles have already been screened of nonessential details, and many of the situations contain conflict elements (necessary in stories and dramatic sketches) already established in the articles.

Three circumstances are less favourable: journalism plays up the freakish and bizarre—two types of material not satisfactory for amateurs in imaginative expression; news items normally place the climax at the opening, but stories and plays usually build up to one near the end; and most material in news columns is stated in summarising form, not in the dramatised manner of stories and plays.

Several Difficulties: There are difficulties, too. Me is rarely available to buy enough copies to make full use of periodicals. Storage space soon becomes a problem. Along with usable material the columns carry some items which are objectionable.

Unavoidably there is something opportunistic about day-by-day uses of periodicals. Pupils and teachers must work with what happens to come along. They cannot predetermine news or newsworthy events. Mostly they must keep alert, ready to benefit from whatever happens to be suitable.

SCHOOL AND CLASSROOM NEWSPAPERS

When a class or school publishes a paper the pupils' activities centre in the production side rather than in the role of reader because a large number of the children help prepare each issue. Pupils' experiences differ according to the situation—whether the paper is edited by a classroom staff or a general school staff; whether it is a weekly, a monthly, or a publication issued on special occasions only; and whether it is printed in school or by a commercial press.

In the early grades a newspaper is likely to be in the form of hand written columns, written in manuscript form on ruled paper and pasted on a large sheet or cardboard that has the paper's name lettered or printed at the top.

Whatever the situation, there is motivation for all staff members to be accurate and prompt in doing their share of the work. Those who write and distribute copies enjoy the action involved. When the teacher knows, the basic techniques of news editing there are exceptional chances for interest and learning to develop simultaneously, because school journalism appeals widely to the natural interests of children.

Management and Planning: If mismanaged a classroom or school paper can become a crushing burden for a few people and especially for the teacher. When this happens something is wrong with the planning. Or perhaps the paper is being published too much for the public or for the school administration instead of for the school as a whole. To be an educative enterprise it must be the product of group cooperation and fit rather comfortably into the normal work load of the day. It should provide some fun too, even though the work is exacting. If no solution to burdensomeness is discovered the publication should probably be discontinued.

Preplanning in specific detail usually clears the way for group cooperation. If the enterprise is a group's first venture in newspaper publication, further planning and some readjustments of earlier plans may be necessary as the project develops.

During preplanning the group can decide on the paper's name, the number of pages, what sections shall be established (general news, sports, poetry, and other features), how many reporters, editors, and assistant editors are needed, whether the paper shall be handwritten, mimeographed or printed, and where the duplicating or printing can be done. Then there are business considerations: the source of the materials needed, the cost, and the duties of the business and circulation managers. A visit to a newspaper office clarifies some techniques and duties.

Individual Competence: Individual responsibility in a group enterprise is the key to smoothness in publication. Many factors are interrelated. Accuracy, dependability, and promptness turn out to be the most valuable traits of good staff workers.

New staff members learn much about their jobs through the problems of publishing their first issue. Those who continue working on a series of issues get to know some things very well—perhaps through embarrassment resulting from inaccuracies, poor proofreading, or from carelessness in duplicating, distributing, or financial accounting. Reporters discover the importance of getting all the facts and veryfying them before handing in a final copy. Reporters and editors become more apt at sorting material, choosing what is important enough or suitable for publishing and what is not, and also at distinguishing between personal opinion and objective news. All writers discover the value of using simple language to state facts and opinions clearly.

Policy on News: One practical problem regarding news interest faces all school editors. Many of the events to be reported are known to the reader before the paper is issued. How, then, shall reporters prepare write-ups which will interest readers and yet be acceptable as news reporting? This is a problem for group discussion and staff ingenuity.

Objectives in School Journalism

Elementary school newspaper activity can aim at numerous objectives related to language arts in general as well as to the special demands of journalism. These objectives are realistic in the grades because there is nothing mysterious or especially difficult about procedures in the newspaper craft. Moreover it is just about as easy for children to write an article or edit a paper in a correct way as it is for them to blunder through procedures that are incorrect.

Accurate and Full Information: Reporters and editors discover that they must obtain all the basic facts which readers look for in a news article. In their first ventures they are likely to overlook some important aspect of their assigned topic or forget to mention the names of people who had important connections with the event reported. They improve rapidly if they assume that the readers know very little or nothing about the topic, and then write the article so fully and clearly that these readers will understand it and get the information they want.

Staff workers must develop a sense of accuracy. What has been published has been published—mistakes included. Although a reporter can spin a page of copy from half-knowledge, he can weave a true news story only from facts. Careful rechecking for accuracy in the final copy spares the staff embarrassment after the news story has been published.

Fact Versus Opinion: Beginners confuse factual news and personal opinion or editorialising. Breaking away from straight news reporting they step out on the page and make a personal appeal to the reader: "Everybody should come to the meeting," or "We wish to thank all the committee members." Sometimes they introduce their personal opinion: "She gave a fine talk on . . . ." They could remain within the framework of objective news by saying something like, "The chairman said he hoped that everybody would come to the meeting," "The officers said 'thank you' to all the committee members," or "Those who heard her said she gave a fine talk."

The distinction between reporting facts and expressing editorial opinion is rather difficult for pupils to maintain. A reporter may wish to make the write-up lively and informal, or at least "different." Or he may want to do a little boosting for some person or organisation. Or if careless or lazy, he finds it easier to write an opinion than to do the telephoning and legwork necessary to get the facts. Also there may be the general feeling that a school paper, like some small-town weeklies, should be "folksy" and (taking on the nature of magazines) mix opinion with news.

A teacher does the young reporter a kindness by starting him in the right technique. Straight news reporting is a kindness to the reader also when it spares him from the surfeit of article after article of saccharine sweetness. For if a paper allows opinion in one news article it must, in fairness, allow it in all articles. And if it praises everything it may as well praise nothing.

Organisation: Young reporters can learn the way a news article is supposed to be constructed. Properly written, a news story tells its essential in the opening paragraph—the lead. This lead, telling the *who, what, where,* and sometimes *why* of the situation, gives the article an arrangement that is the opposite of what pupils find in literary stories, which usually develop a climax near the end.

The most important information (who, what, where, when, why) is told in the first paragraph. People's names are given in full.	Three pupils from the fourth and fifth grades went to Baton Rouge yesterday on a trip that they won in the essay contest on "The Importance of Voting in State Elections." They are Sally Endres from Grade 4 and Patty Herbert and Philip McNice from Grade 5. Mrs. Gordon Straus took them to the city in her car and will be with them throughout the trip.	The first sentence opens with an aspect other than the time of the event. Paragraphs are short. Two sentences open with elements other than the subject, providing variation from other sentence openings.
Essential facts are given fully enough for a stranger to understand the article.	In the capital they will visit the Governor's office and see the legislature in session. They plan to return tomorrow evening. Next Monday, in the school assembly, they will tell about their experiences.	
	The contest was sponsored by the Good Citizen League. Thirty-three essays were handed in from grades four and five.	The last paragraph contains information that could be omitted with least loss, should lack of space force a cutting.
	The news story is written from a third-person point of view. There is no editorialising.	

Fig. 6.1: Points to observe when writing news articles.

Pupils can understand the two practical reasons for putting the most important information at the beginning: to give a reader the gist of the article very quickly; and to allow the printer making up the news page to shorten an article, if necessary, by his usual procedure of dropping the last few lines—which, therefore, should not contain the most essential facts of the write-up.

Figure 6.1 illustrates several news-writing techniques that young learners can begin acquiring.

The Opening: The phrasing of the opening sentence of a news article deserves attention. Two practical and easy suggestions can be observed. First, start some write-ups with words other than *the, they, a,* or *an* because a page full of such openings is monotonous for readers. Instead of beginning with, "A puppet show called 'Three Showmakers' will be . . . ," the reporter could say, " 'Three Showmakers', a puppet show, will be . . ." or "As the first puppet show of the year. . . ."

Second, avoid opening with mention of the *time,* unless it is especially important. Usually it is not that important, particularly if the event already has happened. Yet amateurs are inclined to start with the time: "Tomorrow night a puppet show called . . ." or "Last night a puppet show . . . ." This tendency is understandable. Such an opening is an easy (really lazy) way for a reporter to break into the subject. Also it looks like a method of avoiding the *a, an,* or *the* opening.

Interviews: Interview assignments involve a cluster of language arts skills: planning the interview, phrasing questions well, listening accurately, being courteous in speech and manner, taking notes carefully, and shaping material into a readable article. The writer has a delicate problem in trying to represent faithfully what has been said, because statements inaccurately quoted or cited out of original context can embarrass the person who has been interviewed.

An interview writer has greater freedom than a news writer in organising his article. He has a body of material, including most likely, a quotation or two. He can arrange that material pretty much as he wishes, and as he shapes it into a good write-up he has opportunity to use his highest sense of composing.

Two suggestions may guide the interview writer. First, he should avoid the beginner's tendency to give too much space to explaining why he chose to interview this person or to telling how he managed to arrange the visit. Second, he ought to include a few direct quotations if possible, to help make the interview seem like a real visit.

The Reader: The practice of keeping the intersts of the other person in mind—important in all writing and speaking—is a major objective for reporters and editors. Reporters wonder how they can open and develop topics so as to link up with readers' experiences and interests. They try to state the news and editorials with plain words in straightforward sentences. In order to be understood easily, and because they wish their article to be read to the end, they continue thinking about their readers throughout the composing of the item, not merely in the opening sentence or paragraph.

This objective of journalism, once attained, benefits the pupil in all his speaking and writing.

Examples, Quotations, and Dialogue: Newspaper columns tell about specific, tangible things: people, meetings, days of the week, events, quotations from people, reported conversations, and travel. Examples, quotations, and dialogue make articles concrete and, very likely, interesting. A pupil who has discovered their value in news items, interviews, or editorials is prepared to be specific and concrete in all his writing and speaking, both factual and imaginative.

Assured Interpretation: "What is the most mistaken, absurd, or foolish meaning that somebody (bright or stupid) could give to this statement?"

That question or one similar to it is a good one for newspaper writers and editors to ask regarding all final copy. It is a precautionary test. A sentence or paragraph that at first seems foolproof to the writer might be taken to mean something very different by a reader.

Writers and editors must judge each one of their statements severely—the more severely because they are prejudiced in its favour. Since they already know what it is supposed to say, they tend to interpret it in the way they want it to be understood. Embarrassed by some statements that they published, they may agree on the venerable advice good for all writers and speakers: compose sentences in such phrasing that they not only can be understood, but also cannot be misunderstood.

Punctuation, Spelling, and Capitalisation: Editors and proofreaders soon become sensitive to punctuation and spelling. Their reader-critics see to that. Editors, in turn, ask reporters to be careful. Periods, commas, colons, question marks, and quotation marks are the punctuation symbols which they work with most as they try to make their writing clear to the general reader. Spelling requires constant watchfulness. Editors who have worked on several isues and teachers who have advised staffs for some time know of a dozen or more words which reporters tend to misspell. Once the reporters master those words, spelling improves notably.

As for capitals, reporters tend to use far too many. The staff ought to establish a clear policy about which kinds of words should be capitalised. Few capitals rather than many are preferable.

Regarding both punctuation and spelling the staff should try to be not only correct but also consistent. Neat, legible handwriting in copy given to the typist or printer reduces the likelihood of errors.

Nicknames, Slangs, and "Columns": A newspaper staff discovers that slang and nicknames look more crudely brash in print than they sound when spoken. Such words glare from the page. Editors are wise, therefore, in admitting them cautiously.

Control of their use becomes particularly important when a newspaper has a special "column". Whenever school newspapers are published, there always is somebody who wants to start a personal column. Once started, the column can degenerate quickly into slang, cheap compliments, and gossip. Statements that were intended to carry no offense may pain the person referred to. What was put in as a joke may cause a sting. The writer must learn that the charm of a personal column is in the chatty, friendly manner of saying things, not in sensational ways of getting attention.

To be remembered, too, is the fact that a classroom or school newspaper gets into the hands of the public. Innocent-looking items, caught up by people outside the school, may be embarrassing. No staff can expect to publish a newspaper that will be restricted to school consumption only.

Advertisements: If a school newspaper carries advertisements, the advertising editors have a chance to gain profitable experiences in phrasing as well as in layout. Much thought can go into developing suitable wording. Also the display should be a genuine advertisement, not a mere announcement, as too many school newspaper advertisements are. Editors are challenged to use words and space effectively.

Original Writings: The presence of a school newspaper induces pupils to compose poems and stories for publication. It is desirable that a paper provide an outlet for original work, but literary editors must maintain respectable standards if their department is to survive.

Editorial standards should correspond to the suggestions on imaginative expression. Especially should verse be withheld when it presents nothing more than a prose idea set up in lines of four beats each and rhyming in couplets. Authors usually are willing to revise a piece if they see prospects of publication. Because of this the newspaper editors are in an exceptional position for improving the standards of imaginative expression in a school.

PUPIL ACTIVITIES

1. You and our friends can prepare somethig like a newspaper on a large cardboard. Mark off columns with ruled lines. That will be your page. Then write news items and headlines on paper strips that will fit into the columns you drew, and paste the strips wherever you want them. You can plan the page carefully.

The columns should be made somewhat wider than the usual columns of a newspaper.

If you wish you could prepare an issue that celebrates a special event like the first airplane flight, the end of the Revolutionary War, or the launching of the first submarine driven by atomic power.

2. Read a news item four or five times. Then you will see how the reporter put the article together. You can notice what he reported first, what second, what next. Also you can see how he worded the sentences.

The first time a person reads an item he usually gives most of his attention to what it says. That is the reason why you may have to reread it a few times in order to notice *how* the news was said.

3. Be on the lookout for a news article which does not tell you all the facts that you would like to know. Maybe it does not tell where or when a certain meeting is to be held or who is planning it. When you find such an article, decide how you would have written it. What would you have added so that readers would get all the information they need?

4. Visit a newspaper or magazine office and printing plant when you have a chance. How many different kinds of work do you see being done there? How does the visit help you understand more about the magazines and newspapers which you see at home and school?

5. You will enjoy seeing typewritten copies of news stories that are to be set up for a newspaper. If you visit a newspaper office you can see such copies. Some pages will be marked with revisions or with directions to the typesetter. Can you find out what those marks mean?

6. Arrange with your teacher to have a newspaper writer visit your classroom or be interviewed on the school television. Plan your questions carefully.

7. Once in a while we find a newspaper article that seems unfinished. A few sentences or a paragraph is missing. Maybe the article ends right in the middle of a sentence.

This happened, most likely, because the printer who made up the paper did not have enough space to put in the whole article. So he omitted some of the last lines and nobody had time to rewrite and reset the article.

Collect a few examples of such cut-off articles. Do they show you one reason why the most important news is told at the beginning of an article?

8. A good many people who write for newspapers and magazines or edit them check their sentences with this question: "What is the most foolish or absurd meaning that somebody

could give to this statement?" They do this becuase they expect many people to read what is printed, and they are afraid that somebody will either misinterpret it or give it an absurd meaning. Therefore they double-check their statements and change them if necessary.

How do you double-check what you write?

9. Select ten or twelve news articles and see how well their headlines fit the write-ups. How many of the headlines give a reader a correct idea of what is in the article? How many make you expect to find something which is not actually there?

What are some things that the person who writes the headlines must think of when choosing what to say and the words to use?

10. How well do you like the way the front page of your favourite newspaper is planned or laid out? Would you make any changes, if you were planning it?

How is the editorial page planned?

You will be able to find nicely planned pages in magazines, too. The advertising pages also have interesting layouts.

11. Interviews often are especially interesting to read. The interview might be with a nurse, a teacher, a mailman, a soldier, an inventor, a politician, an author, an actor, or other persons who are doing something that people like to hear about.

Have you noticed how those interviews are written? Did the writer put in a few quotations from the person interviewed? What other things make an interview pleasant to read?

12. How fast can you read an article in a newspaper? Can you read a news article faster than you can read a story in a book? Does the narrowness of the newspaper column help you read rapidly?

Some people read news columns without moving their eyes much to left and right, at least not along every line. They zig-zag their way down the page. Because the column is narrow they keep their eyes focused rather near the middle of the column.

13. Have you found where to look in your newspaper for opinions about television programmes and new books?

STUDY ACTIVITIES FOR TEACHERS

1. "I guess they don't like us down there at the newspaper office. I send in news about our programmes and they always change it. When it comes out in the paper it doesn't say at all what I wanted it to say."

That is a familiar complaint. A check into the situation usually discloses that the original writer did not know how to write news articles. The copy sent in was not organised properly and contained editorialising opinion. Perhaps it was written from "we" and "you" viewpoints ("We hope that . . ." or "You are invited . . .").

Someone from the editorial staff had to rewrite the item, and in the process changes occurred. The changes did not please the original writer, but the rewrite man probably did as well as he could with the material at hand.

After acquiring the technique of news writing, do you find that your news items get published almost as you sent them in? Do you then feel more confident when advising pupils who write for a school paper?

2. What observations can be made on these:

(a) Does the headline writer's quest for short, hard-hitting words increase the use of such words in everyday speaking and writing?

(b) Has the narrowness of the newspaper column encouraged the trend toward shorter sentences and paragraphs?

(c) Do the characteristic phrasings and rhythms that people meet repeatedly in headlines tend to influence readers' phrasings and rhythms in speaking and writing?

3. Write-ups in small-town weeklies are likely to differ from those in daily newspapers. How many of the differences are due to (a) the circumstance that the newspaper appears only once a week? (b) the reporting of a good many events which readers know about before seeing the paper? (c) the presence of

dailies in the area served by the weekly? (d) the busy life of the editor?

4. By comparing the results of similar kinds of material presented through different media one can test the effects of various forms of presentation. Ideally the same material should be available in seven forms: handwritten, typewritten, mimeographed, set up in leaflet form, in a newspaper, in a magazine, and in a book.

Which form of recording seems to have most prestige among average readers? Which has the least?

Are people more inclined to believe something when it is presented in some one form than when it is presented in another? Are there traces of popular respect for *anything* that gets printed? (One person remarked: "That was printed; therefore it must be true.")

VIEWPOINTS TO EMPHASISE THROUGH TEACHING AIDS

1. *One should read newspapers and magazines discriminatingly.*

(a) A poster containing several newspaper clippings. Caption: What happens in your mind when you read these? *or* What questions do you bring to these?

(b) Headlines and articles detached from each other but mounted on bulletin board or poster. Pupils read the two separately. Questions: Do headlines and articles agree? How much does the headline tell?

(c) Drawings in the form of animated cartoons showing what goes on in a careful reader's mind during the reading of parts of a newspaper or magazine.

2. *It is convenient to know where to look for specific kinds of items and what to expect to find when looking at a particular part of the paper.*

(a) Copies of public newspapers.

(b) Copies of good school newspapers, or photostat copies of such papers.

3. There are differences between newspapers and magazines.

(a) Copies of newspapers and magazines.

(b) Items from newspapers and magazines. Can pupils tell which articles are from newspapers? Which are from magazines? (Articles are typed, so that pupils cannot use such identifying clues as kind of type and paper.)

4. News articles are organised and stated in a special way.

(a) A poster containing a news clipping or, better, an enlarged photostatic copy of a news clipping. Space around the clipping is wide enough to carry various comments on how the article is written. From each comment a line or arrow leads to the appropriate part of clipping.

(b) Projector showings of well-written clippings and also of ones that are not entirely satisfactory.

(c) Any clipping which reports something that the pupils are interested in but which does not adequately cover the event. The pupils are vexed because it does not tell them all that they wish to know.

(d) A poster carrying two write-ups of a school event. One is satisfactory; the other is not written in a correct technique for a news item. Caption: You are editor. Which write-up would you print?

5. Many factors work together in producing a newspaper or magazine.

A poster with a heading like: These seven work in a newspaper or magazine office.

Sketched or shown in cutouts beneath the heading are personifications of some or all of these:

Mr. (or Miss) Fact-finder	Mr. Proofreader
Mr. Good Writer	Mr. Business Manager
Mr. Planner	Mr. Circulation Manager
Mr. Printer	

INQUIRIES AND PROBLEMS FOR STUDENTS

1. Look through an issue of a good daily newspaper, marking whatever material you believe would be useful in

language arts, particularly for teaching vocabulary development, spelling, punctuation, factual speaking and writing, sentence construction, paragraphing, or imaginative expression. Which of your findings might you use in a fourth grade? In a sixth-grade?

2. What proportion of newspaper readers seem alert to differences between objective reporting and editorialising? Between impersonal news reports and by-line articles? How many readers note the adequacy or inadequacy of headlines as clues to the actual content of articles?

3. Try to find out whether a newspaper page looks like a strange jumble of items to childre. At what age do pupils begin seeing some news stories in the perspective of day-by-day developments? Could the medley of newspaper reports on diverse activities, events, facts, and opinions be considered a kind of stream-of-consciousness representation of the world?

4. "Journalism is literature in a hurry." What are some implications of that statement?

5. A fifth grade wants to start a classroom mimeographed newspaper. You are to be the advisor. How would you and the class proceed in the planning? What points of advice would you give to reporters?

6. Pupils inclined to be "flowery" in their writing tend to have difficulties in preparing satisfactory news write-ups. Why?

7. Decide on index headings for a personal file of newspaper clippings that might be usable in teaching language arts. Establish at least ten headings. (If you start collecting items, be selective; avoid making your file a catchall.)

LANGUAGE

Language is fundamentally a code or, as Cherry prefers, an "organically developed system." It consists of units which, in accordance with recognised rules and habits, can be grouped into patterns that convey meaning. The English language is such a system, its main units being phonemes, morphemes, words, inflectional forms, accents, junctures, pitches, and sentence patterns. Modern English relies much on position also—the particular location of a word, phrase, clause, or intonation signal in a statement.

Presumably, then, the pedagogy of teaching the English language should be largely a matter of helping children learn more about the units of the system and how to organise those units into intelligible patterns. Such presumption is reasonably correct. But teaching language patterns and usage is more complicated than might at first be supposed. One reason is that language, though a system in itself, is closely related to whatever message it carries. Indeed, the transmittal of messages may be considered the main reason for the existence of language. Furthermore, language is interwoven with a society's culture and outlook. And, causing a third complication, language serves as an instrument for thinking and for analysing environment and experience. All these enlarge the scope of what the teacher must consider. They also complicate the situation when teachers and pupils, for certain purposes and at certain times, wish to view language as a discrete phenomenon, a code that has an existence of its own.

Uniquely Human

Language, as understood in the present discussion, is uniquely human. Other creatures than man have languages of sorts. Much has been observed regarding the signal systems used by bees, crows, and dolphins, for example, but, as Cherry notes: "A hen can set her chicks scurrying up to her, by clucking—communication established by a releaser mechanism—*but human language is vastly more than a complicated system of clucking.*" Only human language has the elaborate equipment, oral and written, to state cumulative information and reflections from the past as well as the present and to project into the future. Animal language is limited to immediacy. "The animals are not phonetically defective but semantically blocked," says Jacobs. "Their speech is hence an unchanging dialect, incapable of variation or improvement, consisting of a limited repertory of vague interjections which are not intended to convey knowledge but merely to voice subjective fears."

Language Study

The origin of human language antedates known history by many thousands of years, but records of systematic study of langauge start relatively late. Evidently such study occurred in India as early as the fourth or fifth century BC, though mainly as an aid in explaining the Vedas. Somewhat later the Greeks analysed their language, particularly in relation to poetry. Greek interest in oratory, and a similar interest among Romans, stimulated studies in rhetorical aspects of language, with emphasis on the rat of composing well in prose. Medieval and Renaissance scholars continued to cultivate rhetoric and studied grammar as related to Latin. They gave little time to formal study of their native vernacular languages.

In the eighteenth century, students of language began devoting more attention to English, codifying its grammar, formalising and prescribing usages. With the late nineteenth century and the first half of the twentieth came new aspects of language study. Sociology, anthropology, psychology, and acoustical physics raised questions and revealed previously unobserved facts related to the nature of language. Clyde Kluckhohn, Lucien Levy-Bruhl, Otto, Jespersen, George Boas, Ludwig Wittgenstein, Alfred Korzybski, Edward Sapir, Benjamin Lee Whorf, Leonard Bloomfield, Charles Fries, Henry Lee Smith, George L. Trager, and Noam Chomsky are key names in these developments. Today teachers of language benefit from cultural anthropology, semantics, and descriptive linguistics.

Linguistic and Academic Problems

Problems of teaching the English language stem from two sources, one linguistic, the other academic. Linguistic ones arise from the structure of English, especially from the irregularities which still persist in the conjugations and declensions; from the complex nature of words and of the functional shifts which words may experience through their varied uses in sentences; and from the cultural involvements of language. Academic problems develop when teachers lack adequate knowledge of the nature and functions of language, sentences, classes of words, and signals that convey meaning in speech and writing.

Teachers and pupils can generate excitement in working with language. Such excitement is likely to flourish when the class discovers new expressional possibilities in English. When there is limited success or even failure in teachng grammar, the trouble often comes from lack of linguistic knowledge; probably too much time is being spent on picayune issues, too little on long-range values of language.

Teaching the resources of the English language and their use is more complicated, by far, than teaching the mechanics of writing, spelling, and social and business letters. In its way of demanding an instructor's scholarship and resourcefulness it ranks with the teaching of literature or imaginative expression.

An Entity

Language is an entity having an existence of its own. In spite of its involvement with the culture of people who use it and with the burden of information or ideas that it carries, language can be viewed as a phenomenon in itself. A language—the English language here—is a system embodying certain structural principles. These principles remain the same, regardless of whether language says "Please pass the bread." "Life is but a walking shadow," "Man, get hep!" or "He who rides a tiger fears to dismount." Basic patterns of English structure are common denominators through all kinds of verbal expression, utilitarian and literary. Those will be observed in the following interrelated chapters on structure and usage, words, and constructing ideas with language.

PROFESSIONAL RESEARCH

As part of professional growth in language arts, teachers can do three things related to research: keep up-to-date on new findings as reported in professional literature, be judicious about the validity of what is reported, and do some research themselves. Doing these three, a teacher is likely to discover that, in addition to professional growth, she gains considerable pleasure. Certainly she is freed from the sense of monotony which some teachers complain of in teaching elementary grades.

Means of keeping up-to-date on reported research are widely available. Among the best are the monthly publications of the National Council of Teachers of English *(Elementary English, The English Journal,* and *College English)* and occasional Council bulletins. The New England Association of Teachers of English issues *The English Leaflet. Research Helps in Teaching Language Arts,* an Association for Supervision and Curriculum Development bulletin, furnishes a convenient survey of recent findings, and the *Encyclopaedia of Educational Research* gives liberal space to all aspects of language arts. Textbooks also report on research and offer advice.

A bit of skepticism is wholesome among claims of "research says." Research in language arts involves both human beings and an art—two entities ill adapted to scientific exactitude. Present are such variables as personalities of teachers, health of pupils, classroom conditions, the time of day when experiments occurred, home environment, individual interests, variations in sundry personal factors (even when intelligence scores of experimental and control groups correspond), and differences in taste and personal judgment regarding literary selections. These variables influence the validity of findings, even under "controlled" conditions. In addition there are questions as to whether the samplings studied were extensive enough to represent the population, geographic areas, or time span considered in the research. Too often conclusions are claimed from insignificant data.

These difficulties suggest why research has concentrated on topics that provide objective measurements: word counts in letters, notes, compositions, and stories; spelling; reading; errors in mechanics of punctuation and grammar. At the present stage of research there are few valid findings on how children form concepts of classes of words and patterns of expression, on the nature and growth of appreciation, or on how to test whatever growth in appreciation may have occurred during a year.

With much research yet to be done, a teacher can be encouraged to attempt some personally. She owes it to the profession as well as to herself. Professionally she should be exacting at all steps in the research, avoiding flimsy methods of judging results and being cautious in attributing to a particular child the findings which seem to be valid for a group. For herself a research project may be a rejuvenator. It may keep her interested in her work when some colleagues are tiring of "teaching the same elementary stuff over and over again." Research gives new dimensions to her enterprise of teaching.

Teachers usually have opportunities to report their findings, if they wish, at professional meetings in central school districts or regional or state conferences. Among publications that accept reports on research are local school bulletins, state educational magazines, and magazines of the National Council of Teachers of English, of state organisations affiliated with the National Council, of the New England Association of Teachers of English, and of professional groups connected with the National Education Association and the Association of Supervision and Curriculum Development.

If teachers wish suggestions regarding topics needing research, they can find many in professional literature, notably in publications of the National Council of Teachers of English and in magazine-article listings in the *Educational Index*. A topic should be chosen thoughtfully because when so many potentially useful projects need to be done, a teacher would not wish to spend time on research which would yield little more than statistical proof of what is known already.

PARENTS AND THE LANGUAGE ARTS

What language arts teachers teach is one thing; what the parents think is being taught may be something very different. Pupils, the most likely informants, often speak vaguely at home about what happens in school. "Of, we took a trip," they report, or "We sat on the floor and pasted," or "We played." They rarely tell the purpose of the activity or what they learned from it. Asked what they did in reading, their reply might be: "Oh, we didn't *have* reading today," even though there may have been much informal reading during school hours.

Demagogues from the general public take up their cue at this point. Being interested in damaging a school system or a particular administration they exploit parent' doubts regarding the teaching of language arts "fundamentals." The clamour may be for "more grammar"—meaning more formal grammar—even though experience demonstrates that formal grammar is not the most efficient route to satisfactory language usage.

When instructional methods change from those which parents and other adults knew in their school days the school has a public relations obligation to inform responsible adults about the nature of the changes and the reasons for those changes. Some schools send a handbook to all parents; others inform the public through the parent-teacher association.

In the classroom, teachers can help by making sure pupils know the purposes and values of daily activities. By whatever why it is accomplished, informing the school constituency is a public relations aspect of teaching.

EMANCIPATION OF THE PUPIL

The emancipation of the pupil from the need of a teacher's guidance in language usage, choice of books, and enjoyment of literature is an ideal objective. Its attainment never is assured, but some instructional procedures excel others in developing it.

Pupil independence is furthered when the teacher moves opportunely between (1) her inclination to help pupils with their problems or tell them whatever they ask about, and (2) her better judgment, which counsels her to let pupils discover and formulate some things for themselves, even though the process may require more time for both pupil and teacher. Many children like to be "told," especially the very ones most needing the experience of working independently. A teacher should have no apologies for ceasing to help pupils while their problem still seems a bit "hazy" to them.

There is a natural tendency to dispense quantities of information ready-made. In many instances this should be curbed. The conventional classroom situation provides some inducement toward independent thinking but it rarely makes independent thinking a major objective. The usual situation does not preclude a pupil's emancipation; neither does it encourage it. Material which "informs" a child directly may not be best for nurturing his ability to make individual inquiry or to develop opinions independently.

Pupils need emancipation in literature too. The instructor should avoid doing all the "appreciating" herself. It sometimes happens that teachers make the classroom enthusiasm for a selection so personal that their pupils, though enjoying literature in class, may be disappointed by the comparatively small amount of pleasure they derive when reading a selection alone. Those pupils have become so dependent on experiencing literature at second hand that they cannot generate momentum for themselves.

Teachers should hope that a pupil will become something more than a mirror for their academic faces. A child ought to become more, also, than a reflector of textbooks. There should be evidence that he knows what is in the book, but a greater concern to teachers is whether flashes of light illuminated the pupil's mind.

NOT BY CHECK ALONE

Amid the challenges of the classroom situation an instructor, sometimes becomes a better teacher than she might have thought possible. For that enhancement she is indebted to her profession. Teachers of language arts live not by paycheck alone. Newer ideas about the organismic development of children have made teaching more clearly creative than it used to be. When conditions are right, teachers are released from being disciplinarians; they become "gardeners" instead.

Particularly is this true in teaching a subject like language arts. This rich subject does fine things to the mind, just as a resourceful mind does fine things to this responsive subject. There is interplay of material over mind and of mind over material. The teacher draws sustenance from her role as intermediary between two stimulating forces: between language arts—a radiant facet of human achievement—and great numbers of dynamic young people whose native interest in the subject awaits development.

INQUIRIES AND PROBLEMS FOR STUDENTS

1. Many teachers prefer that pupils learn through problem-

solving types of experiences rather than through hearing or reading direct statements of what is to be learned. How can the problem method be used in language arts?

2. "We live our way into thinking far more than we think our way into our living," said Whiting Williams, as quoted by Ordway Tead. How might this statement influence the classroom methods of a language arts teacher in the middle grades? In the upper grades?
3. "Learning by doing is a sound principle only if the doing is good doing." What do you think of this caution from Aldous Huxley?
4. Identify some aspects of speaking and writing instruction that, because of their nature, are more or less mechanical. How can a person teach and conduct drills on those mechanical items without allowing the instruction to become mechanical?

COMMUNICATION

Teachers agree that at least four elements should be present to make a communicative situation: The pupil ought to have facts or ideas to express, a reason for saying or writing them, enough linguistic ability to speak or write understandingly, and a person or persons to hear him or to read what he writes. Two additional elements are highly desirable in the receivers of the communication: attentiveness in listening and efficiency in reading.

A listener or reader seems to be rather unimportant, though, for children in two circumstances: Young children often chatter in monologue fashion, with no serious thought of communicating, and pupils sometimes (but by no means always) compose stories and poems with less intent of communicating to someone else than of saying what they feel impelled to say.

Two unfavourable circumstances reduce the zest which normally exists in a communicative situation. First, pupils do most of their speaking and oral reading before captive audiences; and second, they do almost all their talking and writing on topics which, they are aware, are more fully known by the teacher than by themselves. It is a happy occasion when the pupil has something which his classmates are eager to hear or read and which he knows is also informative to the teacher. Such occasions are unfortunately rare, and one of a teacher's major endeavours is to have them happen more often.

The chapters of this Part discuss five of the elements associated with communication: the subject-matter that pupils speak or write, motives for expression, the hearers and readers, discriminatory listening, and skills of speaking and writing. Discussions of grammar, usage, and some aspects of composing are deferred to Part III, "language". Reading is referred to occasionally, but there is no attempt to discuss it fully because any such attempt would require a book in itself.

Most of the speaking and writing done in the classroom is factual. Even in corridors and on playgrounds informative speech predominates, though fragmentary and mingled with shouts and exclamations.

Fortunately the experience of teaching the much-needed factual type of communication can be stimulating even though some professional opinion labels it a pedestrian chore. The stimulus comes from the artistic possibilities inherent in the many variables which teachers and pupils work with. These variables and possibilities are present, whether the topic happens to be factual, like "How Colours Protect Insects," "How to Fire and Glaze a Clay Bowl," "Shapes of Poems as Seen on the Page," and "Four Sentences Made from Eight Different Words," or a venture into imaginative expression through a story on "Why the Robins Came Back" or a poem on "Hammers Pounding."

Though her job of teaching communication is complicated, the teacher can find help in her pupils' traits and needs. Children, like adults, have many things they really want to tell, write, listen to, or read. They have a feeling for communication, and they are beginning to discover the importance of speech and writing as factors in human personality. School offers counterparts to the needs and traits of normal children.

Successful teachers note what a child brings with him and what the school can offer him, then find efficient ways of bringing the two together.

The teacher of communication enjoys a second advantage—the active nature of speaking, writing, listening, or reading. There are tangible things to do in both factual and imaginative expression. Profitable activities abound, not only for pupils but also for teachers. This is evident from the suggestions in the following chapters.